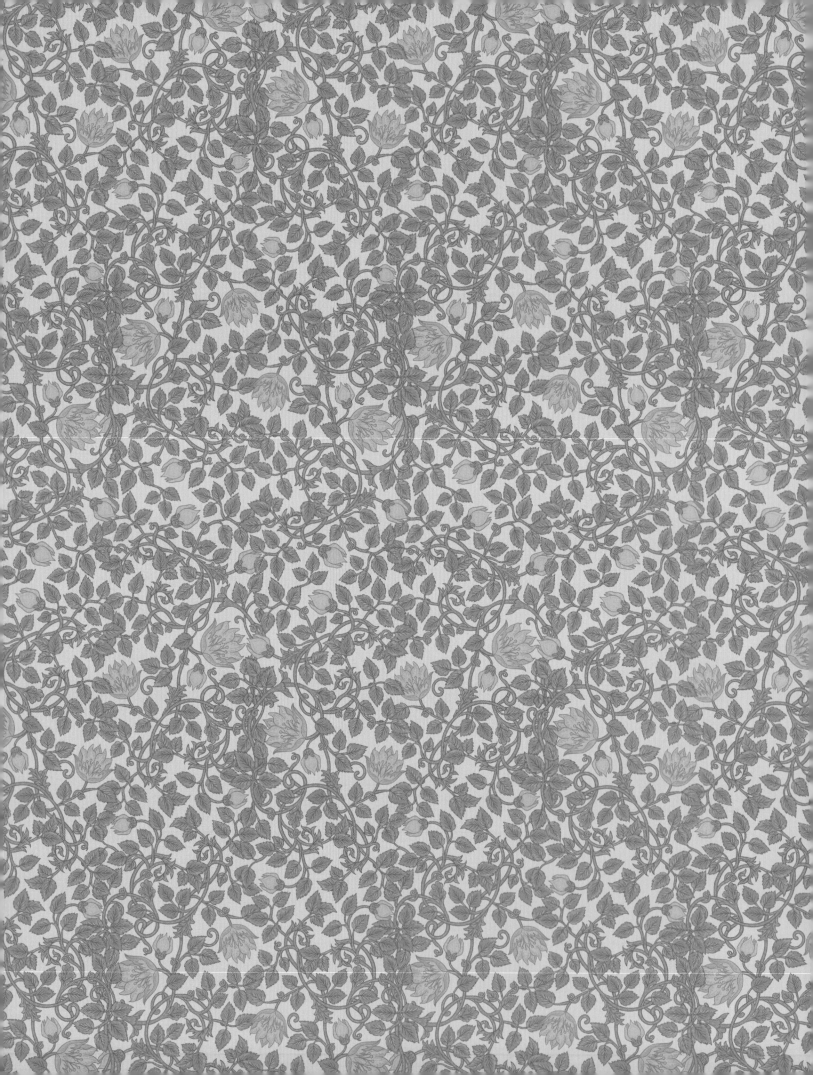

Visual Encyclopedia

Jane Austen

TITAN
BOOKS

Gwen Giret & Claire Saim

Visual Encyclopedia

Jane Austen

Illustrations by Sophie Koechlin

TITAN
BOOKS

Contents

Contents

Foreword

"**As** a lover of Jane Austen, it remains a daily joy to work in her treasured home and to be surrounded by the sights that inspired her as she wrote and revised all six of her novels. Over the two centuries since their publication, those books have travelled far beyond Chawton, being translated into many languages across the world.

Her genius was to create stories and characters that are universal, that cross the boundaries of time and language to speak directly to us, in a way that still feels immediate, relevant and constant.

...

...

The French were the very earliest beyond her native country to fall in love with her works. Today, they are amongst the many visitors from across the globe who come every year to this special place in order to walk in her footsteps.

The House tells us much about Jane Austen, a multi-faceted, driven woman, whose ambition and drive to succeed in her writing remains as inspirational as her novels are influential. It was such a treat to meet with Claire and Gwen to talk all things Jane Austen and I know that this book will take you on a fascinating journey into Jane Austen's world. 99

Lizzie Dunford
DIRECTOR OF JANE AUSTEN'S
HOUSE IN CHAWTON

Introduction

1

Jane Austen is currently the only female writer to be re-imagined as a Funko Pop figurine. Not even Mary Shelley or Agatha Christie managed this feat.

6

The number of works completed and published by the British novelist Jane Austen, including two published posthumously. Add to that a stunning novella, *Lady Susan*, and two other promising novels that she barely began, as well as her early works —the famous Juvenilia— and a few notes, essays and snatches of correspondence.

41

Jane Austen died young, five months before her forty-second birthday, probably of Hodgkin Lymphoma, cancer or tuberculosis. The mystery has not really been solved. Her body lies beneath a modest black slab in Winchester Cathedral.

90000

Records show that this is the total estimated amount, in today's pound sterling, that Jane Austen earned during her lifetime. She took a certain pride in being a woman and earning her own money.

20000000

It is estimated that *Pride and Prejudice* has sold an estimated twenty million copies worldwide since it was first published in 1813, when only fifteen hundred copies were printed.

Why is Jane Austen still the object of so much fascination around the world? Her first texts bear no signature other than *By a lady* and initially met with only relative success. Yet other remarkable women writers, such as her contemporaries Fanny Burney, Maria Edgeworth and Regina Roche, widely read and recognised in their time, do not enjoy such a fervent and passionate legacy today.

So how did Jane Austen survive two centuries of history to become a key figure in both literature and pop culture? A certain wet shirt no doubt has something to do with it —don't worry, we'll come back to that— as does the romantic image of Britain, with its light dresses, ribbons and chiffon, sunny country outings and delicate china.

There are many reasons for this infatuation... and the feelings associated with this status reinforce the reputation and influence that Jane Austen continues to inspire. Her female characters are adept at wresting the smallest snippets of freedom and happiness from their fate. Her non-conformist male heroes are not to be outdone, far from it. And let's not forget her biting irony in describing the failings of her time, both great and small.

Set aside your prejudices and be transported into another world...

Jane Austen is without doubt the best-known British novelist in the world. And yet, if you put her in her Georgian context, she was just a country girl. Loved by her family, happy, devout, uncomplicated, but undoubtedly with dreams of surpassing her condition, she was a woman, she was single, she was not rich.

In a world where appearances counted for so much and where a woman had so little room to develop, Jane Austen constantly pushed back the restrictions of her era, on the strength of her talent alone.

PART I

Jane Austen

A woman of her time

Born to a good family

Jane Austen came from what is known as a "respectable background". Although not very wealthy, her family was close-knit and content. Rather unusually at the end of the 18th century, her parents attached great importance to the education of their two daughters. Going from a child playing in the country lanes of Hampshire to a talented novelist at her desk, was a long journey. Yet everything she came into contact with at every stage of her life contributed to her education and development.

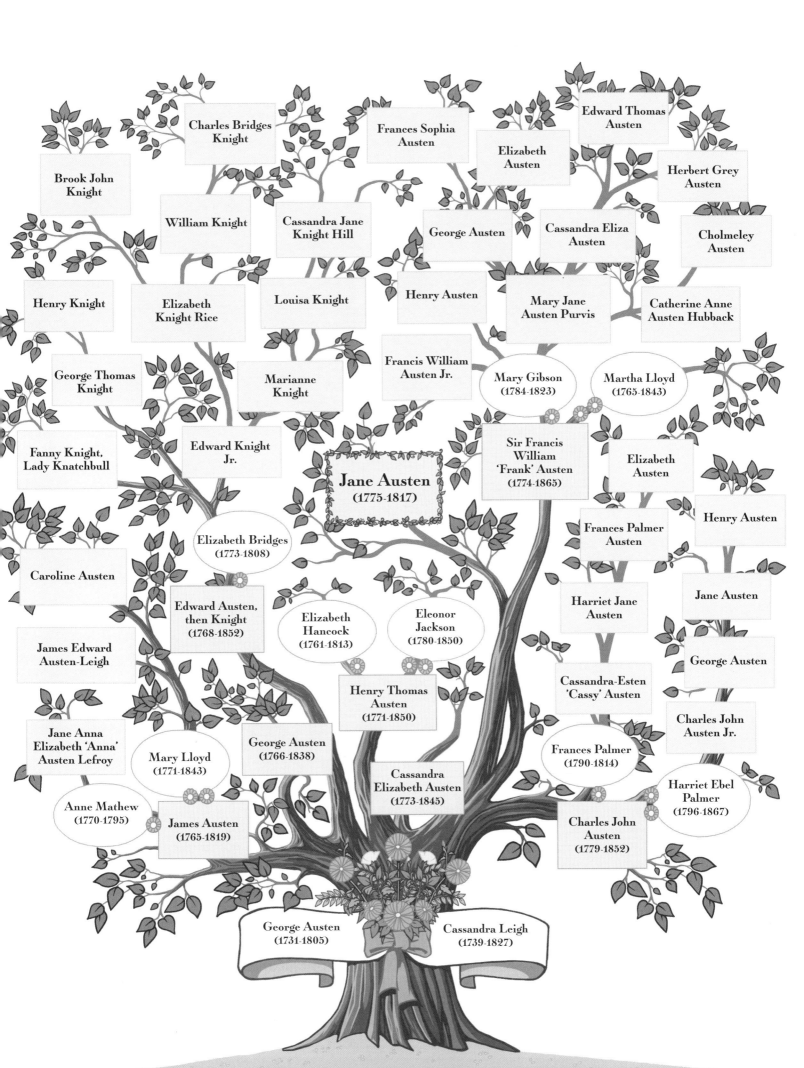

Charles Bridges Knight

Brook John Knight

Frances Sophia Austen

Edward Thomas Austen

Elizabeth Austen

Herbert Grey Austen

William Knight

Cassandra Jane Knight Hill

George Austen

Cassandra Eliza Austen

Cholmeley Austen

Henry Knight

Elizabeth Knight Rice

Louisa Knight

Henry Austen

Mary Jane Austen Purvis

Catherine Anne Austen Hubback

George Thomas Knight

Marianne Knight

Francis William Austen Jr.

Mary Gibson (1784-1823)

Martha Lloyd (1765-1843)

Fanny Knight, Lady Knatchbull

Edward Knight Jr.

Jane Austen (1775-1817)

Sir Francis William 'Frank' Austen (1774-1865)

Elizabeth Austen

Henry Austen

Elizabeth Bridges (1773-1808)

Frances Palmer Austen

Caroline Austen

Edward Austen, then Knight (1768-1852)

Elizabeth Hancock (1761-1813)

Eleonor Jackson (1780-1850)

Harriet Jane Austen

Jane Austen

James Edward Austen-Leigh

Henry Thomas Austen (1771-1850)

Cassandra-Esten 'Cassy' Austen

George Austen

Jane Anna Elizabeth 'Anna' Austen Lefroy

Mary Lloyd (1771-1843)

George Austen (1766-1838)

Frances Palmer (1790-1814)

Charles John Austen Jr.

Cassandra Elizabeth Austen (1773-1845)

Anne Mathew (1770-1795)

James Austen (1765-1819)

Harriet Ebel Palmer (1796-1867)

Charles John Austen (1779-1852)

George Austen (1731-1805)

Cassandra Leigh (1739-1827)

A COUNTRY GIRL

J ane Austen was a child of the winter cold. In her biography of the novelist, Claire Tomalin recounts[1] that the month in which Jane was born was particularly harsh. In the remote Hampshire village of Steventon, a mother of six prepared to give birth again. She was thirty-six years old. The baby to be born would leave her mark on the history of world literature, and no one in this household would ever be aware.

It was a birth like any other, on Saturday 16 December 1775. A clergyman's wife gave birth in the countryside, without any special help or doctor present. Mrs. Austen was sure that Jane arrived a month late. This is part of the family's story[2]. All went well, and the baby stayed in the warm for part of the winter with her mother, who rested, while Philadelphia Hancock, Mr. Austen's sister, took care of the household. Reverend Austen baptised his daughter at home, she then would have a bigger celebration in the spring.

Little Jane looked a lot like her brother Henry, who was four years older. She was a pretty baby, with a round face, full cheeks, and beautiful hazel eyes, just like Mr. Austen. She had a quiet childhood with loving parents and siblings. The only unusual fact that may come as a surprise is that Mrs. Austen did not look after her children from the age of three months until they were around eighteen months old. They spent this phase of their lives in the village, with a wet nurse. This was not considered abandonment: it was simply part of their upbringing.

Did this forced separation heighten Jane Austen's sensitivity? It is possible that this form of exclusion, however involuntary, may have been at the root of what shaped her personality and her strong attachment to her family, particularly her sister Cassandra. But this method also allowed the Austen family to better manage their time with their numerous children and the young students at the rectory.

---

[1] *Jane Austen, A Life,* Claire Tomalin, Penguin, 2000.
[2] Medically speaking, a pregnancy lasts between forty-one and forty-two weeks i.e. around nine lunar months. If the pregnancy continues beyond this point, there is a risk of complications. This was not the case here. Mrs. Austen just miscounted.

JANE'S PARENTS

Old black and white photograph of England and Wales: Stoneleigh Abbey

MRS. AUSTEN was born Cassandra Leigh, into a Warwickshire aristocratic family, something she took a certain pride in. One of her ancestors was the Lord Mayor of London who proclaimed Elizabeth I Queen of England, which did not prevent Jane Austen from viciously denigrating the monarch later in her parody *History of England*[3]. In August 1806, Jane Austen, her sister Cassandra and their mother travelled to this side of the family to visit a cousin, the Reverend Leigh. He had just inherited the prosperous Stoneleigh Abbey, which dated back to medieval times. Today, this estate is open to visitors and is proud of its connection with the famous novelist.

For more information, visit stoneleighabbey.org.

Cassandra Leigh's father, the Reverend Thomas Leigh, taught at All Souls College, Oxford, while one of her uncles, Dr Theophilus Leigh, was President of Balliol College, also in Oxford. The latter said of his niece Cassandra, the future Mrs. Austen, that she was one of the most brilliant minds he knew. She loved to write, especially poetry. It was when she was in Bath with her sister, also named Jane, that her father died suddenly. This hastened her decision to marry the Reverend George Austen. Mrs. Austen's sister, who was reputed to be very beautiful, married Dr Cooper, a clergyman living near Bath. Among the ancestors in whom Mrs. Austen held much pride was her namesake, a duchess, Cassandra Willoughby (unsurprisingly we come across this surname in a Jane Austen novel)[4].

GEORGE AUSTEN and his sisters lost their parents when they were very young. Their mother died giving birth to her youngest daughter, Leonora. Once their father had died, his second wife wanted nothing to do with them, and the Austen children were left to fend for themselves. They were taken in by different aunts and uncles, and

separated. George Austen worked hard and eventually won a scholarship to Oxford to study theology.

At the age of twenty-four, he was ordained in Rochester, Kent. He's said to have been handsome, with bright hazel eyes and curly hair. His career was exemplary, thanks to his hard work and resilience. Winning another scholarship, he continued his studies at Oxford University. He would no doubt have crossed paths with Cassandra Leigh when she visited her uncle, the President of Balliol College.

Thanks to his uncle Francis Austen[5], George Austen was finally given his own parish in 1761. It was in Deane, Hampshire. A second parish was added later, thanks to a wealthy Knight cousin. This was Steventon, where Jane Austen was born. George was thirty-two when he finally got married, Cassandra Leigh was twenty-four. We know that the young bride wore a red travelling outfit. The ceremony took place in Bath on 26 April 1764. Despite hesitation, calculations and agreements, in the end, they were a happy, well-matched couple.

---

[3] See the chapter "*Juvenilia*" in Part II.
[4] It's the surname of a character in *Sense and Sensibility*.
[5] This uncle's wife was also called Jane (née Chadwick), and was one of Jane Austen's godmothers.

AN AUNT IN PRISON

In the summer of 1799, the wife of Mrs. Austen's brother, Jane Leigh-Perrot, found herself arrested for shoplifting, and was even thrown in jail due to a simple piece of black lace. Was it foolishness? Kleptomania? A mistake? More likely it was dishonesty on the part of the accusers and a miscarriage of justice. The shopkeeper, Elizabeth Gregory, a haberdasher and milliner, and her sales assistant swore that they saw her put the fabric in her pocket. And that's where it was found, along with a piece of white lace that Mrs. Leigh-Perrot paid for. A complaint was lodged.

At the time, this type of petty theft was a serious matter, as lace was very expensive. Mrs. Leigh-Perrot risked deportation to Australia and even hanging. For this wealthy, well-to-do lady in her fifties, it was disgrace. She remained in detention for almost seven months, refusing the offer of a visit from her nieces Cassandra and Jane, judging that it was not a suitable place for young ladies. Constantly supported by her husband and family, at her assize trial on 29 March 1800, she was finally declared innocent.

JANE'S BROTHERS

Jane Austen had six brothers, five older and one younger.

JAMES, an Oxford graduate like his father, had a reputation for being serious, conscientious and earnest, although he liked to joke around with his family. In love with his cousin Eliza Hancock during his teenage years, he travelled to France with her family. He came back enthralled. But he ended up marrying Anne Mathew while he was a curate in Deane. Together they had little Anna, who would later become Anna Lefroy, dear to the hearts of Cassandra and Jane Austen. After the death of his first wife, he married Mary Lloyd, a sister of Jane Austen's friend Martha Lloyd. He had two children with her, including the famous James Edward Austen-Leigh, the author of *A Memoir of Jane Austen*, her first biography. When his father, the Reverend George Austen, retired in 1800, he naturally succeeded him as parish priest of Steventon. He remained there until his death at the age of fifty-three.

GEORGE was certainly the most secretive and mysterious brother, about whom little is known. Jane Austen probably communicated with him in sign language[6]. There is no formal indication that he was deaf and dumb, but in a letter of 1808, Jane Austen mentions that she "spoke with her fingers"[7]. While he was with the wet nurse, it became clear that he was not as fit as his brother James. He suffered from convulsions. Mrs. Austen recognised the same symptoms she had observed in her own brother Thomas, who had been brought up outside the family. Little George was entrusted to a family in the village. As an adult, his younger brothers continued to look after him until his death at the age of seventy-two. We don't know exactly what was wrong with him, perhaps he had a birth defect.

---

[6] Biographer Claire Tomalin speculates that Jane Austen learned sign language so that she could communicate with George, Claire Tomalin, *op. cit.*
[7] *Jane Austen's Letters*, Deirdre Le Faye, Oxford, 2011.

EDWARD 's life was unusual, and may seem surprising in such a close-knit family. The Austens had wealthy cousins, the Knights, a family originally from Kent. Jane Austen's father already owed the parish of Steventon due to the generosity of his wealthy cousin by marriage, Thomas Knight II. The Knight family visited the Austens en route to their honeymoon. Edward was twelve years old at the time. Thomas and his wife Catherine Knatchbull immediately took a liking to him and took him on their honeymoon. Thereafter, the couple visited the Austens regularly and their attachment to the well-behaved Edward grew.

As the years went by, it became clear that the couple would have no children. The Knights suggested to the Reverend Austen and his wife that they take care of Edward's education in the manner of a 'gentleman'. What would later become a true adoption took place in stages. At first, the young boy travelled regularly with them, before returning to his parents for a while. He was finally adopted at the age of sixteen. The Knights took him to France on a major trip from the east to the south of the country. They passed through Reims, Châlons-sur-Marne, Dijon, Mâcon, Lyon, Avignon, Nice and Agen. Later, they sent him on a 'Grand Tour', the educational and cultural journey that all rich young men from good families took, during which he travelled through Switzerland, the Kingdom of Saxony and Italy.

It was also agreed that in order to inherit, Edward would have to change his surname. In this way, his descendants would be able to continue to pass on the Knight name. It seemed that Mrs. Austen accepted this arrangement more readily than her husband. Mrs. Austen's opinion would prove to be correct when future circumstances required the Knight heir to use his fortune to ensure the welfare of his family. Throughout his life, he remained close to his natural family, and never changed his behaviour towards them. He married the daughter of a baronet, Elizabeth Bridges, with whom he had eleven children. Widowed at the age of forty, he never remarried, as he had been very attached to his wife. He died peacefully at the age of eighty-five, on his estate at Godmersham in Kent.

A STRONG WOMAN:
JANE AUSTEN'S GREAT-
GRANDMOTHER, ELIZABETH
WELLER

Elizabeth Weller, George Austen's grandmother, was a woman of great courage who left her mark on the family's history. In 1693, she married the son of a cloth merchant, John Austen. In the beginning they were financially comfortable, but her husband was not in good health. The mother of seven children, Elizabeth found herself widowed at an early age. She had debts and her in-laws turned their backs on her. But that wasn't a problem for her! She was strong and took matters into her own hands. She found work at a boarding school. In exchange, her seven children received a home and a good education. One of her sons, William, became a doctor. He married a widow who already had a son, and together they had four more children[8], including Jane Austen's father, George.

HENRY is often described as Jane Austen's favourite brother. It is said that they were physically very similar. Like his older brother James, he was an Oxford graduate. Handsome, intelligent and cultured, Henry had it all. He was best known for his constant support of his younger sister's ambition to be published. Henry was essentially her agent. He joined the militia for a time, then became a banker, but went bankrupt in 1816. His first marriage was to his childhood sweetheart, Eliza, his beautiful cousin. With her, he went to France between 1802 and 1803 during the Treaty of Amiens, to try to recover part of the estate of her first husband, the Comte de Feuillide. Once widowed, he eventually embarked on the career in the church that he had dreamed of as a young man. Seven years after Eliza's death, he married a completely different, very pious woman, Eleanor Jackson, the niece of the former vicar of Chawton. She wrote a religious essay, *An Epitome of the Old Testament*, in 1831. In 1840, he became involved in the fight against slavery. He ended his life modestly at

---

[8] The first-born did not survive long.

the age of seventy-nine in Kent, at Tunbridge Wells, very close to Tonbridge, the home village of the Austen family. He had no descendants.

FRANCIS arrived just before Jane Austen in the order of siblings, and they were very close during their early years. As a little boy, he was boisterous. Later, she admired him for his brilliant career as an officer in the Navy. He was brave, resilient and dashing. He remained very attached to his family throughout his life. Extremely devout, he was known for never using foul language and for always kneeling in church. He fell in love with a young lady from Ramsgate, Mary Gibson: they got engaged and exchanged many letters. They married just as Francis was receiving some financial rewards for his bravery and war record. They had eleven children together, but Mary died giving birth to the last, a daughter, who also died a few weeks later. Not wanting to be left alone, he found solace in a marriage of convenience to Martha Lloyd, sister of Mary Lloyd who married his brother James. Martha Lloyd was sixty-three and her husband forty-nine. It was more of a partnership arrangement than a marriage of love. Martha gained status and financial security, and Francis gained a housekeeper to bring up his many children. He ended his career as an Admiral of the Fleet, knighted as Sir Francis Austen, and Martha became Lady Austen. He was buried in Portsmouth when he died at the venerable age of ninety-one. We know that he kept his precious correspondence with his sister Jane throughout his life, which was eventually destroyed by one of his daughters.

CHARLES was the youngest Austen. His sisters Cassandra and Jane called him "our beloved little brother". He was described as cheerful and mischievous. Like Francis, he had a brilliant career in the Navy. Separation from the family was hard, especially for Charles, who enlisted at the age of just fifteen when war was looming. While stationed in Bermuda, he met his first wife, Frances "Fanny" Palmer, with whom he had four children. When she died in childbirth, he married her sister, Harriet. They were the daughters of the Attorney General of Bermuda. With Harriet, he also had four children. One of their daughters, Cassandra-Esten "Cassy", was bequeathed the small portrait of her aunt Jane, now on display at the National Portrait Gallery. Charles continued his military career for a long time. He died in service from an attack of cholera in Burma, aged seventy-three. His body was not repatriated.

JANE AND CASSANDRA, A UNIQUE BOND

When Jane Austen was born on a cold December night, Cassandra was almost three years old. Her parents were delighted at the arrival of a little sister for their first daughter, whom they affectionately nicknamed Cassy. Reverend Austen even joked that the baby was a "toy" for her older sister. For him, they became Cassy and Jenny.

As was often the custom in families of the gentry, the eldest daughter took her mother's first name. Cassandra Elizabeth Austen was born on 9 January 1773 in Steventon. Her middle name was after Mr Austen's grandmother, that courageous ancestor. Because of the age difference of just a few years, Cassandra and her little sister had a close relationship from the start. They never liked to be separated. "If Cassandra were going to have her head cut off, Jane would insist on sharing her fate."[9] Throughout their lives, they would share the same room, the same bed, exchange secrets, laughter, sorrows and dreams.

---

[9] This anecdote comes from Anna Lefroy, Jane and Cassandra's niece, and is reported in *Jane Austen, A Life*, Claire Tomalin, *op. cit.*

CASSANDRA'S TRAGIC ENGAGEMENT

Among the pupils attending the school run by Reverend Austen at Steventon Rectory, four young boys from the same sibling group, the Fowles, became close friends with the Austen children. They came from Kintbury in Berkshire. Among them, Thomas in particular struck a close friendship with James, the eldest of the Austen boys. By the time Thomas and Cassandra reached adolescence, their childhood friendship had developed into deeper feelings. She was only nineteen when they got engaged, Thomas was eight years older. The engagement remained secret for two years, but became official in 1795. They were aware that for financial reasons, marriage was not on the agenda any time soon. This future union was welcomed by both families.

After studying at Oxford, Thomas Fowle became the protégé of his cousin, the wealthy Lord Craven. He offered the young man a parish in Allington, Wiltshire. But Thomas was penniless, and his vicar's salary could not provide Cassandra with the life he wanted to give her. The engaged couple spent Christmas 1795 together at the Fowle family home. He then embarked for the West Indies as a chaplain in the war against the French. Lord Craven promised him a parish in Shropshire when they returned to Ryton. Thomas Fowle hoped to return to England with what he needed to settle down comfortably with Cassandra. We can't help but see a parallel with *Persuasion*. Did Jane Austen imagine a happy ending for her sister?

Misfortune struck the Austen and Fowle families. In May 1797, while everyone was waiting for news of Thomas' imminent return, a shocking letter arrived. It announced news that Thomas had died in February, on his way to Santo Domingo. The young man died of yellow fever. His body was thrown into the sea. James, his best friend, was devastated by the news. Cassandra withdrew into a world of grief and dignity, eliciting the compassion of everyone around her.

Thomas took care to draw up his will before leaving. He bequeathed everything he owned to Cassandra, including £1,000[10] which would help the young woman through many difficult times, particularly the death of her father, the Reverend Austen. Cassandra believed that there was only one love for each person. She decided to mourn this love for the rest of her life, and to devote herself entirely to her family. Jane Austen admired her courage and fortitude, and perhaps drew inspiration from her when she imagined the character of Elinor Dashwood in *Sense and Sensibility*.

It was said that CASSANDRA was pretty, but too serious, even cold and withdrawn, whereas her sister Jane was cheerful, and loved to laugh and entertain. One thing is certain, the two sisters were close companions, complementary to each other. For Cassandra, the loss of the man she loved undoubtedly impacted her. Her younger sister became the centre of her life, and she never stopped encouraging her, supporting her and making her daily life easier so that she could write. They had a close bond, understanding each other without needing to talk.

Later, Mrs. Austen, her daughters and lifelong friend Martha Lloyd lived together in Chawton Cottage for eight years. After Jane Austen's death in 1817, Mrs. Austen's death ten years later, at the venerable age of eighty-seven, and Martha Lloyd's marriage, Cassandra Austen remained alone in Chawton Cottage for almost eighteen years. It was during this period that she decided on and selected the information that the world was entitled to know about her sister's life. She became the guardian of Jane's memory, taking with her the most precious of their secrets and memories. Cassandra died on 22 March 1845, aged seventy-two, probably of a stroke. The two sisters were not reunited in death, as Cassandra is buried in Chawton House cemetery, next to her mother.

---

[10] The equivalent of £144,000 in today's money.

Tombstones of Mrs. Austen and Cassandra at Chawton House.

CASSANDRA AND JANE, TWO TRUE FICTIONAL HEROINES

Cassandra and Jane's bond is often compared to Jane Austen's extremely strong sisterly duos, such as Elinor and Marianne or Jane and Elizabeth[11]. This affection, this trust, this feeling of being part of the other person makes them true heroines of the novels.

In 1919, Eleanor Holmes Hinkley, author and cousin of the American poet T. S. Eliot, wrote *Dear Jane*, the first fictional account of Jane Austen's life. This play in three acts tells the story of the attachment between the two sisters. In the story, the novelist turns down three marriage proposals, including one inspired by the Harris Bigg-Wither anecdote[12]. In reality, Jane Austen preferred to stay with her sister.

The play was first performed in Boston in 1922, then in New York in 1932. It was directed and performed by one of the greatest actresses of the 1930s, Eva Le Gallienne, who took the role of Cassandra. Her stage partner, in the role of Jane Austen, was Josephine Hutchinson. The two women had played famous couples on several occasions, notably Wendy and Peter Pan, to whom Eva Le Gallienne lent her androgynous physique[13].

The latest inspiration is *Miss Austen* (Flatiron Books, 2020) by Gill Hornby. The British novelist gives us the portrait of an ageing Cassandra, whose final task is to preserve her sister's memory. The book was adapted by the BBC for a television series in 2024 "starring Keeley Hawes and Rose Leslie."

---

[11] The heroines of *Sense and Sensibility* and *Pride and Prejudice* respectively.
[12] See the section entitled "A time for love".
[13] At the time, the two actresses were at the centre of a scandal when it was discovered that they were lovers. But this in no way impacted their careers, and in fact made Eva Le Gallienne one of the first queer personalities of the 20th century.

ELIZA, THE BELOVED COUSIN

The destiny of this key figure in the Austen family is like a real adventure novel, the kind that a teenage Jane liked to pastiche in her early writings. ELIZA was bound to have had a considerable influence on her little cousin, who was fond of her anecdotes and accounts of her travels, from India to France, via the hustle and bustle of London life. Jane Austen dedicated the text *Love and Friendship* to her[14].

_____

[14] See the chapter on *Juvenilia* in Part II .

Warren Hastings gave the child a substantial dowry. Philadelphia, Eliza, Hancock and Hastings all travelled to meet George Austen's wife Cassandra after the couple's wedding. Philadelphia and Eliza didn't return to the colonies. A few years later, Warren Hastings became the first Governor General of British India and, once widowed, ended up marrying Baroness Von Imhoff. As for Mr. Hancock, he died in Calcutta in the year that Jane Austen was born.

In 1779, Philadelphia decided to go and live in Paris because it was cheaper than London, but also so that her daughter could learn French. There, Eliza met the handsome Jean-François Capot de Feuillide, captain of Queen Marie-Antoinette's Dragoon Regiment. He went by the title of Count. She married him in 1781. This was enough to fuel Jane Austen's vivid imagination. Suffice to say that this relative appeared exotic to her little cousins in rural England. Eliza had a son, Hastings François Louis Eugène Capot de Feuillide, whom she gave birth to in England[16], risking her health on a chaotic journey from the south of France.

In 1786, Philadelphia, Eliza and little Hastings spent Christmas with the Austens. Henry was there, a handsome teenager already grown up. He found his cousin truly fascinating. The eldest, James, was also increasingly interested in the beautiful Countess. Eliza was fluent in French, refined and well-travelled. She talked about faraway places, the Indies, castles, the king and queen of France, the aristocracy and her new life in London.

Her husband visited her regularly in England, staying for long periods. He supported his wife when she gave birth to a stillborn child. But the French Revolution led to the fall of the monarchy and the hunting down of the nobility. The Comte de Feuillide was arrested and guillotined in 1794. Eliza was thirty-three at the time. Pregnant again, she suffered a miscarriage when she learned of her husband's death. Her mother had died of breast cancer two years previously. Distressed, she found refuge in Steventon, as well as immense comfort in her uncle and her cousins, who adored her.

Her mother was PHILADELPHIA Austen, a strong-willed woman and Mr. Austen's older sister. An apprentice milliner at fifteen and worthy heiress to her grandmother Elizabeth, at twenty-two Philadelphia took her destiny into her own hands and decided to leave for India. She was not rich, but she knew her own beauty. She had no choice but to get married, and above all not to be picky. Men went to India to make their fortune, women went to find a husband who had made a fortune. Her uncle Francis Austen facilitated her journey, obtained the necessary permits and arranged a marriage. It was a difficult journey and took six long months. Nothing is known about the conditions of her arrival, but the fact remains that in February 1753 she married Tysoe Hancock, a doctor with the East India Company.

After this, the story becomes a little confused. We know that Philadelphia became close to Warren Hastings, godfather to her daughter Elizabeth Hancock[15] who was born in December 1761. Was Eliza the daughter of Hancock or of Hastings, who was also married? Doubts always remained, fuelled by the fact that

---

[15] At first she was known as Betsy, but when she reached adolescence she chose the diminutive Eliza.
[16] Some sources claim that he was born in Calais, but it is unclear.

Henry had been in love with his beautiful cousin for a long time. But James declared himself first. Eliza asked for time to think. Like Mary Crawford's character in *Mansfield Park*, she did not see herself as the wife of a man embarking on a career in the church. In 1797, she finally chose Henry, ten years her junior, who was a banker at the time. The marriage was a happy one, although Eliza suffered another tragedy when she lost a son in 1801. The marriage lasted only sixteen years, as Eliza died in 1813, aged almost fifty-two.

Austen scholar Deirdre Le Faye has also produced an extensive bibliography of Eliza in *Jane Austen's 'Outlandish Cousin': The Life and Letters of Eliza de Feuillide* (The British Library, 2002). Eliza is also a character in *Jane Austen: A Play*, written by Helen Brown, great-great-grand-niece of Jane Austen, in 1939.

THE GRAVE OF ELIZA, COMTESSE DE FEUILLIDE

Eliza Austen's grave is located in the small cemetery of St. John-at-Hampstead, north of London. It's in a quiet corner of the town, far from the hustle and bustle of the crowds, in the heart of Hampstead village, wedged between the trendy boutiques and the beautiful houses of the district. 'Refined' is the word that springs to mind. That was certainly the word used to describe Eliza when she was alive. In the tranquillity, her tombstone on the ground is surprisingly discreet.

Beneath the half-faded inscription, which was nevertheless restored in 2013 by the London branch of the Jane Austen Society, are buried two of the strongest figures in the Austen family, Eliza and her mother Philadelphia. With them lies little Hastings, who was in poor health all his life. Remarkably, in the 1970s, this grave was found by chance by Deirdre Le Faye, as a member of the Camden History Society. In 1995, she edited the reference edition of Jane Austen's letters, which remains the authority today.

PHILADELPHIA HANCOCK
26 - 2 - 1792
AGED 61

HER GRANDSON
HASTINGS CAPOT DE FEUILLIDE
25 - 6 - 1786
9 - 10 - 1801

HIS MOTHER
ELIZABETH AUSTEN
25 - 4 - 1813

AGED 50[17]

Inscriptions on Eliza's grave

---

[17] There is a slight discrepancy of two years in relation to her real age, and the error is no doubt due to the funeral parlour at the time.

In the footsteps of Jane Austen

Various places in England are marked
by the indelible imprint of Jane Austen.
These southern English locations: rural Hampshire,
the bustling spa town of Bath, quiet Chawton and Winchester
(now known as the city of her final resting place),
are an ideal tourist route.

STEVENTON: THE HAPPY YEARS

In 1768, after four years of marriage, George and Cassandra Austen moved to Steventon in Hampshire, a modest community of around thirty families. The presbytery was at the end of the village, in a shallow valley dotted with elm trees. The house had red tiles and brick walls. The ground floor comprised a small and a large living room, a kitchen and Mr. Austen's study. Upstairs, there were seven bedrooms and three attic rooms. It was a relatively simple but comfortable home.

However, Mr. Austen's clerical activity did not bring in enough money to support his wife and three children. James, the eldest, was born in 1765, and George a year later. The third little boy, Edward, entered the Austens' lives in 1768, the year they moved to Steventon. In order to increase the family's income, Mr. Austen, an Oxford graduate, decided to take in boarders to prepare them for university. In addition, one of his uncles, Francis Motley Austen, gave him the rectory at Deane, less than two

kilometres away, which added a few extra benefits to the household.

In 1771, little Henry came into the world, followed by the family's first daughter Cassandra in 1773, and a year later Francis. Large families were commonplace, and Mr. and Mrs. Austen chose not to sleep in separate bedrooms. She soon became pregnant again and gave birth to a second girl, a strong, healthy baby. Jane Austen was born on 16 December 1775 during a severe winter that prevented her from being christened in church in the days following her birth[18]. Her arrival was a great joy for little Cassandra, almost three years old, who would find an ideal playmate in Jane. Four years later, when Mrs. Austen no longer expected to have children, the youngest, Charles, made his appearance.

Jane Austen's early years were spent in a warm and loving environment. In 1783, Cassandra and Jane, aged ten and

---

[18] This was postponed until 5 April 1776.

seven, were sent to school in Oxford in the company of Jane Cooper, their cousin. A few months later, Mrs. Ann Cawley, their rigidly-mannered governess, moved with her charges to Southampton. Unfortunately, typhus was spreading very quickly that year, wreaking havoc. The three girls contracted the disease, but Mrs. Cawley did not consider it necessary to notify their families. Jane Cooper, the eldest, took it upon herself to contact her mother. Mrs. Cooper and Mrs. Austen immediately travelled to Southampton to collect all three of them for treatment. Jane Austen was the sickest and narrowly escaped death. Mrs. Cooper, however, was not so lucky. She caught a fever and died shortly afterwards.

Despite this sad episode, Mr. and Mrs. Austen decided to enrol twelve-year-old Cassandra at the Abbey School in Reading in the spring of 1785. Jane Austen was only nine years old and her parents saw no need to send her there too. However, they didn't take into account the young girl's steely will. Not wanting to be separated from her sister, nothing would change her mind. Her parents eventually gave in and her wish was granted. The school was run by Mrs. La Tournelle, who was French in name only. Also known as Sarah Hackitt, this very active woman in her forties couldn't speak a word of French. She loved the theatre, but that was the sum of her skills.

Like most young girls, the two sisters learnt writing, history and geography, sewing, drawing, music and dance. After morning prayers and lessons, the girls could enjoy their free time as they pleased. Cassandra and Jane were happy there. But boarding school was expensive, and their parents took them back to Steventon in the autumn of 1786. From then on, their education took place at home. They learnt some Latin and Italian and took music and singing lessons. Jane Austen received music lessons until she was at least twenty.

At the age of eleven, she met Madam[19] Lefroy, her new neighbour. Madam Lefroy had three children of her own, but Jane Austen quickly befriended the woman who was twenty-six years her senior. Madam Lefroy was a passionate reader, and no doubt advised the future novelist on her reading. In 1789, the Deane rectory had some new tenants: the Lloyd family. The daughters, Martha, twenty-three, and Mary, eighteen, quickly formed a bond with Cassandra and Jane, then aged sixteen and thirteen. That same year, the Austens also met the Bigg sisters, Catherine, Elizabeth and Alethea, who lived in Manydown, a few miles from Steventon.

Jane Austen made her debut into society in 1792, at Enham House near Andover. She loved to dance and go to parties. In Basingstoke, seven miles away, a ball was held every month. No doubt Jane Austen attended as often as she could.

It was in Steventon that the young teenager began to write the short texts now known as *Juvenilia*. In 1795, she tried her hand at an epistolary novel with *Elinor and Marianne* (now known as *Sense and Sensibility*). In 1796, a few months after meeting Tom Lefroy, her alleged childhood sweetheart, Jane Austen drafted the beginning of a novel, *First Impressions* (the original title of *Pride and Prejudice*). The following year, she decided to transform *Elinor and Marianne* into prose. Between 1798 and 1799, she began writing *Susan* (which later became *Northanger Abbey*). She drew her inspiration from the people she met, the people around her, her neighbourhood, but also from her travels with her family in Kent, Hampshire and the capital.

---

[19] Commonly called Madam, without an e, not Mrs.

A NEW LIFE IN BATH

Bath is located in Somerset, in the south-west of England. Originally a sacred Celtic site, the spa town was founded by the Romans from 50 CE onwards. In the 18th century, the town was mainly occupied by holidaymakers seeking the health benefits of the water. But it was also, above all, the place to be for members of high society in search of entertainment.

Jane Austen went there at the end of 1799 with her brother Edward, who was suffering from gout. On this occasion, she wrote to her sister saying how much she appreciated their situation. These few weeks spent in Bath were pleasant, the activities and society contact refreshing for this young twenty-four year old woman.

However, at the beginning of December 1800, Mr. and Mrs. Austen announced suddenly that they were leaving Steventon to move to Bath, at which Jane Austen nearly fainted. Even though she had fond memories of time she spent in this town, she couldn't imagine leaving her childhood home, the place where she was born, grew up, got up to mischief, met so many friends and cherished all the wonderful times she spent there.

However, the decision was not hers to make. All the Austen boys, grown up and mostly married, had left home and only Cassandra and Jane, unmarried, were still in the care of their parents. In a letter, however, Jane Austen confided that she did eventually come to terms with the idea of moving. They left the rectory in the spring of 1801, leaving the place to James, who had become a churchman. He succeeded his father at the rectory in Steventon.

The Royal Crescent

What you might think is a series of thirty identical houses is just an illusion. Between 1767 and 1774, only the façades of this "crescent" were built by the developers, and they resemble each other perfectly. The future buyers then hired an architect for the rest of their house. If you venture to the rear of the Crescent, you'll notice differences in the height of the roofs and the number of windows. Today, Number 1 Royal Crescent is a museum that gives an insight into the daily life of an 18th century house. A wide range of furniture, paintings and historical objects can be seen there. Wander through the dining room, the boudoir, the study, the bedrooms, the kitchen, the servants' quarters and don't miss the top floor, from which you can admire the remarkable view.

Information at: no1royalcrescent.org.uk

After living at number 1 Paragon with Mrs. Austen's relatives the Leigh-Perrot family, they moved to 4 Sydney Place.[20] Jane Austen approved of this choice. Before moving in, she said: "It would be very pleasant to be near Sydney Gardens! We might go into the Labyrinth every day".[21] These gardens were a place for meeting up and where events took place. Concerts, galas and fireworks displays were organised here. During her stay in 1799, the novelist told Cassandra: "The fireworks were really beautiful and surpassing my expectation".[22]

Jane Austen loved walking and regularly took walks in and around the city: Weston Village, Lyncombe Hill, Widcombe. She liked to go to the Royal Crescent when the conditions were right: "We didn't walk long in the Crescent yesterday, it was too hot and not crowded enough".[23] The Circus, arranged like a perfect circle, and the Georgian Garden nearby were undoubtedly places she liked to frequent.

In Bath, Jane Austen visited her acquaintances regularly. After one of these visits, she wrote to her sister, who was away visiting a friend: "Another stupid party last night [...] I cannot anyhow continue to find people agreeable; I respect Mrs. Chamberlayne for doing her hair well, but cannot feel a more tender sentiment".[24] The novelist also attended plays and balls at the Assembly Rooms.

Since 1799, a few months before she left Steventon, Jane Austen's literary activity seemed to be non-existent. Between 1802 and 1803, she copied out *Susan* (the future *Northanger Abbey*) with the intention of having it published, and her brother Henry took charge of selling the copyright to a London publisher, Crosby & Co. The novelist took up her pen again in 1804 and began work on *The Watsons*. A few months later, in early 1805, Mr. Austen died suddenly, probably of an acute bacterial infection.[25] The news came as a shock to the whole family. What's more, it meant that Mrs. Austen and her two daughters no longer had an income, and their meagre savings would not provide enough support. Nevertheless, the Austen family was close-knit, and the brothers provided help and financial support. The three women stayed in Bath and moved to 25 Gay Street, then

---

[20] A plaque on the house states that Jane Austen lived there from 1801 to 1805.
[21] *Jane Austen's Letters*, Deirdre Le Faye, *op. cit.*
[22] *Ibid.*
[23] *Ibid.*
[24] *Ibid.*
[25] Mr. Austen is buried in St. Swithin's Church, Bath.

in January 1806 to Trim Street. Jane Austen stopped writing *The Watsons* and never returned to it.

A few months later, Francis, in the Royal Navy, returned to England and received prize money for his captures at sea. He was thus able to marry the woman of his heart, Mary Gibson. Francis, who was due to leave again soon, suggested to his mother and two sisters that they stay with his love in Southampton, so that she would not be alone. The offer was enthusiastically accepted and the move took place in October 1806. Two years later, Jane Austen told her sister about the thrill of escaping from Bath.

Daily life in Southampton was relatively quiet, punctuated by visits and occasional trips to see family members. After living there for three years, they left in June 1809.

Did you know?

Two of Jane Austen's novels are largely set in Bath: *Northanger Abbey* and *Persuasion*. In the first, Catherine Morland is delighted with the activities on offer in the city. At a ball, she meets Mr. Tilney through the master of ceremonies of the Assembly Rooms: Mr. King. This famous Mr. King was indeed master of ceremonies at the Lower Rooms between 1785 and 1805, and then at the Upper Rooms. In the second novel, Anne Elliot goes to Bath with a little less enthusiasm, preferring the joys of the countryside to the spa town's activities.

Based on these two writings, *Northanger Abbey*, written before the Steventon move, and *Persuasion*, written at the end of her life, some speculate that Jane Austen really did enjoy the few weeks she spent in the spa town, but that overall, the years she lived there were not the happiest.

THE ASSEMBLY ROOMS

In 18th century Bath, there were two Assembly Rooms: the Lower Rooms and the Upper Rooms. Comprising several rooms, they were notorious social meeting venues where balls and card games were organised. They were also great locations to have tea with new acquaintances.

The Lower Rooms, built in 1708, were located in the 'lower' part of the town. The ballroom was twenty-seven metres long and eleven metres wide, and the walls were decorated with numerous paintings. There were also two tea rooms, a games room and an eighteen-metre-long card room. Unfortunately, they were destroyed in 1820.

The Upper Rooms opened their doors in September 1771, competing with the Lower Rooms with their more majestic architecture. Measuring thirty-two metres long and twelve metres wide, the ballroom was richly decorated with portraits painted by Gainsborough and five magnificent chandeliers. An octagonal room led to the ballroom, tea room and games room. These are the current Assembly Rooms that can be admired[26] when you visit Bath.

Concerts and balls were held at least twice a week. The dances began at six o'clock in the evening and lasted until eleven o'clock at night. During one ball, Jane Austen was astonished: "There was only one dance, danced by four couples. Think of four couples, surrounded by about an hundred people, dancing in the Upper Rooms in Bath!"[27]

Additional information:
Take a look at the logbook for the Bath Jane Austen Festival (an event not to be missed!), where you'll find information about getting to Bath and places to visit there (page 255).

---

[26] The Assembly Rooms are not currently open to the public. The National Trust is looking into the possibility of offering visitors a new experience. A reopening has been announced for 2026. The Fashion Museum, which was housed in the Assembly Rooms, is currently being moved to a building in the city centre. Check out their collection at **fashionmuseum.co.uk**.
[27] *Jane Austen's Letters*, Deirdre Le Faye, *op. cit.*

CHAWTON: THE CALM YEARS

After Southampton, and Francis' marriage to Mary Gibson, the women of the Austen family and Martha Lloyd began looking for a cheaper place to live. Edward Knight, the heir to the wealthy family that adopted him when he was sixteen, offered them the chance to choose between two of his houses. One was in Kent, in the village of Wye, near his Godmersham estate, where he lived for much of the year with his numerous offspring.[28] The other was in Chawton, Hampshire, the county where Jane Austen was born and where she had been so happy. "The home of a favourite author is always of great interest to those who love the books that have been written there",[29] her niece Caroline would later write. That's why today Chawton is an essential place for understanding Jane Austen.

In 1809, the family chose Chawton in Hampshire. The six-room cottage had a lot going for it. It was not far from London; and was also close to Steventon, where James Austen worked. It was also pleasantly close to Chawton House, where Edward and his family stayed when they came to the area. Martha Lloyd, a long-time friend and housekeeper,[30] joined Mrs. Austen and her daughters in the house. Mrs. Austen enjoyed gardening, while Cassandra and Martha kept Jane comfortable so that she could write in peace.

The previous year, 1808, Edward Knight had commissioned some renovation and refurbishment work. The windows and wallpaper were replaced, the water pump repaired and the garden landscaped. So the house was safe and

---

[28] At the time, his wife Elizabeth had just died giving birth to their eleventh child.
[29] *My Aunt Jane Austen, A Memoir*, Caroline Austen, 1867.
[30] She had been living with them in Southampton.

comfortable. The four women did not own a vehicle as such, although they regularly used a small cart[31] pulled by a donkey. Their pace of life was modest, but sufficient. In 1814, however, neighbours at Chawton Cottage challenged Edward Knight's right to the entire Chawton estate. This trial lasted for years, but finally recognised the totality and validity of his inheritance.

Our Chawton home - how much we find
Already in it to our mind,
And now convinced that when complete,
It will all other Houses beat
That ever have been made or mended,
With rooms concise or rooms distended.[32]

Jane Austen wrote this little poem for her brother Francis in July 1809, to congratulate him on the birth of his son. That was how happy she was to live in this pretty cottage in Chawton, where she could settle down and relax.

In this inspiring setting, Jane Austen's creativity blossomed and flourished. She went back to her old writings and started new ones. It was a haven of peace for her. We recognise details of this house when she describes Barton Cottage, the home of the Dashwood sisters, in *Sense and Sensibility*. She lived there for eight wonderful years, before illness finally caught up with her.

---

[31] It is still kept at the cottage in Chawton.
[32] *Jane Austen's Letters*, Deirdre Le Faye, *op. cit.*

A DAY IN THE LIFE OF JANE AUSTEN AT CHAWTON

When she was not visiting relatives or acquaintances, Jane Austen was happy to take part in everyday tasks. She started her day practising the piano. Despite the presence of a cook, a maid and a valet, it was she who took care of breakfast for the household at around nine o'clock in the morning. Because of the imposing fireplace in the middle of the room, which generated an impressive amount of ash and could therefore cover the ground floor with soot, the kitchen had a separate entrance door. So you had to go through the garden to get to it. Jane Austen boiled water for tea and toasted some bread.

Jane Austen's writing table at Chawton

When she was working on her novels, patiently copying sheet music or dealing with her correspondence in the morning, she sat in the dining room, near the window, on a small table that benefited from the sun's rays at this time of day. She also enjoyed watching the hustle and bustle of the crossroads and the passing carriages. In the afternoon, the light was better in the small lounge. Sometimes she embroidered and played cup-and-ball to relax.

When the weather was fine, she might go to Alton, a thirty-minute walk away. She would buy sugar and tea and order wine. If necessary, she would stock up on ink and paper, unless she had brought back enough from London or Martha had made some. Life was peaceful, they dined early and went early to bed. Sometimes in the evening, to the delight of her audience, Jane Austen read passages from her works aloud. In the opinion of all those around her, she was particularly good at it. She shared a bedroom with her sister Cassandra, as they had always done.

Kent and Godmersham Park

Kent is an important location in the Austen family history, and a must for anyone wishing to make a pilgrimage in the footsteps of the British novelist. Jane Austen travelled there many times, and her father was born in the county, in the market town of Tonbridge. In fact, as you walk through the town, in the shadow of the imposing medieval castle, you can't help thinking that she too must also have wandered there, on the arm of Cassandra, along the River Medway.

Some seventy kilometres further west, not far from Canterbury, lies the Godmersham Park estate in the town of the same name. It was the principal residence of Edward Knight, who inherited it from his adoptive parents. This beautiful Palladian-style residence was built in 1732. Jane Austen spent long periods there. While there, she befriended Anne Sharp, her niece Fanny Knight's governess. This relationship was an important one in Jane Austen's life, for after her death Cassandra took care to leave a small legacy to Anne Sharp in memory of this friendship. Novelist Gill Hornby recounts this encounter from Anne's point of view in her novel *Godmersham Park* (Penguin Books, 2022).

Today, the building is home to the Association of British Dispensing Opticians. It is not open to the public, but you can admire the manor house and its gardens from the outside. These can be visited on National Gardens Scheme days in April and June, information at **ngs.org.uk**. If you look closely at the current £10 note with Jane Austen, you'll recognise Godmersham, discreetly depicted on her left.

WINCHESTER, OR THE END OF THE JOURNEY

The capital of Hampshire, Winchester, is a centuries-old city, dating back to Roman times. Before the Norman invasion, it had even been the capital of England during the Saxon era. The earliest remains of a church, Old Minster, date from before 650. It became a cathedral in 660, dedicated to St Swithun.[33] Jane Austen's last text, dictated to Cassandra three days before her death, is a short poem about this saint, whose feast day falls on 15 July.[34] Jane Austen spent her last days in this city steeped in history, completely unaware of how much her presence would bring prestige to it.

In 1817, Jane Austen knew she was very ill. Being farsighted, she had already secretly drawn up her will on 27 April and left it, unwitnessed, in her writing desk in Chawton. She made her sister executor of her will, which was unusual for the time since it was customary for this role to be held by a man.

---

[33] St Swithun was bishop of Winchester Cathedral in the 9th century.

[34] Destiny? Jane Austen's parents were married in the church of St Swithun (also spelt Swithin) in Bath, and Mr. Austen is buried there, **stswithinswalcot.org.uk**.

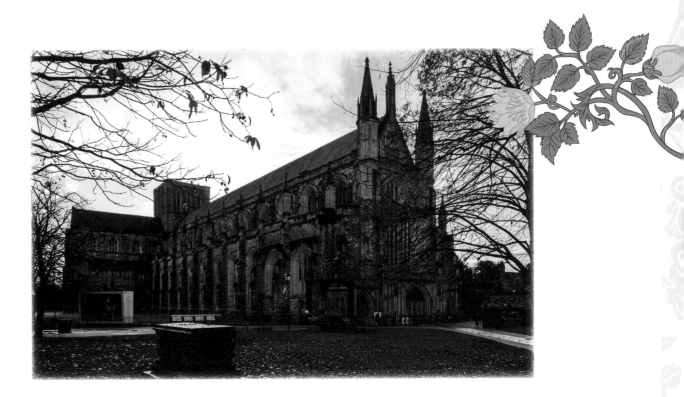

Jane Austen had already experienced illness. During their childhood, the Austen sisters narrowly missed succumbing to a typhus epidemic while at boarding school in Southampton. Later in her adult life, the novelist was seriously affected by whooping cough, as well as by frequent ear infections. From the letters that have survived, which describe these various inconveniences, we can see a strong tendency to joke about them as much as possible, and rarely to complain about them.

We may never know the real cause of Jane Austen's death. Addison's disease, tuberculosis and stomach cancer have all been suggested. However, recent research suggests that it could have been Hodgkin Lymphoma.[35] There are several strong indications that this was the case. Jane Austen began to weaken around 1813. First, she suffered from facial neuralgia, forcing her to walk around with a small cushion against her cheek to rest her head. She also suffered from severe itching. These pains were probably caused by persistent shingles, due to an immune deficiency, a symptom of Hodgkin Lymphoma.

JANE AUSTEN'S WILL

I, Jane Austen, of the Parish of Chawton, do by this my last Will & Testament give and bequeath to my dearest sister Cassandra Elizabeth everything of which I may die possessed, or which may be hereafter due to me, subject to the payment of my Funeral Expenses, & to a Legacy of £50. to my Brother Henry, & £50 to Madame Byion[36] which I request may be paid as soon as convenient. And I appoint my said dear Sister the Executrix of this my last Will & Testament.[37]

Jane Austen, 27 April 1817

---

[35] A form of cancer of the lymphatic system, it was first identified by the English physician Thomas Hodgkin in 1832. Today, it is very well-treated with chemotherapy and radiotherapy.

[36] Madame Byion or Bigeon is Eliza Austen's former French chambermaid, the ex-Comtesse de Feuillide.

[37] *The Life of Jane Austen*, John Halperin, Johns Hopkins University Press, 1984.

After 1815, a nasty bout of conjunctivitis took its toll, preventing her from reading and, above all, writing. Henry Austen's correspondence also confirms the deterioration in his sister's health in 1816. Although Jane Austen's successive biographers agree that this date marks the beginning of her illness, it may simply be the moment when she agreed to talk about her condition and her family realised that she was not well.

Her health declined slowly but steadily, with a few periods of calm that gave her family cruel hope. The Austen sisters tried unsuccessfully to take a spa treatment at Cheltenham in Gloucestershire, which specialised in skin diseases. Before returning to Chawton, they stopped off in Steventon and Kintbury to greet the family of Thomas Fowle, the fiancé Cassandra had never forgotten. Back home, Jane Austen could barely walk. However, so as not to deprive her mother of the comfort of the only sofa, she used three chairs to lie down.

The novelist fought with all her might, amid fevers and lethargy. Alton's apothecary, William Curtis, declared himself totally incompetent to help her. The family tried everything, clinging to the slightest hope. It became imperative to leave Chawton in search of a cure. On 24 May 1817, very ill, Jane Austen went with Cassandra to Steventon. Their brother James lent them his carriage to reach Winchester, and the two women were escorted by their nephew William and their brother Henry. The journey was difficult, the weather was bleak and it was pouring rain. In this larger town there was a hospital, better-trained carers and, above all, a renowned doctor known to the family, Dr Gyles-King Lyford.

Thanks to lifelong friends Elizabeth Heathcote and Alethea Bigg, Jane Austen and Cassandra moved close to him, to 8 College Street with Mrs. David. At times Jane seemed better, but then the fever and aches came back, all the time stronger. Her brother James travelled back and forth to Winchester frequently and kept the family informed.[38] When her condition worsened further, Mary Lloyd Austen, James' second wife, was called in to help, as the nurse had been caught sleeping.

The plaque on the front of the house reads:
"In this house Jane Austen lived her last days and died 18 July 1817".

Mary, Cassandra and her maid took turns working through the night.

In the end, the disease prevailed. Jane Austen died in her sister's arms at half past four in the morning on 18 July 1817. She was only forty-one years old. The pain of those who knew her was immense, Cassandra's unfathomable. She closed Jane's eyes and cut a few strands of her hair to give to loved ones. Women were not allowed to attend funerals, as they were considered too sensitive. Jane's coffin was accompanied by three of her brothers, Henry, Edward and Francis, as well as her nephew James Edward. On the morning of 24 July, Cassandra watched the funeral procession pull away, and when it reached the corner of the street, she realised that she had lost her sister. She wrote to her niece Fanny: "She was the sun of my life, the gilder of every pleasure, the soother of every sorrow... it is as if I had lost a part of myself. I loved her only too well, not better than she deserved".[39]

---

[38] The distance is around sixteen miles, or just over an hour with a galloping horse.
[39] *The Life of Jane Austen*, John Halperin, *op. cit.*

Thanks to the intervention of her brother Henry Austen, who called on his ecclesiastical connections, on Thursday 24 July 1817 Jane Austen was discreetly buried, not in a simple cemetery, but in the north wing of the prestigious Winchester Cathedral, which was already very popular at the time, attracting many tourists from all over the country.

On the floor of the cathedral,[40] the black marble plaque affixed by the family reads:

In Memory of
JANE AUSTEN,
Youngest daughter
of the late Rev. GEORGE AUSTEN,
formerly Rector of Steventon in this County.

She departed this Life on the 18th of July 1817,
aged 41,
after a long illness supported with
the patience and the hopes of a Christian.

The benevolence of her heart,
the sweetness of her temper, and

the extraordinary endowments of her mind
obtained the regard of all who knew her and
the warmest love of her intimate connections.

Their grief is in proportion to their affection
they know their loss to be irreparable,
but in their deepest affliction they are consoled
by a firm though humble hope that her charity,
devotion, faith and purity have rendered
her soul acceptable in the sight of her
REDEEMER.

A second copper plaque was added to the north wall in 1872, financed by the profits from the sale of James Edward Austen-Leigh's *A Memoir of Jane Austen*.

JANE AUSTEN
known to many by her writings,
endeared to her family
by the varied charms of her character
and ennobled by Christian Faith and Piety,
was born in Steventon, in the county of Hants[41]
Decr XVI MDCCLXXV,
and buried in this cathedral
July XXIV MDCCCXVII.
"She openeth her mouth with wisdom,
and in her tongue is the law of kindness."
Prov. XXXI v. XXVI

---

[40] **winchester-cathedral.org.uk**.
[41] Abbreviation of Hampshire.

JANE AUSTEN IN LONDON

"Here I am once more in this city [London], Scene of Dissipation & vice, and I begin already to find my Morals corrupted."[42]

Jane Austen never lived in London, but she visited the English capital on many occasions. In 1796, she stayed there with her brothers. They lodged in a hostel on Cork Street in Mayfair. Today it is home to the Burlington Arcade, which overlooks Piccadilly. **Information at burlingtonarcade.com.**

Henry Austen lived briefly at 10 Henrietta Street. A plaque marks the spot where Jane Austen visited him during his wife Eliza's illness. The building is close to two theatres, Drury Lane and Covent Garden, where the novelist and her family attended performances. A little further on, at the Lyceum, she saw *Hypocrite*, a play adapted from Molière's *Tartuffe*. Today, this dwelling is located just above a colourful pub, the *Mrs. R!OT*.

Henry and Eliza Austen lived for a time at 64 Sloane Street in Kensington and Chelsea. There is also a blue plaque there commemorating Jane Austen's visit. The building was renovated in 1897 by the architect Fairfax Blomfield Wade-Palmer. Henry Austen moved to 23 Hans Place in the same neighbourhood after his wife's death. His sister very much appreciated the small garden nearby. In 1815, when he was ill, the novelist stayed on to look after him, while work began on getting *Emma* published.

When Jane Austen wanted to buy tea, she always went to Twinings on the Strand, at number 216. This veritable institution was opened in 1706 by Thomas Twining. Tea was expensive at the time, not least because it was top quality and because the import tax was very high. Despite these constraints, this venue was a great success. As well as Jane Austen, the shop also counted the painter William Hogarth among its famous regulars.

Twinings' flagship shop in London

---

[42] *Jane Austen's Letters*, Deirdre Le Faye, Oxford University Press, 2011.

Hatchards is famous for being London's oldest surviving bookshop. In 1797, at the age of twenty-nine, John Hatchard opened this shop in Piccadilly, a fashionable district. According to the shop's records, it was here that Jane Austen bought her copy of Ann Radcliffe's *Mysteries of Udolpho*, which inspired *Northanger Abbey*. Today, this bookshop is also known for selling first and rare editions –if you're lucky, you might be able to pick up a Peacock edition of *Pride and Prejudice*.

Information at hatchards.co.uk.

50 Albemarle Street was home to publisher John Murray. In 1815, he took on the publication of *Mansfield Park* and *Emma*. At the time, this publishing house was an incredible literary hub, the star of which was undoubtedly Lord Byron, the most popular living poet. John Murray wrote to him in September 1817, just after Jane Austen's death, to inform him that he was about to publish two new novels by "the ingenious author of *Pride and Prejudice*".[43] A little later, in 1859, this publishing house brought out a landmark work, Charles Darwin's *The Origin of Species*. The Murray Press brand still exists today, as a subsidiary of the Hachette group.

For more information, visit johnmurraypress.co.uk.

When she was in London, Jane Austen never missed an exhibition at Somerset House. At the time, the prestigious Royal Academy of Arts was based there. Today it stands opposite Hatchards Bookshop in Burlington House on Piccadilly. In May 1813, the novelist enjoyed a retrospective exhibition at the Pall Mall art gallery, also known as the British Institute. There, she amused herself by finding a portrait that would catch her eye as Elizabeth Bennet, now Mrs. Darcy, whom she imagined dressed in yellow. Created especially for the two-hundredth anniversary of *Pride and Prejudice* by the University of Austin in Texas, *What Jane Saw* is an online reconstruction of the exhibition of paintings by Sir Joshua Reynolds.

For more information, visit whatjanesaw.org.

Jane Austen is buried in Winchester Cathedral, but London's Westminster Abbey also pays tribute to her in Poets' Corner. A commemorative plaque places her in good company, alongside Charles Dickens, George Eliot, the Brontë sisters and Lewis Carroll.

For more information, visit westminster-abbey.org.

Did you know?

THERE ARE THEMED JANE AUSTEN WALKS IN LONDON

London Walks offers original tours of the English capital, and the one devoted to Jane Austen reminds us that although she was a country girl, her literary life was linked to London. The walk begins at the very spot where stagecoaches arrived from Hampshire in the Regency era. The rest of the tour focuses on the various London locations evoked in *Sense and Sensibility*, with a short detour to see the building where her publisher was based, as well as some of the shops in Old Bond Street that the novelist once visited.

For more information, visit walks.com.
Online calendar of walks.

---

[43] *A Chronology of Jane Austen and Her Family*, Deirdre Le Faye, University Cambridge Press, 2013.

A time for love

Throughout her life, Jane Austen remained single.
When you consider the wonderful love stories that populate her
novels, the question arises: was she inspired by what she read,
by the affairs of the heart of those around her, or by her own
experience? Thanks to her correspondence and information
gleaned from biographical writings, a number of conclusions
can be drawn.

TOM LEFROY, A FAILED LOVE AFFAIR?

Thomas Langlois Lefroy was born in 1776 in Limerick, Ireland, less than a month after Jane Austen's birth. In 1790, at the age of fourteen, he entered Trinity College Dublin. An ambitious and hard-working student, he went to London in 1793 to study law at Lincoln's Inn, graduating two years later. His great-uncle Benjamin Langlois, who paid his school fees, described him as a young man with wit and common sense.

In January 1796, Tom travelled to Ashe, not far from Steventon, where the Austen family lived. He then visited his uncle, Mr. Lefroy, the rector of this parish. His wife, Madam Anne Lefroy, was a close friend of the novelist. The young man took advantage of this respite to take part in some of the local festivities. This is how he met Jane Austen.

In a letter to her sister Cassandra, the young woman described the ball that had taken place the day before: "I am almost afraid to tell you how my Irish friend and I behaved".[44] This handsome and pleasant friend was none other than Tom Lefroy. The two young people only saw each other at three balls and during a visit to the Austens' house. Their last meeting took place at a reception in Ashe the day before Tom Lefroy's departure. In the same letter, Jane Austen added: "The Day is come on which I am to flirt my last with Tom Lefroy, & when you receive this it will be over. My tears flow as I write, at the melancholy idea".[45] Ironic? Real grief? Perhaps a mixture of the two. She seemed to oscillate between attraction, amusement and indifference towards the young man.

Did you know?

Directed by Julian Jarrold in 2007, the biopic *Becoming Jane* is based on Jane Austen's correspondence and her alleged love affair with Tom Lefroy. Anne Hathaway stars opposite James McAvoy.

BECOMING JANE

---

[44] *Jane Austen's Letters*, Deirdre Le Faye, *op. cit.*
[45] *Ibid.*

One thing is certain: if Jane Austen and Tom Lefroy did have feelings for each other, fate destroyed the beginnings of their romantic relationship. Mr. and Madam Lefroy took the initiative to send their nephew back to London quickly. Without a fortune and with twelve children, the young man's family was counting on him to marry a woman from a wealthy background. As their eldest son, he was responsible for providing for them. And without a dowry, Jane Austen was not the wife they hoped for.

In 1797, Tom Lefroy became engaged to Mary Paul, the sister of one of his school friends. In the autumn of 1798, he returned to Ashe to visit his aunt and uncle, but did not see Jane Austen. She writes to Cassandra: "of her nephew [Madam Lefroy] said nothing at all [...]. She didn't mention his name once and I was too proud to make any enquiries."[46] She added that she had heard from their father that Tom had been called to the Bar and was on his way to Ireland.

Tom Lefroy and Mary Paul married in 1799. After the sudden death of her brother, the young woman became sole heir to the family fortune. The couple had eight children.[47] Tom Lefroy began a long and distinguished career in law and became Chief Justice of the Supreme Court of Ireland. He died in 1869 at the age of ninety-three. At the end of his life, he revealed to his nephew that he had indeed fallen in love with Jane Austen, but that she had been a childhood love.

A SPECIAL FRIENDSHIP

Anne Brydges Lefroy was an important figure in Jane Austen's life. Twenty-six years her senior, Madam Lefroy had a very good relationship with the novelist and her family. She was a beautiful, talented woman and an eloquent speaker. She was very involved in local life. She taught the village children to read and write, and took charge of inoculating them against smallpox after Dr Edward Jenner's discovery.

What role did Madam Lefroy play in the story of Jane Austen and Tom Lefroy? We don't know if it was really her decision to cut short her nephew's stay to prevent an unhappy marriage with her dear friend. In any case, the relationship between the two women does not seem to have waned. In 1804, on Jane Austen's birthday, Madam Lefroy died tragically in a riding accident. Four years later, the novelist dedicated a poem to her, which reveals a deep attachment:

"The day returns again, my natal day;
What mix'd emotions with the Thought arise!
Beloved friend, four years have pass'd away
Since thou wert snatch'd forever from our eyes. –
[...]
Angelic Woman! past my power to praise
In Language meet, thy Talents, Temper, mind.
Thy solid Worth, they captivating Grace! –
Thou friend and ornament of Humankind! –."[48]

---

[46] *Ibid.*

[47] The biopic *Becoming Jane* plays on the ambiguity of the first name of Tom Lefroy's eldest daughter, who is also called Jane, as a tribute to the novelist. However, she is more likely to have been named after Mary Paul's mother.

[48] *Juvenilia, Jane Austen*, 10-18, 1999. The complete poem is freely available on the Internet: **janeausten.co.uk/blogs/jane-miscellany/to-the-memory-of-mrs-lefroy**.

THE MYSTERIOUS SAMUEL BLACKALL

In 1797, Madam Lefroy invited one of her acquaintances, Samuel Blackall, with a view to a possible courtship with Jane Austen. The twenty-six-year-old was studying at Emmanuel College, Cambridge. He was tall, good-natured and had a generous heart. Nevertheless, courtship was not one of his skills, and his ostentatious manner was hardly an advantage. His visit was brief, and even though Madam Lefroy invited him back the following Christmas, he apologised for not being able to grant her request. In a letter to her sister, Jane Austen expressed her relief at the situation, saying that "our indifference will soon be mutual".[49]

HARRIS BIGG-WITHER, ALMOST A FIANCÉ

In 1802, now living in Bath, Jane and Cassandra took advantage of a trip to visit very close friends Catherine and Alethea Bigg[50] and there was plenty to enjoy with them. A few days after their arrival, their brother Harris proposed to Jane Austen. Her answer was yes! Harris, six years her junior, was plain and awkward. He stammered and lacked self-confidence, but he was heir to the family fortune. They already knew each other, his sisters were her friends... And above all, the young woman was twenty-seven and already considered an old maid. This proposal seemed to be the chance of a lifetime. It was certainly an unexpected opportunity: the security of having a roof over your head to house your family, the freedom to maintain your own home – what an exciting destiny!

But the very next morning, in a complete turn of events, Jane Austen retracted her answer. It is said that it's best to sleep on it, but what was going on in her head? Several theories have been put forward, but none of them has been proven. Fear of non-existent love? Being separated from Cassandra? Not having the freedom to write? Whatever the reasons, the two sisters left Manydown immediately to go to Steventon. They asked their brother James to drive them back to Bath within the hour, without giving any explanation. Jane Austen would only confess a few years later the reason for her sudden departure, not daring to face the eyes of her brothers at the time, ashamed as she was to remain a burden on them.

It is not known whether Jane Austen saw the young man again after this incident, but the Bigg and Austen sisters always kept in touch. Harris married Anne Howe Frith two years later, with whom he had ten children.

A DARK-EYED STRANGER

From Cassandra's recollections, we learn that during a family trip to Devonshire, Jane Austen met a charming man. It is likely that this episode took place between 1801 and 1804, but Cassandra does not give a date. She explains only that the attachment between her sister and this man was mutual, and that the man was so attracted to Jane Austen and so in love with her that he insisted on knowing where the Austens were going on holiday next. However, some time later, the tragic news came that this stranger had died. There is no certainty as to the identity of this holiday love, except that this man could, perhaps, have been the chosen one of Jane Austen's heart.

---

[49] *Jane Austen's Letters*, Deirdre Le Faye, *op. cit.*
[50] Only the father and the Bigg boys added the name Wither to their surname, in homage to the last owner of Manydown Manor.

FLIRTATIONS, REAL OR IMAGINED?

Marriage without love? Impossible for Jane Austen. Choosing celibacy did not make her unhappy; she found fulfilment for her life in her writing. However, she was also a flesh-and-blood human being, sensitive to the compliments and attention she could elicit. She wasn't always indifferent to the attractive gentlemen who crossed her path.

• Probably before 1796, Jane Austen met Edward Taylor, a relative of her brother Edward's wife. She mentioned him only a few times, but in one of her letters,[51] she confided to her sister that she had contemplated with melancholy pleasure the beautiful black eyed-gaze of this young man, with whom she was in love.

• In a letter dated January 1796, she mentioned[52] a certain Charles Powlett who tried to kiss her at a ball.

• Edward Bridges, the brother of Edward Knight's wife, fell in love with Jane and probably asked her to marry him. To Cassandra, she wrote: "I wish you could accept Lady Bridges' invitation, because I cannot accept her son Edward's".[53]

• At a party in 1806, a member of parliament, Robert Holt Leigh, fell in love with the young woman's pretty face and gave her a few signs of his admiration. But the story ended there, they never saw each other again.[54]

• At the age of thirty-six, Jane Austen met William Seymour, her brother Henry's lawyer. He found her charming and was seriously thinking of asking her to marry him. However, he never did.[55]

Did you know?

Mr. Austen, a clergyman, officiated at baptisms, deaths and marriages in Steventon Rectory. Jane Austen, then aged fifteen, was already dreaming of love and romance, and of meeting her Prince Charming. The solution: to get married! And nothing could be simpler: she took her father's register and had fun entering a number of fanciful names, as if she were getting married. She published the banns of Henry Frederic Howard Fitzwilliam of London and Jane Austen of Steventon, Edmund Arthur William Mortimer of Liverpool and Jane Austen of Steventon and finally Jack Smith and Jane Smith, née Austen.

[51] *Jane Austen's Letters*, Deirdre Le Faye, *op. cit.*
[52] *Ibid.*
[53] *Ibid.*
[54] *Jane Austen at Home*, Lucy Worsley, Hodder & Stoughton, 2017.
[55] *Jane Austen, A Family Record*, Deirdre Le Faye, Cambridge University Press, 2004.

JANE AUSTEN, LOVE ADVISOR

When Jane Austen took up her pen to offer advice to her beloved nieces, Anna Austen Lefroy and Fanny Knight Knatchbull, she never hesitated to speak her mind.

ANNA AUSTEN was the eldest daughter of James Austen, the novelist's brother, and his first wife, Anne Matthews. Born in 1793, Anna lost her mother when she was just two years old. James entrusted her to his own mother and his two sisters, Jane and Cassandra. They took her in for two years before their brother married Mary Lloyd.

When she was sixteen, Anna became secretly engaged to the Reverend Michael Terry. He was twice her age and handsome, he had a comfortable life, but James refused the match for no apparent reason. A few weeks later, Cassandra pleaded Anna's case with James, who agreed to give her permission. Anna visited her fiancé's family for three days, but realised that she was not in love. This time, the relationship was well and truly over.

In 1813, she announced to her family that she wished to marry Benjamin Lefroy, the youngest son of Madam Lefroy. He was tall and good-looking with good manners, but he was unemployed and didn't know what he wanted to do in life. Jane Austen was worried about the couple. She felt their tastes and temperaments were too different. Nevertheless, the two young people announced their engagement on 7 August 1813 and married in the autumn of 1814. After the wedding, Jane Austen wrote mischievously to her niece: "I rather imagine indeed that nieces are seldom chosen but out of compliment to some aunt or another".[56]

FANNY KNIGHT, born in 1793, was the eldest daughter of Edward Knight, Jane Austen's brother. This much-loved niece kept a diary that tells us a great deal about her and the whole Austen family. In her correspondence, the novelist gave her niece a great deal of valuable advice about love. At the age of nineteen, she fell under the spell of Mr. John Pemberton Plumptre of Fredville. They met again two years later at parties at which Mr. Plumptre paid her much attention. But some time later, Fanny's feelings began to fade. Jane Austen reassured her and advised her not to go any further unless she was certain of his attachment. Her aunt remarked: "nothing can be compared to the misery of being bound without love – bound to one, and preferring another; that is a punishment which you do not deserve".[57]

But at twenty-four, Fanny worried that she hadn't yet found a husband, regretting that she may have missed her chance with John Plumptre. However, a new young man appeared on the scene, a certain Mr. Wildman. Jane Austen told her niece that she must not throw herself wholeheartedly into the relationship if the young man has no feelings for her. "To you I shall say, as I have often said before, do not be in a hurry, the right man will come at last", and the novelist added that she will soon meet the one who will be attached to her in such a way that "you will feel you never really loved before".[58] Unfortunately, in 1820, at the age of twenty-seven, Fanny married a lonely and morose widower, Sir Edward Knatchbull.

[56] *Jane Austen's Letters*, Deirdre Le Faye, *op. cit.*

[57] *Pas de femmes parfaites, s'il vous plaît* (No perfect women, please), Exclusive Collection of Letters, L'Orma, 2020.

[58] *Ibid.*

Portrait of a Lady

If there is one literary figure about whom little or nothing is known, it is Jane Austen. We have a vague idea of her looks and general appearance. Specialists have worked hard researching as much information and detail as possible about the 'real' Jane Austen. In the absence of reliable portraits and precise descriptions, all we have is a set of presumptions.

AN ENIGMATIC APPEARANCE

We will never really know what Jane Austen looked like. However, the description provided by Caroline Austen, the daughter of James, the novelist's elder brother, gives us a glimpse. Caroline was only twelve when she lost her aunt, so she admitted that these were mostly childhood memories. However, she conceded that she admired her and remembered her as a beautiful woman. "Her face was rather round than long—she had a bright, but not a pink colour—a clear brown complexion and very good hazel eyes... She was not, I think, a perfect beauty, before she left Steventon she was established as a very pretty girl."[59] She also added that although her aunt always wore a bonnet, she remembered her darkish brown, curly hair.

A little further on, Caroline Austen added that her aunt read wonderfully, that she had a beautiful voice and used the right intonations, just like in the theatre. James Edward Austen-Leigh, Caroline's brother and the only one of the novelist's nephews to attend her funeral, remembers her as "an intelligent character, [...] always kind, compassionate, amusing...".[60] One relative provides us with a few details about her looks, the other a few details about her personality.

Anne Hathaway, *Becoming Jane*, 2007

From her correspondence with her sister Cassandra, we also know that she was cheerful, lively and spontaneous, and that she loved to dance. Above all, she had a wicked sense of humour and remarkable powers of observation.

BIOPICS

Jane Austen has been represented on screen four times. The first time was in Julian Jarrold's 2007 film *Becoming Jane*, with Anne Hathaway in the title role and James McAvoy as Tom Lefroy. This fictionalised biopic explores the relationship between Jane Austen and "[her] Irish friend".[61] In 2008, Olivia Williams took on the role of the novelist in Jeremy Lovering's TV film *Miss Austen Regrets*. The plot revolves around several members of the Austen family, including Cassandra and Jane's beloved niece, Fanny Knight. Although she does not appear on screen, Jane Austen is also mentioned several times as a very active character in the world in the hit BBC series *Doctor Who*, and in season 2 of *Good Omens* (Neil Gaiman has publicly stated that Jane Austen has been a powerful source of inspiration). She also appeared in 2024, played by Kendra Anderson in David Weaver's Hallmark TV film *Love & Jane*, and by Patsy Farran in Aisling Walsh's *Miss Austen*.
In France in 2008, playwright, actress and theatre director Céline Devalan wrote the play *Les Trois Vies de Jane Austen (Jane Austen's Three Lives)*, with Lesley Chatterley and the participation of Élodie Sörensen, which focuses on the destinies of a young 21st century woman and Jane Austen when she met Tom Lefroy. Céline Devalan played the role of Jane Austen. This fully French creation has played for several seasons in Paris at the Théâtre Essaïon and at the Avignon Festival.

[59] *My Aunt Jane Austen, A Memoir*, Caroline Austen, 1867.
[60] *A Memoir of Jane Austen*, James Edward Austen-Leigh, Richard Bentley & Son, 1869.
[61] *Jane Austen's Letters*, Deirdre Le Faye, *op. cit.*

PORTRAIT GALLERY

Portrait dated 1804

Portrait dated 1810

The only real image whose authenticity is not in dispute is a pencil and watercolour miniature by Cassandra Austen, probably dating from 1810 or 1811. Jane Austen's sister was no novice, taking drawing lessons in earnest with the Franco-English watercolourist John Claude Nattes. This portrait, which is always surprisingly small when you first see it, has belonged to the National Portrait Gallery in London since 1948. Cassandra also painted another image of her sister around 1804, showing her in a blue dress from behind. This painting is now owned by a private collector.

While no accurate portrait of Jane Austen has survived, it is clear that the same is true of her sister Cassandra. A great niece recalls a vague memory of her as "a pale old lady with black eyes, a large aquiline nose and a very gentle smile".[62] We might wonder why, when there are portraits of the brothers, there is no representation of the daughters in the family. At the time, commissioning a painting was expensive. The men in the Austen family had their portraits painted once they were well-established in their professional lives and able to commission them. Only Edward, adopted by the wealthy Knight cousins, is the subject of an imposing portrait in his teens. Women usually ordered them as gifts when they got engaged. There is no record of any portrait of Cassandra for her fiancé Thomas Fowle, but that doesn't necessarily mean that there wasn't one. As far as Jane Austen is concerned, we know that she did not like to show off, preferring to observe others rather than be admired.

Information on npg.org.uk

---

[62] Quoted by Claire Tomalin, *op. cit.*

In 1944, a bookseller found a treasure in a second-hand shop: volumes one and two of the second edition of *Mansfield Park* (1816). In the middle of the pages of one of the volumes, he discovered this silhouette. This new "portrait", entitled *L'Aimable Jane* (in French), is now in the National Portrait Gallery, listed as "identity uncertain". Yet it is the symbol that unites all Janeites.

This other silhouette was presented to the Dean of Winchester in 1936 by Miss Jessie Lefroy, a descendant of the Austen family. On the back of the sheet, it is written that this is a self-portrait of Jane Austen, painted in 1815. There is no proof that this is really the novelist, even though the document came from the Austen family archives.

Does this painting represent Jane Austen as a teenager? There's certainly a gentleness in the dark eyes, a mischievous little smile, a certain assurance in the posture. This painting is the *Rice Portrait*, named after the family who inherited it, descendants of the Austens. The painting was commissioned by Francis Austen, Jane Austen's wealthy great-uncle. The painter has also been identified as Ozias Humphry. In July 1788, a twelve-and-a-half-year-old Jane visited this wealthy ninety-year-old patriarch. She spent a month in his beautiful red-brick home, Red House, at Sevenoaks in Kent with her parents and sister, Cassandra. Posing for a painting at this time was a real possibility. But why not with Cassandra?

A photograph of this painting was chosen by Lord Brabourne, Jane Austen's great-nephew, when his great-aunt's letters were first published in 1884, which was a form of recognition in itself. However, the much-respected National Portrait Gallery in London refuses to recognise its authenticity and refutes the idea that it could represent Jane Austen. Yet in 2017, the equally respected Royal Mint printed a small booklet to accompany the issue of collector coins on the theme of Jane Austen, and used the *Rice Portrait* as an illustration. **Read the whole story on thericeportrait.com**

This portrait was reproduced in France by the painter Félix Vallotton, in the form of an engraving. It was used to illustrate the first French-language article devoted to the English novelist by Théodore Duret, *Miss Austen*, in *La Revue Blanche*, published on 15 July 1898.

Two Jane Austens?

You may have noticed that in this little world, the same first names were often passed down within the same generation. In the course of her research, Austen scholar Deirdre Le Faye discovered the existence of another Jane Austen, a second cousin on a different side of the family. She was also born in 1775,[63] but in Kippington, Kent. Her father was Francis Austen, Jane Austen's great-uncle, who commissioned the *Rice Portrait*. This distant cousin married William John Campion on 10 January 1797, with whom she had nine children, including Mary Anne, their eldest daughter. In the 1980s, after meticulous investigation, Deirdre Le Faye concluded that Mary Anne Campion was the true model for the *Rice Portrait*. But it could just as easily be the cousin of the same name, since an X-ray eventually revealed that the name 'Jane Austen' is inscribed on the back. The mystery remains. As for the fate of this "second Jane", she lived quietly with her family on the estate of Danny House in Sussex, where she died peacefully in 1857 at the age of eighty-two.

In 2011, Paula Byrne was working on a biography of Jane Austen. Her husband returned from an auction with a present for her, an early 19th century portrait of a woman with "Jane Austin" written on the back. Despite the different spelling, she was immediately convinced that this was a previously unknown image of the novelist, depicted writing and self-confident. The building on the right has been identified as St. Margaret's Church in Westminster. A real investigation began to find out whether this drawing represented Jane Austen, and also to determine whether it was made with her as a live model, and not as a tribute after her death. The results of this research were released in December 2011 in a BBC documentary. While Paula Byrne remained confident, the consulted experts were unable to give a firm verdict. You can see the portrait in a video on YouTube: *The Real Jane Austen: A Life in Small Things, Paula Byrne.*

The painter Andrew James produced a watercolour at the request of James Edward Austen-Leigh in 1869, while he was writing *A Memoir of Jane Austen*. The aim was to create a portrait of the novelist based on the memories of the last generation who knew her, her nieces and nephews. This miniature currently belongs to a private collector. The drawing is the origin of the face of Jane Austen that is currently seen on ten pound notes.

This engraving is based on the previous portrait, and the artist is anonymous. It was used as the frontispiece to the first edition of *A Memoir of Jane Austen*, published in 1871. This design quickly became a reference image.

---

[63] Some biographies say she was born in 1776.

STATUES

10 POUND NOTE

On 24 July 2013, the Bank of England announced that the new face chosen for the £10 note was Jane Austen. The note was officially released on 14 September 2017. In the top right-hand corner, the drawing of a small open book with the novelist's initials is featured.

Below, a quill pen frames a sketch of the entrance to Winchester Cathedral, with a transparent portrait of Elizabeth II. At the bottom right of the novelist's face is her signature, a copy of the one on her will.

On the left, you can see a woman writing, who is Elizabeth Bennet, the heroine of *Pride and Prejudice*. Just below is Godmersham Park, the home of Edward Knight, Jane Austen's brother. Finally, one sentence illustrates the note: *"I declare after all there is no enjoyment like reading!"*[64] The choice of this quotation gave rise to a little controversy, since the character who utters it is Caroline Bingley,[65] who is not, strictly speaking, a great reader.

In the same year, the Royal Mint issued two £2 collector coins featuring Jane Austen's silhouette and signature.

The various statues of Jane Austen are considered to be tributes, and are not particularly intended to resemble her.

In Basingstoke, a small town not far from Winchester, a bronze statue of the novelist stands in the Market Square opposite the Willis Museum of Local History, housed in the old Town Hall. During the Regency period, these were Assembly Rooms, which Jane Austen frequented to dance and meet her circle of acquaintances. She also visited the square regularly to pick up books from the lending library. Commissioned by the Hampshire National Trust, the statue marks two hundred years since the novelist's death. Created by local artist Adam Roud, it was unveiled in July 2017 by the Countess of Portsmouth during a small ceremony.

To find it, when you arrive in Basingstoke by train, you have to cross the entire shopping centre opposite the station and follow the signs to Historic Basingstoke Wote Street. A miniature version of this statue can be admired in the cemetery of Chawton House, the former residence of the Knight family, which is both a museum and a study and conference centre.
Information on chawtonhouse.org

Since 2014, the Jane Austen Centre in Bath has also had a wax statue, modelled on those found at Madame Tussauds and the Musée Grévin. It is the work of costume designer Andrea Galer who is also a forensic artist trained by the FBI. Galer drew inspiration from various family portraits and descriptions.
Information on janeausten.co.uk

---

[64] *Pride and Prejudice*, Jane Austen.
[65] A secondary character in *Pride and Prejudice*.

JANE AUSTEN THROUGH BIOGRAPHIES

A glance at the reference list reveals an almost inexhaustible supply of biographies, essays and manuals of all kinds devoted to the English novelist.

- The first official biography was by her nephew James Edward Austen-Leigh, *Jane Austen A Memoir*, originally published in 1871.

- From 1935, the academic Lord David Cecil taught a course on Jane Austen at Cambridge. He published the bulk of his notes in two books, including a landmark biography, in the UK in 1978, *A Portrait of Jane Austen* (Will and Wang, 1978).

- In 1984, John Halperin published *The Life of Jane Austen* (Johns Hopkins University Press).

- In 1997, Claire Tomalin made history with *Jane Austen: A Life* (Viking, 1997).

- Carol Shields wrote a biography named *Jane Austen* (Viking, 2002).

- Isabelle Ballester's French documentary *Les Nombreux Mondes de Jane Austen* (The Numerous Worlds of Jane Austen) mixes the novelist's biography with that of her characters (Les Moutons électriques, 2009).

- Fiona Stafford wrote *Jane Austen: a Brief Life* (Yale University Press, 2017).

- *Biographics Austen* by Sophie Collins unpacks the life of Jane Austen through diagrams and charts (GMC Publications, 2017).

- Catherine Rihoit offers a novelised French biography with *Jane Austen, un Cœur Rebelle* (Jane Austen, A Rebel Heart, Écritures, 2018).

- Nicole Jacobsen and Devynn Dayton take us on an illustrated English tour with *Jane Was Here* (Hardie Grant, 2020).

- There is also an English collection devoted to Jane Austen, *Jane Austen for Dummies*, by Joan Elizabeth Ray (For Dummies, 2006).

- Paula Byrne's biography is entitled: *The Real Jane Austen: A Life in Small Things* (HarperCollins, 2013). She is also the author of *Jane Austen and the Theatre* (Bloomsbury Academic, 2003), reprinted as *The Genius of Jane Austen: Her Love of Theatre and Why She Works in Hollywood* (Harper Perennial, 2017).

- The latest biography is by historian Lucy Worsley,[66] *Jane Austen at Home: A Biography* (St. Martin's Griffin, 2021).

[66] Several of her programmes are available on YouTube.

Jane Austen, reader and author

Born to a family that placed great importance on the education of girls, the young Jane Austen learned at an early age to develop her literary skills and artistic gifts. The Austens encouraged reading, intellectual curiosity and open-mindedness. This education, which was so unusual for the time, undoubtedly encouraged her growing talent.

A FAMILY OF SCHOLARS

The Austens were great lovers of novels and were not ashamed to admit this. At the time, this literary genre was not considered noble reading, unlike poetry. In the evenings, Mr. Austen read books aloud to his family. In 1801, he had no fewer than five hundred volumes in his library, to which his children had free access. Among the novels, Jane Austen mentions in a letter[67] that her father was reading *The Midnight Bell* (1798) by Francis Lathom, which she mentions in *Northanger Abbey*. The shelves also feature works by the poet William Cowper, James Boswell's *Life of Samuel Johnson* (1791) and Samuel Egerton Brydges' *Arthur Fitz-Albini* (1798). On the subject of the latter, we learn that Mr. Austen considered it terribly badly written.

Apart from novels, the Austen family loved the theatre and even staged their favourite plays. In fact, James was the main initiator of this: each of the plays was accompanied by a prologue and an epilogue written in verse by him. In 1782, he chose Thomas Francklin's *Matilda, A Tragedy* (1775). Two years later, he revived a comedy by Richard Brinsley Sheridan, *The Rivals* (1775). At Christmas 1787, when Eliza de Feuillide, their exotic cousin, was staying at Steventon, the whole family performed Susanna

Centlivre's comedy *The Wonder: A Woman Keeps A Secret!* (1714). Other plays, such as Henry Fielding's *Tom Thumb* (1730) and Isaac Bickerstaffe's *The Sultan* (1775) were also performed, but the festivities came to a halt some time later.

James was a student at Oxford University at that time and had other ambitions. With the help of his brother Henry, also at Oxford, he launched a weekly magazine: *The Loiterer*, and sold it for 3 pence. It comprised essays and stories mostly written by James —only one issue is credited to Henry. The subjects: portraits of human nature, customs and entertainment in Oxford... The first issue was published on 31 January 1789. After sixty issues, the adventure came to an end in March 1790, when James graduated and left university.

Mrs. Austen also had some literary talent and regularly wrote poetry. One of her cousins, Cassandra Cooke, published a book in 1799 entitled: *Battleridge: An Historical Tale Founded on Facts*. It's not surprising that, growing up in such a world, Jane Austen fell in love with books.

CIRCULATING LIBRARIES

In the 18th and 19th centuries, books were expensive and circulating libraries were an alternative to buying them. In return for an annual or monthly fee, reading enthusiasts accessed a wide range of books.

These libraries could be located in premises dedicated exclusively to this activity, and sometimes also offered products for sale, such as perfumes. Others could be found in a local shop, such as a cloth merchant or milliner, allowing them to increase their income. They were also meeting places, where you could meet friends and catch up on the latest gossip.

Until this point, reading had been almost exclusively the preserve of men. Young girls learned to read and write, but what was the point of them learning more than they needed to? And what about the entertainment provided by novels that might corrupt their morals? Through the circulating libraries, where anyone could take out a subscription, women finally had the opportunity to access this pleasure. Even though Mr. Austen's library was stuffed full of books of all genres, Jane Austen was a regular subscriber, especially after she left Steventon.

---

[67] *Jane Austen's Letters*, Deirdre Le Faye, *op. cit.*

JANE AUSTEN'S LIBRARY

Two books from Jane Austen's childhood have survived the passage of time: John Newbery's *The History of Little Goody Two-Shoes* (1765) and *Fables Choisies*, a little book of French grammar that she received for her eighth birthday, based on fables by La Fontaine. Her cousin Eliza gave her *L'Ami des Enfants* (1782) by Arnaud Berquin for her eleventh birthday. This little collection of stories and sketches is designed to teach young children about generosity, charity and good behaviour. No doubt Jane Austen, who admired her cousin, was quick to read it.

Did you know?

One of the possible sources of inspiration for the couple in *Pride and Prejudice* is undoubtedly the famous *Much Ado About Nothing* (1598-1599) by William Shakespeare, whose work the entire Austen family, like all self-respecting Britons, admired. In this delightful comedy, the couple Beatrice and Benedict never stop putting each other to the test, and neither is afraid to tell the other the truth, in the manner of Elizabeth Bennet and Mr. Darcy.

James, arguably the second literary child of the Austen family, greatly influenced his younger sister's tastes. In the biographical notice written by Henry Austen for the publication of *Northanger Abbey* and *Persuasion*, we learn that Jane Austen's favourite poet was William Cowper, whom she quoted regularly in her novels. Her favourite prose writer was Samuel Johnson. The novelist's copy of *Elegant Extracts* (1771), an anthology in prose form written by several authors, which she later gave to her niece Anna, belongs to the Jane Austen's House Museum.

Among her other reading, Jane Austen admired Frances Burney, citing her as the best of English novelists, and she also found much entertainment in the novels of Ann Radcliffe. She read works by Charlotte Smith, Maria Edgeworth, Charlotte Lennox, Regina-Maria Roche and Sarah Harriet Burney (Frances Burney's half-sister); poetry by Robert Burns, William Wordsworth, Lord Byron and George Crabbe; and plays by Richard Brinsley Sheridan, Richard Cumberland and William Shakespeare.

Although Jane Austen enjoyed Henry Fielding's *The History of Tom Jones, a Foundling* (1749), she preferred Samuel Richardson's *The History of Sir Charles Grandison* (1753) and his other works. Laurence Sterne's *The Life and Opinions of Tristram Shandy, Gentleman* (1759) and *A Sentimental Journey through France and Italy* (1768) were also among the books she read.

In *The History of England: From the Earliest Times to the Death of George II* (1771) by Oliver Goldsmith, Jane Austen wrote comments in the margins, recriminating the Whig party[68] and perhaps revealing some political opinions. In volume two of her *Juvenilia*, the novelist parodies this work and writes her own *History of England*. It is clear from her text that she is siding with the Stuarts against the Tudors. She also read *Mary Queen of Scots Vindicated* (1790) by John Whitaker.

---

[68] English political party opposed to royal absolutism.

With unlimited access to her father's books and to circulating libraries, these works only represent a small proportion of the novelist's reading.[69] The titles and authors cited come from her correspondence, that of her friends and family, and from recollections. For cash flow reasons, this fabulous family library ended up being completely dispersed. Unfortunately, most of the books were sold when the Austens moved to Bath.

JANE AUSTEN'S FAVOURITE CONTEMPORARY AUTHORS

The books Jane Austen read during her life strongly influenced her style, her themes and were of inspiration to her generally. Here are the portraits of some of the authors of her time.

Her name and her novels are regularly mentioned in the letters and novels of Jane Austen, who loved to read her stories. Born to a family that loved reading and writing, FRANCES 'FANNY' BURNEY (1752-1840) did not learn to read and write on her own until the age of eight. Aged fifteen, she wrote her first story, which she was forced to throw into the fire when her stepmother found out about it. A few years later, she began writing *Evelina* and offered it to publishers without revealing her true identity. The book was published anonymously in 1778. However, her name was soon revealed and her company sought out. Cassandra Cooke, one of Mrs. Austen's cousins, was a friend of hers. However, there is no indication that the two novelists ever met. Frances Burney published several novels, the most famous of which, after *Evelina*, were *Cecilia* (1782) and *Camilla* (1796).

Did you know?

CAMILLA BY FRANCES BURNEY

In 1795, to guarantee the printing costs of her new novel *Camilla*, Frances Burney proposed it as a participatory project. Around one thousand people subscribed, including novelists Maria Edgeworth and Ann Radcliffe, as well as "Miss J. Austen, Steventon". It was probably with her father's money, but Jane Austen was keen to contribute to the project and acquire the famous author's new novel. Her copy is now in the Bodleian Library, Oxford.

---

[69] Godmersham Park, the home of her brother Edward Knight, also had many books that Jane Austen may have consulted. Browse the library at **readingwithausten.com/index**.

The poet LORD BYRON (1788-1824) was world-famous, not only for his writings, but also for his travels across Europe. He travelled from Portugal to Greece, via Switzerland, where he met Mary Shelley, author of *Frankenstein or The Modern Prometheus*, a novel published the same year as *Persuasion* (1818). His most remarkable

work is *Don Juan* (1824), an epic poem of over five hundred and fifty pages. Jane Austen and Lord Byron never met, yet they shared the same publisher, John Murray. In a letter from the publisher to the poet, Murray confided that he would soon be publishing two new novels by Miss Austen, who had died six weeks earlier.

Did you know?

Lord Byron was the father of a famous thinker, mathematician and scientist. Born in London in 1815, Augusta Ada Byron, who became Lovelace after her marriage, was the daughter of Anne Isabella Milbanke, Baroness of Byron and Baroness of Wentworth, who was also a mathematician. Lady Byron encouraged her daughter's passion for science at an early age. Ada was brilliant and met the inventor and mathematician Charles Babbage at the age of seventeen. Both were working on a kind of "analytical machine", for which Ada invented a programme in 1840 that enabled her to carry out repetitive tasks, which would give rise to computer programming just over a hundred years later.

WILLIAM COWPER (1731-1800) was one of the most renowned poets of his time. He began writing at the age of thirty-nine and paved the way for Romanticism. His scenes of everyday life in the English countryside probably inspired Jane Austen. Henry Austen called him his sister's favourite poet, and she often quoted him in her novels. In his verse, William Cowper regularly denounced slavery and campaigned for its abolition. His

major work was published in 1785: *The Task: A Poem, in Six Books*.

MARIA EDGEWORTH (1768-1849) was an Anglo-Irish novelist and essayist who met a number of authors during her literary career and maintained friendly relations with Sir Walter Scott throughout her life. Her first novel, *Castle Rackrent* (1800), was an immediate success. She wrote many other novels, essays and stories, including *Belinda* (1801), *Ennui* (1809) and *The Absentee* (1812). When *Emma* was published, Jane Austen asked her publisher, John Murray, to send a copy to Maria Edgeworth, who unfortunately found the novel uninteresting.

Originally a playwright, HENRY FIELDING (1707-1754) abandoned this career after a law passed in 1737 censored plays that targeted the British government. In 1741, he published his first epistolary novel, *Shamela*, which parodied one of Jane Austen's favourite books, *Pamela or*

Virtue Rewarded (1740) by Samuel Richardson. Henry Fielding's most acclaimed work is *The History of Tom Jones, a Foundling*, published in 1749.

SAMUEL JOHNSON (1709-1784) had many strings to his bow: poet, biographer, lexicographer and essayist. After working as a teacher, he tried his hand at writing and became a journalist. His biggest project came to fruition in 1755 after some ten years' work: a dictionary of the English language.[70] He was Jane Austen's favourite author.

As a young man, SAMUEL RICHARDSON (1689-1761) gave his pen to help the young ladies around him answer the love letters they received. He became a publisher of various newspapers, including that of the House of Commons, and of various works. In 1740, at the age of fifty-one, he wrote his first book in epistolary form, *Pamela; or, Virtue Rewarded*, considered to be the first sentimental novel. A sequel was published a year later. His greatest success was *The History of Sir Charles Grandison* (1753), one of Jane Austen's favourite novels.

ANN RADCLIFFE (1764-1823) was a pioneer of the Gothic novels in vogue in the late 18th century. Five of her works were published during her lifetime. The first three were published anonymously, but she defied any prejudice she might encounter by adding her name to the second edition of her third novel. Her most remarkable story is *The Mysteries of Udolpho* (1794), which makes an important appearance in *Northanger Abbey* as it is Catherine Morland's bedside book. *The Italian*, published in 1797, is another of the author's landmark novels. Thanks to the income from her books, Ann Radcliffe travelled extensively in Europe and England with her husband. As a journalist and then editor-in-chief, he always supported her in her work.

The novelist was a great admirer of SIR WALTER SCOTT's work, but in a letter to her niece Anna, she wrote: "[He] has no business to write novels, especially good ones. —It is not fair.— He has Fame and Profit enough as a Poet, and should not be taking the bread out of other people's mouths".[71] A lawyer by profession, the Scotsman Sir Walter Scott (1771-1832) had a passion for literature and history. He began his career as a poet and his first major success, *The Lay of the Last Minstrel*, a medieval tale, was published in 1805. He wrote many poems, including the famous *The Lady of the Lake* (1810), before turning to prose. His first novel, *Waverley* (1814), was published anonymously and received widespread acclaim. *The Antiquary* (1816) and *Ivanhoe* (1819) are among a long list of published novels. Sir Walter Scott worked with several publishers, including John Murray, Jane Austen's publisher.

---

[70] Since 1928, the English dictionary of reference has been published by Oxford University Press.
[71] *Jane Austen's Letters*, Deirdre Le Faye, *op. cit.*

A LONG ROAD TO PUBLICATION

Jane Austen wrote her first books in 1787, which were published posthumously as *Juvenilia*. In 1792, in the third volume, Mr. George Austen wrote a short note: "Effusions of Fancy by a **very Young Lady** Consisting of Tales in a **Style entirely new**".[72]

After writing poems, a few short texts and epistolary stories, Jane Austen chose to use prose in all her novels, bringing a new style to the genre. In most of them, the novelist made little use of long descriptions. Her greatest assets are her subtle analysis of the characters' personalities and their social relationships. Jane Austen pokes fun at the shortcomings of the society around her, choosing her words carefully. Her biting irony also comes through in her correspondence: "Mrs. Hall, of Sherborne, was brought to bed yesterday of a dead child, some weeks before she expected, owing to a fright. I suppose she happened unawares to look at her husband".[73]

What makes her work unique, however, is her free indirect discourse. This literary device is characterised by the absence of an introductory verb or inverted commas and the use of the third person. The narrator combines her voice with the words and thoughts of a character, without specifying who the speaker is. The distinction can be subtle, and Jane Austen often uses this technique to poke fun at the intimacy between narrator and character. Although she did not invent it, she was one of the first authors to use it throughout her career.

CASSANDRA'S MEMORANDUM

Probably while writing the biographical note on Henry Austen that precedes *Northanger Abbey* and *Persuasion*, Cassandra wrote down the dates on which her sister's novels were written. These few lines were the starting point for the study of Jane Austen's literary chronology.

"*First Impressions was begun in October 1796 Finished in August 1797 – Subsequently published, with modifications and contractions, under the title Pride and Prejudice. Sense and Sensibility was begun in Nov. 1797 I'm sure a similar story and characters were written earlier called Elinor and Marianne. Mansfield Park, was begun somewhere around Feb. 1811 – Completed shortly after June 1813. Emma was begun on 21 Jan. 1814, completed on 29 March 1815. Persuasion was begun on 8 August 1815 and completed on 6 August 1816. Northanger Abbey was written around 98 & 99*[74]."

---

[72] *Jane Austen, A Life*, Claire Tomalin, Viking Books of London, 1997, *op. cit.*
[73] *Jane Austen letters*, Deirdre Le Faye, *op. cit.*
[74] *Jane Austen A Family Record*, Deirdre Le Faye, Cambridge University Press, 2004.

The novelist dealt with four publishers in the course of her life. In 1797, Thomas Cadell received the manuscript of *Pride and Prejudice*, but did not read a single page. He returned it as soon as he received it. In 1803, Richard Crosby bought the copyright to *Northanger Abbey*, but left it to gather dust until it was bought back by Jane Austen in 1816.

The first publisher to take an interest in her stories was Thomas Egerton, who published *Sense and Sensibility* (1811), *Pride and Prejudice* (1813) and *Mansfield Park* (1814). After negotiations with Egerton for a second edition of *Mansfield Park*, Jane Austen turned to John Murray. He published *Emma* (1815) and then *Northanger Abbey* and *Persuasion* (1818) posthumously. All her novels were published on a self-publishing basis, which means that Jane Austen covered the printing costs and the publisher earned his commission on sales. The only exception was the sale of the copyright to *Pride and Prejudice*.

Jane Austen compared her writings to precious little pieces of ivory. After her death, her family worked to ensure that the treasure represented by her works continued to be known, and helped to create her legend. The choices made would play a decisive role in the reception of her work for years to come. Particular attention was paid to the various editions, especially the illustrated editions. The first of these was French. This was *La Famille Elliot*[75] in 1821, with an engraving on the front cover by Charles-Abraham Chasselat, the historic illustrator of Molière, Racine and Voltaire.

The first illustrated English edition was published by Richard Bentley in December 1832. Richard Bentley offered £210[76] to the rights holders and paid £40[77] to his former publisher, Egerton. Ferdinand Pickering was the first to illustrate *Sense and Sensibility*. The following year, Bentley had the idea of reissuing all the novels in a collector's edition. This was a success, especially as it was the first time that all of Jane Austen's novels had been brought together in a single collection. The boxed set contained five volumes, as *Northanger Abbey* and *Persuasion* were grouped together as posthumous works. The ten illustrations give the book a misleading Victorian connotation, which would later perpetuate the confusion that classified her as a writer of that era. It was the publisher and illustrator who took over for four decades.

---

[75] *Persuasion.*
[76] Just over £30,000 in current value.
[77] Just over £5,500 in current value.

The first woman to illustrate Jane Austen's novels was Christiana Mary Demain Hammond, alias Chris. She worked for two different publishers: *Emma* in 1898 and *Sense and Sensibility* in 1899, for George Allen, and finally *Pride and Prejudice* in 1900 for Gresham Publishing. Like many of the women who in one way or another crossed Jane Austen's path, Chris' destiny was far from ordinary. Her mother died young, but she benefited from lessons by her governess. She attended Lambeth School of Arts and then spent three years at the Royal Academy School. But her poor health prevented her from continuing her studies. She then began illustrating books. For the first time in a Jane Austen novel, she introduced images of death and war.[78]

THE PROBLEM WITH FRENCH TRANSLATIONS

Since 1813, there have been some thirty French versions of Austen's works, but the task is a complex one, given Jane Austen's precise and meticulous style. Translators have often chosen to delete passages, condense the story or transform the narrative devices, thereby altering the original meaning. The Swiss translator, Isabelle de Montolieu, even took the liberty of changing the ending of *Sense and Sensibility* to meet the expectations of the French public, who were looking for sentimental novels at the time.

Some of these texts are still used by publishers, and although recent versions have appeared, they have not always been an improvement. Vocabulary has evolved and the perception of the context of the time is different. One solution was to enrich the story with prefaces and explanatory notes to enlighten the reader. To date, the most faithful translations have been published by Gallimard in 2000 and 2013 in La Bibliothèque de la Pléiade, despite a desire to emphasise morality rather than the author's ironic pen.

In the majority of translations, the emphasis is on the sentimental side, where the main themes are material concerns, the love story and its happy ending. A whole section of the novels is sacrificed, the part that brings out the sharpness of her pen, so good at depicting the small and large failings, of her time in particular, and of human nature in general. All too often we lose sight of her incredible *tour de force*, which is both subtle and skilful in playing with both form and content. In this polished writing, precious and precise as "two inches of ivory",[79] every word counts, and no word is ever chosen at random.

---

[78] The death of Jane Fairfax's father in *Emma*, for example.
[79] *Jane Austen's Letters*, Deirdre Le Faye, *op. cit.*

THE RECEPTION OF HER WORKS

Whether the reviews were positive or negative, Jane Austen always put her heart into writing her novels. However, as a young author, she must have been somewhat impatient to find out what her readers thought of the stories she had so painstakingly committed to paper. Here are some of the opinions of her entourage, literary critics and various authors of the time.

Sense and Sensibility

In 1812, the journal *Critical Review*, which specialised in literary, political and scientific debates, was full of praise for the novel. In their opinion, it was well-written and the characters were portrayed in a natural way. Jane Austen was described as a writer who knew how to mix common sense with lightness. Many passages from the book were quoted.

In her correspondence, Princess Charlotte, daughter of the Prince Regent, confided to a friend that she had enjoyed *Sense and Sensibility*, in particular because she saw herself in the reckless personality of Marianne Dashwood.[80]

Henry Crabb Robinson, a lawyer, diarist and one of the founders of the University of London, disliked the novel entirely, finding it far inferior to *Mansfield Park* and *Pride and Prejudice*.[81]

Pride and Prejudice

Critical Review was as enthusiastic about Jane Austen's work as ever: "We cannot conclude, without repeating our approbation of this performance, which rises very superior to any novel we have lately met with in the delineation of domestic scenes. [...] There is not one person in the drama with whom we could readily dispense;— they have all their proper places".[82]

Maria Edgeworth, the famous novelist, took great pleasure in reading *Pride and Prejudice* and urged her friends and family to buy it and make up their own minds.[83]

One of Jane Austen's greatest admirers, the poet and novelist Walter Scott, wrote in his diary that he had read the book at least three times. In his opinion, her inimitable talent lay in her descriptions of ordinary life, which he marvelled at every time. Walter Scott even concedes that the author knew how to make everyday life and ordinary characters interesting far better than he did. He also noted that he was saddened by her early death.[84]

---

[80] *Letters of The Princess Charlotte 1811-1817*, Home & Van Thal, 1949.
[81] *Henry Crabb Robinson on Books and Their Writers*, J.-M. Dent & Sons, 1938.
[82] *Critical Review*, March 1813.
[83] *Letters from England 1813-1844*, Maria Edgeworth, Oxford University Press, 1971.
[84] *The Journal of Sir Walter Scott*, Anderson, Oxford University Press, 1972.

Mansfield Park

In a letter to her sister,[85] Jane Austen wrote that their brother Henry was enjoying the novel more and more as he read it. He found it in no way inferior to the previous two. He praised the fine descriptions of the characters and proclaimed Henry Crawford as a kind and intelligent young man.

Her uncle and aunt, Mr. and Mrs. Cooke, also praised the book, and particularly Jane's treatment of clergymen.[86]

Her brothers, Francis and Edward, did not recognise the qualities of *Pride and Prejudice* in this novel, but they did like the character of Fanny Price, and especially the descriptions relating to the Navy. The character of Mrs. Norris made them laugh with her ferocity.[87]

Edward Knight's son George admits to having a soft spot for the beautiful Mary Crawford. His sister, Fanny Knight, liked her namesake, but not the end of the novel, like her aunt Cassandra.[88]

The publisher, Thomas Egerton, conceded that it had purely literary qualities, no weaknesses in structure, and was a good moral take.[89]

Maria Edgeworth said that she found the story very entertaining.[90]

The Prince Regent's librarian, James Stanier-Clarke, said that *Mansfield Park* unquestionably represented Jane Austen's genius.[91]

Emma

After a detailed summary of *Emma*, *The Quarterly Review*[92] stated that although the subjects were relatively simple, the accuracy with which Jane Austen described them was bound to delight readers. The reviewer said that the narration was neat and comic, and quoted dialogue taken from the book, but warned that this extract could not do justice to the author's talent.

Jane Austen's brother Francis was extremely fond of the book, finding it wittier than *Pride and Prejudice*.[93] Fanny Knight, her niece, could not stand the heroine Emma. She found the character of Mr. Knightley charming, and thought that she would like Jane Fairfax more if she knew more about her.[94]

After reading it a second time, Miss Bigg, one of Jane Austen's friends, liked Miss Bates much better than she did the first time. She liked all the Highbury characters, except Harriet Smith.[95]

Did you know?

ABOUT MANSFIELD PARK AND EMMA

In a small eight-page notebook, Jane Austen patiently copied out the opinions of her readers. This precious document, signed by her, is now carefully preserved in the British Library in London.

Extracts from this notebook can be seen on the British Library website bl.uk/collection-items/opinions-by-various-people-of-jane-austens-work.

---

[85] *Jane Austen's Letters*, Deirdre Le Faye, *op. cit.*
[86] *Ibid.*
[87] Opinion collected in a notebook by Jane Austen.
[88] *Ibid.*
[89] *Ibid.*
[90] *The Life and Letters of Maria Edgeworth*, Augustus Hare, Edward Arnold, 1894.
[91] *Jane Austen's Letters*, Deirdre Le Faye, *op. cit.*
[92] This was a literary and political periodical founded and published by John Murray, who also published *Emma*.
[93] Opinion collected in a notebook by Jane Austen.
[94] *Ibid.*
[95] *Ibid.*

Persuasion and Northanger Abbey

The British Critic New Series published an article on these last two books in 1818. They mourned Jane Austen's death and provided some biographical details. They went on to highlight the novelist's humour and talent for observation. However, the editor added that she lacked imagination. In his opinion, *Northanger Abbey* was one of Jane Austen's best works, despite its flaws: the incidents are unlikely, General Tilney's reaction implausible, and the scenes in the abbey lack care. Regarding *Persuasion*, although they felt it had some merit, they felt that the morality of following one's inclination rather than prudence was not common sense.

In general terms, the *Edinburgh Magazine* recognised the discernment, subtle irony and tone of purity of Jane Austen's writing, but lamented the simplicity of her stories. As far as the novels were concerned, the magazine didn't bother to give a separate review. They only commented that the former was the most animated and the latter the most pitiful, and warned the readers that those seeking religious opinions would be disappointed.

Maria Edgeworth finds General Tilney's behaviour in *Northanger Abbey* unacceptable. In *Persuasion*, she greatly appreciated the wonderful love story of the two heroes and found it very well written. She also admired Captain Wentworth's behaviour in the scene with the Musgrove children. Nevertheless, she found the first fifty pages devoted to the Elliot family completely unnecessary.[96]

Henry Crabb Robinson was disappointed by these two books. He found the characters to be unpleasant and insignificant. He conceded, however, that his declining judgement may not have been reliable.[97]

Although Jane Austen was recognised by some of her peers during her lifetime, she did not begin to achieve a degree of fame until the end of her life, albeit within a limited circle. After the dedication she offered to the Prince-Regent in the first edition of *Emma*, in 1816, the secret of her anonymity, which she cherished above all else, was revealed. But it wasn't enough to make her a celebrity, like Charlotte Brontë a few years later. Unlike the story in the biopic *Becoming Jane*, she never rose to fame as a novelist. It was only after her death in 1817, and the posthumous publication of her last two novels, *Northanger Abbey* and *Persuasion*, that she began to become truly famous, her reputation gradually spreading across borders. Today, she is the most quoted British author in the world.

[96] *The Life and Letters of Maria Edgeworth*, Augustus Hare, *op. cit.*
[97] *Henry Crabb Robinson on Books and Their Writers*, *op. cit.*

Jane Austen

AS SEEN BY SOME MODERN AUTHORS

It is amusing to note that the English novelist Charlotte Brontë (1816-1855), who wrote one of the most beautiful love stories of all time, *Jane Eyre* (1847), never appreciated Jane Austen. In January 1848, in an exchange of letters with the literary critic George Henry Lewes, she admitted that she did not like Austen's prose at all, especially as her correspondent held it in high esteem. Is Charlotte Brontë offended at being compared to the country gentry with whom she seems to have so much in common? The fact remains that she found Jane Austen lacking in poetry, even though she recognised certain qualities in her: *"Miss Austen, being as you say without 'sentiment', without poetry, may be —is sensible, real (more real than true) but she cannot be great".*[98]

A Room of One's Own, an essay written in 1929, British author Virginia Woolf (1882-1941) seems to settle the question between these two novelists. Referring to her reading of *Jane Eyre*, she says of Charlotte Brontë: "The woman who wrote those pages had more genius in her than Jane Austen; but if one reads them over and marks that jerk in them, that indignation, one sees that she will never get her genius expressed whole and entire".[99] Virginia Woolf, a harsh critic, described *Pride and Prejudice* as "a good book".[100] For her, Jane Austen was on a par with Shakespeare, because she writes "without hatred, without bitterness, without fear, without protest, without preaching", and even emphasises that she "permeates every word she writes".[101]

[98] *The Brontës: A life in Letters*, edited by Juliet Baker, The Overlook Press, 1997.
[99] *A Room of One's Own*, Virginia Woolf, Hogarth Press, 1929.
[100] *Ibid.*
[101] *Ibid.*

The American author Mark Twain (1835-1910) was Jane Austen's most irreverent critic. In 1896, he wrote an essay (unfinished) on the novelist, and more specifically on *Sense and Sensibility*, criticising her inability to make people appreciate her characters, who were bland, obnoxious and crude. In 1898, he wrote to a friend: "I haven't any right to criticize books, and I don't do it except when I hate them. I often want to criticize Jane Austen, but her books madden me so that I can't conceal my frenzy from the reader...".[102] His virulence peaked when he read *Pride and Prejudice*, and he said that his only wish was to dig up the novelist and beat her over the skull with her own shin-bone...[103]

In his *Journal*, the French writer André Gide, winner of the Nobel Prize for Literature in 1947, recounts how he bought a copy of *Pride and Prejudice* in Algiers on 16 January 1929. He wrote that he saw the novel as an "exquisite mastery of what can be mastered."[104]

In 1948, the Russian writer Vladimir Nabokov, famous for *Lolita* (1955), taught a course in literature at Cornell University. The American novelist Edmund Wilson suggested that he include *Mansfield Park* in his programme. Initially reluctant, he was persuaded and literally fell under the spell of Austen's style, in particular her sense of irony, which he described as "a peculiar dimple"[105] and Jane Austen achieves this, he says, by "stealthily introducing a touch of delicate irony into the midst of the components of a simple informative sentence".[106] He dissects this novel, or rather this "fairy tale",[107] as he idealises it, with obvious relish, not hesitating to consider it a masterpiece.

[102] *The Complete Letters of Mark Twain*, Echo Library, 2007.
[103] *Ibid.*
[104] *Journal, 1889-1939*, André Gide, Gallimard, 1939.
[105] *Lectures on Literature*, The Estate of Vladimir Nabokov, 1980
[106] *Ibid.*
[107] *Ibid.*

WOMEN WHO WRITE ARE DANGEROUS: A PANORAMA OF WOMEN'S LITERATURE IN THE 18th AND 19th CENTURIES

Most of them were ostracised for years, yet they wrote and established themselves as intellectuals and women of letters. They say that women who read are dangerous, but women who write are even more so!

Whether they preceded Jane Austen (1775-1817), were her contemporaries or followed her, between France and Great Britain, these women, here under their pen names, have left their mark on the history of literature and knowledge.

Gabrielle-Suzanne de Villeneuve
(circa 1695 -1755), France

Émilie du Châtelet
(1706-1749), France

Jeanne-Marie Leprince de Beaumont
(1711-1776), France

Marie-Jeanne Riccoboni
(1713-1792), France

Hannah More
(1745-1833), Great Britain

Félicité de Genlis
(1746-1830), France

Charlotte Smith
(1749-1806), Great Britain

Elizabeth Craven
(1750-1828), Great Britain

Élisabeth Guénard
(1751-1829), France

Frances 'Fanny' Burney
(1752-1840), Great Britain

Elizabeth Inchbald

Elizabeth Inchbald
(1753-1821), Great Britain

Anne-Jeanne-Félicité Mérard de Saint-Just
(1755-1830), France

Elizabeth Hamilton
(circa 1757 -1864), Great Britain

Jane West
(1758-1852), Great Britain

Adélaïde Gory-Decour
(circa 1759 -1825), France

Mary Hays
(1759-1843), Great Britain

Helen Maria Williams
(1759-1827), Great Britain

Mary Wollstonecraft
(1759-1797), Great Britain

Adélaïde de Souza
(1761-1836), France

Ann Radcliffe
(1764-1823), Great Britain

Ann Radcliffe

Regina-Maria Roche
(1764-1845), Great Britain

Germaine de Staël
(1766-1817), France

Félicité de Choiseul-Meuse
(1767-1838), France

Eliza Fenwick
(1767-1840), Great Britain

Constance de Salm
(1767-1845), France

Maria Edgeworth
(1768-1849), Great Britain

Germaine de Staël

Sophie Cottin
(1770-1807), France

Dorothy Wordsworth
(1771-1855), Great Britain

Jane Porter
(1775-1850), Great Britain

Sophie Gay
(1776-1852), France

Claire de Duras
(1777-1828), France

Frances Talbot
(1782-1857), Great Britain

Lady Caroline Lamb
(1785-1828), Great Britain

Lady Caroline Lamb

Marceline Desbordes-Valmore
(1786-1859), France

Marie d'Heures
(1786-1845), France

Élise Voïart
(1786-1866), France

Mary Russell Mitford
(1787-1855), Great Britain

Mary Russell Mitford

Alida de Savignac
(1790-1847), France

Virginie Ancelot
(1792-1875), France

Louise d'Estournelles de Constant
(1792-1860), France

Mary Shelley
(1797-1851), Great Britain

Comtesse de Ségur
(1799-1874), France

Marie-Sophie Leroyer de Chantepie
(1800-1888), France

Delphine de Girardin
(1804-1855), France

George Sand
(1804-1876), France

Elizabeth Barrett Browning
(1806-1861), Great Britain

Elizabeth Gaskell
(1810-1865), Great Britain

Ada Lovelace
(1815-1852), Great Britain

Charlotte Brontë
(1816-1855), Great Britain

Charlotte Brontë

Emily Brontë
(1818-1848), Great Britain

Anne Brontë
(1820-1849), Great Britain

It is not widely known that Jane Austen's work was not limited to her six novels. Of course, it was these that made her famous, in particular *Pride and Prejudice*, which is undoubtedly the most popular. But the novelist also distinguished herself in many other ways, notably through her short stories, fairy tales, parodies and theatre sketches. Her surviving letters also shed valuable light on her character and her approach to her art.

## PART II

The world of Jane Austen

Jane Austen's novels

During her short career as an author, Jane Austen only had
time to produce six major completed novels.
Each of them is a milestone in the history of world literature.
While there are similarities between them, they all have their
own originality that sets them apart and makes them unique.

Sense and Sensibility

The human soul would not exist without emotions and feelings. In the strict and measured society of the Regency period, sense prevailed over sensibility. In *Sense and Sensibility*, Jane Austen does not oppose these two qualities. She examines them together, observing them through two contrasting characters. Whether sense or sensitivity prevailed, she realised that one could not exist without the other. Pushed to the limit, these opposite sides of the same coin break down resistance, leaving the hearts of two young girls sorely tested.

Incipit 1811

The family of Dashwood had been long settled in Sussex. Their estate was large, and their residence was at Norland Park, in the centre of their property, where, for many generations, they had lived in so respectable a manner as to engage the general good opinion of their surrounding acquaintance.

WHAT'S IT ABOUT?

When Henry Dashwood dies, the peace and quiet of Norland Park is overturned. The entire estate and inheritance goes to John, his son from a previous marriage. Elinor and Marianne are forced to leave with their mother and youngest sister, Margaret.

The precariousness of Mrs. Dashwood's life prevents her from finding a home that lives up to her expectations. She has no choice but to accept a proposal from one of her cousins, Sir John Middleton, who owns a modest house, Barton Cottage, on his land.

This earnest gentleman, a somewhat intrusive but considerate neighbour, regularly invites his female relatives to entertain them, in particular the older sisters, two pretty young unmarried women, Elinor and Marianne. Just before leaving Norland Park, Elinor develops a tender attachment to a charming young man, while her sister Marianne, having just arrived in her new surroundings, is rescued like a fairytale princess and has eyes only for her rescuer.

The two sisters' approach to reality could not be more different. While one is forced to hide the turmoil of her heart in order to put on a brave face and remain in control of herself, the other expresses her passion and shows off her happiness with carefree abandon. But life throws them a few curveballs, and the young women learn the hard way that sometimes the right balance of behaviour is needed.

Character Gallery
THE LADIES

ELINOR DASHWOOD: nineteen years old, the eldest daughter in the Dashwood family.
Described as a pretty girl, Elinor has a delicate complexion and a graceful physique. Intelligent, sensible and always down to earth, the young woman may be considered the most mature member of the Dashwood family. Her clear-headedness and practical sense prove indispensable in managing the household, as her mother lacks the skills required to cope with their new financial situation. Elinor is respectful and always listens to those around her. Her mother and Marianne, who are both very emotional, think she is insensitive. But Elinor is just as capable of deep feelings. She simply knows how to control her emotions and doesn't believe she needs to show them.

MARIANNE DASHWOOD: seventeen years old, a younger daughter in the Dashwood family.
Even prettier than her elder sister, Marianne has a dark complexion, beautiful dark, lively eyes and a gentle smile. She's intelligent, engaging and has a zest for life. Despite her common sense, the young woman is reckless and listens to her feelings. With no caution, she expresses her joys and sorrows with excessive passion, without worrying about the opinion of others. Marianne admires those who share her tastes in reading, music, the picturesque. She excels at the piano and transports her audience with her beautiful voice. However, despite her generosity and friendliness, she has no tolerance for those who lack passion.

MARGARET DASHWOOD: thirteen years old, the youngest in the Dashwood family.
This young lady only makes a few appearances and little information is given about her. Playful by nature, she wants to be worthy of her sisters and does what is expected of her. Her temperament is closer to that of Marianne.

MRS. DASHWOOD: aged forty, mother of Elinor, Marianne and Margaret.
Similar to Marianne, Mrs. Dashwood is very sensitive, and no one can reason with her. She is cheerful, welcoming and generally has an enduring faith in life and happiness. But on the other hand, if her happiness is shaken, she is inconsolable and wallows in the deepest distress. Caring and loving, she is committed to making her daughters happy.

FANNY DASHWOOD: **sister of Edward and Robert Ferrars and wife of John Dashwood.**
Fanny does not have many good qualities. Friendliness, sympathy and intelligence are alien to her. When her father-in-law died, she wasted no time in taking over Norland Park from her husband. She shows no tact or compassion for her mother-in-law and sisters-in-law. Fanny exerts much influence over John. They have one child, Harry, aged four.

MRS. JENNINGS: **the mother of Lady Middleton and Mrs. Palmer.**
A woman of a certain age, Mrs. Jennings has a pleasant manner and is always in a good mood. She never stops talking and joking. A matchmaker at heart, she loves to tease Elinor and Marianne about potential future husbands and prides herself on being very perceptive when it comes to love. A widow, Mrs. Jennings has enough dower to live relatively comfortably.

LADY MIDDLETON: **aged twenty-six or twenty-seven, wife of Sir John Middleton.**
Her beautiful face, elegance and tall stature are impressive. However, her perfect education contrasts with her dull, banal conversation, and her good manners with a cold, reserved attitude. As mistress of the house, Lady Middleton enjoys entertaining and proudly displays her skills. She derives a great deal of pride from her four children, who are nevertheless boisterous and far too spoilt.

CHARLOTTE PALMER: **younger sister of Lady Middleton and wife of Mr. Palmer.**
Charlotte is pretty, small and chubby. Several years younger than Lady Middleton, she is the exact opposite of her sister. Charlotte's manners are less polished, but she is more endearing and welcoming. She's cheerful, friendly and full of kindness. She laughs incessantly and never takes offence at her husband's unsympathetic remarks, which she actually finds amusing.

LUCY STEELE: **aged twenty-two or twenty-three years old, she is a relative of Mrs. Jennings.**
Lucy has a lively gaze and is a pleasing young woman to look at. Without being particularly graceful, she is naturally at ease in society. Her lack of intelligence doesn't prevent her from being good company, as long as the conversation doesn't drag on for too long. Her artifice conceals her lack of moral rigour and honesty.

ANNE STEELE: **Lucy's elder sister.**
At nearly thirty, Anne is still single. Unfortunately, her looks don't do her any favours. Her vulgarity and silliness do not add to her appeal. Without much intelligence or common sense, she often makes her sister uncomfortable.

MRS. FERRARS: **mother of Fanny Dashwood, Edward and Robert.**
Small in stature, this woman has a pale complexion and an expressionless face. Her erect posture gives her a haughty air that perfectly suits her pride and sense of superiority. The rare appearances by Mrs. Ferrars, who doesn't say much, are testament to her narrow-mindedness and arrogance.

Character Gallery
THE GENTLEMEN

EDWARD FERRARS: twenty-four years old, the eldest brother of the Ferrars family.

Although not very handsome, with no confidence in himself or his judgement, this young man is charming in his own way. He is shy, modest, calm and discreet. Nonetheless, when he feels comfortable, he is outgoing. What's more, he is kind and respectful and has a real sense of morality. Edward candidly admits to being an idle person with no ambitions. He is currently without a profession and totally dependent financially on his mother, who has her late husband's fortune at her disposal. The only interest he has is for the Church, but those close to him feel that this is not distinguished enough for Ferrars. His dearest wish is simple domestic happiness.

JOHN WILLOUGHBY: a young man of twenty-five.

John is the most perfect Prince Charming. Attractive, distinguished and gallant, to complete the picture, he has a perfect education and warm manners. His outspoken, lively nature makes him pleasant company. Always cheerful, he enjoys music, dancing, hunting and taking advantage of the pleasures life has to offer. Although not particularly wealthy, he has an estate, Combe Magna, in Somerset. He is related to Mrs. Smith, a respected old lady from the Barton Park area. She is the owner of Allenham, a majestic old manor house. With no direct descendants, she intends leaving her property to John Willoughby.

COLONEL BRANDON: thirty-five or thirty-six years old, a close friend of Sir John Middleton.

Physically, the colonel is not very handsome and, at first glance, lacks vitality. His serious expression and taciturn demeanour don't do him justice. However, in reality and when he feels confident, he is courteous and kind. His solid education and experience of the world make him pleasant company. Naturally reserved, he has a good heart and is highly regarded. He is a generous man who is concerned for the people he cares about. Colonel Brandon owns the Delaford estate.

SIR JOHN MIDDLETON: about forty years old, a relative of Mrs. Dashwood.

This cordial, friendly and kind man is highly respected by those around him. He regularly invites his neighbours over, always looking to entertain and be entertained. He is sometimes forceful and gets close to overstepping the bounds of propriety, but his warm demeanour and constant cheerfulness usually excuse him. He has a lot of land around Barton Park and enjoys hunting.

JOHN DASHWOOD: Mr. Dashwood's son from his first marriage.

Although he is not a deeply wicked man, John is somewhat selfish under the influence of his wife. Married very young to Fanny and still in love, he lets his feelings get the better of his reason, and his naivety the better of his commitments. Inheriting the Norland estate further increased his fortune.

THOMAS PALMER: aged twenty-five or twenty-six, husband of Mrs. Palmer.

His incompatibility with his wife could not be more obvious. Looking serious and constantly ill-tempered, Mr. Palmer is disdainful. This arrogance demonstrates his sense of superiority. He takes little or no trouble to respond when spoken to and retreats into a corner to avoid dealing with those around him. As well as being ill-mannered, he has little regard for his wife.

ROBERT FERRARS: younger brother of Edward Ferrars.

This young man has little more to him than his looks. He has an ordinary physique and is content to follow fashion. Robert is particularly arrogant and selfish. He thinks he's more intelligent than his brother, for whom he has little respect.

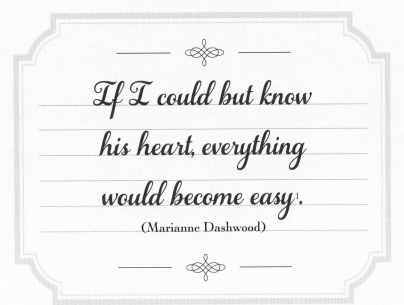

Sense and Sensibility
IN A NUTSHELL

If I could but know his heart, everything would become easy.[1]
(Marianne Dashwood)

A BRIEF OVERVIEW

In 1795, Jane Austen began writing this story of two sisters, which, according to her niece Caroline, was first written in the form of letters. It was simply titled with the names of the main characters, *Elinor and Marianne*, like most novels of the period, such as Frances Burney's *Evelina* (1778) or *Camilla* (1796). It was in 1797 that the book took on its current prose form. After the setbacks with *Pride and Prejudice*, which was rejected without explanation by the publisher Thomas Cadell in 1797, it was not until 1809-1810 that the novelist seemed to regain hope of being published.

After starting it in Steventon, her childhood home, she took the manuscript with her to Chawton, her final home. The biggest change she made was in the title, which became *Sense and Sensibility*. As attached as she was to Elizabeth Bennet, Jane Austen also spoke of "my Elinor" and confided to her sister Cassandra: "I am never too busy to think of S&S. I can no more forget it than a mother can forget her sucking child..."[2]

Henry Austen approached the London publisher Thomas Egerton, a cousin of his mother's, who accepted the novel on condition that it was published on a self-publishing basis: he didn't want to take any risks. Jane Austen had to pay the costs of printing and advertising, and for each copy a commission was paid to the publisher, who was responsible for distribution and sales. The novelist anticipated that sales would not cover the expenses involved. In preparation, she set aside some money from her meagre savings. She went to London with her brother and his wife Eliza to correct the proofs in March 1811. The initial release was scheduled for May of that year. However, for no apparent reason, it was postponed until the end of the year. We only know that in April Henry urged the printer to bring out the book as soon as possible. The first advertisements appeared in the *Star* and *Morning Chronicle* newspapers on 30 and 31 October, then throughout November.

[1] *Sense and Sensibility,* Jane Austen, T. Egerton, 1811. *op. cit.*
[2] *Jane Austen's Letters*, Deirdre Le Faye, Oxford Editions, 2011.

Jane Austen was thirty-six at the time. One of her novels had finally been published. Her hours of work were rewarded. Prejudice against women writers prevented her from adding her name, but she was keen to make it known that the author was a woman. The cover read: *"By a lady"*. This anonymity was also a choice, and she forbade her entire family from revealing the secret. In 1812, in a letter to one of her correspondents, Princess Charlotte wrote that the Duke of York had told her that the author of the book was a certain Lady A. Paget. Jane Austen's true identity was not yet public.

Sense and Sensibility was published in three volumes at 15 shillings each, with a print run of between seven hundred and fifty and one thousand copies. The first edition sold out in July 1813 and earned her £140, or around £20,600 today. Not only did this cover the costs she incurred, but it also generated a profit. A second print run was scheduled for the end of 1813, again on a self-publishing basis. She earned £12 in March 1816, which she invested in her brother's bank, and £19 in March 1817.

The first French translation appeared in 1815, by Isabelle de Montolieu, under the title *Raison et Sensibilité ou Les Deux Manières d'Aimer*. The translator did not bother to mention Jane Austen's name and took the liberty of making a few changes, including altering the ending.

RAISON
ET
SENSIBILITÉ,
OU
LES DEUX MANIÈRES D'AIMER.
TRADUIT LIBREMENT DE L'ANGLAIS,
PAR
Mᵐᵉ ISABELLE DE MONTOLIEU.

TOME PREMIER.

À PARIS,
CHEZ ARTHUS-BERTRAND, LIBRAIRE,
RUE HAUTEFEUILLE, Nᵒ. 23.
1815.

AN ANONYMOUS LETTER

In December 1811, about a month after the publication of *Sense and Sensibility*, Jane Austen received an anonymous letter:

To Miss Jane Austen the reputed author of Sense and Sensibility, a Novel lately published:

On such Subjects no Wonder that she shou'd write well,
In whom so united those Qualities dwell ;
Where 'dear Sensibility', Sterne's darling Maid,
With Sense so attemper'd is finely pourtray'd.
Fair Elinor's Self in that Mind is exprest,
And the Feelings of Marianne live in that Breast.
Oh then, gentle Lady ! continue to write,
And the Sense of your Readers t'amuse and delight.
A Friend. "[3]

In fact, the author of this lovely poem was none other than her older brother James. Is this a joke between them? Did Jane Austen tell him that she very much "hoped" to have a secret admirer? Still, the attention is both amusing and touching.

[3] The letter comes from Mary Lloyd's diary, which is transcribed in *Jane Austen, A Family Record*, Deirdre Le Faye, Cambridge University Press, 2004.

THE BIG PICTURE

The gentry

In Jane Austen's time, England was divided into several social classes. If we disregard royalty, the highest class was the nobility. It was characterised above all by titles, which were hereditary: dukes, marquesses, earls, viscounts and barons. People could even hold several titles. Members of the nobility held political power and could sit in the House of Lords. The gentry, who were less well-to-do, included baronets, knights, esquires and gentlemen. The first three were titles, but only that of baronet was inherited. The gentry was made up of three levels of class: upper, middle and lower. Finally, the bottom rung of the ladder was made up of workers, peasants, domestic servants and shopkeepers, and the poor who had no profession.

Like the nobility, the gentry were landowners, but they had no political power. They lived off the earnings generated by their business without having to get their hands dirty. Farmers paid them rent for accommodation, to raise livestock and cultivate the land. Part of the harvest went back to the owners for their own use, but the resale of these products and others, such as wood, increased their income. Finally, the men could invest money to guarantee a regular income. However, the resources and standard of living varied greatly, depending on the family's background or the size of the land. Jane Austen's family belonged to this social class, as do the majority of her characters.

INHERITANCE

There were several ways of passing on your property. In *Sense and Sensibility*, Henry Dashwood, his wife and daughters are taken in by a paternal great-uncle. He writes a will in which we learn that on Henry's death, all his property will go to John, his son from his first marriage. The old uncle is keen for the estate to be passed on to little Harry. Mr. Henry Dashwood thinks he will live long enough to see his daughters settle down and not have to worry about their future. Unfortunately, he left this world very quickly. His wife and daughters have to vacate the premises.

In a will, you could choose which assets went to whom. This meant that the estate could be divided up for the benefit of several people, but the property then lost its value, and the family's wealth and power were diminished. For this reason, the principle of primogeniture, or entail, was favoured.

The first option was based on choosing a single beneficiary. It could be absolute primogeniture, in which the inheritance went to the eldest child, regardless of sex. Male primogeniture favoured the son or sons first, then the daughters if their brothers were deceased or if there were simply no male descendants.

Lastly, agnatic primogeniture was the most discriminatory with regard to females. No daughter could inherit the estate. When the father died, the estate had to revert to a man, a son, nephew or cousin, even a very distant relative. There was a duty to preserve the family heritage in the same lineage. This act was based on the fact that when a woman married, all her property reverted to her husband. The family name disappeared forever.[4]

As far as entail was concerned, the aim was to ensure that the heir could not dispose of his assets as he wished. This contract covered all the real estate, land and property, which the owner could not sell, divide or transfer. The family estate became an entity in its own right. There were several types of entail: for male heirs only, for female heirs only or those that followed certain criteria. Moveable assets, such as jewellery, furniture or money, were independent and could be passed on to the heirs of one's choice.

Widows were entitled to a dower. The husband could indicate in his will that his wife would inherit part of the property until her death. The heir would then receive his full inheritance.

---

[4] However, some families adopted the wife's name if it was more prestigious.

Those who were not fortunate enough to be born into a 'respectable' family might have an opportunity to rise to the rank of gentleman. Families who made a fortune, particularly in commerce, could pay for their sons to learn the basics, a good education and good manners, and above all to develop and maintain new social relationships. Finally, the essential condition for gaining a foothold in the gentry was owning land.

From that moment on, the activity from which the estate was financed had to be discontinued. A gentleman didn't work. Having a working male relative was always a stain on the pedigree of any self-respecting gentry family. Nevertheless, honourable relations and a possible marriage to an influential member of this social milieu could mitigate the stigma.

Men's professions

When the family chose a single heir, only the eldest was guaranteed to receive the income associated with the estate. The younger brothers had no option but to take up a trade. However, the choice was limited to a few activities considered appropriate to their social status: the army, the Church or the law. Other professions, such as banking or medicine, were also accepted as long as the practitioner did not receive a salary as such.

The army

Young men with no military experience or training could join the cavalry or infantry of the regular army. But to be considered a gentleman, it was not enough to be a soldier. You had to be an officer, and to become one, you had to buy a commission from the army or another officer. This was a perfectly normal and acceptable procedure at the time.

Only wealthy men could afford this, as it was very expensive. It was believed that having the ability to pay for a rank in the army meant that "rich" men who were sufficiently "educated" would protect the nation. In addition, investing this money would make them more responsible, helping them maintain good behaviour. It also ensured that they had an income when they decided to leave the army.

Poor people who signed up were not considered. A few soldiers could nevertheless hope for promotion based on their courage, but this was a rare occurrence, and luck —i.e. good connections— was often essential. Sometimes, when a superior retired or died suddenly, the immediate need to replace him was an opportunity for a deserving soldier to get the position.

In the late 18th century, a number of laws were passed to regulate the conditions for joining the army. The minimum age for entry was sixteen, and the purchase of a commission to obtain a higher rank could only be made after two years' service. The aim was to ensure that officers were able to rise through the ranks by gaining real experience, rather than just paying to climb the ladder. Another law allowed soldiers to enlist for a limited time. Previously, joining the army meant a lifetime commitment, but the government understood that this might make volunteers reluctant. They promised a retirement pension to all those who made a long-term commitment: this argument convinced men to defend their country over a long period.

The standing army should not be confused with the militia. All men between the ages of eighteen and forty-five were required to be ready to join the militia in times of war. Only Church clergy were exempt. It was the parish that was responsible for gathering the necessary men, and it risked a fine if it did not meet the quota required by the government.

The militia maintained order in the absence of the army, while they were away fighting the enemy on the battlefield. Militiamen were stationed throughout the country, particularly in the south to protect the coast. Unlike the regular army, commissions for officer ranks could not be bought. A militiaman's rank depended on the size of his family's land holdings or whether he earned a regular income.

The Church

To become a clergyman, the first step was to study at Oxford or Cambridge and obtain a degree. Clergy were then qualified to administer the sacraments. They began by being an assistant, and could then be ordained from the age of twenty-four.

Clergymen had to find a religious parish in which to officiate. This was a position in a parish that provided a presbytery, where they could live with their family, and land that they could rent. Their income came mainly from the tithes they collected. However, a single parish was often insufficient to support a family, and it was common to own at least two. Jane Austen's father was a clergyman at Deane, bought by her uncle Francis Motley Austen, and at Steventon, where the whole family lived, passed on to him by his cousin Mr. Knight.

A high-ranking contact could enable you to enter ecclesiastical life immediately after ordination. Without connections, it could take several years before you had the opportunity to take charge of a parish. In *Sense and Sensibility*, Edward Ferrars plans to take holy orders, but even though his family is very wealthy, they oppose him and do not help him.

The activities of a clergyman included ordinary duties, baptisms, marriages and deaths. They officiated every Sunday, visited the poor and took part in local life. They reviewed the repair and maintenance needs of the church and roads. They decided on the acts of charity to be undertaken.

Once his parish had been acquired, the clergyman was there for life. He could not be removed or replaced. Only his death or his wish to pass it on to someone else disengaged him from clerical life. When Jane Austen's father retired, his eldest son, James, took his place.

Did you know?

"A MEETING WAS INEVITABLE"[5]

Generally used in the army, duelling was also practised in the highest social circles. Although illegal for many centuries, it was nonetheless commonplace. This meeting between two men was an opportunity for them to defend their honour or right a wrong. Whoever was called to the duel had a choice of weapon, usually a sword or a pistol.

The motivation was not necessarily to cause death. With a pistol, if you were not a good shot or if the weapon was faulty, you could miss your opponent. A "duel across a handkerchief", however, was a pistol duel that resulted in certain death. Each man had to hold a corner of the same handkerchief. Physical proximity increased the chances of hitting your target. Some sword fights could be broken up after a few scratches, but they could also produce serious injuries. Since duelling was forbidden, killing someone during a duel could result in the death penalty.

[5] *Sense and Sensibility, op. cit.*

Law

Studying law was a major financial investment, which considerably reduced the number of applicants. Ideally, you studied at university and then joined the Inns of Court[6] for three years. Interested parties could also apply directly to one of these institutions, but the time limit was extended by two years. There was no specific programme and students had to learn on their own. However, they spent time in contact with professionals and took part in meals, which sometimes included lectures and mock hearings.

After three to five years of study, the Inns of Court decided which students would be called to the bar. They could then practise as lawyers. With experience, they could progress and even become judges. Those who were not fortunate enough to be selected could become a notary or agent, the intermediary between clients and lawyers. They were the only members of the legal profession to be considered gentlemen, as they did not receive a salary but rather a bonus.

---

[6] There were four legal institutions in London: Gray's Inn, Inner Temple, Lincoln's Inn and Middle Temple.

THE GRAND TOUR

The Grand Tour was seen as an essential stage in a man's education. Before, after or instead of university, wealthy young men were sent across Europe to further their education. Under the responsibility of a tutor, they visited the most influential regions and cities in the fields of art and culture. They attended concerts, observed and admired works of art from the classical and Renaissance eras, and visited ancient sites. In this way, they deepened or acquired new intellectual and cultural knowledge. The Grand Tour could last up to five years! Such experiences were an asset for their future.

These "tourists" went mainly to Italy and France. They visited Florence, Venice, Naples and their archaeological sites. Paris was a very popular destination. They could leave their luggage there for a few weeks or even several months. Switzerland, Germany and the countries of Eastern Europe might also be part of their itinerary.

Thanks to the generosity and fortune of his adoptive parents Thomas and Catherine Knight, Edward Austen was sent to Europe to further his education. He was eighteen and kept a diary of his adventures. He discovered Switzerland and Italy, and spent a year studying at the University of Dresden.

It was common for young men to bring back a portrait of themselves from their trip, as well as 'objets d'art' that they could later display in their homes. Edward Austen was no exception, returning to England with a superb full-length portrait of himself. This painting is on display at Chawton House.

Men's education

School in Jane Austen's time was not regulated as it is today. Social class, family wealth and parental expectations all played a part in inequalities in boys' education. The ages and subjects taught were very random.

Very young boys were usually educated at home, by their parents or a governess. Around the age of four or five, they learnt the rudiments of reading, writing and mathematics. From the age of six or seven, children were taught by tutors or sent to a small school often run by clergymen. In Steventon, Mr. Austen took in and taught several children to supplement his income. Teaching became diversified to include history, geography, science, Latin, literature and philosophy. They also learnt about good manners, dance, music and sport.

A few years later, if the family was unable to pay the wages of a tutor, the pupils entered a boarding school, such as Eton or Westminster. The lessons were similar to those studied previously. Others chose specialised schools such as the Royal Naval Academy, where Francis and Charles Austen were admitted to join the Navy.

Around the age of eighteen, young men enrolled at university to obtain a degree and consider a career. The most prestigious were Oxford and Cambridge. They rejected students who did not adhere to Church of England doctrine. These students had to join dissenting academies.[7]

The poorest pupils could be awarded a scholarship. They remained isolated, however, and were likely to be bullied by their peers who were privileged by birth.

The London season

The London season was the time of year when society's elite gathered in the capital. It happened when Parliament was in session, from November to July. Beyond politics, it was an opportunity for politicians and their families to meet up with friends, organise receptions, attend balls, and go to the opera or theatre. All these social events were also an opportunity to forge new connections.

Single men took advantage of these entertainments to search for and perhaps find the one they would fall in love with, or failing that, a well-bred woman with a pretty penny to her name. For the young women, this season was all about making their entry into the world and letting people know that they were available on the wedding market.

In *Sense and Sensibility*, Mrs. Jennings invites Elinor and Marianne to spend a few weeks at her home in London. Above all, she wants to entertain and be entertained. What was the point of staying in a house in the country during those long winter months with nothing to do but play cards and try to keep warm by the fire, when the city offered so many attractions? The young women aren't going there to "enter the world" or to find a husband, as Elinor's heart is already set on a certain Mr. F. and Marianne's on the one who occupies her thoughts.

At the end of the season, it was time to get away from the hustle and bustle and take a rest. Families returned to their county to enjoy the fresh air and, for the gentlemen, to go hunting.

---

[7] Schools run by non-conformist Protestants.

ADAPTATIONS

The earliest recorded adaptation was an American series recorded by NBC in 1950, about which little information remains. Since then, several adaptations have been made.

Sense and Sensibility, BBC, 1971, 180 minutes

Divided into four episodes, this mini-series was broadcast on television.

Directed by: David Giles

Script: Denis Constanduros

Cast: Joanna David (Elinor Dashwood), Ciaran Madden (Marianne Dashwood), Isabel Dean (Mrs. Dashwood), Milton Johns (John Dashwood), Robin Ellis (Edward Ferrars), Michael Aldridge (Sir John Middleton), Patricia Routledge (Mrs. Jennings), Richard Owens (Colonel Brandon), Clive Francis (John Willoughby), Frances Cuka (Lucy Steele).

Anecdotes:

♦ Denis Constanduros wrote the screenplay for this adaptation, as well as the 1981 adaptation of *Sense and Sensibility*.

♦ Joanna David, seen here in the lead role, would go on to play Mrs. Gardiner in the 1995 version of *Pride and Prejudice*.

Sense and Sensibility, BBC, 1981, 174 minutes

This mini-series was made up of seven episodes of around thirty minutes each.

Directed by: Rodney Bennett

Script: Alexander Baron, Denis Constanduros

Cast: Irene Richard (Elinor Dashwood), Tracey Childs (Marianne Dashwood), Diana Fairfax (Mrs. Dashwood), Peter Gale (John Dashwood), Bosco Hogan (Edward Ferrars), Donald Douglas (Sir John Middleton), Annie Leon (Mrs. Jennings), Robert Swann (Colonel Brandon), Peter Woodward (John Willoughby), Julia Chambers (Lucy Steele).

Anecdotes:

♦ Irene Richard, here Elinor, played Charlotte Lucas in the 1980 version of *Pride and Prejudice*.

♦ Donald Douglas (Sir John Middleton) played Mark Darcy's father in the *Bridget Jones* adaptations.

♦ The exterior scenes in London were actually shot in Bath.

♦ In 1981, the summer season in Devon was particularly rainy, which gave a real authenticity to the majority of the scenes shot in the rain.

Shooting locations:

♦ **Babington House** in Babington, Somerset, is the location for **Norland**, the home of John and Fanny Dashwood. Built around 1705, the manor house first belonged to the Babington family and then to the Knatchbull family. In 1998, it was bought by the private club Soho House, when it was converted into a hotel. Many celebrities have chosen to hold their weddings here, including Eddie Redmayne in 2014.
Information at sohohouse.com/houses/babington-house

• **Came House** in Dorchester, Dorset, is a country house built in 1754. In the 1830s, a stunning domed winter garden was added. The plans were signed by Charles Fowler, who was also the architect of Covent Garden Market in London. The house was used for the **Barton Park** scenes, and the nearby thatched cottage was used as the modest home of Mrs. Dashwood and her daughters. Came House is a private property that opens its doors to those seeking a fairytale wedding.

For more information visit camehouse.co.uk

• **Crowcombe Court** in Crowcombe, Somerset, is a house built in the mid-18th century in the Baroque style. This sumptuous venue is accessible if you are planning your wedding there. In the adaptation, it was used as Mrs. Jennings' London house.

Information at crowcombecourt.co.uk

Sense and Sensibility, BBC, 1995, 136 minutes

This adaptation was the first to be made for the big screen.

Directed by: Ang Lee

Script: Emma Thompson

Cast: Emma Thompson (Elinor Dashwood), Kate Winslet (Marianne Dashwood), Gemma Jones (Mrs. Dashwood), James Fleet (John Dashwood), Hugh Grant (Edward Ferrars), Robert Hardy (Sir John Middleton), Elizabeth Spriggs (Mrs. Jennings), Alan Rickman (Colonel Brandon), Greg Wise (John Willoughby), Imogen Stubbs (Lucy Steele).

Anecdotes:

- The director, Ang Lee, did not read *Sense and Sensibility* before receiving the script. He was chosen because, as a Taiwanese national, his outside perspective was an asset to the film.

- It was Emma Thompson's adoration for Jane Austen that won her the offer to write the screenplay. It took her five years to put the finishing touches to it. During the writing process, the actress slept with the novelist's letters beside her.

- At one point, she thought she had lost the file on her computer, but Stephen Fry located it after a seven-hour search. He is thanked in the credits.

- In the novel, Elinor Dashwood is nineteen years old. Emma Thompson was thirty-six at the time of filming.

- While writing the script, Emma Thompson was already imagining Hugh Grant in the role of Edward Ferrars, without knowing whether he would accept the part. The Jane Austen Society contacted one of the film's producers to complain that the actor was far too handsome to play the character.

- In the diary she kept during filming, Emma Thompson recounts that kissing Hugh Grant was fun and adds, "Glad I invented it. Can't rely on Austen for a snog, that's for sure."[8]

- Colonel Brandon was due to be played by Hugh Laurie, but the actor was finally chosen to play Mr. Palmer.

- Amanda Root was the first choice for the role of Marianne, but the actress had committed herself to the adaptation of *Persuasion*.

- Kate Winslet was being considered for the role of Lucy Steele, although she wanted the part of Marianne. During her audition, she pretended that her agent had sent her to play Marianne. And that's how it happened!

- Willoughby saves Marianne in the pouring rain, but more than fifty takes were needed for this scene and Kate Winslet ended up suffering from hypothermia as a result.

- Kate Winslet and Emma Thompson chose to live together for the duration of the shoot to help them form a sisterly bond.

- The film was nominated for and won several major film awards. It won the Golden Bear and a Bafta for Best Film. It won Best Drama and Best Screenplay at the Golden Globes. And it won an Oscar® for Best Adapted Screenplay!

- At the Bafta awards, the Best Actress went to Emma Thompson and the Best Supporting Actress to Kate Winslet.

---

[8] *Sense and Sensibility. The Screenplay and Diaries*, Emma Thompson Bloomsbury, 1995.

Did you know?

JANE AUSTEN BROUGHT TO LIFE IN A SPEECH

At the Golden Globes, *Sense and Sensibility* won Best Screenplay. Emma Thompson took to the stage to receive the award and delivered a memorable speech,[9] voicing what Jane Austen might have said in a letter after such an evening. Extract:

"Four A.M. Having just returned from an evening at the Golden Spheres, which despite the inconveniences of heat, noise and overcrowding, was not without its pleasures. Thankfully, there were no dogs and no children. (...)

P.S. Managed to avoid the hoyden Emily Tomkins who has purloined my creation and added things of her own. Nefarious creature."

Shooting locations:

• **Saltram House** in Plympton, Devon, was **Norland Park**, the home of John and Fanny Dashwood. An amazing fact is that Jane Austen herself visited her friend there, the second wife of the Earl of Morley, who owned the manor at the time. Designed by architect Robert Adam in the 18th century, it retains its period architecture, a collection of paintings and ceramics and much of its original furniture. The library contains numerous works, including a copy of the *Nuremberg Chronicle* from 1493. The manor house is open to visitors and a tea room awaits you for a delicious tea time experience.

Information at nationaltrust.org.uk/visit/devon/saltram

• Flete Estate in Holbeton is a vast estate with breathtaking views over the River Erme estuary in South Devon. Several houses dot the landscape, including **Efford House**, which served as the backdrop for **Barton Cottage**. The front façade is deceptive and gives the appearance of a modest thatched cottage, but in reality the house is much more impressive. Another house hosted the team for the drawing room scenes in Mrs. Jennings' London house. **Mothecombe House** was built in 1710 in the sublime Queen Anne style. Its gardens are open every Tuesday from April to September. The homes on the estate are now hotels, providing a warm and calming environment. Easily accessible, the nearby beaches are the icing on the cake.

Information at flete.co.uk

[9] Available on YouTube.

♦ **Mompesson House**, in Salisbury, Wiltshire, built in 1701, is unique in that it is part of the cathedral precinct. For six hundred years, it has been home to the oldest clock in the world still in use. Several families came one after another, until the house was bought by Denis Martineau. The sale was accepted on condition that he bequeathed it to the National Trust on his death. Surprise! In 1975, when the owner died, he left an empty house. Two years later, after refurnishing and redecorating the main rooms, the organisation opened the doors of Mompesson House to visitors. These premises were used as the backdrop for Mrs, Jennings' London house. The garden is a haven of peace, and at the far end, the small tearoom is the perfect place to end your visit. The site is closed on Wednesdays and Thursdays, so please check the opening times before you visit.
Information at

nationaltrust.org.uk/visit/wiltshire/mompesson-house

♦ **Compton Castle** in Marldon, Paignton, Devon, is a majestic medieval manor house dating from the 14ᵗʰ century. It is used for **Combe Magna**, the Willoughby estate. Open Tuesday to Thursday from April to October.
Information at nationaltrust.org.uk/visit/devon/compton-castle

♦ The Palmers' estate, **Cleveland**, is represented in the film by **Montacute House**, a masterpiece of Elizabethan architecture. Situated in Montacute in Somerset, the manor house dates back to the end of the 18ᵗʰ century. The first occupant was Sir Edward Phelips, a great lawyer and prominent member of the English government. He was most famous for his part in the prosecution of Guy Fawkes and his followers in the Gunpowder Plot, a failed attempt to blow up the English Parliament in 1605. The house has huge windows all along the façade, letting light into the long gallery that stretches for fifty-two metres. You can admire portraits of the most famous English monarchs, Henry III, Elizabeth I and James I. Some of the paintings are the property of the National Portrait Gallery, with which Montacute House has a partnership. The gardens are also exceptional. One remarkable feature is the huge yew hedge, which suffered a harsh winter in the 1940s. Bent under the weight of the snow, the hedge became deformed in a curious way, and the organisation has since insisted that it be maintained as it was. The site is open to visitors all year round.
Information at

nationaltrust.org.uk/visit/somerset/montacute-house

Sense and Sensibility, BBC, 2008, 174 minutes

This mini-series is the latest to date. It was made up of three episodes, each lasting around an hour.

Directed by: John Alexander

Script: Andrew Davies

Cast: Hattie Morahan (Elinor Dashwood), Charity Wakefield (Marianne Dashwood), Janet McTeer (Mrs. Dashwood), Mark Gatiss (John Dashwood), Dan Stevens (Edward Ferrars), Mark Williams (Sir John Middleton), Linda Bassett (Mrs. Jennings), David Morrissey (Colonel Brandon), Dominic Cooper (John Willoughby), Anna Madeley (Lucy Steele).

Anecdotes:

♦ Andrew Davies included several scenes that are not in the novel to develop and highlight the characters and feelings of Colonel Brandon and Edward Ferrars. The scene in which Edward is cutting logs shows his frustration and his way of venting it.

♦ Mark Williams, who plays Sir John Middleton, is an historical weapons enthusiast. He suggested that the director add a scene in which he hunts with Colonel Brandon, an opportunity for him to show off his talents.

♦ Charity Wakefield (Marianne) played the piano herself. She practised all the songs on an electric piano that she bought especially for the shoot.

♦ The scene of Elinor standing in a cave is entirely improvised. The inclement weather interrupted the planned sequence. The camera continued to roll and the scene was included in the mini-series.

Shooting locations:

♦ An imposing building stands on the grounds of Hartland Abbey, in Hartland, Devon. A former monastery built in the 11th century, it was sold in 1583 by Henry VIII to William Abbot, who converted it into a manor house. It is open to the public from April to September, and numerous events are organised there, including open-air theatre productions in the summer. The brochure can be downloaded from their website. On the same estate is **Blackpool Mill Cottage**, which was used for **Barton Cottage**. This charming house dates back to the 15th century. Now converted into a rental property, it sleeps up to eight people and is perfect for relaxing and taking a break from the outside world, as the owners have chosen not to install internet or cable. You can take a stroll along the coastline, where many of the scenes were filmed.
Information at hartlandabbey.com/blackpool-mill

Ham House

• **Ham House**, in Richmond, Surrey, is a 17th century manor house on the banks of the River Thames. In 1626, King Charles I presented his friend William Murray with the precious house. Murray made a number of changes. His daughter, the future Duchess of Lauderdale, inherited the estate. She continued to add to its furnishings and decorations. A 3D virtual tour of the "green cabinet" is well worth the time. Most of the furniture in this room is original, including the small Japanese wardrobes. A miniature of Elizabeth I is also on display. The outside of the house is the setting for **Cleveland** and the inside for **Norland**. The site is open all year round, with the exception of a few dates.

Information at

nationaltrust.org.uk/visit/london/ham-house-and-garden

• **Wrotham Park**, in Barnet, Hertfordshire, is the location for **Norland**. The building was constructed in 1754 for Admiral John Byng. Unfortunately, he had little or no opportunity to stay there: after a failed expedition to Minorca, he was sentenced to death in 1757. Despite a major fire in 1884, the house retains its original architecture. It still belongs to the Byng family. It is not open to the public, but can be hired for private events.

Information on wrothampark.com

Did you know?

♦ *Kandukondain Kandukondain* is a modern Indian adaptation of *Sense and Sensibility*, released in 2000. The colourful story was adapted as a musical.

♦ *Scents and Sensibility*, released in 2011, is a ninety-minute American film loosely based on the novel.

♦ An American-Mexican version was released in 2011. In *From Prada to Nada*, two Mexican-born sisters live in Los Angeles. Broke following the death of their father, they have to move in with their aunt.

♦ *Elinor and Marianne Take Barton* is a 2014 web series comprising thirty-two episodes of around five to ten minutes each. Marianne Dashwood is at university and shares her daily life and moods in the form of a vlog.[10]

♦ *Sense, Sensibility & Snowmen* is a 2019 Canadian film about the Dashwood sisters, in this case Ella and Marianne, who run a party-planning business. They're excited about Christmas, but one of their customers, Edward Ferris, causes trouble.

WHEN *SENSE AND SENSIBILITY* INSPIRES CONTEMPORARY WRITERS

♦ *The Dashwood Sisters' Secrets of Love*, by Rosie Rushton. Ideal for teenagers. (Published on September 5, 2006 by Little, Brown Books for Young Readers)

♦ *Sense & Sensibility*, adapted by Nancy Butler and illustrated by Sonny Liew. This book presents the original novel in comic book form. It is split into five volumes. (Marvel, 2010)

♦ *Colonel Brandon's Diary*, by Amanda Grange. The author's imagination takes the reader into the Colonel's past and his relationship with Eliza, from their first meeting to their last, and then invites us to discover the turmoil that besets him when he meets Marianne. (Berkley, 2009)

♦ *Sense and Sensibility*, by Joanna Trollope. This novel is part of the Jane Austen Project undertaken by Harper Collins to revisit and modernise Austen's works. (HarperCollins Publishers Ltd, 2013)

♦ *Constance et Séduction*, by Jess Swann. This modern retelling is the only French production. (Artalys, 2015)

♦ *Willoughby's Return: A Tale of Almost Irresistible Temptation*, by Jane Odiwe. This sequel focuses primarily on Marianne and her new life, but also gives a starring role to Margaret, the youngest of the Dashwood sisters. (Sourcebooks Landmark, 2009)

♦ *Sense and Sensibility*, by Po Tse. For Manga fans. (Manga Classics, 2001)

♦ *A Dashwood of Sense and Sensibility*, by Anyta Sunday. This is the sixth volume in the *Love, Austen* series, a modern gay adaptation. A French translation is currently being published by MxM Bookmark. (Anyta Sunday, 2021).

---

[10] Available on YouTube.

Pride and Prejudice

Pride and Prejudice is the most popular, the most famous, the most adored of Jane Austen's novels. What's all the fuss about? What is so special about this book that it is often used as a gateway to the Austen world in particular, and to British culture in general? While the power of *Pride and Prejudice* as a novel left its mark at the time, this love story has stood the test of time and continues to fascinate and inspire more than two hundred years after its publication.

Incipit 1813

It is a truth universally acknowledged, that a single man in possession of a good fortune, must be in want of a wife.[11]

WHAT'S IT ABOUT?

In the heart of the modest market town of Meryton, in Hertfordshire, all the inhabitants are in uproar. While the arrival of the militia has upset everyone's routine, the new tenants of the most beautiful property in the neighbourhood have also disrupted this peaceful corner of the countryside. Among them, one particularly distinguished gentleman stands out, Mr. Darcy. He seems to have it all: looks, youth and wealth. Yet, his behaviour is most unpleasant: he snubs people he doesn't know.

[11] *Pride and Prejudice*, Jane Austen, T. Egerton, 1813.

However, his interest is soon piqued by a young lady from the local gentry, Elizabeth Bennet, renowned for her frankness and sharp wit. Unimpressed and totally unaware of the emotion she is arousing, she naturally takes a dislike to him from the moment they first meet. The bold young woman, with her outspoken temperament, never fails to give him a piece of her mind, challenging his convictions.

In the meantime, she meets a dashing officer who is both pleasant and sociable, and who has no trouble winning everyone over. But first impressions can sometimes be misleading, especially when you listen to prejudice rather than common sense, and when pride takes precedence over feelings.

"I hope M.ʳ Bingley will like it"

Hugh Thomson's illustration for an 1894 edition of Jane Austen's novel shows Mr. and Mrs. Bennet with their daughters Jane, Elizabeth, Mary, Kitty and Lydia.

Character Gallery
THE LADIES

ELIZABETH BENNET: **a graceful young woman with lovely dark eyes.**

Sweetly nicknamed Lizzy by her family, or Eliza or Miss Eliza by her friends, she is just twenty years old. The Bennets' second daughter, she is a firm favourite of her father who is delighted by her sense of humour and quick wit. Deeply honest, impulsive, cheerful, sunny, mischievous and intelligent, she likes to think with her heart rather than her head. This tends to confuse her as to how to judge those around her. She's convinced of her common sense, and she's never afraid to say what she thinks, whoever she's talking to. She is also very aware of the lack of education and good manners of a number of people close to her.

JANE BENNET: **Elizabeth's elder sister.**

This pure soul sees good everywhere, even in the meanest characters. She and Lizzy have a close relationship, and as well as sisters they are close friends. Jane is also very modest and reserved. She doesn't dare express her feelings

Did you know?

HOW WAS A LADY ADDRESSED DURING THE REGENCY PERIOD?

The first-born daughter was called by her surname only. So, in the Bennet household, we have a Miss Bennet (Jane), a Miss Elizabeth, a Miss Mary, a Miss Catherine and a Miss Lydia. In the Bingley family, the second daughter, Caroline, is called Miss Bingley because her older sister is already married.

The Bingley sisters address Elizabeth as Miss Eliza: what looks like affection is actually contempt in disguise. They haven't known each other long enough for this degree of intimacy. This reveals that they consider her inferior to them.

easily, even if it means suffering for it. Mrs. Bennet despairs that her daughter, so outrageously beautiful, is not already married, at the age of almost twenty-three.

CHARLOTTE LUCAS: **Elizabeth's best friend.**
At twenty-seven, Miss Lucas considers herself a burden on her family because she is still single. A close friend of the Bennet sisters, she has found a confidante in Elizabeth and never hesitates to tell her what she thinks. She is very perceptive, with a great capacity for analysis and a pragmatic mind. She doesn't let her feelings rule her. She is said to have an ordinary appearance, but a good heart.

LYDIA BENNET: **the youngest member of the Bennet family.**
All Lydia thinks about is fun, flirting and dancing. At almost sixteen, pretty, fresh-faced and tall, the mischievous teenager lives in her own little world of laughter and fun. Often rude, she is also stubborn, carefree and gossipy. Lydia is her mother's favourite, and her mother recognises herself in her. She ignores her whims and overlooks all her faults.

CATHERINE BENNET: **a younger sister in the Bennet family.**
Two years older than Lydia and just as scatterbrained, they are inseparable, but she tends to follow her little sister's lead. It's not easy to assert yourself, or simply to be heard, in a family where, whether they want to or not, the girls are all competing for a successful marriage. Those close to her affectionately call her Kitty.

MARY BENNET: **the ugly duckling of the Bennet family.**
Mary doesn't seem very smart, quick-witted or friendly. She enjoys reading, but lacks a critical eye. She plays the piano with good technique, but lacks sensitivity. Caught between two slightly superficial younger sisters and two remarkable older sisters, she struggles to find her place, sometimes blundering, sometimes unlucky.

MRS. BENNET: **a mother on the verge of a nervous breakdown.**
With five daughters to support, this constantly anxious woman considers herself to be eternally misunderstood. She is acutely aware that when her husband dies, the family's lifestyle will be considerably reduced. The potential marriage of her offspring becomes a real obsession for her, at the risk of annoying everyone around her. Like Elizabeth and Lydia, she's not afraid to speak her mind, although her remarks often verge on the ridiculous. She is reputed to have been very beautiful in her youth, but never very subtle, and above all unable to control her emotions.

MRS. PHILLIPS: **maternal aunt of the Bennet girls.**
Mrs. Bennet's sister lives in Meryton. An avid gossip, she's always up to date with the latest happenings. She is a great hostess, inviting the most eminent members of the militia as soon as they arrive in town. Her husband, a former clerk, is a solicitor.

MRS. GARDINER: **aunt by marriage to the Bennet girls.**
Married to the brother of Mrs. Bennet and Mrs. Phillips, she is the proud mother of four young children, who adore their cousins, especially Jane. Born in Derbyshire, close to Mr. Darcy's estate, Pemberley, she feels nostalgia for her region. She is very fond of her niece Elizabeth, whom she considers like a daughter. Sweet and intelligent, she is also perceptive when it comes to matters of love.

Did you know?   WHO WAS THE REAL LYDIA BENNET?

Jane Austen may have been thinking of one of her acquaintances, Mary Pearson, renowned for her beautiful dark eyes and cheerful disposition, when she describes the whimsical character of Lydia Bennet. In the summer of 1796, the pretty, frivolous Mary was briefly engaged to the handsome Henry, the novelist's favourite brother, then a soldier in the militia. The young people met in Rowling, Kent.

Despite the break-up of the engagement, apparently at Henry's instigation, the two women kept in touch for a few years, exchanging a handful of letters. They then ceased all relations, although they lived in Southampton for the same short period. We know that Mary Pearson ended up marrying someone else in 1815.

ELIZABETH KNIGHT: A STRONG-WILLED WOMAN

Lady Catherine de Bourgh is a perfect caricature of the noble lady who believes herself superior to everyone else by virtue of her birth alone, with her unfailing bad faith, her unbearable temper and her shameless manners. To create this ferociously funny character, even though she didn't know her personally, Jane Austen found a valuable source of inspiration in Elizabeth Knight (1674-1737), a legendary figure in the Knight family whose portrait still stands proudly at Chawton House. The lady demanded that the parish bells be rung every time she rode in the carriage.

In a Georgian England where women had few prerogatives and were constantly under the control and authority of men, Elizabeth Knight skilfully manoeuvred to gain as much freedom and independence as possible. She inherited the estate of Chawton House on the death of her brother. It was not usual for a woman to own land and property in the 18th century, particularly because the laws of succession favoured men. In some families, however, when there were no male descendants, women could inherit.

Elizabeth married twice: first to her cousin Edward Woodward Knight, and then to a man called Bulstrode Peachey Knight.[12] She had no children with either of them. Widowed each time, her wealth increased. At the end of her life, she found herself at the head of a considerable fortune, which she bequeathed in her will to a distant relative, Thomas Brodnax. In those days, it was easy to change your surname, and Knight was a natural choice. Later, his son bore the same name, Thomas Knight. It was this famous Thomas, the Austens' cousin, who adopted Edward, one of Jane Austen's older brothers.

CAROLINE BINGLEY: **younger sister of Mr. Bingley.**

Affable at first sight, elegant, refined and always at the cutting edge of fashion, she nevertheless despairs of not already being married, despite her influential connections. Appearances count for a lot to her, especially since she's set her sights on winning over the heart of Mr. Darcy. She spares no effort to achieve this. She openly mocks Elizabeth Bennet, whose behaviour she strongly disapproves of, at every opportunity.

LOUISA HURST: **elder sister of Mr. Bingley.**

As spiteful as Caroline, she has a marriage of convenience with a moderately wealthy man who seems to have neither education nor manners. She spends her time following her brother around, with the aim of keeping as much company as possible with Mr. Darcy, thus encouraging the union of her sister with him.

GEORGIANA DARCY: **Mr. Darcy's little sister.**

Barely sixteen, she lives with her brother, whom she adores, either in London or in Pemberley. A virtuoso pianist and experienced harpist, she rarely goes out, devoting herself entirely to her art. Shy, emotional and fearful, she is nonetheless warm and kind when she feels confident. Born into a particularly wealthy family, she is also a very prominent heiress.

LADY CATHERINE DE BOURGH: **Fitzwilliam Darcy's maternal aunt.**

Lady Catherine's sister is Lady Anne, Mr. Darcy's mother. Extremely wealthy, noble by birth and by her marriage to the late Lord Lewis de Bourgh, she has only one daughter, also named Anne, whom she hopes will marry her nephew. Self-righteous, easily provoked and fundamentally indiscreet, she thinks she's entitled to everything and is always right. She lives in the superb Rosings Park in Kent.

---

[12] In these two unions, each of Elizabeth's husbands added his wife's name, Knight, to his own. This was common practice at the time, especially if the wife's name was prestigious, as was the case in this family.

Character Gallery
THE GENTLEMEN

FITZWILLIAM DARCY: a bachelor with an exceptional fortune.

The first thing that people notice about him is his superb presence. Tall, infinitely handsome, rarely smiling, this young man of twenty-eight impresses everyone who meets his penetrating gaze, except Elizabeth Bennet. Heir to an immense fortune, including the incomparable Pemberley Estate, he represents one of the most desirable families in England. He is not a nobleman, although his mother was an earl's daughter. Rumour has it that he owns half of Derbyshire and, not least, has one of the most impressive libraries in the country. He prefers to keep his distance from strangers, which gives him a haughty and seemingly unapproachable air. Orphaned at a very young age, he had to face up to major responsibilities, which shaped his distrustful temperament. As a result, he trusts his common sense more than his heart.

CHARLES BINGLEY: gentleman from the North of England.

Described as personable, elegant, pleasant, cheerful and humble, he has the ability to quickly win over all hearts, especially those of the small circle of Meryton residents. His fortune, inherited from his father, came from trade. His origins don't stand in the way of his close friendship with Mr. Darcy, whose advice he follows blindly.

COLONEL FITZWILLIAM: cousin of Mr. Darcy.

A military man in his thirties, courteous and cultured, he is Mr. Darcy's cousin on his mother's side and is the youngest son of an unfortunate earl. Although he finds Elizabeth Bennet very likeable and no doubt to his taste, he knows that he is obliged to marry a lady with a generous dowry.

MR. BENNET: father of the five Bennet daughters.

This man is a respected and respectable member of the local gentry. Calm, teasing and quiet, this philosopher with an exaggerated sense of humour takes pleasure in taking refuge in his library at the slightest opportunity. Stuck in a mismatched marriage, he puts on an unflappable front to cope with the gloom of his daily life.

WILLIAM COLLINS: a devoted vicar.

A heavy, pompous young man of around twenty-five, he has a high opinion of himself. He now lives and works in Kent, on the estate of Lady Catherine de Bourgh. He visits his cousins in order to choose a wife from among them. With a certain pretentiousness, he thinks he is making up for the wrong that will be done to them when he inherits all their property.[13]

SIR WILLIAM LUCAS: neighbour of the Bennets.

Freshly knighted, Sir Lucas, a wealthy former merchant, is a courteous and debonair friend of the Bennets. Very happy with his new status, he doesn't particularly take any misplaced pride in it, but rather a certain satisfaction that he tries to share with as many people as possible.

Did you know?

WHO WAS THE REAL MR. DARCY?

The rumours continue, and it's impossible to know for sure who was the inspiration behind the character who has become a household name among fictional heroes. While it may have been thought that Tom Lefroy, one of Jane Austen's childhood sweethearts, inspired some of the features of this perfect gentleman, recent research has explored a different avenue.

In 2015, the academic Susan Law proposed the name of John Parker, the first Earl of Morley, a former university friend of Henry Austen. Morley's second wife, Frances Talbot, also a novelist, was friends with Jane Austen. There are even rumours that the Countess of Morley may have been behind the origins of *Pride and Prejudice*, since the description of the main character matches that of her husband.

Another intriguing fact is that, according to Dr Susan Law, during part of the writing of her novel, Jane Austen visited the Morley family at Saltram House in Devon. No formal proof, only speculation: the mystery remains unsolved.

---

[13] The law specifies that on the death of Mr. Bennet, his estate passes, not to his daughters, but to the nearest male heir. This man is Mr. Collins. His father, who died a few years earlier, was Mr. Bennet's cousin.

MR. GARDINER: **maternal uncle of the Bennet girls.**
Mrs. Bennet's brother lives in the City of London. He earns his comfortable lifestyle from commerce. He is fairly well off, but not well enough to be part of the gentry. Although a father of four, he has not forgotten his nieces. Jane and Elizabeth are his favourites. Generous and devoted, he has a simple, frank and honest nature. He loves angling.

GEORGE WICKHAM: **a fine officer.**
New to the Meryton area, George is a member of the militia, but originally from Derbyshire. A childhood friend of Mr. Darcy, he no longer has any contact with him. Taking advantage of his good looks, he loves to flirt, and there isn't a single girl in the area who doesn't feel some attraction for him. Talkative when it comes to recounting his misfortunes, he easily attracts sympathy.

Did you know?

THE PRESENCE OF THE MILITIA AND THE WAR AGAINST FRANCE

Jane Austen began writing what would become *Pride and Prejudice* in the late 18th century, at the height of the Napoleonic Wars. There were fears of an invasion from the south of the country, which partly explains the presence of the military in this region. One of Jane Austen's cousins, from Hertfordshire, himself joined a militia in Derbyshire in 1794-1795. A source of inspiration for Mr. Wickham?

Pride and Prejudice
IN A NUTSHELL

You must allow me to tell you how ardently I admire and love you.[14]
(Mr. Darcy)

"No, no; stay where you are," Elizabeth told them.

Illustration by Hugh Thomson for an 1894 edition.

[14] *Pride and Prejudice*, Jane Austen, T. Egerton, 1813, *op. cit.*

A BRIEF OVERVIEW

It is universally acknowledged that *Pride and Prejudice* is, without doubt, Jane Austen's most famous novel. She was particularly fond of it, calling it "my darling child".

Jane Austen began work on the novel in October 1796. At the time, she was the same age as her heroine, Elizabeth Bennet, almost twenty-one. The original title, *First Impressions*, refers to the encounters and emotions between the main characters, which form the core of the plot. She drew inspiration for her work from her reading: the expression "first impressions" also appears in Ann Radcliffe's *The Mysteries of Udolpho* (1794) and in a novel by Samuel Richardson, *The History of Sir Charles Grandison* (1753), Jane Austen's favourite.

From a note in Cassandra Austen's handwriting, now in the archives of the Morgan Library in New York, we know that she completed the first draft in August 1797. No trace remains of this first draft. For some years, this novel existed only in the privacy of the Austen family, where it was read regularly and particularly appreciated. In 1800, author, poet and translator Margaret Holford Hodson published *First Impressions: Or, the Portrait*, which forced Jane Austen to think of another title.

How did the novelist go from *First Impressions* to *Pride and Prejudice*? The combination of these two concepts may seem surprising, but it was not new at the time. It had already appeared, for example, in Oliver Goldsmith's *History of England* (1764), which a teenage Jane Austen amused herself by imitating in her own *History of England*, a short parody now part of *Juvenilia*. This combination of words can also be seen in Fanny Burney's *Cecilia* (1782). The novel was so popular at the time that the expression "pride and prejudice" became commonplace.

Similarly, the opening sentence of *Pride and Prejudice* pastiches an expression common in the 18th century, mainly used in moralising texts. Jane Austen's father had many of these books in his library, which he made available to his daughters. These works include *the Memoirs of General Fairfax* (1776). In this text, we find a turn of phrase that probably gave the novelist the idea for her incipit, fuelled by her acute sense of irony, but which also unwittingly left its mark on the history of literature: "It is a truth universally acknowledged and universally confirmed...".[15]

Pride and Prejudice was the first of Jane Austen's works that she envisaged publishing. The original text was cut by at least a third. The choice of publisher fell on Thomas Cadell. Both bookseller and publisher, his books included works by the famous Scottish poet Robert Burns, and novelists Fanny Burney, Hannah More and Charlotte Smith. In 1797, he refused to pay any attention to *First Impressions*. Despite a flattering letter from Jane Austen's father and an offer to publish on a self-publishing basis, the manuscript was returned without explanation. We suspect that Thomas Cadell did not even read it, as it was returned with the words "Declined by Return of Post".

In his letter, Mr. Austen even compared the manuscript to one of his daughter's favourite and best-selling novels, Fanny Burney's *Evelina* (1778). But the fashion at the time was for gothic novels, with thrills and chills, suspense and trails of blood through secret passages. There seemed to be nothing stimulating for a publisher of the time in this story about country gentry, in which very little actually happens. The time was not yet ripe for character studies. Fortunately, Jane Austen was not discouraged, and was constantly supported by her family.

Is *Pride and Prejudice* a mature novel? Begun in the padded comfort of Steventon and finished in the cosy tranquillity of Chawton, the work evolved, grew and matured, just like its author. From 1809 onwards, Jane Austen devoted herself to revising the manuscript. The sales of *Sense and Sensibility*, published in 1811, were satisfactory, which convinced her publisher, Thomas Egerton, not to publish

---

[15] Information quoted by Pat Rogers, in his *Introduction* to the edition of *Pride and Prejudice*, Cambridge University Press, 2006.

on a self-publishing basis, but to buy the rights to *Pride and Prejudice* for 110 pounds.[16]

On the day of its publication, 28 January 1813, an advertisement appeared in *The Morning Chronicle*. As a selling point, the front cover states "By the author of *Sense and Sensibility*". The book, published in three volumes, was well received by critics and the public alike. One thousand five hundred copies were sold in six months. Although she still preferred to remain anonymous, Jane Austen could finally consider herself a writer. She made a living with her writing.

In the Austen family, it was customary to write your name on the books you owned. In a three-volume first edition of *Pride and Prejudice* from 1813, Jane Austen's sister wrote, "Cass. Elizth Austen", on the flyleaf of volume II. Cassandra Austen was her sister's most loyal ally and supporter. This first published copy contains five corrections in her own hand. This shows her commitment and attention to detail, and above all to every stage. In a letter to Cassandra dated 29 January 1813,[17] we learn that Jane Austen pointed out a few typos in her novel, precisely those highlighted by her sister. But they were not corrected in the second printing in October.

The precious annotated volume of this very first edition belonging to Cassandra has been passed down through the Austen and Knight families. It was eventually purchased at auction by the Harry Ransom Center in Austin, at the University of Texas, where it remains to this day.

French translations were not long in coming, with a few extracts appearing in the Genevan periodical *Bibliothèque Britannique*, edited by Charles Pictet, from 1813. But it was in 1821, four years after the novelist's death, that the first complete French version was published, entitled *Orgueil et Prévention* and authored by an Englishwoman, Eloïse Perks. The first German translation appeared in 1830. An illegal copy, without the authorisation of the rights holders, appeared in Philadelphia, in the United States, in 1832-1833, under the title *Elizabeth Bennet or Pride and Prejudice*. The Austen family, who held Jane

Austen's memory and work dear to their hearts, were not aware of it at the time, and so did not benefit from it.

In 1894, Hugh Thomson made his mark on the collective memory with the famous Peacock Edition. This is undoubtedly the most famous edition of *Pride and Prejudice*, and the one that paved the way for all kinds of marketing around Jane Austen's work. Hugh Thomson illustrates one hundred and sixty sentences from the book, not including headings and ornaments, in the body of the text. He continued to build on this success with the other five novels, published between 1896 and 1898.

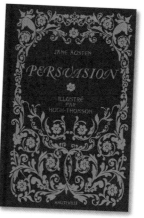

---

[16] Around £16,500 today.
[17] *Jane Austen's Letters*, Deirdre Le Faye, Oxford, 2011.

Hugh Thomson's illustration for an 1894 edition of Jane Austen's novel depicts **Mr. Darcy** proposing to **Elizabeth Bennet.**

Is Elizabeth Bennet the perfect heroine?

In a letter to Cassandra dated the day after the book's publication, 29 January 1813, Jane Austen shows that she is particularly attached to Elizabeth Bennet. She sees her as "as delightful a creature as ever appeared in print"[18] and even says that she can't understand anyone who doesn't love her. This character perfectly illustrates one of the principles dear to Jane Austen's heart: don't marry without love. Marrying well meant looking for your equal. This idea was incredibly innovative in Regency English society, where a woman was still considered dependent on a man.

From the very first pages, Elizabeth Bennet emerges as a particularly daring and combative female character. This heroine is no damsel in distress, quite the contrary. Even though she makes mistakes, she is always in control of her destiny and her choices. From the beginning of the novel, she admits without batting an eyelid that she attributes Mr. Darcy's pride to his social position, his wealth and his perfect looks: "...I could easily forgive his pride, if he had not mortified mine".[19] Without seeming to, and probably without realising it, she let slip a secret from her heart. The opinion of this enigmatic gentleman matters to her, or she wouldn't have been so mortified.

The rest of the plot is based on this first unfavourable impression. Vexed, Elizabeth Bennet catalogues, categorises and finally judges him without trying to understand him or change her perspective. For his part, Mr. Darcy goes to great lengths to revise his convictions, shaken by the strength of his feelings and the female resistance he encounters for probably the first time in his life. Elizabeth Bennet has to go through a phase of cruel disillusionment in order to mature. In so doing, she reveals her inner richness and leaves an indelible mark on the history of literature.

---

[18] *Jane Austen's Letters*, Deirdre Le Faye, Oxford editions.
[19] *Pride and Prejudice*, Jane Austen, *op. cit.*

HISTORY

Social relations during the Regency period

During the Regency period, relationships between people from the same world were highly codified. You only met people from the same background as you. Fortunately, the gentry's social boundaries were quite broad, allowing it to encompass a rather diverse range of social variations. As gentlemen, Mr. Bennet and Mr. Darcy belonged to the same environment and could socialise without offending etiquette. As Elizabeth Bennet rightly pointed out to Lady Catherine de Bourgh on the question of their respective social status: "He is a gentleman; I am a gentleman's daughter; so far we are equal".[20]

Mr. Bennet and Mr. Darcy are at opposite ends of the spectrum. Whereas Mr. Darcy is known to earn £10,000[21] per year, Elizabeth's father has an income of just £2,000[22]. A landowner, Mr Bennet manages his Longbourn House estate, which is a manor house. He rents out plots and farms to his tenant farmers and has no need to work. Although his income seems modest compared with others, it is honourable and sufficient for a perfectly respectable life in the Hertfordshire countryside.

At the Meryton ball, Elizabeth Bennet almost chokes with shame and indignation when the son of her father's cousin, the vicar Collins, wishes to introduce himself to the nephew of his patroness, Lady Catherine de Bourgh. He is wrongly convinced that his connection with this diligent lady is enough. This is not the case: "To approach Mr. Darcy without introduction would be considered as an impertinent freedom, rather than a compliment to his aunt".[23] You couldn't talk to someone you didn't know without being introduced to them by a third party. As a man of the cloth, and heir to Longbourn, Mr. Collins is also part of the gentry. But he has no authority to speak to Mr. Darcy without being introduced to him first. His gesture

---

[20] *Pride and Prejudice*, Jane Austen, *op. cit.*
[21] Approximately £1,475,000 today.
[22] Approximately £260,000 today.
[23] *Pride and Prejudice*, Jane Austen, *op. cit.*

Games during the Regency Period

There is a lot of card-playing in the novel, particularly at parties with militia officers. It was a very popular way for men and women to spend time together. They played vingt-et-un (twenty-one), whist (the forerunner of bridge), faro, piquet, commerce and fly. These were gambling games where the stakes were high, which is why Elizabeth Bennet declines the invitation from Mr. Bingley's sisters.

Chess and dice were particularly popular indoor games at the time. Some homes also had a billiards room for men only. But they often simply enjoyed mental games. In *Emma*, for example, the characters play charades and riddles. In the Austen family, they loved the game we know as Mikado. In Regency England, these were called *spillikins*, and the sticks were pretty objects made of wood or ivory.

appears very rude. The person with the highest social status may take the lead, but never the other way round.

Once they had had a chance to introduce themselves and meet each other without upsetting etiquette, they could exchange a few words. But social interaction remained limited: meeting up at balls, private or public, or at dinner parties at neighbours' houses. As pointed out by Mrs. Bennet in Meryton, the Bennets visit no fewer than twenty-four families, which makes Mr. Darcy smile and Miss Bingley gloat. They are used to far more numerous and varied London gatherings.

The Cloak-Room at the Clifton Assembly Rooms, Bath, England.
Oil painting by Rolinda Sharples, 1817.

In *Pride and Prejudice*, neighbours often visit each other, in what were known at the time as "morning calls", which generally took place between eleven and three o'clock (the morning could be extended!) and should not exceed an hour and a half. At the beginning of the novel, Mrs. Bennet is worried that she won't be able to be introduced to Mr. Bingley at the next ball. Fortunately, her husband takes the initiative and makes a famous morning call to Bingley. As the town's leading gentleman, he has every right to go straight to his new neighbour's house to welcome him. That way, the next time he would be able to introduce Mr. Bingley to anyone, including his wife and daughters.

Coming too early could interfere with the intimate activities of the home, and coming too late could be seen as trying to get a dinner invitation, which was very impolite. They always brought calling cards, in case the family was away or couldn't receive guests. On the other hand, it would be shocking if a single man left his card with an unmarried lady - it just was not done. And what can we say about Mr. Darcy, who often seeks the company of Elizabeth Bennet, alone and without a chaperone? Is he looking for a wife?

A young, accomplished woman according to Mr. Darcy

"I cannot boast of knowing more than half a dozen, in the whole range of my acquaintance, that are really accomplished."[24]

When Mr. Darcy is trying to attract Elizabeth Bennet's attention; he is painting a picture of the ideal woman. A little earlier, his friend Mr. Bingley spoke of women's ability to do needlework, and Mr. Darcy, his sister Georgiana's musical talents. Miss Bingley approves!

During Regency times, in the gentry, little importance was attached to the education of girls, as they were destined only to become good wives. In wealthy families, a mother was not even expected to educate her own children, as was the case in *Mansfield Park*. Boys could hope to study at university, consider a career, or take up respectable occupations linked to their social status, such as managing their land and estate.

Quiz

Mr. Darcy has a very specific idea of the perfect lady. Would you like to claim that title?
Just tick the boxes!
If you meet all the criteria, you (might!) have a chance with Mr. Darcy!

○ A natural disposition to needlework

○ Artistic skills (music, singing, drawing, dancing)

○ Proficiency in modern languages
—usually French and Italian. Be careful not to perfect your Latin or Greek, or you'll end up looking like a "bluestocking" (intellectual woman)

○ Graceful attitude

○ Elegant speech

○ Literary culture

"She is tolerable," Darcy said of Elizabeth.

Elizabeth Bennet hears Mr. Darcy at the ball. Illustration by Hugh Thomson from an 1894 edition of Jane Austen's *Pride and Prejudice*, first published in 1813.

[24] *Pride and Prejudice*, Jane Austen, *op. cit.*

Education in the strict sense ended for girls at around the age of eight. They then went on to perfect their skills in the areas mentioned above by Mr. Darcy and Miss Bingley, with the sole aim of pleasing a potential husband. This is precisely the point against which Mary Wollstonecraft, philosopher, essayist, freethinker and mother of the equally famous Mary Shelley, revolts. Inspired by French Enlightenment theories, she defended her avant-garde convictions in *A Vindication of the Rights of Women* in 1792.[25]

It is not clear whether Jane Austen ever read this subversive text, which was ahead of its time. But there's no doubt that the way she tackles these issues, with her characteristic fine, well-placed humour, admirably conveys the essence of her thoughts on this unfair inequality between the sexes. In fact, Mary Wollstonecraft and Jane Austen have at least one important thing in common. Both couldn't help but make fun of James Fordyce's famous *Sermons to Young Women* (little texts on how young girls should behave), read in *Pride and Prejudice* by the pedantic vicar Collins, for what he thinks is the good of his cousins.

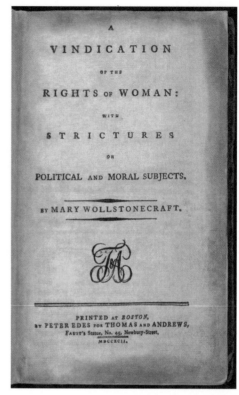

Title page of the first American edition of *A Vindication of the Rights of Woman* by Mary Wollstonecraft. 1792.

Music in the Regency period

Music played an important role in education. As Lady Catherine de Bourgh, a paragon of good advice of all kinds, is quick to point out: "There are few people in England, I suppose, who have more true enjoyment of music than myself, or a better natural taste".[26] She also adds that, "she cannot expect to excel if she does not practice a good deal".[27] Need we point out that neither the lady in question nor her aristocratic daughter received any musical education? In the case of the daughter, Anne, her poor health is cited as an excuse for this failure; in the case of Lady Catherine, on the other hand, we do not know why, as a noblewoman, she did not have access to music lessons. She is suspected of not having had the desire to "excel" in the first place.

Jane Austen loved music, so it was only natural that her characters should be drawn to it. Georgiana Darcy is an accomplished pianist, as is Marianne Dashwood in *Sense and Sensibility* and Jane Fairfax in *Emma*. Jane Austen herself was of a perfectly respectable standard in piano playing. She began taking lessons at the age of nine, at the Abbey School in Reading, and then with one of Winchester Cathedral's assistant organists, Dr. George Chard. She loved copying sheet music. The archives at Chawton House hold all her notebooks. You can even find a *Marseillaise* copied in her handwriting, under the title *The Marseillaise March*. She didn't like to make a spectacle of herself and only played for her nearest and dearest, especially in the mornings. Sometimes she even sang.

[25] *A Vindication of the Rights of Women*, Mary Wollstonecraft, Thomas and Andrews, 1792.
[26] *Pride and Prejudice*, Jane Austen, *op. cit.*
[27] *Ibid.*

Did you know?

THE PIANOFORTE REVOLUTIONISED MUSIC

Throughout history, this instrument has revolutionised the art of music. Born of the desire to give more nuance and power to its ancestor, the harpsichord, it was invented by the Italian Bartolomeo Cristofori in the early 18th century. It was subsequently perfected in Germany and France by eminent organ builders. But it was really in England that the mechanical part was developed that made this instrument so famous. Johannes Zumpe, born in Germany, emigrated to England and, towards the end of the 18th century, launched the English square piano, which was more compact, simpler and more affordable. The instrument became extremely popular. At Chawton, Jane Austen played a William Stodart square piano.

When imagining the Regency era, you have to imagine a world completely different from our own. There was no electricity, no devices to detract from human presence, the ambient noise was mainly that of everyday life, and music as entertainment required effort. This role fell mainly to the women of the household. After all, being trained in the musical arts was one of the attributes expected of them when they got married. Most gentry homes had music rooms, as was the case at Chawton. These rooms featured one or more instruments, such as the pianoforte, harp, flute and violin.

These were played to practise, to entertain friends and family, to express their mood with happy or melancholy tunes, but also to dance and have fun. Among the most popular composers of the time were Wolfgang Amadeus Mozart, Joseph Haydn, Ignace Pleyel and Ludwig van Beethoven. Jane Austen was particularly fond of Scottish and Irish folk music.

JANE AUSTEN'S PLAYLIST

Title	Duration	Artist(s)	Year
# *Robin Adair* (*Irish Folk*)	2:28	Charles Coffey (music) Lady Caroline Keppel (lyrics)	1750
# *Piano Concerto No. 1*	19:43	Joseph Haydn	1756
# *Piano Concerto No. 23: II Adagio*	8:03	Wolfgang Amadeus Mozart	1786
# *The Erl-King*	4:09	John Wall Callcott (music) Matthew Lewis (lyrics)	1797
# *Piano Sonata Op. 20*	26:07	Jean-Baptiste Cramer	1800

ADAPTATIONS

Pride and Prejudice *was the first of Jane Austen's novels to arouse interest in theatre and film. There have been no fewer than thirty adaptations, in all styles, genres and periods.*

Pride and Prejudice, BBC, 1938, 55 minutes

This very first version has completely disappeared. It was shot under live studio conditions, and the resources of the time did not allow it to be recorded. Because of the TV film's short running time, the plot was considerably tightened.

Directed by: Michael Barry

Script: Michael Barry

Cast: Curigwen Lewis (Elizabeth Bennet), Andrew Osborn (Mr. Darcy), Antoinette Cellier (Jane Bennet), Barbara Everest (Mrs. Bennet), Allan Jeayes (Mr. Bennet), Eileen Erskine (Lydia Bennet), Lewis Stringer (Charles Bingley), André Morell (Mr. Wickham), Helen Horsey (Charlotte Lucas).

Anecdotes:

♦ This TV film was broadcast only twice on live television, on 22 and 27 May 1938.

♦ It was the second classic of English literature to be adapted by the newly-formed BBC, after *Jane Eyre* in 1937. Welsh actress Curigwen Lewis played the lead role Elizabeth Bennet each time.

♦ The script is so condensed that the characters of Mary and Kitty were left out.

♦ Michael Barry, one of the BBC's most influential early producers, directors and writers, also directed and produced the first adaptation of *Emma* in 1948.

♦ London beat Hollywood in the race against time! In 1936, the BBC learned of MGM's plans to adapt *Pride and Prejudice*. They had to act quickly to reclaim this landmark British novel, before the Americans got hold of it. This undoubtedly explains the very short format of this version: there was not enough time to develop the details.

♦ The script and filming instructions are in the BBC archives.

♦ This very first adaptation was only seen by a small number of viewers. Viewing conditions were not optimal in 1938. At the time, there were very few television sets: there were just over 1,300 in the whole country. The screens were also very small, barely thirty centimetres diagonal.

FOUR DECADES OF ADAPTATIONS

Over almost forty years, *Pride and Prejudice* was constantly reinvented in a variety of forms, on television, film, radio and on stage. On television, this was the most prolific period for adaptations, with at least a dozen. Paradoxically, these have almost all disappeared.

In Italy *Orgoglio e Pregiudizio* (1957),[28] in the Netherlands, *De vier dochters Bennet* (1961),[29] in Spain, *Orgullo y Prejuicio* (1966), in Canada - starring Patrick Macnee as Mr. Darcy - (1958) and in Venezuela (1979). The Americans produced two more version, including a play filmed in colour in 1956. This was an episode of NBC's *Matinee Theater*. The script was by Helen Hanff, the celebrated author of the novel *84 Charing Cross Road*. This script now belongs to the New York City Public Library. The BBC repeated this experiment with two longer serials, in 1952 and 1958, using the same script. No recordings were made at the time, and no copies exist, just a few publicity photographs. The next series was produced in 1967, to mark the 150th anniversary of Jane Austen's death. This was the last black and white version. A copy is held at the British Film Institute in London.

[28] You can watch the original version on YouTube.
[29] Also available on YouTube, with English subtitles.

Pride and Prejudice, MGM, 1940, 118 minutes

This American version was the very first to be made for a large audience, as it was released on the big screen. Production began in 1936, but studio disputes delayed filming. The film is in black and white. The action is set in the Victorian period and takes many liberties with the novel's storyline.

Directed by: Robert Z. Leonard

Script: Aldous Huxley and Jane Muffin

Cast: Greer Garson (Elizabeth Bennet), Laurence Olivier (Mr. Darcy), Maureen O'Sullivan (Jane Bennet), Mary Boland (Mrs. Bennet), Edmund Gwenn (Mr. Bennet), Ann Rutherford (Lydia Bennet), Marsha Hunt (Mary Bennet), Heather Angel (Kitty Bennet), Bruce Lester (Mr. Bingley), Edward Ashley (Mr. Wickham), Karen Morley (Charlotte Lucas), Edna May Oliver (Lady Catherine de Bourgh), Frieda Inescort (Miss Bingley), Melville Cooper (Mr. Collins).

Anecdotes:

♦ The film was released on 26 July 1940 in the United States and the United Kingdom. But it was not until the end of the Second World War that it could be seen in France (1945), Germany (1946) and Poland (1948).

♦ The screenplay was by a great name in British literature: Aldous Huxley, author of the dystopian *Brave New World* (1931). He also contributed to the screenplay of *Jane Eyre*, based on Charlotte Brontë's novel, in 1944.

♦ Australian Helen Jerome was the author of a play inspired by *Pride and Prejudice*, which formed the basis of the screenplay for this film. This play was first performed in Philadelphia in 1935. It was at this point that MGM bought the rights for $50,000 on the advice of Harpo Marx, one of the famous Marx Brothers. He loved this theatrical adaptation. The story doesn't end there: in 1959, Helen Jerome's play became *First Impressions*, a Broadway musical with sixteen songs. But the show was a monumental flop.

♦ In 1940, this feature film won its first Oscar® for best set design for an Austen adaptation. Some of these sets, props and costumes had already been used on the set of *Gone with the Wind* (1938), which also won the Oscar® for Best Set Design a year earlier.

♦ Clark Gable was MGM's first choice for the role of Mr. Darcy. Vivien Leigh, his co-lead in *Gone with the Wind*, was considered for the role of Elizabeth Bennet. However, her extra-marital relationship with Laurence Olivier discredited her in the eyes of the producers.

♦ Laurence Olivier was Greer Garson's mentor during her theatre studies in London. She is known as the oldest actress to play Elizabeth Bennet. She was thirty-six at the time.

♦ Following the release of the film, the book became increasingly popular in the United States. In the decade that followed, it was reprinted more than twenty times.

Pride and Prejudice, BBC, 1980, 265 minutes

This is the fifth BBC version, but this time in co-production with Australian television. It was also the first colour mini-series, in five episodes.

Directed by: Cyril Coke

Script: Fay Weldon

Cast: Elizabeth Garvie (Elizabeth Bennet), David Rintoul (Mr. Darcy), Sabina Franklyn (Jane Bennet), Priscilla Morgan (Mrs. Bennet), Morey Watson (Mr. Bennet), Nathalie Ogle (Lydia Bennet), Tessa Peake-Jones (Mary Bennet), Clare Higgins (Kitty Bennet), Osmund Bullock (Mr. Bingley), Peter Settelen (Mr. Wickham), Irene Richard (Charlotte Lucas), Judy Parfitt (Lady Catherine de Bourgh), Marsha Fitzalan (Miss Bingley), Malcolm Rennie (Mr. Collins).

Renishaw hall

Anecdotes:

♦ Elizabeth Garvie is best known for her on-stage performances. The role of Elizabeth Bennet was her very first television role.

♦ David Rintoul played Mr. Darcy. In the film *Legend of the Werewolf* (1975), he crossed paths with another Mr. Darcy, Peter Cushing, who played the role in a 1952 BBC adaptation, of which no trace remains today.

♦ Judy Parfitt (best known for her role as Sister Monica Joan in the series *Call the Midwife*) is still the youngest to play Lady Catherine. In 1980, she was only forty-five years old.

♦ Fay Weldon, the screenwriter, was a feminist novelist who was very popular in the 1980s. In 1984, she published an epistolary novel, *Letters to Alice: On First Reading Jane Austen*. In this autobiography of sorts, she corresponds with a fictional niece, Alice, in the manner of Jane Austen with her own nieces.

♦ Most of the costumes, especially the dresses, come from the 1972 BBC soap *Emma*.

♦ In its original version, the full title of this mini-series is *Pride and Prejudice or First Impressions*. A tribute to Jane Austen's first choice of title.

Shooting locations:

♦ **Renishaw Hall** in aptly-located Derbyshire, was used as **Pemberley**. Built in 1625, the castle was owned by the Sitwell family until the current heiress, Mrs. Alexandra Hayward, daughter of Sir Reresby Sitwell. The estate, famous for its Italian-style gardens, can be visited from mid-March to early November, but is also open for some Christmas events. Afternoon tea at Café Renishaw can be booked twenty-four hours in advance. For more information, visit renishaw-hall.co.uk

♦ **Thorpe Tilney Hall** (perhaps an unintentional reference to *Northanger Abbey*, where the hero is Henry Tilney), in Lincolnshire, is the setting for **Longbourn**, the Bennet estate. It was also used in the 1995 BBC version. The manor house was built in 1740 and originally belonged to the Whichcote family. After the First World War, it was bought by the Stockdale family, who restored it. It is not open to the public.

♦ **Well Vale** in Alford, also in Lincolnshire, became **Netherfield Park** for the duration of the shoot. Little is known about this venue, which is not open to the public. Located in the hamlet of Well, the manor house dates back to the early 18th century.

Pride and Prejudice, BBC, 1995, 327 minutes

This was the BBC adaptation that completely revolutionised the perception of *Pride and Prejudice* and rekindled an interest in Jane Austen, fifteen years after the previous version. It is also the most faithful to the novel.

Directed by: Simon Langton

Script: Andrew Davies

Cast: Jennifer Ehle (Elizabeth Bennet), Colin Firth (Mr. Darcy), Susannah Harker (Jane Bennet), Alison Steadman (Mrs. Bennet), Benjamin Whitrow (Mr. Bennet), Julia Sawalha (Lydia Bennet), Lucy Briers (Mary Bennet), Polly Maberly (Kitty Bennet), Crispin Bonham-Carter (Mr. Bingley), Adrian Lukis (Mr. Wickham), Lucy Scott (Charlotte Lucas), Barbara Leigh-Hunt (Lady Catherine de Bourgh), Anna Chancellor (Miss Bingley), David Bamber (Mr. Collins), Emilia Fox (Georgiana Darcy), Joanna David (Mrs. Gardiner).

Anecdotes:

* This adaptation was made possible by the tenacity of producer Sue Birtwistle. *Pride and Prejudice* had always been her favourite book, and it was her dream to see a faithful version of it on the small screen. It was she who persuaded Andrew Davies to write the screenplay.

* Andrew Davies was also a lecturer. He taught English literature, including a famous course on *Pride and Prejudice,* at the University of Warwick between 1971 and 1987.

* Rehearsals and filming lasted five months. Jennifer Ehle (Elizabeth Bennet) appears in virtually every scene. Every morning, she started her day at 5.30am. Transforming herself into a young woman from the Regency period took about two hours, even though she wore a wig.

* In 2020, during the Covid pandemic lockdown, the actress launched her YouTube channel, "Jennifer Ehle, Reading From My Car etc," where she read the whole of *Pride and Prejudice,* in short sequences, at home and in her car, with her dog.

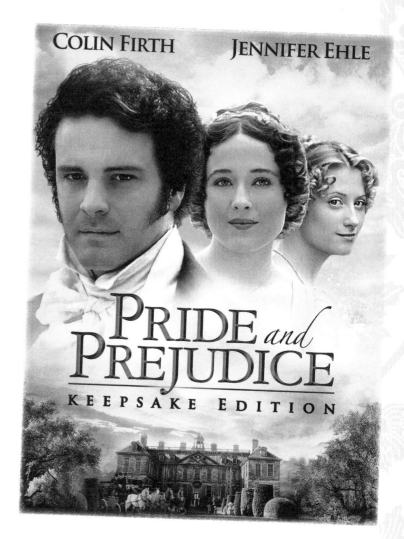

* Emilia Fox and Joanna David, who played Georgiana Darcy and Mrs. Gardiner respectively, are mother and daughter. Emilia's cousin Laurence Fox played Jane Austen's suitor in Julian Jarrold's *Jane* (2007), while her other cousin, Jack Fox, appears in *Welcome to Sanditon.*

* Susanna Harker, here Jane Bennet, is the daughter of actress Polly Adams, who was Jane Bennet in the 1967 version. During filming in the summer and autumn of 1994, the young actress hid her early pregnancy with loose Regency-style dresses and scarves.

- Julia Sawalha (Lydia Bennet) and Colin Firth (Mr. Darcy) were born on 9 and 10 September respectively. The whole team prepared a birthday party for them on the set. They blew out their candles in period costume.

- Alison Steadman admitted that she had never read the book before being cast in the role of Mrs. Bennet. When she finally read it, she compared her character to "a box of chocolates", because she found her character so well written, so detailed and descriptive that she knew how to play her.

- Anna Chancellor is linked to Jane Austen in many ways. Here she played Miss Bingley. She was the voice-over in the 2002 documentary *The Real Jane Austen*. More importantly, she is a descendant of Edward Knight, Jane Austen's brother.

- The delicate green porcelain decorated with flowers and butterflies used by the Bennet family is a reproduction of a late Regency model from a Staffordshire tableware manufacturer. The Mottahedeh brand produced it between 1988 and 1995, under the name 'Cornelia Green'.

- During filming, the entire village of Lacock in Wiltshire was transformed into Meryton, the Bennet's town.

- Before the final episode was broadcast, the BBC switchboard exploded with calls from viewers desperate to know if the ending was a happy one.

- On the day of the final episode, motorways were hit by terrible congestion. No one wanted to miss the last episode, but the rush to get home caused traffic jams.

- The novel was republished in the UK. Twenty thousand copies were sold every week after the series was broadcast.

- When the video box set was released, the twelve thousand copies in stock sold out in just two hours. Other copies were made in a hurry, and fifty-eight thousand were sold by the end of the first week.

- Colin Firth's Mr. Darcy made a memorable appearance in Greta Gerwig's global hit *Barbie* (2023).

Did you know?

Colin Firth, made famous by Jane Austen

Colin Firth was born in the Hampshire market town of Grayshott. It is located just a few miles from another village in the same county, Chawton, very popular with Janeites. He struggled to accept the role of Mr. Darcy, he did not feel worthy of it. He said he was too impressed by Sir Laurence Olivier's performance in the 1940 version. In fact, he drew his inspiration from Olivier's acting, the way he talked, the way he held himself and even the way he dressed. The actor admitted that he had never read Jane Austen before agreeing to play Mr. Darcy. He thought it was "literature for young girls". But once he started the book, he couldn't put it down. The mini-series was such a success that Colin Firth was forced to step back and take refuge for a while in Tunisia. His film career took off and has never let up since. Colin Firth can be seen as Mr. Darcy on four occasions, including his role as Mark Darcy in *Bridget Jones's Diary* (2001), *Bridget Jones: The Edge of Reason* (2004) and *Bridget Jones's Baby* (2016).

Mr. Darcy's wet shirt

A myth is about to crumble. The famous scene with the wet shirt is not in the novel. Similarly, there are never any kisses of any kind in Jane Austen's books, so now you know! So what's all this about a wet shirt? This is called the 'white wet shirt effect' it was the first time that an adaptation of *Pride and Prejudice* offered a sexual and sensual portrayal of Mr. Darcy. This version, and this scene in particular, are at the origin of what has subsequently been called Darcymania and, more generally, Austenmania.

SEQUENCE ANALYSIS. This 'wet white shirt effect' developed in two stages. In episode 1, Mr. Darcy takes a bath. Don't get excited, that's not in the novel either. He finishes bathing, he's wet. We see him get up from the bath (he remains decent, calm down). Dressed in a bathrobe, he looks out of the window at Elizabeth Bennet playing with a Dalmatian in the park. This is the first interaction between a half-naked, wet Mr. Darcy and Miss Bennet, except he's the only one who knows it.

Episode 4 brings the second interaction. The evocative power of seduction is pushed to the limit. The hero is dishevelled and completely soaked in his white shirt. Some purists also criticised the sheer fabric of Elizabeth Bennet's immaculate dress. Did the costume designers do this deliberately, as an echo of the famous wet shirt that hints at the body without revealing it? Nonetheless, we get a glimpse of her long legs through a petticoat that was far too thin for its time. The two protagonists are at the height of their sex appeal, while respecting the rules of propriety.

BUT BACK TO OUR WET SHIRT. First of all, you should know that the initial script by Andrew Davies called for Mr. Darcy to be completely naked! Elizabeth Bennet was to discover him in his birthday suit at a bend in Pemberley Park. It's easy to imagine how embarrassed he would have been. However, at that time, it was neither rare nor strange for men to bathe naked in the open air. At the beach, for example, men and women were kept quite separate. So it wouldn't be so incongruous for a landowner such as Mr. Darcy to enjoy the coolness of the lake on his estate on a hot summer's day.

During filming, the producers decided that such a scene was not appropriate. What's more, Colin Firth himself was not comfortable with filming in the buff, and he had already had doubts about accepting the role. The idea of nudity was therefore abandoned and the script rewritten. Andrew Davies describes this scene as a compromise between himself and Colin Firth.[30] The outfit worn by Mr. Darcy doesn't hide his muscled physique, but it does give him a certain modesty. The gentleman has the grace to be embarrassed, because he is caught unprepared in a situation over which he has no control.

He may not be naked physically, but he is morally, and above all symbolically. For the first time, he has found himself in an inferior position to Elizabeth Bennet, as if caught at fault. He appears vulnerable, almost caught in a normal act. Yes, dear Elizabeth Bennet, you who dare not set eyes on him, Mr. Darcy is a flesh and blood human being, bursting with hormones. He has just taken a dip in the lake to soothe his sweaty body, which drips when he gets out of the water. He is cruelly lacking

---

[30] Anecdote reported by Claire Harman in *Jane's Fame*, Canongate, 2009.

in self-confidence in that moment. He looks very sheepish at being caught, even mortified, because here, in front of him, is the young woman who occupies all his thoughts and desires.

Believe it or not, the aim of the script, at this precise moment, was not an attempt at seduction. The scene is meant to be funny, even embarrassing. The script suggests that Mr. Darcy seems a bit of a ninny, all wet and sloppy. However, as soon as the episode was broadcast, it had the opposite effect. He doesn't look ridiculous at all. He becomes touching, almost fragile, and above all incredibly charming. This scene was a landmark. Indeed, it is a milestone in the history of Austen adaptations, and has become a veritable trope in the romantic comedy genre. There's a before and after the "wet shirt". Nothing will ever be the same again.

The scene was then repeated, copied or parodied in several films and television series:

♦ Hugh Grant, in *Bridget Jones's Diary* by Sharon Maguire (2001), falls in the water and his shirt gets soaked.

♦ In a comic scene in Beeban Kidron's *Bridget Jones: The Edge of Reason* (2004), Hugh Grant and Colin Firth splash each other while fighting in a fountain.

♦ In Richard Curtis's *Love Actually* (2004), Colin Firth can't escape a scene where he dives in fully clothed (into a pond this time).

♦ In Gurinder Chadha's *Bride and Prejudice* (2004), William Darcy (Martin Henderson) also gets wet.

♦ Colin Firth once again parodies himself in a comic scene in Oliver Parker and Barnaby Thompson's film *St. Trinian's* (2007). The dog belonging to one of the characters is called Mr. Darcy.

- In the series *Sense and Sensibility* (2008), Dan Stevens chops wood in the rain, wearing a sodden white shirt. The script is by Andrew Davies, the "inventor" of the wet shirt.

- In Dan Zeff's mini-series *Lost in Austen* (2018), heroine Amanda Price (Jemima Rooper) is obsessed with this scene and asks her Mr. Darcy (Elliot Cowan) outright to jump into the lake.

- In Jerusha Hess's *Austenland* (2015), Jane Hayes (Keri Russell) literally lives in an Austenian world. At the beginning of the film, she watches this scene from *Pride and Prejudice* on television. Later, a male character falls out of a boat. Finally, she lives her dream in a reversed fantasy. With her clothes clinging to her body in the pouring rain, she becomes the object of admiration of the gentlemen around her.

- In Burr Steers's *Pride and Prejudice and Zombies* (2016), Mr. Darcy (Sam Riley), professional zombie hunter, takes a dip to calm his nerves.

- In season 2 of Chris van Dusen's *Bridgerton* (2022), Anthony Bridgerton (Jonathan Bailey) falls into the water dressed to the nines and emerges with a wet white shirt clinging to his body.

LET'S DECONSTRUCT THE MYTH IN ITS ENTIRETY: Colin Firth never dived into the lake! In the *making-of* feature, we learn that an experienced stuntman performs the scene, because of the risk of infection from bacteria in the water. It's a lot less glamorous than we imagine! Colin Firth simply threw himself on a big blue gym mat and swam in a pool at the Ealing studios in West London. Thanks to some effective editing and suggestive music, you really get the impression that he's the one jumping in.

We learn a lot about this scene in *Bridget Jones: The Edge of Reason*, Helen Fielding's second instalment. For Bridget, it's a real obsession. As a journalist, she interviews Colin Firth *himself* in the novel and loses her composure. The anecdotes that are reported are authentic, such as the fact that the stuntman was only allowed one take because of the insurance, and that Mr. Darcy's shirt had to keep being sprayed to stay wet.

In the collective imagery of the Janeites (but not exclusively), Mr. Darcy in a wet shirt is now considered a fantasy. To mark the two hundredth anniversary of *Pride and Prejudice* in 2013, a statue of the character in this iconic scene was installed in London's Serpentine Lake in Hyde Park, then toured the country, ending up in Lyme Park, where it all began. Made of fibreglass and polyester, in full colour, and standing over three metres high, this monumental statue of Mr. Darcy in a wet shirt is the work of a team of three sculptors, led by Toby Crowther. It took them almost two months to complete. The statue was then flown to Melbourne, Australia, to the superb estate of Rippon Lea House & Gardens, which is the setting for Aunt Prudence's house in the *Miss Fisher Murder Mysteries* series. It is currently held in the archives of the Australian National Trust.

Mr. Darcy's white shirt,[31] made of ordinary linen, has had plenty of time to dry and belongs to the BBC's costume collection - and there were several of them on the set. This genuine piece of television history is regularly shown at exhibitions. One of the latest of these exhibitions took place in Chawton in 2022, and drew the admiring gaze of Queen Camilla, a great admirer of Jane Austen's work, and Colin Firth's Darcy.

---

[31] You can buy an almost identical shirt on the website **darcyclothing.com.**

Shooting locations:

♦ **Belton House** in Lincolnshire, became **Rosings Park**, Lady Catherine's stronghold. Since the 17th century, this imposing estate has belonged to the Brownlow family, who have taken great care to decorate and develop it over the generations. An Italian garden provides a pleasant backdrop to the park. The objects and paintings there are worthy of a major museum, including an extraordinary collection of silver tableware, porcelain from China and Japan, and porcelain from the Sèvres factory in France, dating from 1790-1791. If you're feeling peckish, the Stables Café serves delicious snacks. The sites, managed by the National Trust, are open from mid-March to late December.

Information on nationaltrust.org.uk/belton-house

♦ **Lacock Abbey**, in Lacock, Wiltshire, lent its sumptuous interiors as **Pemberley**. Administered by the National Trust, the site has a rich history. Originally a convent founded in memory of her husband by the formidable Countess of Salisbury in 1232, it became a Tudor manor house under Henry VIII. Part of its cloisters can still be seen today. During the Victorian period, the house was inhabited by William Henry Fox Talbot. A mathematician and astronomer, he was a pioneer in the field of photographic development. In 1835, he invented the principle of the positive negative, which enabled multiple prints to be made. He was also the first to publish a commercial book containing photographs, *The Pencil of Nature* in 1844. A small museum is dedicated to his work. The property has been used as a film location for other famous productions, including the *Harry Potter* series and *Downton Abbey*. Open from early March to late December.

Information on nationaltrust.org.uk/lacock

Lacock Abbey

◆ **Lyme Park**, near Manchester in Cheshire, is famous as "**Pemberley 1995**", for the outdoor scenes. Owned by the Legh family since the 14th century, it was transferred to the National Trust in 1946. Surrounded by 700 hectares of parkland, it is located in the heart of the Peak District. Lyme Park represents six centuries of English history, from the time of King Edward III of the Plantagenet dynasty, with an architectural style ranging from Palladian to Baroque. In the 18th century, the famous Italian architect Giacomo Leoni gave it a Mediterranean feel with the addition of Italian marble, a Renaissance-style portico and iconic statues. The library is famous for its collection of over eight hundred period books. A gallery houses an impressive collection of clocks of all sizes, assembled in the 20th century by Sir Francis Legh. The most precious timepiece is a pendulum clock from 1658, made by Ahasuerus Fromanteel. Fancy a little snack after your walk? The Timber Yard café awaits you. The site can be visited from mid-March to late December.

Information on national-trust.org.uk/lyme-park

Lyme Park

◆ **Old Rectory**, Teigh Oakham, Leicestershire, became **Hunsford**, Mr. Collins's vicarage. Little is known about the history of the building, except that it dates back to Georgian times. It was built in 1740. The good news is that for the last dozen years, the site has offered bed and breakfast accommodation. Located in a secluded hamlet, it's a peaceful spot, ideal for relaxing and unwinding.

Information and hire at

teigholdrectorybedandbreakfast.org.uk

◆ **Sudbury Hall** in Sudbury, Derbyshire, serves as the interior settings for **Pemberley**. The estate has been managed by the National Trust since 1967. In the 17th century it belonged to the Baron Vernon family. The red brick manor house has two storeys, a turret and a domed roof, giving it a solemn, classical feel. The interior is richly decorated. A famous painting can be seen here, *Louisa Barbarina Mansel, Lady Vernon* (whose name may have inspired Jane Austen to create her character Lady Susan Vernon), painted by Thomas Gainsborough. Visits must be booked in advance.

Information at

nationaltrust.org.uk-sudbury-hall-and-museum-of-childhood

Sudbury Hall

Pride and Prejudice, Universal Pictures/Focus Features, 2005, 127 minutes

This is the first British adaptation (albeit co-produced with the USA and France) for the big screen. It was also Joe Wright's first feature film, who found himself involved in the project somewhat by chance, even though at the time he had not read the book and had only seen the 1940 American version.

Directed by: Joe Wright

Script: Deborah Moggach and Lee Hall

Cast: Keira Knightley (Elizabeth Bennet), Matthew Macfadyen (Mr. Darcy), Rosamund Pike (Jane Bennet), Brenda Blethyn (Mrs. Bennet), Donald Sutherland (Mr. Bennet), Jenna Malone (Lydia Bennet), Talulah Riley (Mary Bennet), Carey Mulligan (Kitty Bennet), Simon Woods (Mr. Bingley), Rupert Friend (Mr. Wickham), Claudie Blakley (Charlotte Lucas), Judi Dench (Lady Catherine de Bourgh), Kelly Reilly (Miss Bingley), Tom Hollander (Mr. Collins), Tamsin Merchant (Georgiana Darcy), Penelope Wilton (Mrs. Gardiner).

Anecdotes:

♦ Keira Knightley is the youngest actress ever to play Elizabeth Bennet. She was only nineteen years old during the filming. She said that since the age of seven she had been fascinated by Jane Austen. This role earned Knightley her first nomination for an Oscar® for Best Actress.

♦ To distinguish itself from the 1995 series, the plot was set in the late 18th century, as can be seen in the choice of costumes.

♦ The first scene of the film shows Elizabeth Bennet reading (and clearly enjoying) a novel entitled *First Impressions*.

♦ Emma Thompson contributed some of the dialogue to the script, but did not wish to be credited.

♦ Joe Wright wanted to show a close-knit, loving Bennet family. There's plenty of interaction between the characters. To help with this, the entire cast met up in Goombridge, Kent, for a huge game of hide-and-seek in the house that serves as the backdrop to Longbourn, the Bennet estate.

♦ Rosamund Pike was Joe Wright's only choice for Jane Bennet, so she gave up the role of Rita Skeeter in the *Harry Potter* films to join the shoot.

♦ The Meryton ball scene was shot with local extras, who naturally blended in with the team of professionals. They have that realistic, authentic and spontaneous feel that the director was looking for.

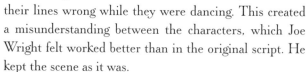

♦ At the ball in Netherfield Park, Rosamund Pike, Keira Knightley and Tom Hollander got the order of their lines wrong while they were dancing. This created a misunderstanding between the characters, which Joe Wright felt worked better than in the original script. He kept the scene as it was.

♦ Finding a new Mr. Darcy turned out to be a complicated matter. Who would follow Colin Firth's masterful performance? The casting choice was for an almost unknown actor, at least on the big screen, Matthew Macfadyen. He had a very different look, to avoid comparison with his predecessor.

♦ The scene of the meeting between Mr. Darcy and Mr. Collins deviates from the script. Matthew Macfadyen and Tom Hollander improvised a moment of pure comedy, playing on their height differences.

♦ Matthew Macfadyen has poor eyesight. In the sunrise scene towards the end of the film, the technical crew had to wave little red flags so that the actor knew where to go in the low light.

♦ A marble bust of Matthew Macfadyen as Mr. Darcy was created especially for the shoot. You can buy a replica for £80 from the Chatsworth shop. The original from the film is in the orangery.

MR. DARCY'S DECLARATION
OF LOVE

In Joe Wright's film, one of the final scenes reaches romantic heights. In the DVD commentary, the director recounts that during filming, one of his assistants watched the scene unfold before her eyes and told him that she dreamt of something like this happening to her in real life. Mr. Darcy is walking in the early hours of the morning, the day is just breaking. As in the scenes at the beginning of the film, we hear birds singing. Mr. Darcy says to his sweetheart: "You have bewitched me, body and soul, and I love, I love, I love you". Although this dialogue does not exist in the novel, Jane Austen does use the term bewitched: "Darcy had never been so bewitched by any woman as he was by her".[32]

---

[32] *Pride and Prejudice*, Jane Austen, T. Egerton, 1813, *op. cit.*

◆ There's no "wet shirt" scene, but Joe Wright still wanted the audience to feel that Elizabeth Bennet and Mr. Darcy were above all two bodies seething with desire for each other. They both end up drenched in a thunderstorm. The director was only sure of this choice of scene when he saw the rushes and noticed the chemistry between the two actors.

◆ In the United States, the film has a different ending to the one we know in Europe. At the time, American test screenings revealed that audiences across the Atlantic were expecting a more conventional and, above all, more glamorous happy ending. While the film was already in post-production, a new sequence was shot with the two lead actors and added to the final American cut. It is available in Europe as an extra on the DVD, and on YouTube.

Shooting locations:

◆ **Basildon Park**, in Lower Basildon, Berkshire, is a Neoclassical manor house. In the film, it's **Netherfield Park**, Mr. Bingley's home. This house was built on the banks of the Thames between 1776 and 1783 by the architect John Carr for Baronet Francis Sykes. Sykes had made his fortune in the East India Company. The Sykes family suffered a reversal of fortune in the 19th century, forcing them to sell the estate to the politician James Archibald Morrison, who had ten children. He soon had new works carried out by his architect friend John Buonarotti Papworth. After the death of James Morrison's last daughter in 1910, the house remained unoccupied for forty years. During the First and Second World Wars, it was requisitioned by the British government. Part of one of the manor's salons was dismantled and bought by the Waldorf Astoria hotel in New York. This hotel has a Basildon Room, with walls, mirrors and a period fireplace. In 1952, Lord and Lady Iliffe invested in the estate to renovate it. The couple donated it to the National Trust in 1978.

Information on nationaltrust.org.uk/basildon-park

Basildon Park

Burghley House

• **Burghley House** in Stamford, Lincolnshire, became **Rosings Park**, the imposing estate of Lady Catherine de Bourgh. In fact, the premises belong to the Marquesses of Exeter family line, the first of whom dates back to Elizabeth I. The family title is still Baron of Burghley, hence the name of the house. Construction began in 1558 and took thirty-two years. The famous architect Lancelot 'Capability' Brown made a number of alterations to the interior and exterior, including the park, stables and bridge. Between 1697 and 1699, the Italian artist Antonio Verrio painted a floor-to-ceiling room here, the Heaven Room, considered to be a Baroque masterpiece. The property is still inhabited by the Burghley family, but is now managed by a voluntary preservation fund. The house is closed on Fridays. The park, restaurant and café are open every day.

Information on burghley.co.uk

• **Chatsworth** in Edensor, Derbyshire, is one of England's architectural gems. It is highly likely that Jane Austen was inspired by it when she described **Pemberley** in her novel, although there is no evidence that she ever visited it. In the film, it serves as a fitting location for Mr. Darcy's house. The majestic staircase of the Painted Hall and the sculpture gallery are clearly visible in the film. The house has belonged to the Dukes of Cavendish since the 16th century. The eleventh Duchess of Cavendish was Deborah, sister of the novelist Nancy Mitford. Today, the twelfth Duke and Duchess of Cavendish live there. The estate is managed by a trust, so they pay rent to live there and their job is to preserve the heritage. The estate is huge, and with its museum-like house, park, gardens, orangery, lake, greenhouses, farm and maze, you could easily spend a whole day there. It's open from mid-March to December, every day.

Information on chatsworth.org

Chatsworth

♦ **Haddon Hall** in Bakewell, Derbyshire, is the location for the **Lambton Inn**. The oldest part dates from the 11th century. The house belongs to the Vernon family. In the 16th century, like Lydia Bennet, the heiress Dorothy Vernon ran away to marry John Manners, the first Earl of Rutland. It was a scandal, because the Vernons were Catholics and the Manners were Protestants. These events inspired a novel by the American writer Charles Major (1902). The Manners family still own the house. Jane Austen may well have visited here, or so the family legend goes. Open every day from April to October: the calendar can be consulted online and changes every year.
Information on haddonhall.co.uk

♦ **Stanage Edge** on Hathersage Moor in Derbyshire, is where Elizabeth Bennet contemplates the immensity and beauty of the Peak District. This is a sandstone rock formation with an escarpment viewpoint. The highest peak is High Neb, at four hundred and fifty-eight metres. The neighbouring village was the inspiration for another great novelist, Charlotte Brontë, for *Jane Eyre* (1847).

♦ **Stourhead Garden** in Warminster, Wiltshire, is the location where Mr. Darcy proposes for the first time, at the Temple of Apollo. Built in 1765, it stands beside the Palladian Bridge in the gardens reputed to be the finest in England. In 1717, wealthy banker Henry Hoare bought the estate from the Stourhead family, who had lived there for seven hundred years. He had the old house demolished and a Neoclassical building constructed between 1721 and 1724. It was his son, Henry Hoare II, who turned the garden into a masterpiece. He devoted forty years of his life to it. The house's library contains nearly five thousand books from the Regency period. The family's last heir donated it to the National Trust just after the Second World War. Open from mid-March to late December.
Information on nationaltrust.org.uk/stourhead

Lost in Austen, ITV, 2008, 180 minutes

In this madcap four-part fantasy, the life trajectories of the characters of *Pride and Prejudice* are thrown off course when a young 21st-century Londoner, and ardent Jane Austen fan, swaps places with a 19th-century Elizabeth Bennet.

Directed by: Dan Zeff

Script: Guy Andrews

Cast: Jemima Rooper (Amanda Price), Gemma Arterton (Elizabeth Bennet), Elliot Cowan (Mr. Darcy), Morvan Christie (Jane Bennet), Alex Kingston (Mrs. Bennet), Hugh Bonneville (Mr. Bennet), Perdita Weeks (Lydia Bennet), Ruby Bentall (Mary Bennet), Florence Hoath (Kitty Bennet), Tom Mison (Mr. Bingley), Tom Riley (Mr. Wickham), Michelle Duncan (Charlotte Lucas), Lindsay Duncan (Lady Catherine de Bourgh), Christina Cole (Caroline Bingley), Guy Henry (Mr. Collins).

Anecdotes:

• The character Amanda (Jemima Rooper) has the same surname as Fanny Price, the heroine of *Mansfield Park*. She works for a company called Sanditon Life, which refers to one of Jane Austen's unfinished novels.

• Amanda uses many pieces from the wardrobe of Elizabeth Bennet (Jennifer Ehle) from the 1995 version of *Pride and Prejudice*.

• Actress Jemima Rooper keeps the same hairstyle throughout the series. She never wears a pretty bun, which was the producers' decision, in order to remind viewers that her character is not from the same era.

• Christina Cole, playing Miss Bingley, comes back as Mrs. Elton, in the 2009 version of *Emma*.

• Director Dan Zeff is no stranger to costume films, notably *Hercule Poirot* and *Miss Marple*.

• For the ball scene, around sixty extras had to be taught the period dances in record time.

• In the middle of November, the team had to organise an outdoor summer wedding. The actors were freezing.

Allerton Castle

Shooting locations:

• **Allerton Castle** in Knaresborough, Yorkshire, was transformed into **Rosings Park**, the home of Lady Catherine de Bourgh. At the time of the Norman Conquest, the castle belonged to the Mauleverer family. It was bought in 1786 by the Duke of York, second son of King George III. It was then bought by Baron Stourton in 1805. The architect George Martin transformed it into a Gothic building in 1843. During the Second World War, it was requisitioned by the Royal Canadian Air Force. A wealthy American bought the estate in 1983. Since then, it has been run by a foundation that oversees its preservation. It is possible to have a very stylish wedding there. The house is open on a very limited number of days: from early March to late October, but only on Tuesday mornings. Guided tours available by prior arrangement.
Information on allertoncastle.co.uk

• **Bramham Park** near Leeds in Yorkshire, is the setting for **Netherfield Park**, the village of Meryton and the lake scene at Mr. Darcy's house. Its first owner, Robert Benson, Lord Bingley (that sounds familiar), made what is known as the Grand Tour in 1697. He visited Europe, studying and honing his artistic tastes, particularly in Italy. These trips gave rise to the desire for a Palladian-style residence and a very large park. The house is built of Magnesian limestone, typical of

this region of north-east England. Lord Bingley had no male successor to bequeath this estate to. The estate then passed into the hands of his son-in-law, George Fox-Lane, who also claimed the title. But he had no male offspring either. The details are unknown, but unusually it was his illegitimate daughter, Mary, who inherited it. This was in the 18th century. She then left it to her husband's nephew, James Fox-Lane, who carried out extensive alterations. The estate is now owned by Nick Lane Fox. The change of surname took place a generation earlier, as could happen when a branch of the family changed its name to inherit a title. The interior is decorated in the Baroque style, as is the park with its chapel, rotunda and colonnaded temple. The site can be visited all year round, but by appointment only.
Information on bramhampark.co.uk

♦ **Cannon Hall Museum** in Cawthorne, Yorkshire, is used for **Meryton's Assembly Rooms**. The origin of the name is thought to come from Gilbert Canun, who was the first owner of the site in the 13th century The estate passed through a number of families until John Spencer, a major figure in the iron industry, bought it in 1660. He made a number of improvements, including a superb library in one of the two new wings he had added. His nephew and heir, Walter Spencer Stanhope, and his wife, Mary Winifred, had so many offspring that they had the house extended to create

more bedrooms. Among the descendants of this family are Gertrude Spencer Stanhope and Evelyn de Morgan, two renowned Pre-Raphaelite painters. At the end of the 19th century, the house was extended to include a ballroom, kitchens and servants' quarters. Elisabeth Fraser Spencer Stanhope, the last of the line, sold the estate to the Barnsley Corporation in 1951. Converted into a museum, the site reopened in 1957. Everything then had to be refurnished. Today, you can admire a major collection of paintings, drawings, ceramics, ironwork and furniture. The park is just as spectacular. Admission is free and the estate can be visited all year round, from Tuesday to Sunday. If you're feeling peckish, the Pavilion Café is the place to go.
Information on cannon-hall.com

♦ **Harewood House** in Leeds, Yorkshire, is **Pemberley** in this version. In the 18th century, Henry Lascelles made his fortune in the sugar cane trade, which involved the slave trade. He became the richest man in England. He bought the land on which his son later built the estate. The current owner is David Lascelles, eighth Earl of Harewood and second cousin of King Charles III. He is a film producer. The house and café are open daily from mid-March until the end of the year.
Information on harewood.org

Harewood House

IF YOU REALLY WANT TO KNOW EVERYTHING: WHEN THE WHOLE WORLD FELL IN LOVE WITH *PRIDE AND PREJUDICE*

- *Pride and Prejudice: A Latter Day Comedy* by Andrew Black (2003) was filmed especially for the Mormon community. In this modernised version, the plot is set in Utah, where Mr. Darcy is a visiting British businessman.

- In 2004, an Anglo-American-Indian film was released, a genre which traditionally features dancing and singing. Although the French title is not very evocative, *Coup de Foudre à Bollywood* (Bollywood Love at First Sight), the English version is based on a play on words, *Bride and Prejudice*. Directed by Gurinder Chadha, the film stars a glamorous but very chaste couple, Indian Aishwarya Rai (as Elizabeth Bennet, renamed Lalita Bakshi) and New Zealander Martin Henderson (William Darcy).

- An Israeli production by director Irit Linur, entitled *What A Bachelor Needs*, was shot in 2008. It's a modernised series in three episodes, in which Mr. Darcy becomes Nimrod Artzi (Dan Shapira) and Elizabeth Bennet, Neta Sadeh (Neta Riskin).

- An American web series caused a stir in 2012. Called *The Lizzie Bennet Diaries*, it ran for one hundred episodes over five seasons. Set in today's world, young Lizzie tells her story through a vlog. She can't escape her smothering mother, who wants more than anything to see her married to a rich man. Created by Bernie Su and Margaret Dunlap, this version was a great success, becoming a book in 2014.[33] It was also the first web series to win an Emmy[34] in 2013.

- In 2015, a ten-part American soap opera by Brian Brough and Brittany Wiscombe, called *Austentatious,* blends several heroes and heroines from the various Austen novels into the modern world, but Lizzie Bennett[35] and William Darcy remain the main characters.

- In England, in 2014, a web series of six episodes, each about ten minutes long, was filmed in Nottingham by Becky Gray, with just three actors in the roles of Mr. Darcy, Elizabeth Bennet and a servant.

- In 2018, Brazil went wild for a telenovela of one hundred and sixty-one episodes, created by Marcos Bernstein. Entitled *Orgulho & Paixao* (Pride and Passion) and transposed to the early 20th century, it is based mainly on *Pride and Prejudice*, but also incorporates other Austen characters, such as Lady Susan and Fanny Price. Elizabeth Bennet becomes Elisabeta Benedito (Nathalia Dill) and Mr. Darcy, Darcy Williamson (Thiago Larceda).

- Several modernised versions were filmed in the United States, such as *Pride and Prejudice, Cut* by Michael Kampa, which features two actors who play in *Pride and Prejudice*. In 2011, Bonnie Mae's *A Modern Pride and Prejudice* was shot entirely in Colorado. There was also a *Pride and Prejudice: Atlanta* in 2019, performed entirely by African-American actors.

- *Pride and Prejudice* is also available in the form of Hallmark Christmas TV films, with their sickly-sweet appeal. These include *Christmas at Pemberley Manor* and *Pride and Prejudice and Mistletoe*[36] in 2018. In *An American in Austen*, by Clare Niederpruem (2024), a young bookshop keeper is suddenly transported in the novel, where she meets all the characters.

---

[33] *The Secret Diary of Lizzie Bennet: A Novel*, by Bernie Su and Kate Rorick, Simon & Schuster, 2014.
[34] Prestigious American television award.
[35] Yes, with two ts!
[36] Based on a novel of the same name by Melissa de la Cruz.

• The LGBTQIA+ community has also embraced the phenomenon, with two productions to its credit. First in 2016, with Byrum Geisler's *Before The Fall*, in which Ben Bennet and Lee Darcy fall in love. In 2022, the Disney+ platform released Andrew Ahn's *Fire Island*, based on the plot of Jane Austen's novel (in broad outline), starring Joel Kim Booster, who also wrote the screenplay.

• While no major French production has ever focused on Jane Austen's work, a fan film, *Orgueil, Préjugés et Sortilèges* (Pride, Prejudice and Spells), made by video professionals (The Cocotte Show Productions), has been available on the YouTube platform since 2021. Produced in part via a crowdfunding campaign, this medium-length film blends the world of the English novelist with that of *Harry Potter*.

Pride, Prejudice and Spells - The Harry Potter Pride and Prejudice fanfilm - YouTube

Did you know?

HAVE YOU HEARD OF ROSINA FILIPPI?

This Franco-Italian actress, who grew up in England, is famous for being the first to adapt Jane Austen for the stage. She proposed a series of extracts as early as 1895, that formed a play. They are taken from *Pride and Prejudice*, *Emma*, *Sense and Sensibility* and *Northanger Abbey*. These texts, entitled *Duologues and Scenes from the Novels of Jane Austen*[37] were published by Joseph Malaby Dent, who also edited Jane Austen's novels at the end of the 19th century. Particular attention is given to the female characters. In 1901, another of her plays, *The Bennets*, was performed for the first time in London. This flamboyant figure on the London stage ended her career as a drama teacher.

---

[37] *Playing Jane Austen* (first published in 1895 as *Duologues and scenes from the Novel of Jane Austen Arranged and Adapted for Drawing-Room Performance*), Rosina Filippi, The British Library, 2019.

WHEN *PRIDE AND PREJUDICE* INSPIRES CONTEMPORARY WRITERS

English-language works

♦ Pamela Aidan imagines the unspoken words and omissions in *Pride and Prejudice* in a four-volume series entitled *Fitzwilliam Darcy, Gentleman* (Atria, 2006).

♦ Elizabeth Aston's vision of the post-wedding period is like a fairy tale: "they got married and had lots of children". Her series consists of six books: *Mr. Darcy's Daughters, The Exploits and Adventures of Miss Alethea Darcy, The True Darcy Spirit, The Second Mrs. Darcy, The Darcy Connection, Mr. Darcy's Dream*, and four Darcy novellas including *Mr. Darcy's Christmas* (Touchstone, 2003-2013).

♦ Jo Baker offers an original perspective, looking at *Pride and Prejudice* through a keyhole. *Longbourn* is written from the point of view of the servants (Vintage, 2014). A feature film is in production with *Bridget Jones's Diary* director Sharon Maguire.

♦ Jennifer Becton looks at the fates of three secondary characters in *The Personages of Pride & Prejudice Collection* of the novels Charlotte Collins and Caroline Bingley and short story *Maria Lucas* (Whiteley Press, 2012).

♦ Richard Galland challenges us to rediscover *Pride and Prejudice* from a new angle. *Pride & Prejudice & Puzzles* reminds us that in Jane Austen's time, mind games, charades and other puzzles were very popular. This book, to be read with a pen in hand, is packed with games and illustrations. A few characters from other novels also make small appearances (Welbeck Publishing Group, 2018).

French-language works

♦ In *Pemberley's Renaissance* (self-published, 2019), Lise Antunes Simoes shows us the daily life of Pemberley's mistress.

♦ Aurore brings the story to life in a three-volume graphic novel, *The Five Daughters of Mrs Bennet* (Soleil, 2019), *Rosings Park* (Soleil, 2021) and *Pemberley* (Soleil, 2023).

♦ The picture book *Où est Lizzie?/Où est Darcy?* (Where's Lizzie/Where's Darcy? 404 Éditions, 2022), by Victoire Bocquillon, Pascale Charpenet and Jenna Lyn Brooks, uses a 'search and find' approach to the key scenes from the novel, including the famous wet shirt.

♦ Michèle Calméjane-Schneiter adapts the story in the form of a *what if...* and roughens up the characters in *Je me souviens de Pemberley* (I remember Pemberley, Edilivre, 2019), and its sequel *Revenir à Longbourn* (Return to Longbourn, Edilivre, 2019).

♦ Charlotte Grossetête translated, adapted and shortened the text for young audiences in a version illustrated by Dogan Oztel (Fleurus, 2015).

♦ Magali Jeannin abridged the text in an adapted version for young people, with an introduction that contextualises the story, *Orgueil et Préjugé* (L'Ecole des Loisirs, 2017). By the way, the word "Préjugé" has lost the 's' on the end.

♦ A *Pride and Prejudice* picture book for children focuses on both the characters and Georgian England, with a short explanatory booklet and games (Quelle Histoire, 2022). An audio version of the text is also available for the "Quelle Histoire" mobile application.

♦ Marie-Laure Sébire wrote *Chroniques de Pemberley* (Pemberley Chronicles, Le Lys Bleu, 2018), imagining what happened after the wedding, and the daily lives of these iconic characters.

♦ Jess Swann's *Amour, Orgueil et Préjugés* (Love, Pride and Prejudice, Les Roses Bleues, 2013) brings the plot to present day Ireland, with a story centred on four sisters.

Suave but stiff.
(if only!?)

Aloof. Unavailable. Ice queen.
(quite fancy a snog though. hmmm!?)

Gorgeous and my boss.
(must NOT sleep with him!?)

RENÉE **ZELLWEGER**   HUGH **GRANT**   COLIN **FIRTH**

BRIDGET JONES'S DIARY

For anyone who's ever been set up, stood up or felt up.

HELEN FIELDING AND MR. DARCY

The Englishwoman Helen Fielding is the author of the most famous retelling of *Pride and Prejudice*. She began *Bridget Jones's Diary* as a column in *The Independent* in 1995. It was an immediate success, giving rise not only to four novels,[38] but also three film adaptations[39] in which she contributed to the screenplay.

When she wrote her novel, Helen Fielding imagined her hero, Mark Darcy, as Colin Firth. In 1999, the second volume, *Bridget Jones: The Edge of Reason*, took the reference further, turning the actor into a character in her novel. Her heroine has the chance to interview him at an iconic meeting, knowing that he is literally her celebrity crush.
In 2001, when *Bridget Jones's Diary* was released, Colin Firth said that he had taken on the role of a modern-day Darcy to free himself from the image of a Regency Darcy, and to break with his own image. In the third film, *Bridget Jones's Baby*, we learn that Mark Darcy's middle name is Fitzwilliam. And the circle is complete!

[38] *Bridget Jones's Diary* (Picador, 1996), *Bridget Jones: The Edge of Reason* (Picador, 1999), *Bridget Jones: Mad About the Boy* (Knopf Doubleday Publishing Group, 2013), *Bridget Jones's Baby: the Diaries* (Alfred a Knopf Inc, 2016).
[39] *Bridget Jones's Diary* (2001), *Bridget Jones: The Edge of Reason* (2004), *Bridget Jones's Baby* (2016).

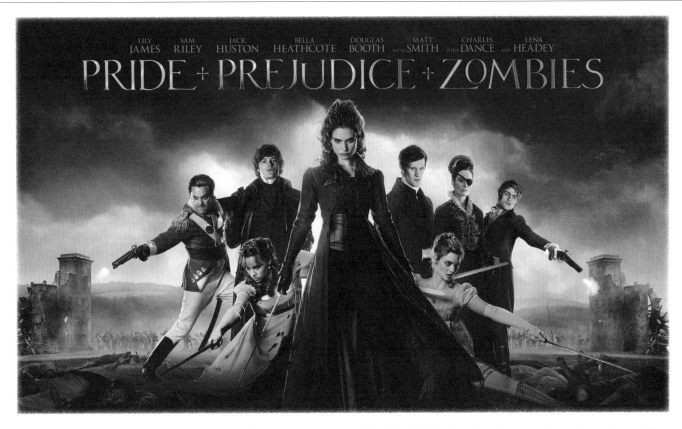

♦ The American Seth Grahame-Smith is the author of a novel that mixes Regency and fantasy, *Pride and Prejudice and Zombies* (Quirk Books, 2009). The author adapted Jane Austen's text, adding an horrific sub-plot. It's a real exercise in style, as it retains eighty-five per cent of the original text. The book was an instant bestseller. Tony Lee and Cliff Richards adapted it into a graphic novel (Del Rey, 2010). A film adaptation of the same name[40] was made in 2016, starring Lily James as Elizabeth Bennet and Sam Riley as Mr. Darcy.

♦ Amanda Grange is passionate about *Pride and Prejudice,* which she constantly adapts in a variety of ways. She takes us into Mr. Darcy's mind with her *Mr. Darcy's Diary* (Robert Hale, 2005). In *Dear Mr. Darcy* (Berkley, 2012), she begins the story before the events of the original book and transforms the text into an epistolary novel. She imagines many of the details that Jane Austen's novel leaves out. Amanda Grange is also the author of, among other works, *Mr. Darcy, Vampire* and *Pride and Pyramids: Mr Darcy in Egypt.*

♦ Mandy Hubbard's *Prada and Prejudice* (Razorbill, 2009) asks the eternal question: what happens to a young lady who finds herself thrust into the Regency period? Does she find her Darcy?

♦ In *Death Comes to Pemberley* (Faber & Faber, 2011), mystery writer P. D. James mixes suspense, elegance and the Regency period. The Darcy couple is well settled in Pemberley when a murder occurs. It involves friends and family, and all the protagonists find themselves embroiled in an investigation. The novel was adapted for the BBC in three episodes in 2013. In the roles of Elizabeth and Mr. Darcy are Anna Maxwell Martin and Matthew Rhys. You can recognise Chatsworth in Derbyshire as the setting for Pemberley.

♦ Kara Louise invites us to a *what if...* with *Only Mr. Darcy Will Do* (Sourcebooks Landmark, 2011). What would have happened if Elizabeth Bennet had refused all the marriage proposals? The answer is in the book.

♦ Australian Colleen McCullough is best known for her international best-seller *The Thorn Birds* (1977). She examines the character of Mary Bennet in *The Independence of Miss Mary Bennet* (Pocket Books, 2009), in which she invents an unusual destiny for her.

---

[40]American-British film by Burr Steers.

◆ Lynn Messina turns the tables in *Prejudice and Pride* (Potatoworks Press, 2015). Darcy is a woman, a wealthy New York heiress and patron of the arts. Bennet, a young man of modest means, works for a small museum in Queens. The action takes place in the present day. She is also the creator of *The Beatrice Hyde-Clare Mysteries* (Potatoworks Press, 2022), which parodies the Lizzie-Darcy relationship in a series of cosy Regency mysteries.

◆ Pamela Mingle, with *The Pursuit of Mary Bennet* (Avon, 2013), gives a voice to a character left out of the original novel, Mary Bennet.

◆ Abigail Reynolds had fun reinventing the original story with minute variations, as in *Mr. Fitzwilliam Darcy: The Last Man in the World* (Sourcebooks Landmark, 2010), *To Conquer Mr. Darcy* (Sourcebooks, 2010) and *What Would Mr. Darcy Do?* (Sourcebooks Landmark, 2011).

◆ In *Eligible* (Random House, 2017), Curtis Sittenfeld plunges the characters from *Pride and Prejudice* into a reality TV show.

◆ Anyta Sunday specialises in gay rewrites of Jane Austen's novels, in a series called *Love, Austen. Bennet, Pride Before the Fall* (Anyta Sunday, 2023) takes up the theme of a thwarted love story.

◆ *Pride and Prejudice* is also available as a manga, drawn by Taiwanese artist Po Tse (Udon, 2020).

◆ American Teri Wilson brings the plot of *Pride and Prejudice* to the modern age in *Unleashing Mr. Darcy* (Harper Collins, 2014) which was adapted into two Hallmark TV films, *Unleashing Mr. Darcy* (2016) and *Marrying Mr. Darcy* (2018). In this story, Elizabeth and Darcy compete in a dog show.

Extract from *The Heartstopper Yearbook*, by Alice Oseman.

Did you know?

ALICE OSEMAN, A *PRIDE AND PREJUDICE* FAN

In the *Heartstopper Yearbook* (Hachette Children's Group, 2022), Alice Oseman makes no secret of her great admiration for *Pride and Prejudice*.

Her first novel, *Solitaire* offers us two heroes who are, in a way, an inverted mirror of Elizabeth Bennet and Mr. Darcy. Victoria "Tori" Spring ironically hates *Pride and Prejudice*. At least, that's what she claims: "The only tolerable character is Mr. Darcy".[41] The original English version echoes Jane Austen's hero's famous line about Elizabeth Bennet: "[S]he is tolerable, but not handsome enough to tempt me".[42] Tori understands Mr. Darcy better than anyone, because she is so similar to him. "I don't see why Elizabeth finds him proud at the beginning, because it's quite clearly obvious that he's just shy", she explains.[43]

In plates published in the mini-comic *The Dream* on Tumblr and Tapas, Alice Oseman also features the two *Heartstopper* heroes, Nick Nelson and Charlie Spring, in a nod to *Pride and Prejudice*. The book is on the school curriculum in Britain, and Nick is forced to read it. Unable to fight off boredom, he falls asleep and finds himself propelled, in a dream, into the middle of a Regency dance class.

[41] *Solitaire*, Alice Oseman, HarperCollins Children Books, 2014.
[42] *Pride and Prejudice*, Jane Austen, Penguin Classics, 2003.
[43] *Solitaire*, Alice Oseman, *op. cit.*

PRIDE AND PREJUDICE AN INFINITE SOURCE OF INSPIRATION

In the fun category, there is a version of *Pride and Prejudice* entirely in emojis, *Pride and Prejudice & Emojis* (Penguin, 2017). What is it like?

You will of course have recognised the novel's opening line: "It is a truth universally acknowledged, that a single man in possession of a good fortune, must be in want of a wife".

In the cute category is *Pugs and Prejudice*, by Eliza Garrett (Wildfire, Hachette UK, 2017). All the characters are lovable pugs, even Mr. Darcy.

There are a number of books for babies and toddlers. From birth, the story is available as a fabric book at **sweetsequels.com**. There is also a collection of *Little Miss Austen* hardback books (Gibbs Smith, 2011), as well as a photo illustrated version with woollen characters by Jack and Holman Wang, *Jane Austen's Pride and Prejudice* (Cozy Classics, 2012).

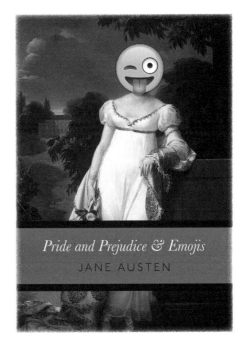

In the entertainment category, there are a few games such as *Jane Austen Matchmaking* and *Jane Austen playing cards*, published by Laurence King.

In the unusual category, is an erotic parody by William Codpiece Thwackery, *50 Shades of Mr. Darcy (Michael O'Mara, 2012)* (the title is evocative).

Mansfield Park

Mansfield Park was Jane Austen's biggest success during her lifetime. Today, however, it is the least popular and, above all, the least well-known of her six novels. To top it all, at the time, the novelist even received an eloquent compliment from James Stanier Clarke, the Prince Regent's librarian. The librarian wrote to her: "Your late works, Madam, and in particular Mansfield Park, reflect the highest honour on your genius and your principles".[44]

From the outside, the heroine, Fanny Price, may seem dull, self-effacing and shy. But open the door of Mansfield Park and meet the woman who, with each passing page, establishes herself as one of Austen's most powerful, feisty and determined figures. Uncompromising, as strong as a lighthouse in a storm, against all odds, she remains steadfastly loyal to her convictions and to those to whom she gives her heart.

Incipit 1814

About thirty years ago, Miss Maria Ward, of Huntingdon, with only seven thousand pounds, had the good luck to captivate Sir Thomas Bertram, of Mansfield Park, in the county of Northampton, and to be thereby raised to the rank of a baronet's lady, with all the comforts and consequences of an handsome house and large income.[45]

---

[44] *A Memoir of Jane Austen*, by James Edward Austen-Leigh. Richard Bentley, 1869.
[45] *Mansfield Park*, Thomas Egerton, 1814.

WHAT'S IT ABOUT?

When Fanny Price arrived at Mansfield Park at the age of nine, it was a heartbreaking change. Although she had left a modest home, it was a place she felt she belonged. She felt of use to her mother who was overwhelmed by multiple pregnancies, and safe with her older brother, William, whom she adored. Her maternal aunts, Lady Bertram and Mrs. Norris, wanting to give the impression that they were helping their sister, decide to take in one of the many mouths to feed. Without further deliberation, they chose Fanny. Naturally unassuming, friendly and helpful, the little girl learns to make herself indispensable, as obliging as a lady's maid. Not quite a maid, but almost.

In this wealthy family, Fanny Price's daily life is not a bed of roses. One of her aunts turns out to be disinterested and the other overbearing. Her uncle, the very formal Lord Bertram, terrifies her. Her cousins make fun of her lack of education, and their older brother Tom, while not mean, barely notices that she exists. In this hostile environment, only one beautiful soul emerges, her youngest cousin, Edmund. On the day he catches Fanny in tears and consoles her, the seeds of an enduring bond take root in the young girl's shattered heart. His gentle admiration blossoms from year to year, in a relationship of trust, kindness and growing affection.

Drawing illustrating chapter 7,
"Mary plays the harp with the greatest obligingness". 1898. H. M. Brock.

Life continues until the young people people are in their prime. The charismatic Henry and Mary Crawford move to the neighbourhood, and the presence of this brother and sister quickly causes trouble, upsetting the peaceful routine of Mansfield Park. Couples form. Attractions, some mutual, some not, shake things up. But in this game of love that owes nothing to chance, the outcome is far from certain. And in this complex web of feelings, only Fanny manages to come out on top.

Character Gallery
THE LADIES

FANNY PRICE: the Bertrams' poor relative.
Fanny is only nine years old when she left Southampton, her parents and siblings to join her maternal cousins in the north of the country. She gets frightened at the slightest thing, cries a lot and stays withdrawn. The little girl grows up in this new family without seeing her family again for years, and no one cares. She quickly becomes indispensable to her aunt, Lady Bertram, who calls on her at the slightest opportunity. Calm, patient and charming, she is also determined. When her conscience demands it, she has no hesitation in stepping out of her natural reserve and expressing her deepest convictions.

MARY CRAWFORD: a beautiful young girl with dark eyes.
Elegant, lively and affable, she arrives in the Bertram neighbourhood with the firm intention of finding a husband, preferably a wealthy one, even though she already had the princely sum of £20,000. She lives with her older, married sister, Mrs. Grant, the wife of the Mansfield Park parish priest. Mary Crawford seems to like Fanny Price, although she doesn't particularly want to be her friend. She likes to slip in a few French words here and there when she speaks.[46]

MRS. NORRIS: eldest daughter of the Ward family and Fanny's aunt.
We don't know her first name. A cantankerous woman, her failure to attract a wealthy gentleman eats her up. Late in life, and mainly out of spite, she ended up marrying vicar Norris, a friend of her brother-in-law, Lord Bertram. Wickedly devious, she never ceases to torment Fanny, but always in subtle ways, so no one can really catch her at it. She has a real talent for making herself feel important, especially when no one asks her to do so. Mrs. Norris never had the joy of being a mother. As a result, she is fully devoted to her Bertram nieces and nephews.

Did you know?

MRS. NORRIS APPEARS IN *HARRY POTTER*!

Do you remember the sneaky cat belonging to the caretaker, Argus Filch? She is called Mrs. Norris, which is a direct reference to Austen's most hated female character. However, this reference goes completely unnoticed in many translations. Most of the proper names were translated, as they are often puns or neologisms, or they contain hidden meanings. For example, in the French edition, the evil feline is known as Miss Teigne (meaning 'nasty piece of work').

LADY BERTRAM: née Miss Maria Ward, younger sister of Mrs. Norris and Fanny's aunt.
In her youth, she was ravishing, attractive enough to please a nobleman with an honourable fortune. Aloof, self-centred and scatterbrained, this incorrigible idler spends most of her day lying on a sofa, petting her pug. No matter! The society of her time considered that she had amply done her duty by giving her husband two sons and two daughters.

MARIA BERTRAM: Fanny's cousin.
Considered the most stunning girl in the county, this young lady is well aware of this and is quietly waiting for the most beneficial match. Frivolous and superficial, she isn't unkind to Fanny, just mocking or indifferent, depending on her mood. Maria is Mrs. Norris' favourite niece, who sees in her all the qualities of a fine lady.

JULIA BERTRAM: Fanny's second cousin.
In the shadow of her beautiful, easily jealous older sister, pretty Julia longs for just one thing: to be noticed for herself. She's not particularly demonstrative towards Fanny. Although she enjoys her company, she never fails to remind her of her place.

---

[46] *In Jane Austen and her predecessors*, Cambridge University Press, 1966, Frank W. Bradbrook observes seventeen occurrences of French words or phrases in *Mansfield Park*, the most for a single Austen novel. For example, there are only seven in *Emma*. In *Mansfield Park*, all these words are spoken by the Crawfords, which is supposed to give us an initial indication of their true nature. In Jane Austen's time, the French were seen as charming and manipulative. Napoleon's influence is felt.

Character Gallery
THE GENTLEMEN

EDMUND BERTRAM: **Fanny's favourite cousin.**
Six years older than his little cousin, he quickly fell in love with her as soon as she arrived at Mansfield Park. Edmund is serious, straightforward and much more mature than his older brother. He set his sights on the priesthood, knowing full well that in his milieu a younger son does not inherit. He has to work, even though he will be given a parish, Thornton Lacey. Edmund never misses an opportunity to think about Fanny, to worry about her and to see to her comfort, especially when their aunt Mrs. Norris does her an injustice. His occasionally rigid side doesn't stop his heart from moving when he thinks he's in love.

TOM BERTRAM: **Fanny's cousin.**
As a first-born son, he bitterly feels the weight of the responsibilities he owes to his family. His weak nature prevents him from dealing with this responsibility fully. He can't resist alcohol or gambling. He's not really unkind to Fanny, but rather distant. No matter how hard his father tries to set him straight, he does as he pleases. He would later own the Mansfield Park estate and the family fortune.

HENRY CRAWFORD: **rich young man from Norfolk.**
Described as ugly, even very ugly, at the beginning of the novel, his physique seems to evolve as his seductive ways turn a few heads. This remarkably smooth talker loves nothing more than flirting, flattery and fawning. As far as he's concerned, there's no need to bother with a wealthy heiress, because he has a comfortable fortune and doesn't fail to make it known.

LORD BERTRAM: **Fanny's uncle by marriage.**
This wealthy landowner is neither harsh nor malicious, despite his very conservative side. He is simply firmly anchored in his superior position and acts according to what seems right to him. Although a baronet, he is by no means a wealthy man. To secure his fortune, he profited from plantations in Antigua, in the Caribbean. He loves his family, but only insofar as they respect decorum and know their place.

MR. RUSHWORTH: **a very well-to-do young man from the neighbourhood.**
On the lookout for a pretty woman to be his wife, he sets his sights on Maria Bertram. He is a good-natured, slightly naive boy who is not very smart and lives with his mother. Deeply in love with his fiancée, he can't wait to get married. To his credit, he is neither handsome nor sharp-witted, but he does have an attractive fortune —£12,000 in annuities— as well as an imposing estate, Sotherton Court. He's the richest Austen gentleman!

WILLIAM PRICE: **Fanny's favourite older brother.**
The young man is only a year older than Fanny. Their relationship is very close, each unconditionally supporting the other. Fanny feels great admiration and love for her brother, who misses her every minute. They write to each other regularly. William is in the Royal Navy, but cannot hope for promotion without a recommendation because of his humble origins.

THE LITTLE TOPAZ CROSS

In May 1801, on receiving a bonus from the Royal Navy,[47] Charles Austen decided to give his sisters, Cassandra and Jane, a cross made of topaz, a semi-precious stone, with a gold chain. In the novel, Fanny Price receives an amber cross from her sailor brother. This fossil resin is less expensive, but proves William's attachment to his youngest sister. It also added an exciting exotic note to Fanny's life, as the jewel came from the far-off land that was Sicily at the time. As for the Austen sisters' crosses, they can now be admired at the Jane Austen Museum in Chawton, and replicas even purchased from the Jane Austen Centre's online shop **janeausten.co.uk/en/pages/jane-austen-online-gift-shop**.

[47] For more information on the Royal Navy, see the section on *Persuasion*.

Mansfield Park IN A NUTSHELL

> *We have all a better guide in ourselves, if we would attend to it, than any other person can be.*[48]
>
> (Fanny Price)

A BRIEF OVERVIEW

When Jane Austen began writing *Mansfield Park*, she did so in the peace and quiet of her cosy cottage at Chawton. The novelist had complete freedom to hone her writing here, despite the constraints of everyday life. It appears that she began this book in February 1811. She had been living in her new home for two years. Buoyed by the success of her previous publications, she was growing in confidence. She took the liberty of exploring the journey of an undoubtedly more complex heroine, in a kind of *Bildungsroman* ("learning novel", in German), as is *Emma*, but with a darker tone here.

If we take the trouble to look into the case of Fanny Price, we can tell a lot about her by simply examining her name. Fanny was the first of her siblings, so she took her mother's name, Frances, as was often the custom at the time. Fanny is its affectionate diminutive version. The eldest cousin, Maria, is also named after her mother, as is Cassandra, in the Austen family. The birth name of Fanny's mother and her aunts —Mrs. Norrish and Lady Bertram— is Ward, which is the name for someone under the care of a guardian. This is precisely Fanny's social condition when she arrives at Mansfield Park. She is told that she owes her presence at the castle only to the generosity of her family, but that she is not and must never hope to become their equal. And yet Fanny Price, if we consider that she represents the name she bears, is the *price*, the one who counts the most, the one who has the most value.

---

[48]*Mansfield Park*, Jane Austen, Thomas Egerton, 1814, *op. cit.*

Did you know?

Fanny Price's story might be compared to a fairy tale. Jane Austen probably drew some of her inspiration from a traditional tale she read as a child, *The History of Little Goody Two-Shoes*. Published in London by John Newbery (1765), it is itself a variation on *Cinderella*. The official authorship of this tale has never been formally established, but it is rumoured to have been written by an 18th century, Irish author, Oliver Goldsmith. Jane Austen owned a copy, in which she inscribed her name.

This tale follows the classic pattern of children's stories in which virtue prevails and wrongdoing is punished. The heroine, Margery "Goody" Meanwell, has only one shoe, but is given a pair of shoes by a wealthy gentleman. She expresses her joy, telling everyone that she now has *two* shoes. She then spends her youth educating poor children, until a rich widower marries her. Her generosity and good deeds are rewarded, just like Fanny Price, so adaptable in character. Today, the expression "goody-two-shoes" is still used to describe a person who always strives to do everything right according to the rules, propriety and morality.

The History of Little Goody Two-Shoes on the British Library website bl.uk/collection-items/the-history-of-little-goody-two-shoes

In the end, Fanny is the anti-Emma. The girl is neither rich, popular nor spectacularly beautiful, at least not enough for the author to point this out. The novel is not named after the main character, but after the place where she transforms from an ugly duckling to a radiant swan. Fanny Price is also one of the rare Austen heroines whom we meet as a child. This is the fundamental theme of *Mansfield Park*: Fanny's intimate metamorphosis from foster child to distinguished young woman, the sweetest of rewards for those who know how to love her.

Jane Austen gives herself the opportunity to explore, in this story, the difficulty of being "a good person". In this, Fanny Price perfectly meets the requirements of the famous "conduct books", published in Georgian times, which indicated the most appropriate and respectable way to behave in society. On the other hand, Fanny allows herself to indulge in romantic feelings, which, before marriage, are forbidden by these same manuals. She thus shows her complexity.

Jane Austen wrote *Mansfield Park* in two years. She put the finishing touches to it, or so she thought, in July 1813. The book was published in May 1814 by her usual publisher, Thomas Egerton, at a price of 18 shillings each. The stock of 1,250 books sold out in six months, earning her around 300 pounds[49], which was financially rewarding, since the total sales of her first four novels had brought her "only" 600 pounds. In 1816, a new print run was required. For this reprint, Jane Austen chose the publisher John Murray, with whom she had already collaborated on *Emma* a few months earlier. Her brother, Henry Austen, handled the transactions and negotiated with this prestigious London publisher, who published not only Lord Byron but also Sir Walter Scott, the two greatest best-selling authors of the time. John Murray accepted, but without taking any risks. The books were still sold on a self-publishing basis, with the slogan "By the author of *Pride and Prejudice*".

[49] Three hundred pounds at the time is the equivalent of almost £40,000 today.

This second publication was released in February 1816. It included some minor modifications, such as changes in punctuation. In addition, special attention was paid to the familiar vocabulary of the Navy, revised with the help of Francis and Charles Austen, the novelist's brothers, officers in the Royal Navy. This is today's authoritative version. Cassandra Austen didn't like the end of the book very much, and took the opportunity to try and change it, but her sister stuck to her guns. In the meantime, a French translation appeared for the first time, in excerpts only, in a Swiss periodical, *Bibliothèque Britannique*, in 1815. Then, in September 1816, a loose translation by Henri Villemain was published in Paris under the title *Le Parc de Mansfield ou Les Trois Cousines*.

HISTORY

The issue of slavery

In the novel, the question of the origin of Lord Bertram's property is not really raised. His business took him to Antigua, in what the English then called the West Indies, the Caribbean, famous for its sugar cane plantations, and therefore a land of slavery. Jane Austen chose Antigua in particular because she had first-hand information from the Langford Nibbs family, who had owned sugar cane plantations in Antigua for three generations, and the Austens were closely connected with them. During his studies at Oxford, her father, George Austen, tutored James Langford Nibbs. Then, in 1760, he became the trustee of his estate in the Caribbean. Finally, James Langford Nibbs was godfather to Jane Austen's brother, James.

The novel is set in 1807. The law abolishing the slave trade had just been passed. Once again, although Jane Austen does not go into detail, she is very aware of the changes in society. Lord Bertram has no choice but to go and supervise the necessary changes himself, which threaten his fortune. Jane Austen is sometimes criticised for staying on the surface of the great historical turning points that marked her time. In fact, she evokes them with subtlety, and it's up to the reader to go in search of the clues between the lines. So, although the theme of slavery is only touched on,

that doesn't mean that Jane Austen didn't read up on the subject. When it was published in 1808, Clarkson's *The History of the Rise, Progress, and Accomplishment of the Abolition of the African Slave-Trade* was an impressive volume that she read and appreciated.[50]

What's more, the choice of the title *Mansfield Park* is certainly not insignificant. The first Lord Mansfield, William Murray, has remained famous. Influenced by the progressive ideas of the Enlightenment, and a powerful magistrate, he ruled in 1772 on the case of Somerset v Stewart. James Somerset was a black slave brought to England by a man called Charles Stewart. He managed to escape his master, who wanted to sell him and ship him back to America. However, James Somerset had the support of high society, who called for his freedom. Indeed, slavery had been formally prohibited on English soil, even though it was still practised in the colonies. In fact, there was nothing in English law to specify that a human being could be sold as property. The case went to court. After a month's reflection, Lord Mansfield decided to grant James Somerset his freedom. Admittedly, this was more a judgement based on the technical aspects of the law than an act of pure generosity, but the foundations for a new way of thinking were laid, and people's consciences were awakened.

---

[50] This text can be consulted on **gutenberg.org**.

DIDO BELLE

Do you know the story of Dido Belle, and her connection with Jane Austen? Dido Elizabeth Belle's life is not as glamorous nor as romantic as depicted in Amma Asante's 2013 film *Belle*. Her father was Royal Navy Captain John Lindsay, Lord Mansfield's favourite nephew. Her mother, Maria, was a former slave, married to a man called Mr. Bell. Nothing very precise is known about the circumstances of Dido's birth. An illegitimate child, she was soon entrusted to the care of the wealthy Mansfield couple, who had no offspring of their own. We don't know if her father ever came to visit her. What's more, he had mixed-race children with other women. We know that her mother, a freedwoman, was also in London at the same time. However, they didn't see each other once the girl reached adulthood. Dido was brought up with her cousin Elizabeth, who was an acquaintance of Jane Austen.

Although well-educated, pampered and luxuriously dressed, she did not enjoy the same privileges as her white cousin, because of the colour of her skin. She was not allowed to eat with the family when they had guests, but had to hide from visitors. When Elizabeth Murray got married, Dido stayed on at her great-uncle's beautiful home, Kenwood House, as a nursemaid. A little later, she married a French servant with whom she had three sons, including twins. She died in 1804, aged forty-three.

It is not impossible that Jane Austen drew inspiration from Dido for her mixed-race character Miss Lambe in *Sanditon*. A parallel with *Mansfield Park* is doubtlessly not accidental either, given the distance kept by Fanny Price's family. Comparing his niece to his daughters, Lord Bertram is careful to point out that "their rank, fortune, rights, and expectations will always be different."[51]

Marriage in the Regency period

Although Fanny Price's arrival at Mansfield Park is due solely to her status as a poor relative, it is also clear from the outset that she is not a potential wife for either of her cousins. As predicted by Mrs. Norris, "of all things upon earth, that is the least likely to happen",[52] since all the children would, so to speak, be raised as brothers and sisters. This is precisely where the problem lies, because Fanny was never considered their equal. She is constantly reminded of how inferior she is to them.

Marriage between cousins was relatively common in this environment and at this time. In *Incest and Influence: The Private Life of Bourgeois England*,[53] the anthropologist Adam Kuper explains that in this world of affluence, during 19th century England, more than one in ten marriages involved a first or second cousin. So the problem here was not being from the same family, but from a different social class. In *Pride and Prejudice*, the maternal aunt of Mr. Darcy encourages his marriage to his cousin Anne. Elizabeth Bennet, meanwhile, is being courted by the son of her father's cousin, Mr. Collins. In the Austen family, Henry fell madly in love with his cousin, the beautiful Eliza de Feuillide, ten years older than him, whom he admired since childhood. He married her in 1797, when she was a widow with a young son.

Mansfield Park offers an anthology of opinions on marriage. Lord and Lady Bertram's marriage was a love match, at least on his side. Henry Crawford believes that the union of two beings deprives them of their freedom to act as they please, and does not wish to settle down until he is obliged to do so. His sister Mary is looking for financial comfort as much as reciprocal feelings, and for her one can't exist without the other. Maria Bertram sees marriage as a transaction, an exchange of courtesies, without any emotional element. Fanny Price knows that she cannot marry without love. If she can't find the love of her heart's desire, she would prefer without hesitation to remain single.

[51] *Mansfield Park*, op. cit.
[52] *Ibid.*
[53] Harvard University Press, 2009.

We are inevitably reminded of the author herself who, like her heroines, cannot conceive of a union without affection. In a letter from the novelist to Fanny Knight, one of her favourite nieces, dated 30 November 1814, she let her heart speak: "Nothing can be compared to the misery of being bound without Love".

Three weeks' banns had to be published in order to marry into the gentry. The main aim of this was to spread the news to as many people as possible at the various religious services, to ensure that neither of them was already married. If you had the means, connections, or both, a dispensation from the banns signed by the Archbishop of Canterbury allowed you to marry without delay. The young bride wore her most beautiful dress. White did not appear until the Victorian era, at Queen Victoria's wedding to Prince Albert. Once the mutual vows had been proclaimed, a woman became her husband's property. The same applied to all her assets and to any children born of the union. This is how the reluctance of some and the hesitation of others was measured, especially as women were expected to stay in their place, produce heirs and not think too much for themselves.

ELOPEMENT AND GRETNA GREEN

In the novel, Julia Bertram finds herself involved in what is known in England as an elopement. The idea was to run away from home, in secret, to get married as quickly as possible, outside the bounds of propriety. This caused a real scandal! Lydia Bennet, in *Pride and Prejudice*, makes this dangerous choice, at the risk of depriving all her unmarried sisters of a respectable alliance.

The young girl finds herself without a chaperone, her virtue threatened, or worse, scorned. If she doesn't get married soon, she will be ostracised from society, with no hope of a new life, and her whole family will be brought down with her. A proper lady is not supposed to have an opinion and should be ignorant of what goes on between a couple until her wedding night. She didn't realise the shame she was exposing herself to by leaving her father's home in secret.

In England, since the Marriage Act[54] established by Lord Hardwicke in 1753,[55] no one under the age of twenty-one, boy or girl, could marry without the consent of their family. The marriage also had to be performed by an ordained priest. The solution to this unfortunate situation? Run away to Scotland! The legal age for marriage there was sixteen. Parental consent and the publication of banns were not required. Secondly, the union had to be consummated quickly, to be indisputable.

Gretna Green is a small village on the road to Carlisle, the first after the border, where runaways flocked. Scottish marriages did not have to be performed by a clergyman. Butchers, bakers, innkeepers, any native of the area could, according to the law of his country, bless a union.[56] But in those days, this task was often left to the blacksmith. In fact, he would be someone you could find most easily, and first. He worked in the centre of the town, at the junction of the five roads known as Headless Cross. This was handy when you arrived from London or any other city in England, at full speed. He was also the most successful, and therefore the most respectable, tradesperson.

These days, it's still possible to get married legally in Gretna Green, as the legislation is fairly flexible. In homage to the ancient tradition, these weddings are still known as "anvil weddings". For more information, visit **gretnagreen.com**.

[54] Before the Act for the Better Preventing of Clandestine Marriage, which was partly introduced to protect gullible young heiresses from dowry chasers, boys could marry at fourteen and girls at twelve!
[55] Since 1929, the legal age for marriage has been eighteen throughout the UK, except in Scotland where it is still possible to marry at sixteen without parental consent.
[56] In the presence of at least two witnesses, who are offered a small fee.

The theatre in the Regency period

Going to the theatre was an extremely popular and very appropriate way to spend a night out. In London, two major venues vied for popularity: Covent Garden and the Theatre Royal Drury Lane. Since King Charles II issued them with royal patents in 1660, they had been the only ones authorised to remain open all year round. In Georgian times, other theatres only opened for six months at a time. This was known as the "season", and it was also the time when young girls were "presented to the world", as the saying went. The season ran from late January to early July.[57] This meant that during this time, wealthy families were in London enjoying the shows. Theatres were not allowed to put on plays every day, so they alternated between pantomimes and musicals, for which the London stage is still famous.

There could be up to twenty thousand people in the theatre every night. A box cost a fortune, at least £2,500 for the season, while the cheapest tickets cost around 10 shillings per performance. In a theatre box, destinies played out. Family, friends, business associates or marriage connections would be invited. It was as much a showcase for talent as it was a hotbed of intrigue. The show wasn't just on stage; you were allowed to arrive late with great fanfare and you could speak out loud. At the Theatre Royal in Bath, built in 1805, or during visits to London, Jane Austen herself liked to mingle with this disparate crowd.

One of the key moments of *Mansfield* Park is undoubtedly the excitement of the play rehearsals. The chosen text is *Lovers' Vows*, by Elizabeth Inchbald. It is a very free adaptation of a German work by August von Kotzebue, *Das Kind der Liebe*, literally "The Child of Love"—first published in 1790. The English version was a huge success. Jane Austen must have seen it in Bath, where it was performed more than fifteen times during her time there. She didn't choose this play randomly. Each of the characters plays a role that reveals a great deal about either their own duplicity or their own naivety. The text of the play does not hesitate to deal with themes considered scandalous at the time: illegitimate children, forced marriages, carnal relations.

Did you know?

JANE AUSTEN WROTE A PLAY

During the Georgian era, it was not uncommon for people to perform in their own homes, with some well-to-do families even having their own small theatres. The Austens did not shy away from this and performed amusing family sketches, often written by a teenage Jane.

Sir Charles Grandison, or, The Happy Man: A Comedy in Five Acts, is a short play written by the novelist, probably between 1790 and 1800, to amuse her friends and family. In it, she parodies one of her favourite authors, Samuel Richardson. The work was long thought to be by Jane Anna Elizabeth Austen, the novelist's favourite niece, commonly called Anna, and also known as Anna Lefroy. She died in 1872 and bequeathed everything she owned of her famous aunt to her descendants. During the 1940s, one of Anna's granddaughters, Louie Langlois, found the original text of the play, which she believed to be by her grandmother, whose handwriting she said she recognised.

One of Jane Austen's most famous biographers, Lord David Cecil[58] had the honour of working on original manuscripts from the 1950s onwards. In autumn 1977, he was part of a team of researchers working on the play. Scientific examination of the paper provides irrefutable proof that the document dates from 1796, in the oldest section, where the handwriting is more youthful. Anna was born in 1793, so it is impossible that she was the author. Since 2004, this document has been the property of the Jane Austen Museum in Chawton.

Fun fact: this play inspired a film. James Ivory's *Jane Austen in Manhattan* (1980) tells the story of a troupe that stages the play in New York.

None of the *Mansfield Park* protagonists who engage in this performance are married and the audience wouldn't have expected them to talk about things considered saucy, especially the candid young ladies. *So shocking!* What should have been an innocent distraction becomes a controversial issue. Edmund and Fanny, aware of these breaches of morality, oppose the project.

Couples come and go, creating unease and confusion in this theatre of emotions. Although the subject may have seemed inappropriate and too daring for Fanny Price, it certainly wasn't for Jane Austen. The novelist had fun with this, using the pretext of the play to evoke these burning themes in the manner of an embedded narrative. With great humour, she lets her characters struggle with the hierarchy of propriety. In this failed attempt at fun, the scene should also be seen for what it is: a group of attractive young people, barely out of their teens, in pursuit of love. Some like each other, others reject each other, and in the cool of November, sensations and feelings are heightened. All things considered, *Mansfield Park* is nonetheless Jane Austen's most spirited novel.

ADAPTATIONS

There have only been two TV versions and one feature film of Mansfield Park. *This is definitely not Jane Austen's most inspiring novel.*

Mansfield Park, BBC, 1983, 261 minutes

This was the very first adaptation of the novel, and to date it is the most faithful. It was not until the 1980s that the BBC took an interest in the adventures of Fanny Price, forty-five years after the very first recorded Austen adaptation, in 1938. The rather long format takes the time to develop the plot over six episodes.

Directed by: David Giles

Script: Ken Taylor

Cast: Sylvestra Le Touzel (Fanny Price), Nicholas Farrell (Edmund Bertram), Anna Massey (Mrs. Norris), Angela Pleasence (Lady Bertram), Jackie Smith-Wood (Mary Crawford), Robert Burbage (Henry Crawford), Christopher Villiers (Tom Bertram), Samantha Bond (Maria Bertram), Jonathan Stephens (Mr. Rushworth), Allan Kedrick (William Price).

Anecdotes:

♦ Samantha Bond, who is playing her very first role in front of the camera here as Maria Bertram, also played Mrs. Weston in the ITV version of *Emma*, in 1996. She is also renowned for her appearances as Miss Moneypenny in several films in the *James Bond* franchise, and Lady Rosamund in *Downton Abbey*.

♦ In the small role of Charles Price, Fanny's younger brother, we recognise Jonny Lee Miller —aged ten during the filming— regular in costume films. He reappeared as Edmund Bertram in the 1999 film adaptation of *Mansfield Park*, and as George Knightley in the 2009 BBC mini-series *Emma*.

♦ Bernard Hepton, alias Lord Bertram, returned to Jane Austen's world in the role of Mr. Woodhouse, in the 1996 TV film *Emma*.

♦ Director David Giles also directed the 1971 BBC series *Sense and Sensibility*.

♦ Nicholas Farrell, pictured here as Edmund Bertram, plays Mr. Musgrove in the 2007 version of *Persuasion*.

Brympton House

Shooting locations:

- **Somerley**, on the border between Dorset and Hampshire - Jane Austen's native region - is the Bertram family's castle. The property can also be seen in the Netflix series *The Crown* and *Bridgerton*. Dating from the Georgian period, this residence has belonged to the Counts of Normaton since the 17th century. King Edward VII was a regular visitor, as godfather to the fifth Earl of Normaton. It is not open to the public and is only hired out for weddings, special events and film shoots. However, nine rooms are also available for tourists to rent, breakfast at the castle included!

  Information on somerley.com

- **Brympton House**, in Somerset, was described as "the most beautiful house in England" by the historian Christopher Hussey, a leading expert on British architecture. Eight hundred years of history have left their mark on this house, from its origins in 1220. The estate is generally not open to visitors, except for twenty-eight days, during which there is free admission to wander around by prior arrangement (calendar available online). In *Mansfield Park*, it serves as the backdrop for **Sotherton Court**, Mr. Rushworth's home. The property can also be seen in the 1994 BBC series *Middlemarch*, based on the work by George Eliot. You can also hire the property for a dream wedding, in which case all the information is available on the website: **brymptonhouse.co.uk**.

  Information on visitbrymptonhouse.com

Mansfield Park, BBC-Miramax, 1999, 112 minutes

This is the one and only film version of *Mansfield Park*.

Directed by: Patricia Rozema

Script: Patricia Rozema

Cast: Frances O'Connor (Fanny Price), Jonny Lee Miller (Edmund Bertram), Sheila Gish (Mrs. Norris), Lindsay Duncan (Lady Bertram), Embeth Davidtz (Mary Crawford), Alessandro Nivola (Henry Crawford), James Purefoy (Tom Bertram), Victoria Hamilton (Maria Bertram), Hugh Bonneville (Mr. Rushworth), Sophia Myles (Susan Price).

Anecdotes:

- We see Fanny Price writing short texts: these are *Juvenilia*, Jane Austen's early works. Patricia Rozema, the director, also wrote the script. She has taken a few liberties with the novel, particularly with the character of Fanny Price, who borrows a few elements from Jane Austen's life.

- Composer Lesley Barber wrote the music. But the director also called on Malian musician Salif Keïta to compose a moving song on the theme of slavery.

♦ Hugh Bonneville, famous for his character of Lord Grantham in *Downton Abbey*, plays Mr. Rushworth. He can also be seen as the Reverend Brook Bridges in *Miss Austen Regrets*, 2007, as well as Mr. Bennet in *Lost in Austen*, 2008.

♦ In this version, Lindsay Duncan plays both Lady Bertram and Fanny's mother, further emphasising their relationship. She also played the formidable Lady Catherine de Bourgh (a character from *Pride and Prejudice*) in *Lost in Austen*.

♦ The film chooses to erase the close relationship between Fanny Price and her brother William in favour of a strong bond between Fanny and her little sister Susan, played by Sophia Myles, an actress familiar with costume dramas.

♦ The role of Lord Thomas Bertram is played by the great British playwright and winner of the 2005 Nobel Prize for Literature, Harold Pinter.

Shooting locations:

♦ **Kirby Hall**, in Northamptonshire, the very region where *Mansfield Park* is set, becomes the Bertrams' home. This Elizabethan manor house, built in 1570, is managed by English Heritage, the organisation that also looks after the little blue plaques that can be seen all over London, indicating where famous people once lived. James I, Mary Stuart's son, was a regular visitor to the castle, which is now partly in ruins. However, some of the rooms still have some fine furniture, including a reproduction of a period four-poster bed,

EMBETH DAVIDTZ   JONNY LEE MILLER   ALESSANDRO NIVOLA   FRANCES O'CONNOR   HAROLD PINTER

MANSFIELD PARK

FOR EVERYONE WHO LOVED "EMMA" AND "SENSE & SENSIBILITY" COMES THE STORY JANE AUSTEN LOVED BEST.

and the gardens are well worth a visit. Kirby Hall can be visited all year round, at weekends and during school holidays.

Information at

english-heritage.org.uk/visit/places/kirby-hall/

Kirby Hall

♦ **Kenwood House**, in North London, is a place not to be missed if you're visiting the capital. Easily accessible and ideally situated in the heart of an immense park, the house dates back to the 17th century, and belonged to the line of the Earls of Mansfield until 1914. Later, as the upkeep was too high, the family sold off plots of land and then some of the furniture. In 1924, Edward Guinness, who had made his fortune as a brewer, bought the property, restored it and bequeathed it to English Heritage, on condition that it remained open to the public free of charge.

Kenwood House

The interior is truly spectacular, in particular the incredible library by Scottish architect Robert Adam, which dates back to the 18th century. The collection of master paintings is also worthy of a major museum. In the film, it's the beautiful mansion belonging to Mr. Rushworth. The estate's volunteer guides happily recount the anecdote that it was Kenwood House that also served as the model, in the novel, for the splendid Rushworth estate, **Southerton Court**.

Kenwood House can also be seen in Roger Michell's film *Notting Hill* (1999), starring Julia Roberts and Hugh Grant. The calendar of days when it is open is available online.

Information at

english-heritage.org.uk/visit/places/kenwood/

Mansfield Park, ITV, 2007, 88 minutes

The latest adaptation of the novel, it was also the first in a series of TV films to be made by ITV as part of the Jane Austen Season in spring 2007.[59]

Directed by: Ian B. MacDonald

Script: Maggie Wadey

Cast: Billie Piper (Fanny Price), Blake Ritson (Edmund Bertram), Maggie O'Neill (Mrs. Norris), Jemma Redgrave (Lady Bertram), Hayley Atwell (Mary Crawford), Joseph Beattie (Henry Crawford), James D'Arcy (Tom Bertram), Michelle Ryan (Maria Bertram), Rory Kinnear (Mr. Rushworth), Joseph Morgan (William Price).

Anecdotes:

♦ Blake Ritson (Edmund) returns in the role of Mr. Elton in the mini-series *Emma*, 2009. It is amusing to note that in both these roles, he is a man of the Church.

♦ Jemma Redgrave (Lady Bertram), niece of the famous actress Vanessa Redgrave, also plays Lady De Courcy in Whit Stillman's *Love & Friendship* (2016) (based on *Lady Susan*). Her uncle, Corin Redgrave, played Sir Walter Eliot in *Persuasion* in 1995. Her aunt Lynn Redgrave appeared in the film *The Jane Austen Book Club* (2007), based on the novel by Karen Joy Fowler. A family affair!

---

[59] It would be followed by *Northanger Abbey* and *Persuasion*.

Newby Hall

Shooting locations:

♦ **Newby Hall**, in Yorkshire, is the only known filming location for this TV film. The action focuses solely on the **Mansfield Park** estate, as the production budget was rather limited. The property is exceptional all the same: it has been in the Compton family for two hundred and fifty years. The current resident, Lord Richard Compton, is a friend of King Charles III, who has his own bedroom there, the Print Bedroom.[60] Newby Hall is an admirable concentration of English art and architecture. Construction began in 1690, under the direction of the famous architect of St Paul's Cathedral, Christopher Wren, and work continued with John Carr and Robert Adam. A little fun fact: Newby Hall has an impressive collection of around a hundred chamber pots, the oldest of which date back to the 16th century! The property was also the setting for *Peaky Blinders* (2012) and the *Victoria* series (2016). You can visit the house in summer, by reservation only.
Information on newbyhall.com

Did you know?

♦ There is a modern web series, dated 2014, inspired by *Mansfield Park*. Entitled *From Mansfield with Love*, is a ninety-six episode vlog featuring Holly Truslove as 'Frankie' Price. You can find out more online at **mansfieldseries.wixsite.com/ mansfieldwithlove**

♦ Also in 2014, BBC Four broadcast and recorded on CD a radio play of the complete text of *Mansfield Park*. There was a prestigious cast, including Amanda Root as the narrator, Felicity Jones as Fanny Price, Benedict Cumberbatch as Edmund Bertram, Jemima Rooper as Maria Bertram and David Tennant as Tom Bertram.

♦ Whit Stillman's film, *Metropolitan* (1991), broadly follows the plot of *Mansfield Park*, transposed to 1990s upmarket New York. The heroine, Audrey, is a committed Janeite. Whit Stillman has never hidden his admiration for the English novelist. To date, he is the only person to have adapted the epistolary short story *Lady Susan* under the title *Love & Friendship* in 2016.

WHEN *MANSFIELD PARK* INSPIRES CONTEMPORARY WRITERS

♦ *Edmund Bertram's Diary*, by Amanda Grange (Berkeley, 2008). This author is a specialist in Austen heroes, giving them a voice in the form of diaries.

♦ *Finley Embraces Heart & Home*, by Anyta Sunday (Anyta Sunday, 2021). This novel is the fourth volume in the *Love, Austen* series. This is a modern, gay and sultry adaptation of *Mansfield Park*.

♦ *Maria Bertram's Daughter*, by Lucy Knight (Meryton Press, 2022). Behind this pseudonym, Helen Crawford, an Englishwoman living in France, proposes a sequel to the original novel, a generation later. She imagines that Maria Bertram had a daughter, Dorothea Rose, whose eventful destiny we follow.

---

60 *Jane Austen's England: A Travel Guide*, by Karin Quint, ACC Art Books, 2019.

Emma

Emma, dear to Jane Austen's heart, is a young person for whom everything is wonderful, she is close to her father, and intelligent enough to accept criticism and challenge herself.

But above all, she discovers love right on her doorstep... Has the English novelist transposed her fantasy of an ideal life onto this delightfully annoying heroine?

Incipit 1816

Emma Woodhouse, handsome, clever, and rich, with a comfortable home and happy disposition, seemed to unite some of the best blessings of existence; and had lived nearly twenty-one years in the world with very little to distress or vex her.[61]

WHAT'S IT ABOUT?

In the small fictional town of Highbury in Surrey, everyone knows everyone else. At the top of the social pyramid, Emma is the focal point of all the plot lines. With this central position, she manipulates her little world without malice, believing she is acting for the benefit of her fellow human beings.

She becomes infatuated with Harriet Smith, a young girl of obscure birth. For Emma, Harriet can be nothing but a gentleman's daughter, so she treats her as such. She charitably decides to find her friend a husband. The lucky man would be Mr. Elton, the parish's new vicar. What Emma doesn't know is that he has his sights set much higher, on the jewel of the county, Emma herself. Emma has sworn never to marry, in order to remain with her father, whom she adores and mothers constantly.

From surprise to disappointment, from intrigue to secret, Emma's world and her deepest convictions are turned upside down. What if the young woman could, in spite of everything (and especially in spite of herself), find love? What if it had been there all along without her noticing? It is said that you only realise the value of what you have when you have lost it. Emma is about to find this out the hard way.

[61] *Emma*, John Murray, 1815.

Illustration from 1816 by Charles Edmond Brock. "So very kind!" replied Miss Bates. "But you are always kind."

A WOMAN'S PERSPECTIVE IN THE REGENCY PERIOD

In Jane Austen's time, a woman was always financially dependent on a father, husband, brother or, worse still, a distant cousin. In the gentry, a woman had virtually no employment opportunities, apart from as a lady's maid or rarely as a seamstress. Mrs. Bates and Miss Bates are striking examples of respectable ladies of the gentry who fell into poverty. When Pastor Bates dies, they find themselves thrown out of the rectory and almost left destitute. Becoming a governess, as Miss Taylor is for the Woodhouse girls, is a last resort. With the exception of Miss Taylor, who becomes the very respectable Mrs. Weston, it was almost impossible to climb the social ladder if you fell from grace. You could be a gentleman's daughter and still be disadvantaged. This is also the case for Jane Fairfax. Born into a good family, she is nonetheless poor. Orphaned, she owes her good education only to the generosity of one of her father's regimental friends. However, she looks for a job as a housekeeper, so as not to be a burden on her family. This is a recurring theme in Jane Austen's work, as she herself, along with her sister and their mother, found themselves in the care of the family's sons.

Character Gallery
THE LADIES

EMMA WOODHOUSE: **a rich, twenty-year-old girl.**
We have no physical description of Emma. All we know is that she's very beautiful and has hazel eyes. The loss of her mother was so long ago that she has no memory of it and has never suffered from it; the comforting presence of her governess, Miss Taylor, has been enough to keep her happy. She has an older sister, Isabella, who is already married. Emma experiences her first heartbreak when Miss Taylor marries and becomes Mrs. Weston. This was the beginning of her vocation as a matchmaker. Emma draws, sings and plays the pianoforte. Everyone around her agrees that she is gifted, although these compliments are not always impartial. She likes her life as it is, and doesn't want to change a thing, feeling perfectly content with her condition. Free, privileged and in control, she lives on the delightful estate of Hartfield with her father, who is accommodating and benevolent. This was the height of luxury for a young woman in 1815.

HARRIET SMITH: **Emma's new friend.**
Although Emma calls her by her Christian name, Harriet addresses her as "Miss Woodhouse", because she is older and socially superior to her. The seventeen-year-old is flattered by her friendship with the most popular lady in the county. A boarder in an institution for young girls, she does not know her father. We know she's not very tall, rather chubby, very pretty, fair-skinned, blonde with blue eyes. As the author derisively points out, it's not her intelligence that strikes you, but the gentleness in her eyes and her good manners. Harriet is a typical "ingenue" in all her glory. She becomes Emma's closest friend, and can refuse her nothing.

MRS. WESTON: **formerly Miss Taylor, governess to the Woodhouse girls.**
For Emma, she's the closest thing to a mother. She got married late in life, to a well-established local widower who had made his fortune in commerce. Symbolically, she is the "mother" who leaves home, instead of Emma, who is of marriageable age. She loves the young girl deeply, sees no faults in her and always praises her big heart.

MISS BATES: **a modest clergyman's daughter.**

Miss Bates lives mainly off the solidarity of her neighbours and friends, even though she has few pretensions. Sweet by nature, she admires Emma. Her sad, dull life leads her to rave about trivial things and to monopolise attention with petty trifles. She lives with her mother, Mrs. Bates, who is very discreet.

MISS JANE FAIRFAX: **Emma's alter ego and niece of Miss Bates.**

From a poor social background, she looks for a job as a governess. Jane is gifted at everything, especially the piano, where her technique and sensitivity shine through. She's tall, elegant, a little cold and reserved, with big grey eyes. There is an unspoken rivalry between her and Emma, particularly for the attention of a certain gentleman. Funnily enough, Jane Austen gave this character her own name.

MRS. AUGUSTA ELTON: **young wife of Mr. Elton.**

Born Augusta Hawkins, she takes the small community of Highbury by surprise. Rather pretty, moderately wealthy, she is full of herself and her origins, which she exaggerates. She is, after all, only the youngest daughter of a Bristol merchant. She quickly takes a liking to Emma, and the feeling is mutual.

Character Gallery
THE GENTLEMEN

MR. KNIGHTLEY: **friend and neighbour of the Woodhouses.**

His first name is George, but Emma calls him Mr. Knightley, as is customary. As the eldest son, he owns the prosperous family estate of Donwell Abbey. His younger brother, John, is married to Isabella Woodhouse, Emma's older sister. George Knightley is a gentleman of about thirty-seven or thirty-eight years old. Little more is known about his physical appearance. Intelligent and cheerful, he doesn't hesitate to tell Emma all that he thinks about her, especially when he doesn't like her behaviour, and he doesn't give her compliments easily. He also appreciates that Emma allows him this freedom of thought in her presence. He trusts their friendship enough to test its limits, but always with the utmost respect and courtesy. What's more, he's very rich!

MR. WOODHOUSE: **Isabella and Emma's father.**

Very attached to his daughters, he has a good heart. He's also a hypochondriac who's sensitive to the slightest thing. A wealthy widower, he has brought up his two daughters alone, with the help of Miss Taylor, the governess.

FRANK CHURCHILL: **a handsome young man of twenty-three.**

A jovial but frivolous young man, he is a son of Mr. Weston's first marriage. When as an infant his mother died, he was adopted by his wealthy maternal aunt and uncle, just as Jane Austen's brother Edward had been adopted by the Knight family. Emma enjoys their —apparently— harmless banter.

MR. ELTON: **Highbury's attractive new vicar.**

Taking over from Vicar Bates, he is described as handsome, well-mannered and articulate. His secret hope is to marry Emma, through whom he also hopes to develop socially. He spares no effort to achieve this.

ROBERT MARTIN: **young tenant farmer of Mr. Knightley.**

Aged twenty-four, he lives with his mother and two sisters. He loves to read, thanks to the influence of Harriet, with whom he is in love. Despite his inferior social position, he maintains a cordial relationship with his landlord, which is almost a friendship.

Emma IN A NUTSHELL

If I loved you less,
I might be able to talk
about it more.[62]

(Mr. Knightley)

He stopped to look the question.

Illustration by Hugh Thomson for an 1896 edition of *Emma*.

A BRIEF OVERVIEW

What if Emma was the image of the carefree young girl the novelist had always dreamed of being? Jane Austen wrote *Emma* in 1815. She was forty years old. We know very precisely from her correspondence that she began writing *Emma* on 21 January 1814 and finished on 29 March 1815. In August or September 1815, she handed the manuscript to her publisher, John Murray, in London. A few years later, James Edward Austen-Leigh, in his biography of his aunt, recalled that she wrote it in the drawing room of Chawton Cottage, constantly interrupted by the comings and goings of people and the sounds of everyday life. You can imagine Jane Austen like this, sitting in front of the window, writing on little scraps of paper with a pen, leaning over her mahogany desk.

[62] *Emma*, Jane Austen, John Murray, 1815, *op. cit.*

Somewhat overwhelmed by the success of *Sense and Sensibility* and *Pride and Prejudice*, she infused her whimsical and gentle irony into this new novel, striking the right note every time. This irony is based in part on the fact that the entire novel is told almost completely from Emma's point of view. Jane Austen does not hesitate to gently tease her main character. We know, however, that she was very attached to her. Indeed, Emma's creator describes her as "a heroine whom no one but myself will much like",[63] aware that the relative perfection of her life had to be balanced by her little blunders, which are themselves absorbed by the path she is taking to improve herself.

It is also Jane Austen's longest novel. But *Emma*'s world is a closed one. Two parishes, a handful of families, a few characters, love entanglements... This is the provincial world as Jane Austen knows it, as she experiences it. The narrowness of the plot leaves plenty of room for the study of characters, their little flaws and their big failings. Apart from a trip to Box Hill, which doesn't go as well as planned, the plot never leaves the fictional village of Highbury.

It is thought that for Highbury the novelist was inspired by the market town of Chilham, near Canterbury in Kent. The name says it all. This ingenious oxymoron reveals that this novel is like a theatre stage, enclosed and out of reach. In any case, it has the sense of a unified place. There is no profusion of words in Jane Austen's work; each one is weighed, deliberately chosen, measured even, like the many tiny clues that she delivers to the attentive reader. In this respect, *Emma* is without doubt her most accomplished novel.

However, Jane Austen's work was still published anonymously. The front cover declared, "By the author of *Pride and Prejudice*". The book was published at the end of 1815, on 23 December, which explains the official date of 1816. That same year, in March, *Emma* was translated into French for the first time, in four volumes, under the title *La Nouvelle Emma ou les Caractères Anglais du Siècle*. Also in 1816, the novel crossed the Atlantic for its first American edition, in Philadelphia. It is very likely that Jane Austen was never aware of this overseas following. Her surviving correspondence makes no mention of this.

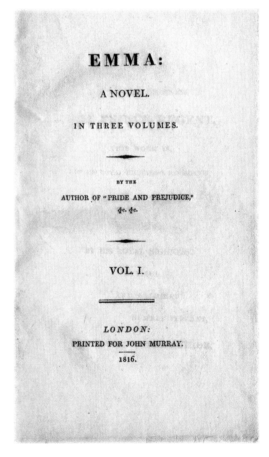

Title page of the first edition of *Emma*. 1815.

---

[63] *A Memoir of Jane Austen, op. cit.*

HISTORY

The Prince Regent

*E*mma is dedicated to the Prince Regent, the Prince of Wales, son of King George III and Queen Charlotte. George III suffered from fits of madness, probably due to a blood disease called porphyria. Considered unfit to govern, it fell to his eldest son to lead the country, under the aegis of Parliament, which signed the Regency Act (1811) in his favour, giving him full authority. In his youth, the Prince Regent was described as a handsome man. Quickly caught up in excesses of alcohol and food, he was not much appreciated by his subjects. A great fan of women, he neglected his own, his cousin, Princess Caroline of Brunswick, with whom he had a daughter, Charlotte.

The period known as the "Regency" in the strict sense - i.e. when the future George IV was Regent - covered the years 1811 to 1820. However, it is customary to date it from 1795, at the first signs of George III's illness, and to place its end in 1837, with the arrival in power of Queen Victoria. These forty years were marked by artistic, cultural and political renewal. One of the most iconic buildings of the era to have survived is undoubtedly Brighton's famous Royal Pavilion, built in the early 19th century. This seaside residence, imposing and exotic, was the setting for memorable banquets, where the Prince Regent liked to surround himself with courtiers. Nowadays, exhibitions are held here, including one devoted to Jane Austen, *Jane by the Sea,* in 2018.

In 1815, Jane Austen met the Prince Regent's librarian, the Reverend James Stanier Clarke, through her brother Henry. Henry Austen had revealed the secret of his sister's anonymity. To be singled out by a member of the Royal Family was an honour that could not be overlooked. In *A Memoir of Jane Austen,* by James Edward Austen-Leigh, the novelist's nephew, he refers to it as "the only mark of distinction ever bestowed upon her".[64] The Reverend told the novelist that His Highness was very fond of *Pride and Prejudice* and *Sense and Sensibility*. He had copies of

these novels in each of his homes. Was the Prince Regent, a Jane Austen "fanboy"? Yes! So much so, that he told her he wanted her to dedicate her next book to him. Jane Austen had no choice, even though she despised the man. She dedicated *Emma* to him, but she used her most powerful weapon, derision, calling herself "a dutiful, obedient and humble servant". The adjective "royal" is used three times, as if to emphasise her status as a mere subject, compared with that of the all-powerful Prince Regent.

Subsequent events confirmed the Prince Regent's interest. He asked James Stanier Clarke to put himself at Jane Austen's disposal during her stay in the capital.

TO

HIS ROYAL HIGHNESS

THE Prince Regent.

THIS WORK IS, BY HIS ROYAL

HIGHNESS'S PERMISSION,

MOST RESPECTFULLY

DEDICATED,

BY

HIS ROYAL HIGHNESSES'S DUTIFUL

AND OBEDIENT

HUMBLE

SERVANT.[65]

THE AUTHOR

---

[64]*A Memoir of Jane Austen, op. cit.*
[65]*Emma, op. cit.*

He invited her to visit the library and the royal flats at Carlton House, a luxurious London residence. The librarian took the opportunity to suggest that Jane Austen should start writing an historical novel about the Saxe-Coburg family, as a present for the Prince Regent's son-in-law, Prince Leopold. The offer was politely declined by the novelist in a letter imbued with the irony and self-mockery that have become her trademark. But a correspondence developed between her and the librarian, who didn't hesitate to offer her his advice and ideas for books and writing lessons. She poked fun at this in a series of short parodies she entitled *Plan of a Novel According to Hints from Various Quarters*. As for the Prince Regent, we can only imagine that he was delighted to receive preview copies of *Emma*, bound in red and gold Morocco leather, no doubt flattered by this lavish dedication to his credit. These first editions are now at Windsor Castle, since Carlton House was destroyed in 1825.

A BRIEF HISTORY

Charlotte, only daughter of the Prince Regent, was heir to the throne of England. The beautiful young princess was extremely popular. Like her father, she loved Jane Austen's novels, and her favourite character was Marianne Dashwood. She married Leopold of Saxe-Coburg, the future King of the Belgians, which was a love match. Sadly, she died the same year as Jane Austen, in 1817, in tragic circumstances: at the age of twenty-one, with her child, a boy, during a harrowing birth. People were in shock, as were her parents and husband, who were grief-stricken. This tragedy finally raised awareness of the need to care for women in childbirth. At that time, none of King George III's sons had any descendants. And yet he was father to fifteen children! Some of them, like Edward, the Duke of Kent, rushed to get married. In 1819, he became the father of a young girl, Victoria, who was to leave an indelible mark on her country.

ADAPTATIONS

Emma, BBC, 1948, 105 minutes

This is the very first black and white adaptation of the novel. At the time, television productions were filmed and simultaneously broadcast live. So there was no room for error! Filming took place exclusively in studios. Unfortunately, all traces of this recording have been lost, apart from a few photos.

Directed by: Michael Barry

Script: Judy Campbell

Cast: Judy Campbell (Emma Woodhouse), Ralph Michael (George Knightley), Daphne Slater (Harriet Smith), Joyce Heron (Jane Fairfax), O. B. Clarence (Mr. Woodhouse), MacDonald Hobley (Frank Churchill), Gillian Lind (Miss Bates), Susan Richmond (Miss Taylor/Mrs. Weston).

Anecdotes:

- The lead role was played by stage actress Judy Campbell, who also wrote the screenplay. You may think you don't know her, but you do! She chose to name her daughter Jane, after Jane Austen. She is the mother of singer and actress Jane Birkin.

- English actress Daphne Slater lends her voice to three major Austen characters. First of all, Harriet Smith in this version of *Emma*. She also played the iconic role of Elizabeth Bennet in the 1952 BBC mini-series *Pride and Prejudice*. Additionally, she played Anne Elliot in the first adaptation of *Persuasion*, in 1960.

Emma, BBC, 1960, 180 minutes

It is known that this six-part television version has completely disappeared, even from the BBC archives.

Directed by: Campbell Logan

Script: Vincent Tilsley

Cast: Diana Fairfax (Emma Woodhouse), Paul Daneman (George Knightley), Perlita Neilson (Harriet Smith), Petra Davies (Jane Fairfax), Leslie French (Mr. Woodhouse), David McCallum (Frank Churchill), Gillian Lind (Miss Bates), Thea Holme (Miss Taylor/Mrs. Weston).

Anecdotes:

- The cast includes Gillian Lind in the role of Miss Bates, a role she played in the very first adaptation of *Emma*, in 1948.

- Australian actress Diana Fairfax returned as another Austen character, Mrs. Dashwood, in *Sense and Sensibility*, in 1981.

- As for the men, the role of Mr. Knightley was played by Paul Daneman, who returned to Jane Austen's world in 1960 as Frederick Wentworth in *Persuasion*.

Emma, BBC, 1972, 240 minutes

This mini-series is the first *Emma* in colour, and it is also one of the longest versions, with six forty-minute episodes.

Directed by: John Glenister

Script: Denis Constanduros

Cast: Doran Godwin (Emma Woodhouse), John Carson (George Knightley), Debbie Bowen (Harriet Smith), Ania Marson (Jane Fairfax), Donald Eccles (Mr. Woodhouse), Robert East (Frank Churchill), Constance Chapman (Miss Bates), Ellen Dryden (Miss Taylor/Mrs. Weston).

Anecdotes:

- Particular attention was paid to the costumes, especially the actresses' outfits, which were reused in other historical productions, notably *Pride and Prejudice* in 1980.

- The screenwriter, Denis Constanduros, went on to write the script for *Sense and Sensibility* for the BBC in 1981.

Did you know?
JANE AUSTEN AND CHURCHILL

Winston Churchill never concealed his admiration for the English novelist. He read her works to give himself courage in times of crisis, in particular *Sense and Sensibility* and *Pride and Prejudice*. But did you know that his daughter Sarah Churchill was an actress and had the opportunity to play the role of Emma? It was in 1957, on the American channel NBC, on *Matinee Theater*. Extracts from plays filmed in the studio were broadcast live, mostly in colour and in costume. We do not know if there is any trace of this particular episode. However, some of these programmes have been preserved by the Library of Congress in Washington. The episodes lasted an hour, and were broadcast almost daily from 3pm to 4pm. The show was very popular on American television throughout its run from 1955 to 1958.

Location: This is the first version of *Emma* for which we have some information about the filming location.

- The **Uppark House** estate at Petersfield in Sussex dates back to the 17th century. It serves as the exterior for **Hartfield**, the Woodhouse family house. The woods, park and house are managed by the

Uppark House

National Trust and can be visited. The owners live on the estate, which is why only a small part of it is open to the public. You can admire a beautiful doll's house there dating back to the 18th century. Near the cosy tea room in the orangery, you can enjoy the second-hand bookshop in the former laundry room. In 1888, the British writer H. G. Wells, then aged twenty, spent the winter there convalescing. He was already familiar with the estate, as his parents worked there when he was a child. The writer made the most of the fabulous library, as well as the telescope. It was undoubtedly a source of inspiration for his novel *The War of the Worlds* (1897). The house is closed for part of the winter.

For more information, visit nationaltrust.org.uk/visit/sussex/uppark-house-and-garden

Emma ITV version, 1996, 107 minutes

Andrew Davies wrote the screenplay, as he had done a year earlier for *Pride and Prejudice,* starring Colin Firth. Kate Beckinsale plays a lively, slightly irritating Emma, as we know her from the novel.

Directed by: Diarmuid Lawrence

Script: Andrew Davies

Cast: Kate Beckinsale (Emma Woodhouse), Mark Strong (George Knightley), Samantha Morton (Harriet Smith), Olivia Williams (Jane Fairfax), Bernard Hepton (Mr. Woodhouse), Raymond Coulthard (Frank Churchill), Prunella Scales (Miss Bates), Samantha Bond (Miss Taylor/ Mrs. Weston).

Anecdotes:

• In 1997, this TV film won two awards at the prestigious Emmy Awards ceremony in Hollywood, in the Best Set Design and Best Costume Design categories.

• The cast includes actress Olivia Williams in the role of Jane Fairfax, who would also play Jane Austen in the 2008 TV film *Miss Austen Regrets.*

• Alistair Petrie, portraying Robert Martin, appears in the Netflix series *Sex Education.* Connor Swindells, also in *Sex Education* —they play father and son in fact— took the role of Robert Martin in the 2020 version of *Emma.*

Shooting locations:

• The elegant **Trafalgar Park**, in Wiltshire, is the setting for the beautiful Woodhouse family home, **Hartfield**. This Georgian country house, previously known as Standlynch Park, dates back to 1733 and belonged to the brother of the famous Admiral Nelson, the Reverend William Nelson. The estate is private and cannot be visited. It is regularly used as a film location. It can also be seen in *Sense and Sensibility* in 1995, as Barton Park, the home of Mrs. Dashwood's cousins.

• If you want to follow the trail of this version of *Emma,* you can visit **Broughton Castle**, the medieval manor house of the Fiennes family, where Nathaniel and Mariette also hold the titles of Lord and Lady Saye and Sele. The property has been in the same family since 1448. Located near Banbury, north of Oxford, this castle, built between the 14th and 15th centuries, is the setting for **Donwell Abbey**, Mr. Knightley's estate. Please note that visits are by prior arrangement only, as the property is inhabited.

Information on broughtoncastle.com

Broughton Castle

Emma, Miramax, 1996, 240 minutes

This is *Emma*'s very first adaptation for the big screen. This American production has an undeniable glamorous side, with a seductive couple created by the main actors.

Directed by: Douglas McGrath

Script: Douglas McGrath

Cast: Gwyneth Paltrow (Emma Woodhouse), Jeremy Northam (George Knightley), Toni Collette (Harriet Smith), Polly Walker (Jane Fairfax), Denys Hawthorne (Mr. Woodhouse), Ewan McGregor (Frank Churchill), Sophie Thompson (Miss Bates), Greta Scacchi (Miss Taylor/Mrs. Weston).

Anecdotes:

- Actresses considered for the role of Emma included Nicole Kidman, Diane Lane, Joely Richardson and Jenny Garth.

- Greta Scacchi, a regular in costume films, plays Mrs. Weston in this film. Twelve years later she played Cassandra Austen in *Miss Austen Regrets*.

- In 1997, Rachel Portman became the first female composer to win an Oscar® for Best Score for the soundtrack.

- Mrs. Bates and Miss Bates, mother and daughter in the novel and the film, are also mother and daughter in real life, played respectively by Phyllida Law and Sophie Thompson, Emma Thompson's mother and sister. For the record, the casting director claimed that he didn't know they were related.

Shooting locations:

- **Donwell Abbey** took on the appearance of the Georgian gem **Claydon House**. A symbol of 18th century extravagance, it boasts some of the most extraordinary interiors in England, including double-height rooms with richly carved ceilings. Owned by the Verney family for over four hundred years, the manor house and gardens are open to the public and managed by the National Trust. In the afternoons, you can enjoy a delicious tea in the Phoenix Kitchen café. The estate is located to the north-east of Oxford, in

Buckinghamshire.

Information at claydonestate.co.uk/your-visit/claydon-house

- **Mapperton,** in Beaminster, Dorset, which is also known as one of England's finest manor houses, was the setting for **Hartfield's** gardens, the Woodhouse estate, as well as the interiors for **Randalls**, the Weston home. This manor house, whose construction began in the 11th century, now belongs to the Earl and Countess of Sandwich. Their ancestor, the Fourth Earl of Sandwich, is famous for putting a piece of roast beef between two slices of bread during a never-ending game of cards. Well, it's actually his valet you have to thank for that! Like many stately homes, Mapperton is closed during the winter season.

Information on mapperton.com

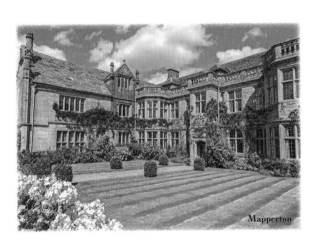

Mapperton

Emma, BBC version, 2009, 240 minutes

This version of *Emma* is spirited and joyful, and owes much to the chemistry between the two main actors, Romola Garai and Jonny Lee Miller. Over the course of four episodes, it takes the time to develop the plot and maximise the number of interactions between the various characters.

Directed by: Jim O'Hanlon

Script: Sandy Welch

Cast: Romola Garai (Emma Woodhouse), Jonny Lee Miller (George Knightley), Louise Dylan (Harriet Smith), Laura Pyper (Jane Fairfax), Michael Gambon (Mr. Woodhouse), Rupert Evans (Frank Churchill), Tamsin Greig (Miss Bates), Jodhi May (Miss Taylor/Mrs. Weston).

Anecdotes:

♦ The screenplay is by Sandy Welch, who also wrote the mini-series *Jane Eyre* (BBC, 2006), based on Charlotte Brontë's novel. She began writing the script for *Emma* in 1995 for the BBC, but the release of the film starring Gwyneth Paltrow and the ITV film starring Kate Beckinsale delayed the adaptation by ten years.

♦ In 2011, Romola Garai received her first nomination in the Best Actress category at the American Golden Globes, thanks to this role.

♦ Romola Garai and Rupert Evans (Frank Churchill) performed the song "The Bluebells of Scotland", written by Dora Jordan in 1800. Dora Jordan, author and actress, is known for having had ten illegitimate children with one of her lovers, the Duke of Clarence, third son of King George III.

♦ Lucie Briars, who plays Mrs Reynolds, the housekeeper, also played Mary Bennet in *Pride and Prejudice* (BBC 1995).

Shooting locations:

♦ One of the main filming locations is the picturesque Kent village of **Chilham**, which is supposed to be **Highbury**. If you happen to be visiting Canterbury, we strongly advise you to make the seven mile diversion. The village is still very much in its original state. It also appeared in some episodes of Agatha Christie's *Hercule Poirot* and *Miss Marple*. The central area of the village is called "The Square". For the shoot, the film crew covered the ground with gravel to hide the traces of the 21st century, and even installed a fountain. The village is very small, but has plenty of places to stay, such as The Church Mouse tea rooms and The White Horse pub, which dates back to the 16th century. Chilham castle is not open to the public. The gardens are, but only in fine weather. The house was built in 1616, on the site of the old castle, and has been owned by the Wheeler family since 2002.

♦ **Loseley Park**, in Guildford, in the beautiful region of Surrey –"the garden of England" in Mrs. Elton's words[66]– is the home of Mr. Knightley, **Donwell Abbey**. The gardens and manor house can only be visited during the summer months (April to August for the gardens, May to July for the interior) but can be hired out for major events, such as weddings. This immense estate, over five hundred years old, now belongs to Alexander and Sophia More-Molyneux. You can dine in the White Garden tearoom.

Information on loseleypark.co.uk

---

[66] *Emma, op.cit.*

Emma., cinema version, 2020, 124 minutes

Anya Taylor-Joy's mischievous performance and the hilarious portrayal of Miss Bates by Miranda Hart, a well-known British comedian, give this version a very funny, offbeat edge. Note the dot after the name Emma in the film's title. It's a little play on words suggested by the film's director, Autumn de Wilde. In American English, the term "period" means a full stop. Since this kind of adaptation is what we call a "period drama", this full stop is a reference to this.

Directed by: Autumn de Wilde

Script: Eleanor Catton

Cast: Anya Taylor-Joy (Emma Woodhouse), Johnny Flynn (George Knightley), Mia Goth (Harriet Smith), Amber Anderson (Jane Fairfax), Bill Nighy (Mr. Woodhouse), Callum Turner (Frank Churchill), Miranda Hart (Miss Bates), Gemma Whelan (Miss Taylor/Mrs. Weston).

Anecdotes:

♦ Screenwriter Eleanor Catton is a New Zealand author whose second novel, *The Luminaries*, was an international bestseller. She admitted that she had never read *Emma* before being recruited for the film.

♦ Johnny Flynn, born in South Africa, is also a singer, songwriter and composer, with his group Johnny Flynn and the Sussex Wit. He wrote and sang the end credits song, "Queen Bee".

♦ The film poster was designed by Autumn de Wilde, who is also a photographer.

♦ The film is notable for a nosebleed scene at a key moment. This detail is a reference to Autumn de Wilde herself, who suffers from frequent epistaxis. Anya Taylor-Joy got a real nosebleed in this scene, which she was very proud of. We don't know the secret of this nosebleed to order!

♦ Anya Taylor-Joy wore a replica of the topaz cross that Charles Austen gave to his sisters Jane and Cassandra in 1801.

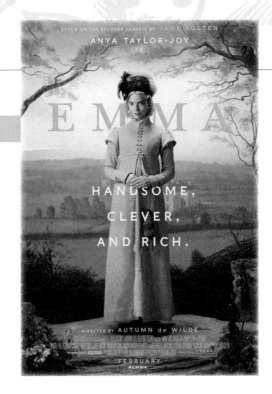

Shooting locations:

♦ **Donwell Abbey,** Mr. Knightley's home is just one of the magnificent places to visit, as is the fabulous **Wilton House,** built on the site of a 9th century convent, in the heart of twenty-one hectares of landscaped parkland. One of the treasures of this venue is undoubtedly the famous Double Cube Room. This piece is a work of art of perfect proportions: eighteen metres long, nine metres wide, nine metres high, a real "double cube". On the wall, a gigantic painting by Van Dyck depicts the fourth Duke of Pembroke and his family. Their descendants own Wilton House today. The estate has regularly been used as a film location for a number of historical films, including *Sense and Sensibility* (1995) and *Pride and Prejudice* (2005), for some interior scenes. Open from May to August, Wilton House is in Wiltshire, near Salisbury. You can have lunch at the friendly Wilton House café, where the local organic ice creams are well worth the trip!

Information on wiltonhouse.co.uk

Wilton House

Chavenage House

◆ **Chavenage House,** in Tetbury, Gloucestershire, is the Westons' home. This beautiful residence also features in the *Poldark* series. Built in the 9th century, before the Norman invasion, the estate belonged to the Godwin family. It was then inhabited by a community of Augustinian monks from Tours, France, before being passed down from generation to generation in the Stephens family, originally from Saint-Étienne, who had bought it at the time of William the Conqueror. It now belongs to the Lowsley-Williams family. Chavenage House can be hired for weddings and visited all year round, but only by prior arrangement, as the family live on site. The Wild Carrot café serves delicious meals here!

For more information, visit chavenage.com

◆ **Firle Place,** Sussex, is used as the Woodhouse family home. This splendid Tudor manor house boasts over five hundred years of history. Since its origins, it has belonged to the Gage family, descendants of a Norman baron who was one of William the Conqueror's companions. Firle Place has one of the most impressive private collections of master paintings, furniture and porcelain, as well as rare tapestries from the Manufacture Royale de Beauvais dating from the late 17th century. The residence, gardens and tea room are only accessible during the summer season.

For more information, visit firle.com

◆ A key scene in *Emma* is the excursion to **Box Hill**. The place really does exist, in Tadworth, Surrey. It's a good place for a walk and a picnic, with memorable views over the region, especially in fine weather. It is managed by the National Trust. In the film, this scene was not shot at the actual location, but at **Leith Hill**, also in Surrey but some 18 miles from the site of the real Box Hill. This location was more convenient for filming and the locations look almost identical.

For more information, visit nationaltrust.org.uk/visit/surrey/box-hill

THE PICNIC AT BOX HILL

What would people eat at a countryside party in the Regency period? Ladies and gentlemen were, of course, completely relieved of domestic duties, as the organisation and preparation of such an event rested solely with the household staff. The staff were responsible for preparing the meals and the equipment needed to ensure the comfort of all the guests. Here is a typical menu from the time:

⤞ MENU ⤟
A Countryside party at Box Hill

For starters:
Vegetable bites
Salmagundi

Main courses:
Pork loin
Roast chicken
Meat pies
Cold meats

Desserts:
Fruit and nuts
Syllabub

Drinks:
Tea, with cream and sugar
Sparkling fruit juice
Light wine

Salmagundi (the word is derived from the French "salmigondis") is a sort of mixture usually made up of salad, meat, seafood, vegetables, flowers, condiments and spices.
Syllabub is a much-loved dessert, invented in the 17th century. Made from curdled cream with fruit juice, it is spiced up with a light alcoholic drink, such as cider or a splash of port.

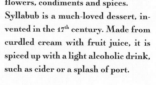

Did you know?

• A Spanish Emma? Yes, there was one! A five-part series was broadcast on Spanish television in 1967 and shot under live conditions.

• The film *Clueless,* released in 1995 and directed by the American Amy Heckerling, starring Alicia Silverstone and Paul Rudd, offers a modernised version of *Emma*. This was the era of the first mobile phones. Emma's name is Cher Horowitz. She is the daughter of a wealthy Californian lawyer. The film went on to inspire a television series from 1996 to 1999, a video game in 2007, a comic book in 2017, and a musical in 2018.

• *Aisha* by Rajshree Ojha, released in 2010, is an Indian version inspired both by the plot of Jane Austen's novel and the film *Clueless* for its contemporary feel.

• There was a web series called *Emma Approved,* starring Joanna Sotomura and Brent Bailey. The seventy-two episodes, each around five to seven minutes long, have been available on YouTube since 2013. Created by Bernie Su, via his Pemberley Digital channel, this series modernises Emma as a life coach who meddles in her friends' love lives.

• In 2015, actress, writer and producer Kelsey O'Brien brought the world of *Emma* to contemporary New York, to the LGBTQIA+ and Wiccan communities with *Enchantments*. A sequel, *Love Magick,* was released in February 2023.

• On a specialist streaming site, you can watch a modernised musical of *Emma* (2018) by Paul Gordon. Link: **streamingmusicals.com.**

WHEN *EMMA* INSPIRES CONTEMPORARY WRITERS

• *Mr. Knightley's Diary* by Amanda Grange (Berkley, 2007). This is a nice variation on the original novel, from the point of view of Mr. Knightley, revealing the secrets of his heart through his diary.

• *Emma: A Modern Retelling* by Alexander McCall Smith (Anchor, 2015). The author of *The Peppermint Tea Chronicles* took a humorous look at Emma in this modern rewrite, while also respecting the plot of the original novel.

• *Emma: An Emotions Primer* by Jennifer Adams and Alison Oliver (BabyLit, 2015). This adorable picture book uses *Emma*'s storyline to help children learn about emotions.

• *Emma* exists in manga! The drawings are by Po Tse, in a highly colourful style. The text follows the plot of the novel in a simplified form, for fans of the genre! (Manga Classics, 2018).

• *Emma* is also available in Marvel comic books. Adapted by Nancy Butler and illustrated by Janet Lee, the series comprises five volumes. (Marvel, Limited series, 2011)

• *Emma*, the play. A French theatrical version of *Emma,* performed in the Paris area in 2007 by the Compagnie du Phénix and adapted and directed by Karima Djelid, focuses on the love triangle. It takes place in a single location, the garden. (Books on Demand, 2019)

• *Emerett has Never Been in Love,* by Anyta Sunday. A modern, gay version of *Emma,* part of the *Love, Austen* collection. (Anyta Sunday, 2022).

Northanger Abbey

Northanger Abbey is often presented as an entertaining parody of the Gothic novel genre, but this story is much more than that. Jane Austen makes a plea, through her own words and those of her characters. She dares the occasional use of the first person at the very heart of the narrative to defend romance literature against prejudice. Because, yes, in those days, writing a novel —especially if you were a woman— was not particularly well regarded or respectable. This bold stylistic choice and this "mise en abyme" device make *Northanger Abbey* her most subversive work.

Incipit 1818

No one who had ever seen Catherine Morland in her infancy would have supposed her born to be an heroine. Her situation in life, the character of her father and mother, her own person and disposition, were all equally against her.[67]

WHAT'S IT ABOUT?

Catherine Morland is a candid young woman with a lot to learn. The opportunity to experience adventure arises when her neighbours, Mr. and Mrs. Allen, invite her to spend a few weeks in Bath. Welcoming this news with joy, she leaves the family and her monotonous daily routine to sample the charm and entertainment of the spa town.

On her arrival, Catherine meets Isabella and her brother John Thorpe, as well as Henry Tilney and his sister Eleanor. Determined to make the most of every moment, she goes to balls, takes walks and visits her new friends. But nothing prepares her for the reality and the shortcomings of society. Her profound naivety and fertile imagination regularly lead her into embarrassing situations. From excitement to disillusionment, the discovery of this new world turns the young woman's expectations and convictions upside down. Will she be able to learn from her mistakes and live up to the role of heroine?

[67] *Northanger Abbey*, John Murray, 1818.

Character Gallery
THE LADIES

CATHERINE MORLAND: **a seventeen-year-old girl.**
Catherine Morland is the archetypal heroine of a novel who goes from being an ugly duckling to a graceful swan. During her childhood, she didn't display the qualities of an accomplished young girl. Boisterous, clumsy and skinny, she preferred to roll around in the grass rather than learn the rudiments of French or arithmetic, even though her parents gave her an education. But at fifteen, the wild little girl with dull hair and coarse features emerged from her chrysalis. Her metamorphosis is motivated by her desire to finally attend a ball. She begins paying attention to her grooming, curling her hair. Now both charming and elegant, she realises that those around her refer to her as a pretty girl. Her affectionate heart and affability complete her transformation. Although still ignorant and immature, Catherine is nevertheless eager to learn and make progress.

ISABELLA THORPE: **twenty-one years old, the eldest of the Thorpe sisters.**
Everyone recognises Isabella's great beauty and beautiful manners. The young woman is elegant and her appearance is very important to her. She loves fashion and Gothic novels and regularly discusses them with her new friend, Catherine. While Isabella appears to be listening to the people she is talking to, in reality she constantly makes the discussion about herself. She loves attention above all else.

ELEANOR TILNEY: **twenty-two years old, youngest of the Tilney family.**
Eleanor has great elegance, a pretty face and, above all, delightful manners. What's more, her education, intelligence and modest nature are widely recognised. Although not an extrovert, she is not shy either, which makes her pleasant company. Eleanor gets on very well with her brother Henry. She is grateful to him for coming to see her regularly at the abbey, where there was little to entertain her.

MRS. MORLAND: **mother of James and Catherine.**
As a mother, Mrs. Morland is kind and good-natured, but she's not very well educated. With a strong constitution, Mrs. Morland gave birth to no fewer than ten children. Very attached to them, she experiences great sadness on the two days before Catherine's departure for Bath, and advises her not to catch a cold and to be vigilant with regard to the nobles and baronets who might perpetrate violence against her.

MRS. ALLEN: **the Morland family's neighbour.**
This woman has no beauty and no talent. She is empty-minded and not inclined to think for herself. Her easy-going character and calm demeanour nevertheless attract sympathy. Mrs. Allen is excited about going to Bath. Being within walking distance of a clothes shop is a dream for her, as she is obsessed with clothing.

MRS. THORPE: **mother of Isabella and John.**
An old friend and schoolmate of Mrs. Allen, Mrs. Thorpe is now a widow without a penny to her name. She has an excellent character and her main concern is her children. She is so proud of her offspring that she never stops praising them. Two other sons are briefly mentioned: Edward, a student at a public school, and William, a sailor. Anne and Maria, just as charming as their eldest daughter Isabella, complete the family picture.

Character Gallery
THE GENTLEMEN

HENRY TILNEY: **a young man of twenty-five.**
This man, while not remarkably handsome, is tall, charming and distinguished. He has a dark complexion, black eyes and brown hair. Henry is friendly, cheerful and very lively. To add to these pleasures, he is a good dancer, intelligent and well-educated. Jane Austen does not skimp on Henry's merits, and he seems to be an almost flawless hero. Tormenting the naïve Catherine Morland is one of the little mischievous tricks to which he has become so accustomed. Catherine, innocent and too gullible, doesn't always immediately understand the secondary meaning. But she doesn't take offence, enjoying his company. Henry is a member of a respectable Gloucestershire family. He works as a clergyman in a rectory in Woodston, where he lives with several dogs. He reads a lot and, extraordinarily, he's second to none when it comes to giving an opinion on the quality of a muslin.

JOHN THORPE: **Isabella's brother and a friend of James Morland.**
This young man is not distinguished by any particular physical qualities. Of average height, John is neither graceful nor handsome, and his attire doesn't help matters. His topics of discussion are carriages, horses, dogs, hunting and money. He loves to boast about all the deals he makes. He is rude and unpleasant to his younger sisters.

JAMES MORLAND: **Catherine's elder brother.**
Although he plays a fairly important role in the novel, we learn very little about James. All we know about him is that he's not very good-looking. He has a close friendship with John Thorpe, whom he met at Oxford. He also has a very good relationship with the Thorpe family, where he spent the last Christmas holidays. He is not particularly close to his sister Catherine, but their reunion in Bath is a warm one.

MR. MORLAND: **father of James and Catherine.**
Richard Morland is a clergyman who is highly respected by his parishioners. He has two ecclesiastical parishes and a considerable fortune. He lives with his wife in Fullerton.

MR. ALLEN: **the Morland family's neighbour.**
Intelligent and honourable, Mr. Allen owns most of the land around Fullerton and, with his wife, lives a stone's throw from the Morland family, with whom they enjoy a good relationship.

GENERAL TILNEY: **Henry's father.**
Mr. Tilney's dual personality leaves his listeners perplexed. Physically, he is tall and very handsome, with good manners. His rank as a general gives him an authoritarian air, and he is pleasant in society. Nevertheless, he is harsh with his daughter, Eleanor, and short-tempered with the servants. He has no sympathy for any lack of punctuality. When this happens, he can become unbearable, flying into a terrible rage. He owns almost all the land around Northanger Abbey along with two vicarages, including the one in which Henry works. He loves gardening and wandering around his gardens and large greenhouses.

CAPTAIN FREDERICK TILNEY: **Henry's elder brother.**
Handsome as he is, the captain never fails to attract the attention of everyone he meets. Nevertheless, he possesses fewer qualities than his brother and sister. His manners are not engaging and his features reveal a certain arrogance. He is proud and thinks above all of his own pleasure.

[I]t is well to have as many holds upon happiness as possible.[68]
(Henry Tilney)

Northanger Abbey
IN A NUTSHELL

A BRIEF OVERVIEW

Although *Northanger Abbey* dates from 1818, the origin of the novel can be traced back to 1798-1799. Jane Austen's imagination was boundless. After writing the first versions of *Pride and Prejudice* and *Sense and Sensibility*, at the age of twenty-three or twenty-four she began work on her third book, then entitled *Susan*, the original name she gave the character of Catherine Morland. By midsummer 1799, the novel was finished. However, a few years later, between 1802 and 1803, she went back to her manuscript and made a few changes. Jane Austen put the finishing touches to her story, which is the shortest of her completed novels, and was satisfied. The next step was publication, but there were many obstacles.

The first attempt. In the summer of 1803, Henry Austen's lawyer, William Seymour, undertook to sell *Susan* and found a buyer with a London publisher, Crosby & Co. The deal was concluded for £10, or around £1,500 in today's money. Richard Crosby therefore held the rights to the novel. He was quick to promote it, and had it listed as "Being Printed" in *Flowers of Literature*, a commercial collection of book extracts and biographies for the publishing world. But this announcement was a lie. The book never went to press and never saw the light of day. At the end of the 18th century, the Gothic novel genre was in vogue. To publish a satire of this kind would have been to act against his own interests and would probably have been a commercial failure. In these circumstances, we can assume that this was the reason why Crosby decided not to publish *Susan*.

The second attempt. Determined to bring the project to fruition, Jane Austen contacted the publisher again in 1809. She wrote to him in April, reminding him that he had bought the rights to her novel and that it was stipulated that it should be published as soon as possible. She offered to send him a copy in case it was lost "through some negligence".[69] She put him on the spot and told him that if he didn't respond, she would take the liberty of submitting it to another publisher.

[68] *Northanger Abbey*, Jane Austen, John Murray, 1815. *Northanger Abbey*, *op. cit.*
[69] *Jane Austen's Letters*, Deirdre Le Faye, *op. cit.*

"Yours truly..." or *"I am yours ..."* was the standard form of address in letters. To her publisher, Jane Austen signed using an alias, Mrs. Ashton Dennis, and indulged in a little wordplay. With a hint of sarcasm, she uses the acronym of this pseudonym to conclude:

[...] I am Gentlemen & c & c

MAD. -

Crosby was quick to respond. Three days later, he wrote that no specific clause had been drawn up and that he was under no obligation to publish the novel. He also warned her that if the manuscript was sold to another publisher, he would take the necessary steps to prevent the sale. To end the matter, he suggested she buy the book back, for the sum he had paid five years earlier. But that was not the end of the story. Jane Austen couldn't afford it.

The third attempt. In 1816, Jane Austen's first two novels were published. It is likely that the success of the sales and the profits received led her to buy the rights to *Susan* back. Henry took it upon himself to meet Crosby and negotiate the purchase of the rights to the novel. According to James Edward Austen-Leigh, Jane Austen's nephew, the publisher was in a hurry to agree to the deal. When the deal was done, Henry proudly revealed that the novel that had gathered dust for years was written by the author of *Sense and Sensibility* and *Pride and Prejudice*. Imagine the shock and despair in Crosby's eyes! Before proposing it for publication, Jane Austen changed the name of her character Susan to Catherine, and consequently also changed the title. We can assume that she made this choice, because in June 1809 another book entitled *Susan* was published by an anonymous author. Her heroine could therefore no longer be called by that name, at the risk of causing confusion.

The novelist was also aware that society had changed. As a result, she wrote a preface in which she explained the misadventures her novel had encountered, and warned readers that in over thirteen years, places, mentalities and works had changed considerably. However, on 13 March 1817, Jane Austen wrote to her niece that "Miss Catherine" had been shelved for the time being and that she did not even know if the book would ever see the light of day. Was she worried about how her novel would be received by readers? Were sales of the second printing of *Mansfield Park* faltering, preventing her from reinvesting? The fact remains that the future *Northanger Abbey* was still not in the shops.

On 20 December 1817, *Catherine* was finally made public, but her author did not witness it. Jane Austen had died five months earlier. The publisher John Murray, published it in conjunction with *Persuasion*, the novelist's last completed work. Both novels are preceded by a biographical notice written by Henry Austen. It seems that it was he who chose to change the title to *Northanger Abbey*, as Gothic novels at the time were usually named after a castle or abbey.

Although the cover still did not clearly mention Jane Austen's name, Henry's biographical notice finally lifted the veil on the novelist's true identity. A first edition of one thousand seven hundred and fifty copies was printed. More than eight hundred copies were sold in the first month. Sales brought Cassandra £515, or around £75,000 today.

'*What an odd gown she has got on*'

Illustration of *Northanger Abbey*, by Hugh Thomson.

A PARODY OF THE GOTHIC NOVEL?

In the late 18th century, the Gothic novel was very popular. Chills, terror, haunted castles and the supernatural captivated readers. One of the most famous writers in this genre was Ann Radcliffe (1764-1823). Her fourth novel, *The Mysteries of Udolpho*, published in 1794, appears at the centre of *Northanger Abbey* as it was Catherine Morland's bedside book. Jane Austen liked Gothic novels, but she had no intention of writing one. She wanted to entertain her readers in her own way. The book does use some of the essential conventions of the Gothic: an old house, secret hideaways, a mystery to be solved... It draws inspiration from them while subverting them to caricature the delusional thoughts of the genre's most fervent admirers. The novelist takes malicious pleasure in abusing and mocking her heroine. From the very first pages, when the Allens and Catherine travel to Bath, they feel disillusioned: "Neither robbers nor tempests befriended them, nor one lucky overturn to introduce them to the hero".[70]

Catherine's all-consuming passion for reading is not without consequences. On the subject of Northanger Abbey, Henry teases her with a frightening picture of the building: "perhaps there may be [...] the remains of some instrument of torture" and tells her that she will eventually discover a mysterious manuscript. The young woman imagines wandering through "long, damp passages, its narrow cells and ruined chapel" and becomes convinced that the abbey is hiding a terrible secret. Her speculations are so extensive that when the truth comes out, she is embarrassed and terribly ashamed. Jane Austen is having fun, but she is also warning us about the dangers in mixing dreams and reality. The unfortunate repercussions caused by the young woman's fantasies are used to teach a few moral lessons.

Jane Austen's satire of the Gothic novel also served as a pretext for defending the genre of novel writing. At the time, historical works, travelogues, poetry and theatre were suitable and respectable reading, but fiction was despised and considered vulgar. The character of John Thorpe declares them to be nonsense and implausible. Determined to express her dissatisfaction, the novelist intervenes in the story herself: "we are an injured body. Although our productions have afforded more extensive and unaffected pleasure than those of any other literary corporation in the world, no species of composition has been so much decried". She adds, through the words of her hero, Henry Tilney: "The person, be it gentleman or lady, who has not pleasure in a good novel, must be intolerably stupid".[71] Jane Austen expresses herself bluntly and with wit.

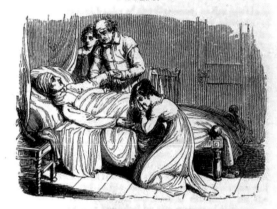

THE

MYSTERIES OF UDOLPHO.

A Romance.

INTERSPERSED WITH SOME PIECES OF POETRY.

BY ANN RADCLIFFE.

VOL. I.

CHISWICK:
Printed by C. Whittingham;
FOR C. S. ARNOLD, TAVISTOCK STREET,
COVENT GARDEN; AND
SIMPKIN AND MARSHALL, STATIONERS' COURT, LONDON.

1823.

Reading corner: in the mood for a thrill?

In addition to Ann Radcliffe's *The Mysteries of Udolpho* (1794) and *The Italian* (1796), here is Isabella Thorpe's recommended reading list:
- *The Castle of Wolfenbach* (1793) and *The Mysterious Warning* (1796) by Eliza Parsons
- *Clermont* (1798) by Regina Maria Roche
- *The Necromancer; or, The Tale of the Black Forest* (1794) by Lawrence Flammenberg
- *The Midnight Bell* (1798) by Francis Lathom
- *The Orphan of the Rhine* (1798) by Eleanor Sleath
- *Horrid Mysteries* (1796) by Carl Grosse.

Although her brother John doesn't recommend it at all, here's a final one:
- *The Monk* (1796) by Matthew Gregory Lewis.

[70] *Northanger Abbey,* op. cit.
[71] *Ibid.*

The three villains in horsemen's greatcoats.

Illustration of *Northanger Abbey*, by Hugh Thomson.

HISTORY

Fashion

"[I am] so tired & ashamed of half my present stock that I even blush at the sight of the wardrobe which contains them."[72]
(25 December 1798)

"Mrs Powlett was at once expensively & nakedly dress'd."
(08 January 1801)

"I cannot determine what to do about my new Gown; I wish such things were to be bought ready made."
(25 December 1798)

"I am quite pleased with Martha & Mrs Lefroy for wanting the pattern of our Caps, but I am not so well pleased with Your giving it to them."
(02 June 1799)

"Mrs Tilson had long sleeves too, & she assured me that they are worn in the evening by many. I was glad to hear this."
(09 March 1814)

Jane Austen's letters contain many references to clothing, and although she seems to have taken an interest in fashion, she is not shy about making fun of it either. In *Northanger Abbey*, she mocks Mrs. Allen and her preoccupation with clothes. She must always be dressed in the latest fashion. At the first ball in Bath, she worries more about the state of her dress than about knowing someone who could introduce her and Catherine to the participants. Mrs. Allen went on and on about the quality of her attire and her impeccable taste.

The other characters are not to be outdone. Isabella is obsessed with a hat she spotted in a shop window, and Catherine is giving serious thought to the outfit she will wear to her next ball. She wants to be seen at her best by a certain gentleman. Jane Austen rightly remarked that: "It would be mortifying to the feelings of many ladies, could they be made to understand how little the heart of a man is affected by what is costly or new in their attire".[73] The novelist does, however, add a slight nuance in the character of Henry Tilney, who, to his credit, is described by others as "an excellent judge in the matter".

---

[72] This quotation and the following ones: *Jane Austen's Letters*, Deirdre Le Faye, *op. cit.*
[73] *Northanger Abbey, op. cit.*

Women's fashion

In the 1780s, the bright colours, ostentation and extravagance of the impressive gowns of recent years were gradually abandoned. It was now the time for simplicity and lightness –a brief respite before the rigid Victorian era. Fashion under the Regency brought a breath of fresh air and comfort, for women did away with corsets!

The inspiration for this fashion dated back to antiquity. Women wore dresses that fit snugly under the bust. They elongated the figure and emphasised feminine lines, thanks to their fluidity and suppleness. White was the colour of choice, despite its tendency to get dirty. However, white and light meant transparent. Of course, it was out of the question to wear a thin dress with a vaporous effect that would reveal every part of your body in the slightest breeze. To remedy this, women wore several layers of fabric.

First of all, underwear. The shirt was the first item of clothing you put on, because it was easier to wash. Women wore linen or cotton bras to replace corsets. Finally, a petticoat, usually made from flannel, linen or cotton, and stockings, made from cotton or silk, complete this first stage.

The empire dress was then slipped over the top. The fabric used was mainly muslin, but tulle, cotton and silk were also popular. In 1808, Jane Austen, aware of the latest trends, informed her sister that "Velvet is to be very much worn this winter".[74] Depending on the activity or the time of day, different dresses were worn: for the morning, walking, riding or even dinner. In simple terms, a day dress had a high neckline and long sleeves. Evening dresses, on the other hand, had a lower neckline and short sleeves. To complete the look, gloves were an essential, and women wouldn't dare show their face without them, depending on the length of their sleeves. During a dance, skin contact between men and women was forbidden.

Day dress, spencer jacket, hat, gloves and reticule

Outside, a coat or jacket was essential. The Spencer jacket emphasised the shoulders. It was a short jacket, fitted under the bust. Its very long sleeves covered the hands almost completely. The jacket was usually dyed a dark colour to contrast with the dress. Depending on the season, hooded coats and very long fleeces –sometimes sleeveless– provided extra protection from the cold. Women also wore long shawls on their shoulders, made of cashmere, silk or chiffon in summer.

[74] *Jane Austen's Letters*, Deirdre Le Faye, *op. cit.*

Shoes and a few accessories completed the outfit. Shoes were in the style of ballet flats: very slim and low, finishing at the ankle. They could be made of silk, velvet or leather. Wooden or leather pads could be fitted underneath to protect them from water or mud. Dresses didn't have pockets, so for accessories small handbags, known as reticules, were used to carry everyday essentials. Paper or silk fans added a touch of glamour.

Hairstyles also became freer. Hair was worn up in a bun and pretty curls framed the face. The finishing touch was a bonnet or hat. It was inappropriate not to wear one when you went out, even though some women took the liberty of going without.

Fan

Embroidered reticule

Umbrella

Gloves

Lightweight shoes

Walking boots

Silk or cotton stockings

SEWING

Sewing work carried out in the home included men's shirts, children's clothes and clothes for people in need. In a letter dated 1st September 1796, Jane Austen proudly announced to her sister that she was the most careful and conscientious worker in the making of Edward's shirts. It was also common to sew small accessories such as hats, or to embellish clothes with simple things like ribbons or flowers. For inspiration and to keep abreast of the latest trends, a number of magazines specialised in fashion, including *The Lady Magazine*, *La Belle Assemblée* and *The Gallery of Fashion*.

For larger pieces, such as dresses or coats, a dressmaker or tailor was called in. Professionals used sheets of paper or fabric directly on the customer to draw the pattern for the garment. This was common practice and was not expensive. In one of her letters, Jane Austen mentions that she paid eight shillings[75] for two pelisses (fur-trimmed jackets). The main cost was the fabric. In *Northanger Abbey*, Henry Tilney is rather proud to explain that he has obtained a superb bargain for his sister, buying real Indian muslin of very good quality at a good price. Old clothes could also be taken back and modified.

---

[75] Twenty shillings was equivalent to one pound at the time.

Men's fashion

Men's fashion moved away from that of previous years with a more streamlined, tailored style. Shirts were made in linen and the neck was covered with a high tie, tied in different ways, in immaculate white. Jackets, in black or dark blue, were cut short at the front and waist with a tail and their stiff collar was set high.

Breeches were longer and tighter, and gradually replaced by trousers made of silk, wool or cotton. During the day, lighter colours were worn. More refined, black was preferred in the evening. During the day, men wore knee-high Hessian boots or Wellington boots, which are lower, mid-calf and tighter. In the evening, shoes were a must.

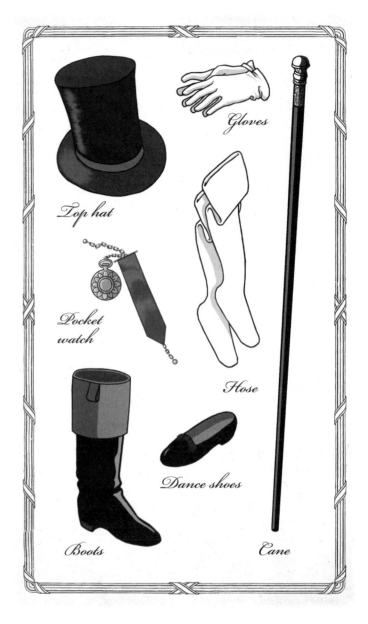

Top hat

Gloves

Pocket watch

Hose

Boots

Dance shoes

Cane

Daywear: top hat, shirt, tie, waistcoat, jacket, long trousers, Hessian boots

As for accessories, men regularly carried a reed or bamboo walking stick. Men also wore a pocket watch, attached with a ribbon or chain —the richest sometimes even wore two! Finally, for the more humorous or outlandish, a monocle was the ideal accessory. Men had short, curly hair with long sideburns. Some people still wore a tricorn or bicorne as a hat, but top hats were beginning to come into fashion.

Did you know?

In 1795, William Pitt, then Prime Minister to George III, imposed a tax on hair powder. Because of the increased cost, but also as a form of protest for some, the population very quickly abandoned the powdered wig, and the tax was a failure. Only the oldest members of society, the military, lawyers and doctors kept their wigs.

Many of these changes were linked to dandyism. The dandy made his first appearance in the 1790s. Elegance was his watchword. His clothes were perfectly tailored to his figure, to show off his good physique. What's more, personal hygiene became essential. For the majority of the population, grooming meant washing their face, hands and arms and putting on perfume to mask any unpleasant odours. The dandy, on the other hand, took a bath in hot water every day and applied neither cream nor perfume. He naturally wanted to be clean.

But this was not just an obsession with appearance. The dandy wanted to demonstrate his self-confidence and self-control through his dress and appearance. It was a personality, an independent state of mind that claimed to be different and superior to others, thanks to a bold simplicity. He flouted popular opinion and made fun of the world around him, but that didn't mean he was disrespectful. Not everyone could be a dandy!

BEAU BRUMMELL, THE DANDY PAR EXCELLENCE

George Bryan "Beau" Brummell was born in 1778. He was the son of Prime Minister Lord North's private secretary. Thanks to this position, the Brummell family lived in relative comfort. Their father's income enabled Beau and his brother to study at Eton,[76] a renowned public school. The young student was soon noticed for his style of dress, his charming manner and his famous repartee. He was fun and cheerful, and was very popular with his friends.

After a brief spell at Oxford, he moved to London. It was a major feat for this young man with no social status to enter the circle of intimates of the Prince of Wales, the future Prince Regent. His uniqueness and elegance, as well as his wit and charm appealed to the Prince, and from then on, all of high society sought his company. Beau's daily routine consisted of attending all the dinners and parties he was invited to, and above all, getting ready. And this process took several hours. In fact, some people witnessed this unparalleled spectacle.

"His look, his hands, his hair, his whole person [is] a work of art patiently elaborated, but where the effort is not felt."[77]

However, underneath all this beauty lay a certain hypocrisy. He was outwardly respectful, but despised the society that welcomed him with open arms. He had no qualms about being sarcastic, even insolent, putting his audience in their place if he felt they were not worthy of his style. He pushed the limits of impertinence with the new Prince Regent and lost his favour after more than fifteen years of friendship. But Brummell's social circle was long established and this didn't stop him from continuing to advance. He had no wife or lover; his only need was himself and the image he projected.

After criticising the nobility for its excesses, he fell into a gambling addiction that he never managed to escape. So much so that in 1816, he went into exile in Calais to avoid prison. He survived thanks to the generosity of his friends, but what little money he received he lost again through gambling. Although he no longer possessed the pomp of yesteryear, he was still himself, charming and eloquent. In 1830, with the help of the Prince Regent —with whom he was never reconciled— he obtained a post as consul in Caen. Despite this work, he was soon ruined and locked up for more than two months due to his debt. His friends helped him out of his predicament. A few years later, living cold in his drab flat, he lost his mind. He had syphilis and could no longer look after himself. He was taken in by nuns at the Saint-Sauveur asylum in Caen, where he died in 1840, aged sixty-one.

[76] Henry Fielding, George Orwell and Princes William and Harry, among others, studied there.
[77] *Brummell ou le Prince des Dandys* (Brummell or the Prince of Dandies), Jacques de Langlade, Presses de la Renaissance, 1985.

Dancing

Jane Austen loved dancing and excelled at it! "There were twenty Dances & I danced them all, & without any fatigue. —I was glad to find myself capable of dancing so much & with so much satisfaction as I did..."[78], she told her sister Cassandra. Dancing and people watching were two of Jane Austen's favourite activities. In her correspondence, she doesn't hesitate to give all the details of the evening, her dancing partners, the people in the audience, their appearance and their behaviour. It was the perfect place to pick up a few ideas.

Balls were an integral part of social life. So you had to have good dancing skills. Not only was it great fun, but it was also a chance to meet new people and potentially meet your loved one. For a young woman, a first ball was her entry into the world. This was a perfect time to make oneself known and show that you were ready to get married.

[78] *Jane Austen's Letters*, Deirdre Le Faye, *op. cit.* 2011.

Families could hire a teacher to ensure that their children learned the different dances. However, if finances didn't allow it, specialist manuals detailed the steps to follow. They also taught the best way to behave. Finally, learning within the family circle was undoubtedly the most accessible and rewarding way.

These moments of dancing with family or friends were often improvised. Formal balls were organised by a neighbour or acquaintance, or held in dedicated public places such as the Assembly Rooms in Bath. Accompanied by Mrs. Allen, Catherine Morland went along and was looking forward to some fun and dancing. However, neither of the women had any connections there. Etiquette required a proper presentation by a mutual acquaintance. In public balls where the crowd was diverse, a master of ceremonies took charge of matching the couples according to their rank and importance, thus initiating the introductions. It was customary to perform two dances, but it was inappropriate, even scandalous, to go beyond this.

It's important to stress that it was the man who chose his partner. Women had the power to decline. However, this was not recommended, particularly when there were a few women present. Refusing an invitation and then accepting another's could be considered offensive to the first gentleman. In the end, women were not free to spurn a man as they pleased, with the risk of being banned from the evening's dancing.

Also, once a woman had made a commitment to a man for a dance, she was not allowed to go back on her decision. When Catherine Morland meets John Thorpe, he invites her to dance with him at the next ball. The young woman,

eager to have a partner as soon as she arrived at the ball, accepted. Just as the festivities are about to begin, Thorpe has the nerve to visit the games room. Catherine is stuck. She is obliged to wait and cannot accept any other invitation. What's more, sitting still is not a comfortable situation. A young woman who did not dance was a woman who was not wanted, she could attract scorn and shame.

Balls were part of the race to get married and, given the social relationships, this was the only time when contact between men and women was permitted. It is only natural, then, that dancing is omnipresent in Jane Austen's novels. Unlike in the adaptations, a dance could last between thirty minutes and an hour. And as dances always went in twos, this time was precious for those who wanted to get to know each other better, but less pleasant for those who didn't enjoy their partner's company. Although most of the dances were not really one-to-one, the pauses allowed a few words to be exchanged.

A final detail that is not to be underestimated was the benefit to physical health. Some dances are so vigorous that they provided sedentary women with an opportunity to exercise. The dancers jumped, twirled, clapped their hands, and it went on for hours! A ball started between 9pm and 10pm and could end very late at night, sometimes even at dawn. To restore one's strength, a meal was traditionally served around midnight. "We began at 10, supped at 1, & were at Deane before 5",[79] said Jane Austen.

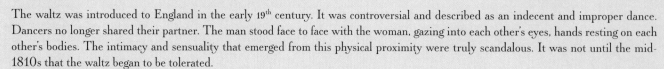

Did you know?

The waltz was introduced to England in the early 19th century. It was controversial and described as an indecent and improper dance. Dancers no longer shared their partner. The man stood face to face with the woman, gazing into each other's eyes, hands resting on each other's bodies. The intimacy and sensuality that emerged from this physical proximity were truly scandalous. It was not until the mid-1810s that the waltz began to be tolerated.

---

[79] *Jane Austen's Letters*, Deirdre Le Faye, *op. cit.*

A few dances

Traditionally, the **minuet** was the dance that opened a ball. After requesting permission from the master of ceremonies, a single couple, standing side by side, performed it in front of the rest of the audience. Relatively difficult to perform, this dance required great mastery and a good deal of concentration. What's more, being in the spotlight could be particularly stressful.

The **contredanse** was a very popular long dance. It was danced in two lines, women on one side and men on the other. Not all the dancers started at the same time. One couple led the dance and choose the different sequences. They took with them the second and third couples, then the third and fourth, and so on.

The **cotillion** made its debut in England in the 1760s. Danced in a square formation, one couple defined the steps, which the other dancers then imitated. Deemed difficult to follow, it was gradually replaced by the **quadrille** in the early 19th century. This dance is very similar to the cotillion, except that it is shorter and the figures are predetermined to simplify it. Jane Austen, however, preferred the cotillion, telling her niece Fanny Knight that the quadrille was far inferior.

As its name suggests, the **scotch reel** is a Scottish dance that was extremely popular at balls. Highly energetic, it was danced in groups of between three and eight people. The participants stood in a circle, twirling, jumping and clapping.

The **boulangere** was reserved for the end of the evening when the guests had run out of energy. Its main feature was that there could be any number of dancers. They stood together in a circle and performed a series of simple steps.

ADAPTATIONS

Northanger Abbey has had relatively few adaptations. These include a few plays, web series, a Spanish mini-series, a film loosely based on the novel, and just two TV films.

Northanger Abbey, BBC, 1987, 88 minutes

Between 1985 and 1998, the BBC launched *Screen Two*, a long series of costume TV films, including *Northanger Abbey* .

Directed by: Gilles Foster

Script: Maggie Wadey

Cast: Katharine Schlesinger (Catherine Morland), Peter Firth (Henry Tilney), Cassie Stuart (Isabella Thorpe), Jonathan Coy (John Thorpe), Philip Brud (James Morland), Ingrid Lacey (Eleanor Tilney), Googie Withers and Geoffrey Chater (Mrs. and Mr. Allen), Greg Hicks (Frederick Tilney), Robert Hardy (General Tilney).

Anecdotes:

♦ After *Northanger Abbey*, screenwriter and novelist Maggie Wadey returned to a new Austen film twenty years later, in *Mansfield Park* (2007).

♦ Robert Hardy was an immensely popular actor on the British stage. He played the very sombre General Tilney in this TV film and the warm Sir John Middleton, cousin of the Dashwood family in *Sense and Sensibility* (1995). Remarkably, his performance as Winston Churchill in *The Wilderness Years* was so acclaimed that he went on to play the political figure in five other films and mini-series.

Shooting locations:

♦ A must-see in Bath. The scenes in the Allens' home were shot at **Number 1 Royal Crescent** in Bath. This magnificent house was restored in the Georgian style and turned into a museum in 1970. Through every room in the house, the museum invites visitors to immerse themselves in the life of an 18th century household.
Information at no1royalcrescent.org.uk

♦ **Bodiam Castle**, in Sussex, is the setting for **Northanger Abbey**. This medieval castle, with its square base, stands in the middle of a moat that is still filled with water. Built in the 14th century for Sir Edward Dalyngrigge, a former knight of Edward III, it was constructed as a bulwark against the risk of French invasion during the Hundred Years' War. While the exterior is majestic, inside most of the walls have collapsed. Climb to the top of the towers to admire the green park and the immensity of the surrounding countryside, then head to the tea room for a bite to eat. Please note opening days. It's best to find out more before your visit, as the castle is home to one of the world's largest colonies of bats: the castle closes its doors to ensure their preservation, particularly during the birth of their young.
Information at nationaltrust.org.uk/visit/sussex/bodiam-castle

Bodiam Castle

◆**Corsham Court**, in Wiltshire, is less than thirteen miles east of Bath. The manor house belonged to the royal family for several centuries. It formed part of the dowry of the queens of England, including two of Henry VIII's wives, Catherine of Aragon and Catherine Parr. The castle was built in 1582, but numerous restorations and improvements have added to its superb appearance, giving it the splendour of the Georgian era. The house has been occupied by the Methuen family for eight generations. Although privately owned, it is open to visitors all year round (Tuesday to Thursday and weekends in high season, weekends only in low season). Measuring twenty-two by seven metres, the portrait gallery is the pride of the house. The collection includes many paintings by Italian, French and Flemish masters. The house also serves as a study and research centre for Bath Spa University, mainly in the field of art. In *Northanger Abbey*, the estate was chosen for **Fullerton Rectory**. Information at corsham-court.co.uk

Corsham Court

Northanger Abbey, ITV, 2007, 84 minutes

This is the latest adaptation of *Northanger Abbey*. It is part of the *Jane Austen Season*, produced by ITV.

Directed by: Jon Jones

Script: Andrew Davies

Cast: Felicity Jones (Catherine Morland), J. J. Feild (Henry Tilney), Carey Mulligan (Isabella Thorpe), William Beck (John Thorpe), Hugh O'Connor (James Morland), Catherine Walker (Eleanor Tilney), Sylvestra Le Touzel and Desmond Barrit (Mrs. and Mr. Allen), Mark Dymond (Frederick Tilney), Liam Cunningham (General Tilney).

Anecdotes:

◆ Unlike the novel, which is partly set in Bath, this TV film was shot entirely in Ireland.

◆ Screenwriter Andrew Davies is no stranger to Jane Austen novels. His credits include *Pride and Prejudice* in 1995, *Emma* in 1996, *Sense and Sensibility* in 2008 and *Sanditon* in 2019. He was also one of the writers of the first two *Bridget Jones* films.

◆ The script for *Northanger Abbey* was written in 1998, but the commercial failure of Miramax's *Mansfield Park* in 1999 initially prevented the producers from launching the project.

◆ J. J. Feild also plays Henry Nobley, a Jane Austen-style hero, alongside Keri Russell in *Austenland* (2013), based on the novel of the same name by Shannon Hale.

◆ Carey Mulligan plays two characters from the Austen world. First the young Kitty Bennet in *Pride and Prejudice* (2005), then here Isabella Thorpe.

◆ Sylvestra Le Touzel (Mrs. Allen) played the heroine, Fanny Price, in the 1983 mini-series *Mansfield Park*.

Shooting locations:

◆ In Dublin, the **King's Inns**, founded in 1541, provided the Allen's house. The establishment was named in honour of King Henry VIII, who granted it a royal licence to teach law.

◆ **Northanger Abbey** is represented by **Lismore Castle**, in Ireland. The first stones were laid in the 11th century to protect the crossing of the River Blackwater. But it wasn't until the mid-19th century that the manor house was designed in the Gothic style. It has belonged to the Duke of Devonshire for three hundred years, a title held by the Cavendish family. They also own Chatsworth House, used as the Pemberley home in *Pride and Prejudice* (2005). Lismore Castle can be rented in its entirety and can accommodate up to twenty-seven people. It is said to have hosted Fred Astaire and John Fitzgerald Kennedy, among others. Located inside the park, Lismore Castle Arts is open from March to October. This is a gallery that presents contemporary art exhibitions.

Information on lismorecastlegardens.com

Lismore Castle

LOOSE ADAPTATIONS

♦ Broadcast on Spanish television in 1968, *La Abadía de Northanger* was a loose adaptation made in black and white.[80] It was divided into ten episodes of twenty to thirty minutes each.

♦ *Northbound* was a 2015 web series comprising thirty-eight episodes averaging four minutes in length.

♦ Another web series of ten mini-episodes, *The Cate Morland Chronicles*, was broadcast in 2016.

♦ *Ruby in Paradise*, released in 1993, is an American film about Ruby, a young woman who goes to a seaside resort to make a fresh start. The story focuses mainly on the character's maturity. Ruby can be seen reading aloud from *Northanger Abbey*.

---

[80] Available on YouTube, as are *Northbound* and *The Cate Morland Chronicles*.

WHEN *NORTHANGER ABBEY* INSPIRES CONTEMPORARY WRITERS

- *Northanger Abbey* by Val McDermid (Harper Collins, 2014). As part of the *Jane Austen Project*, Harper Collins hired the author to adapt the novel with a modern twist.

- *Henry Tilney's Diary* by Amanda Grange (Berkley Books, 2011). Through this diary, the author lifts the veil on Henry's youth, recounts his meeting with Catherine Morland and even attempts to explain General Tilney's tyrannical behaviour.

- *Northanger Abbey*, with author Nancy Butler and illustrator Janet Lee (Marvel, 2012). After *Emma*, the author and illustrator collaborated again to adapt *Northanger Abbey* into a comic book. It is divided into five volumes.

- *Cameron wants to be a Hero,* by Anyta Sunday. A modern gay version of *Northanger Abbey*, in the *Love, Austen* collection (Anyta Sunday, 2002).

Did you know?

Audible, the audiobook platform, has hired a number of celebrities to give voice to Jane Austen's characters. The narrator of *Northanger Abbey* is none other than Emma Thompson, accompanied by Douglas Booth and Eleanor Tomlinson, among others.

Persuasion

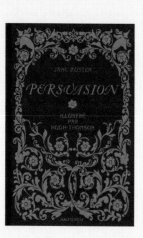

Persuasion is Jane Austen's most accomplished novel in its exploration and description of deep feelings. The most unfathomable aspects of our hearts, which may seem unpretentious, are the essence of this story. Can prudence eclipse passion? Is the constancy of men's feelings comparable to that of women? Whether or not Jane Austen drew her inspiration from the torments of her own heart, *Persuasion* is a remarkable portrait of a woman.

Incipit 1818

Sir Walter Elliot, of Kellynch Hall, in Somersetshire, was a man who, for his own amusement, never took up any book but the Baronetage; there he found occupation for an idle hour and consolation in a distressed one; there his faculties were roused into admiration and respect, by contemplating the limited remnant of the earliest patents.[81]

WHAT'S IT ABOUT?

Eight years previously, Anne Elliot, a baronet's daughter, and Frederick Wentworth, a penniless sailor, fell in love. Although they loved each other deeply, Anne was persuaded by her family to refuse the young man's marriage proposal, on the grounds that he seemed to have no stable situation, no future and no suitable social standing. From then on, communication was severed.

---

[81] *Persuasion*, John Murray, 1817.

In 1814, Sir Walter Elliot, attached to his title of baronet and his position in society, is on the verge of bankruptcy. Unable to restrict his lifestyle, he is forced to rent out his Kellynch Hall estate and move to Bath, a holiday resort where his reputation remained intact. The upheaval in his daily life is made all the more dramatic by the fact that the new tenant is an officer in the Royal Navy, and the baronet hates these new rich. Admiral Croft and his wife, none other than Frederick's sister, take possession of the premises.

Anne and Wentworth's reunion is inevitable. How will the new captain behave after all these years? Will he be quick to forgive Anne, or will he remain indifferent towards her? As for the young woman, is she ready to meet him again without losing her composure, and will she be able to take her future into her own hands?

Character Gallery
THE LADIES

ANNE ELLIOT: **twenty-seven years old, the youngest daughter of the Elliot family.**
Anne has delicate features and soft, dark eyes. Described as a very pretty girl when she was younger, she is now said to have lost all her sparkle. She is renowned for her gentle character, quick wit and modesty. Despite these qualities, her father and elder sister pay her little attention and don't appreciate her true worth. Motherless since she was thirteen, she is very close to her godmother, Lady Russell, who regards her as being her own daughter. Despite being at a critical age for marriage, Anne is still single. Her daily routine consists of doing her father and Elizabeth favours, looking after Mary and her children and visiting Lady Russell. Anne is the oldest heroine in Jane Austen's novels, the most melancholy and self-effacing.

ELIZABETH ELLIOT: **twenty-nine years old, the eldest daughter of the Elliot family.**
Unmarried, she is in no hurry to find a husband, occupying the position of mistress of the house ever since Mrs. Elliot died fourteen years previously. Convinced that she is superior to others because of her social status, she denigrates those around her. Elizabeth only associates with people of her own rank whom she considers worthy of her interest. She has a deep affinity with her father, with whom she spends most of her time.

MARY MUSGROVE: **twenty-three years old, the youngest member of the Elliot family.**
Although described as the least pretty of the Elliot sisters, Mary is the only one to have found a husband. A mother of two, she lives at Uppercross Cottage, near Kellynch, with her husband, Charles Musgrove. His jovial nature doesn't prevent him from constantly lamenting his fate and sinking into melancholy at any moment. Her many antics make Mary the most ridiculous character in *Persuasion*. Jane Austen clearly created her in order to make use of her legendary irony. Although Mary is not completely wicked, she does have the smugness of her father and Elizabeth.

HENRIETTA MUSGROVE: **a twenty-year-old girl.**
The sister of Charles and Louisa, Henrietta is slightly prettier than her younger sister. Although just as cheerful, she has a calmer temperament. She and her sister get on very well with Anne.

LOUISA MUSGROVE: **a nineteen-year-old girl.**
Henrietta's little sister, Louisa has a relatively pleasing physique. Naturally cheerful and enthusiastic, she has a zest for life. Enterprising and reckless, she has no intention of being dictated to. The education the two sisters have received was not brilliant, but their spontaneous manners make them pleasant in society.

MRS. MUSGROVE: mother of Charles, Louisa and Henrietta.

Despite her daughter-in-law Mary's misgivings, Mrs. Musgrove is a kind and caring woman. Her husband, Mr. Musgrove is a wealthy landowner. Warm, cordial and a "bon vivant", he enjoys society and regularly entertains his son Charles and his family. The couple live at Uppercross Hall with their many children, whose happiness is their priority.

LADY RUSSELL: an old friend of Mrs. Elliot and godmother to Anne.

Independent thanks to the fortune she inherited on her husband's death, Lady Russell goes about her business as she pleases. She lives at Kellynch Lodge, a stone's throw from the Elliots' home, where she is regularly in the company of Anne, whom she cherishes dearly.

MRS. PENELOPE CLAY: Elizabeth's friend.

Mrs. Clay is the daughter of Mr. Shepherd, the Baronet's solicitor. A widow, despite her young age, she is rather pretty if you don't mind freckles and puffy wrists, according to Jane Austen's ironic description. She has a quick wit and good manners, and her company is much appreciated by Elizabeth and Sir Walter Elliot.

MRS. SOPHIA CROFT: thirty-eight years old, sister of Captain Wentworth.

Despite her sun-tanned skin due to her many travels in the company of her husband, Admiral Croft, she is still pleasant to look at. Willing, outgoing and caring, she has beautiful dark eyes and a lovely smile. Her presence conveys self-confidence. She and her husband become the tenants of Kellynch Hall.

MRS. SMITH: Anne's former boarding school classmate.

Three years older than Anne, she is a widow, ruined and crippled. She moved to Bath in the hope of regaining her health, which had been impaired by rheumatism in her legs.

LADY DALRYMPLE AND MISS CARTERET: cousins of the Elliots.

Lady Dalrymple, the very wealthy widow of a viscount, and her daughter Miss Carteret go to Bath for the season. Their vanity is a reflection of their high rank in society. Although they are related to the Elliots, they are strangers to them.

Character Gallery
THE GENTLEMEN

FREDERICK WENTWORTH: a remarkably handsome young man of thirty-one.

Although no details are given, we do know that Frederick has a breathtaking physique. Charming, intelligent, quick-witted, enthusiastic, full of zest, approachable, bold, optimistic. So many virtues in one man! Stubbornness and recklessness seem to be his only faults. With no money of his own, he became an officer in the Royal Navy and rose to the rank of captain in just a few years.

SIR WALTER ELLIOT: fifty-four years old, father of the Elliot sisters.

A baronet who reads nothing but the Baronetage, Sir Walter Elliot is proud of his rank and good looks. He despises those who are inferior to him, whether in social status or physically. He can't stop himself from overspending at a time when the accounts are being emptied at breakneck speed. To replenish the coffers, he has no choice but to rent out Kellynch Hall. Widowed many years ago, he has chosen to remain single.

WILLIAM WALTER ELLIOT: **cousin of the Elliot family.**

As a result of the agreement, Mr. Elliot is heir apparent to Kellynch Hall and the title of baronet. While not particularly handsome, he does have a certain charm. He's an intelligent, well-balanced man who will do anything to get what he wants.

CHARLES MUSGROVE: **husband of Mary, brother of Henrietta and Louisa.**

The eldest son of the Musgrove family, Charles goes hunting regularly, probably to escape his wife's constant complaining. He is well-educated, calm and accommodating. Before marrying Mary, his choice had been Anne, who declined his marriage proposal.

CHARLES HAYTER: **a young curate.**

Charles is Louisa and Henrietta's cousin. The Hayter family is not as well off as the Musgroves, and this family connection is not to Mary's liking, as she does not care to be in their company. After completing his studies, Charles found a position as curate in a nearby parish. He courts Henrietta Musgrove in the hope of marrying her.

CAPTAIN HARVILLE: **a friend of Frederick.**

A perfect gentleman, tall, dark-haired and lame from injury, he is retired from the Royal Navy. Feeling useless, he put his energies into furnishing the interior of his Lyme Regis home. His sense of hospitality and that of his wife are a credit to them.

JAMES BENWICK: **a friend of Captain Harville.**

A poet at heart, a gentle dreamer with a melancholy air, Captain Benwick is staying with the Harvilles. His fiancée, Fanny, Captain Harville's sister, died a year earlier while he was at sea. Since then, he has taken refuge in the poetry of Walter Scott and Lord Byron.

Persuasion
IN A NUTSHELL

"*You pierce my soul. I am half agony, half hope.*"[82]

(Captain Wentworth)

---

[82] *Persuasion*, Jane Austen, John Murray, 1817. *Persuasion, op. cit.*

A BRIEF OVERVIEW

Jane Austen's inspiration and imagination never left her. Just four months after completing *Emma*, Jane Austen began writing *Persuasion*. She was forty years old. For the first time, she introduced an older, more mature heroine. The author's own maturity shines through in this novel and its narrative. She also paid tribute to the Royal Navy by introducing officers who were sure to have been inspired by her two brothers, Charles and Francis.

In the space of a year, from 8 August 1815 to 6 August 1816, she wrote this two-volume history, which was to be her last completed work. On 13 March 1817, she sent a letter to her niece Fanny in which she revealed that she had "something ready for publication"[83] and planned to publish the book within a year. A few days later, on 25 March, she wrote to her niece again, warning her not to be impatient to read it. Jane Austen thought that Fanny would not like her new novel. She added: "You may perhaps like the Heroine, as she is almost too good for me".[84]

Her first novels had sold well, as had *Emma*. However, no steps were taken to publish *Persuasion*. In the spring of 1816, the writer was unwell. She breathed her last shortly afterwards, on 18 July 1817, and never saw her work on the shelves of bookshops. *Persuasion* was published posthumously by John Murray in 1818 —along with *Northanger Abbey* and a biographical notice written by her brother Henry. As far as the title is concerned, the information gathered to date is sketchy. Did Jane Austen choose *The Elliots* or *Persuasion* as the title? Was it Henry or her sister Cassandra who decided on the title?

In 1821, Isabelle de Montolieu undertook a "free" translation of the first French edition, under the title: *La Famille Elliot ou l'Ancienne Inclination (The Elliot Family or the Old Inclination)*. Renowned for adapting the story of the novels she translated, Mme de Montolieu made a point of renaming Anne Alice.

An alternative ending?

Jane Austen was dissatisfied, feeling that the ending of her story was insipid and banal. She decided to rework the last two chapters of the second volume, creating the ending as we know it. Most of the original chapter X was deleted and replaced by two new chapters. After a few revisions, the original chapter XI reappeared at the end as chapter XII.

In the first version, Admiral Croft meets Anne in the street and invites her to visit his wife. The couple are wondering whether their lease of Kellynch Hall is about to be terminated. Indeed, a rumour has spread. Mr. Elliot and Anne are engaged! Wentworth, who is present in the flat, is asked by the admiral to speak to the young woman. He wants to be sure that the rumours are true so that he can decide whether to start looking for a new lease. As the admiral leaves the house, the captain, confused, doesn't know how to broach the subject. After a long monologue, he finally gives the floor to Anne, who simply declares that the rumour is totally unfounded. Wentworth's relief is palpable. Pure bliss reigns once again.

In the final version, Jane Austen puts her heroine centre stage, giving her the opportunity to express her view on the constancy of feelings in an intense exchange with Captain Harville. Then comes Wentworth's letter, one of the most beautiful pages in British literature (see the next double-page spread).

These chapters were revealed to the public years later in the second edition of the biography of Jane Austen, written by her nephew, James Edward Austen-Leigh. These thirty-two pages are in draft form, scratched and crossed out. Kept at the British Library in London, the chapters are also available on their website:

bl.uk/collection-items/manuscript-of-chapters-10-and-11-from-jane-austens-persuasion

---

[83] *Jane Austen's Letters*, Deirdre Le Faye, *op. cit.*
[84] *Ibid.*

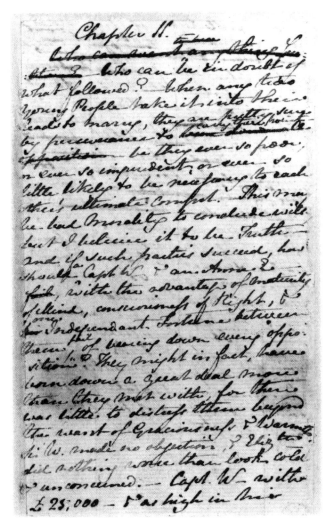

Pages in draft form in Jane Austen's hand, held by the British Library in London.

HISTORY

Jane Austen was no stranger to war. On the contrary, most of her life was punctuated by conflict. Nevertheless, her novels generally show little or no impact of this, with the exception of *Persuasion*. The action takes place in 1814, shortly before the end of the Napoleonic Wars. Despite periods of relative peace, these wars shook the whole of Europe between 1792 and 1815. During these uncertain times, the economic and social landscape was gradually changing. Using only this context as a backdrop, through her characters Jane Austen conveys the repercussions of the war on the small world of the gentry.

A little background

In France, three years after the storming of the Bastille in 1789, Louis XVI was deposed from his throne, bringing the monarchy to an end. The threat of revolution loomed over the European courts, which feared a rebellion by their own people. This is how conflicts broke out in Europe and the colonies. Jane Austen was eighteen when Great Britain, which had no intention of letting the French army invade its kingdom, joined the battle in 1793.

After coming to power as First Consul in 1799 and then Emperor in 1804, Napoleon Bonaparte continued his unrestrained conquest of new territories. Many were annexed, negotiated, exchanged and then repossessed. Peace treaties were signed, then abolished. Truces were just a pretext for rearming. On land and at sea, the war seemed to be unending. For twenty-two years, Europe was torn apart and the hostility between Great Britain and France was at its height. Nevertheless, victory went to perfidious Albion[85] in 1815, defeating the French army at Waterloo (in present-day Belgium).

Seven weeks after Napoleon's defeat, Jane Austen, aged thirty-nine, began writing *Persuasion*, on 8 August 1815, the day after the Emperor sailed to his final exile, St Helena. The island, located in the South Atlantic Ocean, made escape unlikely. Peace seemed to have been established this time. However, the novelist chose to set the action of her novel a year earlier, slightly out of step with current events. She was aware that peace was fragile. Everything could change in an instant. Her contemporaries, reading this story, were also fully aware of this.

[85] French expression coined at the end of the 18th century to describe England in a pejorative way, as a result of the tensions between the two countries at the time.

I can listen no longer in silence.
I must speak to you by such means
as are within my reach. You pierce my
soul. I am half agony, half hope. Tell
me not that I am too late, that such
precious feelings are gone for ever. I offer
myself to you again with a heart even
more your own than when you almost
broke it, eight years and a half ago.
Dare not say that man forgets sooner
than woman, that his love has an earlier
death.

I have loved none but you. Unjust
I may have been, weak and resentful
I have been, but never inconstant. You
alone have brought me to Bath. For
you alone, I think and plan. Have
you not seen this? Can you fail to have
understood my wishes? I had not
waited even these ten days, could I have

read your feelings, as I think you must have penetrated mine. I can hardly write. I am every instant hearing something which overpowers me. You sink your voice, but I can distinguish the tones of that voice when they would be lost on others. Too good, too excellent creature! You do us justice, indeed. You do believe that there is true attachment and constancy among men. Believe it to be most fervent, most undeviating, in

F.W.

I must go, uncertain of my fate; but I shall return hither, or follow your party, as soon as possible. A word, a look, will be enough to decide whether I enter your father's house this evening or never.

86

---

86 Letter from Captain Wentworth, *Persuasion, op. cit.*

VICTORY AT TRAFALGAR AND SAN-DOMINGO!

These two battles are briefly mentioned in *Persuasion*. Without going into further detail, Jane Austen mentions these names, which she may have chosen because of the experience of her brother Francis.

In October 1805, the famous Battle of Trafalgar broke out in southern Spain, near the Straits of Gibraltar. France, allied with Spain, faced Great Britain with thirty-three ships of the line against twenty-seven. In command, Admiral Nelson distinguished himself with an unexpected strategy. He split his fleet in two. The enemy fleet was attacked from both the centre and the left. Cornered, the Franco-Spanish ships were forced to surrender. Seventeen captured ships were credited to the British, who nevertheless suffered a terrible setback. The news of the Admiral's death spread, plunging the sailors into despair. At this time, Francis Austen was in charge of supplies to Gibraltar. Disillusioned, he lamented the loss of Nelson, considered a national hero, but bitterly regretted not having been able to take part in the battle. In *Persuasion*, mention of Trafalgar is made by Anne, who explains that Admiral Croft took part in the battle. However, the glory of this victory did not seem to awaken the Baronet's patriotic fibre or his sympathy for the Admiral, and he made this simple comment: "Then I take it for granted [...] that his face is about as orange as the cuffs and capes of my livery."[87]

Did you know?

- The military strategy employed by Admiral Nelson gave rise to the expression "coup de Trafalgar", which is now used to describe an unexpected and unpredictable move.

- In the 19th and 20th centuries, the British Empire celebrated "Trafalgar Day" every 21 October. This commemoration disappeared following the Armistice of 11 November 1918.

- Nelson's Column in the centre of London's Trafalgar Square is one of the many monuments erected in honour of the brilliant admiral. All over the world, in New Zealand, Ireland and the United States, parks, regions and towns have been named in his honour.

The second conflict took place in February 1806 off the coast of San Domingo in the Dominican Republic. This time, France faced Great Britain alone, with five ships of the line against seven. Preparing to leave the island, the French spotted the British coming towards them at speed. The British fleet, although outnumbered, attacked and won the battle. Francis Austen, then commander of his ship, took part in the battle. He received a gold medal and a vase worth 100 pounds for his bravery. In the novel, this battle off the coast of San Domingo was a triumph for Frederick Wentworth, who was appointed captain as a result.

Royal Navy

The British navy was familiar to Jane Austen. Her brothers, Francis and Charles, were a reliable and inexhaustible source of information for her. They joined the Royal Naval Academy in Portsmouth in 1786 and 1791 respectively. Founded in 1733, this school took in and trained young men from the age of twelve to become officers. The programme was based on both theory and practice, enabling them to learn all the tricks of the trade. The school closed in 1837. More than twenty years later, it was replaced and moved to Portland and then Dartmouth.

Unlike the British Army in which you could buy commissions to progress through the ranks, members of the Royal Navy rose through the ranks on merit and seniority. Starting out as midshipmen, they could rise to reach the highest rank of admiral. Having the right connections or luck on your side, by being in the right place at the right time, were, unfortunately, the best assets for rising up the ranks.

---

[87] *Persuasion*, op. cit.

As well as ordinary wages, battles were an opportunity to make money from the spoils of war. Capturing a ship, cargo or weapons meant bounties, making these conflicts financially attractive. Nevertheless, these captures were largely down to luck. Like Francis Austen at Trafalgar, the sailors were not present at every battle, and defeat, death or the capture of a worthless ship often contributed to their misfortune. The value of the capture depended on the size of the vessel and any goods onboard. Of course, not all crew members shared equally. The fleet commander took the majority, i.e. a quarter of the capture. A captain received three-eighths of the sum (reduced to two-eighths in 1808), and finally, the balance was divided, according to rank, among the remaining sailors.

In *Persuasion*, the only sum we know about is the fortune acquired by Captain Wentworth, valued at £25,000[88] in eight years of service. There is no mention of Admiral Croft's resources, except that they are sufficient to lease Kellynch Hall.

By way of comparison, Francis Austen is said to have earned around £5,000 during his long naval career (seventy-nine years!).[89] As for Jane's brother Charles, after serving his country for sixty-one years, his earnings were estimated at between £2,500 and £3,000.

However, rewards were no substitute for human life. The Napoleonic Wars led to the demise of around one hundred thousand members of the Royal Navy. There were many causes of death, not just combat or shipwrecks. The scourge of the age was disease, including yellow fever, smallpox and typhus. What's more, those that survived these conflicts were left both physically and psychologically scarred by the traumas they experienced.

---

[88] Around £3,660,000 today.
[89] Around £733,000 today, an average of just over £8,600 per year of commitment.

Naval news

It was particularly difficult to get news of officers in wartime. Nevertheless, between 1799 and 1818, the British followed the news through the monthly edition of the *Naval Chronicle*, founded by James Stanier Clarke, the Prince Regent's librarian. Each edition of this chronicle included a list of new ships under construction, biographical memoirs and portraits, naval anecdotes and poems about shipwrecks or battles. Promotions and appointments, marriages and obituaries were also mentioned. However, what was most eagerly awaited was the list of casualties, ship by ship. Family and friends were reassured when their loved ones' names are not included, even though anything could change between the publication of the periodical and the time of reading.

The *Navy List* was another source of information. Designed by David Steel, a London nautical bookseller, this document brought together all the latest news about the ships and officers of the Royal Navy. These unofficial lists were published from 1780 to 1816 and proved to be an invaluable resource throughout the conflicts. In addition, officers' names appeared in order of rank. In this way, readers were kept up to date with their loved ones' career progression. The *Navy List* is also mentioned in *Persuasion*, when the Musgrove sisters set out to find the ships commanded by Frederick Wentworth. Anne Elliot, an assiduous reader, scrupulously scours it, looking for anything that might shed light on the destiny of the man who has never ceased to occupy her thoughts.

Access to these lists was essential for the population to keep abreast of events, but they were also a mine of information for enemy countries. The state of the fleet and the construction of new ships could give them an edge over their rivals.

Reproductions and first editions of these documents can be purchased online.

Self-made men

There is no history, no details of naval life included, and yet the little world of *Persuasion* evolves around this theme to depict a society in the throes of change.

Royal Navy heroes had the chance to progress and achieve a higher standard of living through the bonuses they proudly won in battle. The chance to earn this money provided them with an income, enabling them to support their families or return home to get married. But it also gave access to new opportunities. Admiral Croft rents the majestic mansion of Kellynch Hall, ironically supporting Sir Walter Elliot's declining lifestyle. As for Frederick Wentworth, after earning the rank of captain and pocketing the princely sum of £25,000, he can look forward to a brighter future. He can now choose a wife without worrying about her status or material issues.

However, the upper classes of society did not look favourably on sailors. Several lines in the novel fully illustrate the disdain for those they see as parvenus. Elizabeth Elliot, who lived in Bath at the time, reported that "several odd-looking men walking about here, who, I am told, are sailors".[90] This was not just an observation. Bath was a spa town with a predominantly "respectable" population. Jane Austen reveals the prejudice against these new holidaymakers. Sir Walter Elliot, for his part, expressed his contempt and declared that he objects to this profession: "as a means of bringing persons of obscure birth into undue distinction, and raising men to honours which their fathers and grandfathers never dreamt of".[91] It couldn't be any clearer.

However, these opinions are favourably counterbalanced by other figures who praise the officers. Louisa Musgrove admires them for their character, their devotion to their homeland and the strong fraternal ties they share. Anne, for her part, did not hesitate to voice her opinion in front of her family, letting them know that sailors had "at least an equal claim with any other set of men, for all the comforts and all the privileges which any home can give".[92] Thanks to their actions and merit, as opposed to a family title or heritage, self-made men, in other words men who have succeeded through their own efforts, gradually climbed the social ladder.

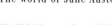

Taxes pouring in

The expenses incurred by successive wars led to a significant increase in taxes. A wide range of goods and commodities were included, including clothing, mail, wine, wallpaper and perfume. Some taxes were tripled or even quadrupled, particularly on horses and vehicles. In 1797, Jane Austen's cousin, Eliza de Feuillide, complained in a letter about the new taxes, fearing that she would have to give up her means of transport. Like Sir Walter Elliot, who also owned a carriage, this contribution to the war effort only increased her debts.

[90] *Persuasion, op. cit.*
[91] *Ibid.*
[92] *Ibid.*

ADAPTATIONS

Persuasion has seen a handful of adaptations. Most of the novel is set in Bath and Lyme Regis, and most of the filming locations were in these two cities.

Persuasion, BBC, 1960-1961, 120 minutes

Broadcast live from 30 December 1960, this adaptation was divided into four black and white episodes. Rumour has it that the mini-series was destroyed or lost.

Directed by: Campbell Logan

Script: Barbara Burnham, Michael Voysey

Cast: Daphne Slater (Anne Elliot), Paul Daneman (Frederick Wentworth), George Curzon (Sir Walter Elliot), Clare Austin (Mary Musgrove), Jill Dixon (Louisa Musgrove), Fabia Drake (Lady Russell), Derek Blomfield (Mr. Elliot).

Anecdotes:

- Scottish director and producer Campbell Logan was no stranger to adaptations. A specialist in BBC television series, he also worked on two other Jane Austen novels: *Emma* in 1960, and *Pride and Prejudice* in 1952 and 1967.

- George Curzon, aka Sir Walter Elliot, also served in the Royal Navy and rose to the rank of *Lieutenant Commander*.

- As for Edward Jewesbury, he not only appeared in this adaptation, here in the role of Charles Musgrove, but also in the 1971 adaptation, where he played the role of Mr. Shepherd.

Persuasion, ITV, 1971, 225 minutes

The first colour adaptation, this mini-series had five episodes.

Directed by: Howard Baker

Script: Julian Mitchell

Cast: Ann Firbank (Anne Elliot), Bryan Marshall (Frederick Wentworth), Basil Dignam (Sir Walter Elliot), Morag Hood (Mary Musgrove), Zhivila Roche (Louisa Musgrove), Marian Spencer (Lady Russell), David Savile (Mr. Elliot).

Anecdotes:

- Although, at twenty-seven, Anne Elliot is the oldest of Jane Austen's heroines, the actress who plays her, Ann Firbank, was thirty-eight at the time of filming.

- Marian Spencer took on the role of mother in two adaptations: Lady Russell in the mini-series and Mrs. Bennet in *Pride and Prejudice* (1958).

- Richard Vernon's role could not have been better chosen. Like his character Admiral Croft, he was also a member of the Royal Navy, as a second lieutenant.

Shooting locations:

• The film crew shot on the sumptuous **Frampton Court** estate in Frampton-on-Severn. It has belonged to the Clifford family for over a thousand years. Comprising several buildings, the manor house and Orangery were used as the backdrop for **Uppercross Cottage** and **Kellynch Hall**. Built in the 1730s, the manor house can be rented privately and comprises seven bedrooms that accommodate up to fourteen people. It combines the elegance of Georgian architecture and the charm of the original furnishings with modern comforts. The Orangery, Cyder House and the old barn are not to be forgotten, the latter being dedicated to weddings. The manor house garden is open to the public on Mondays and Fridays from April to July.

Information on framptoncourtestate.co.uk

Persuasion, BBC, 1995, 104 minutes

This TV film is considered to be one of the most faithful to the novel, even introducing a fragment of the deleted chapter.

Directed by: Roger Michell

Script: Nick Dear

Cast: Amanda Root (Anne Elliot), Ciarán Hinds (Frederick Wentworth), Corin Redgrave (Sir Walter Elliot), Sophie Thompson (Mary Musgrove), Emma Roberts (Louisa Musgrove), Susan Fleetwood (Lady Russell), Samuel West (Mr. Elliot).

Anecdotes:

• At the Jane Austen Centre in Bath, a room with several benches invites visitors to sit down and discover the life of Jane Austen in a documentary presented by Amanda Root, the actress who plays Anne Elliot in this adaptation.

The George Inn

• The ship in the final scene is HMS *Victory*, commanded by the famous Admiral Nelson at the Battle of Trafalgar. Now transformed into a museum at the Portsmouth shipyard, the ship is open to the public every day of the year and presents all aspects of naval life, from the officers' sleeping quarters to the main cabin.

Information on
nmrn.org.uk/visit-us/portsmouth-historic-dockyard/hms-victory

• The poor image quality is due to exposure to natural light. In the night scenes, candlelight was chosen for shooting.

Shooting locations:

• **95 Sydney Place**, Bath, acted as the setting for Sir Walter Elliot, Elizabeth and her friend. Converted into a hotel, the house has been restored to resemble the Regency style as closely as possible. Four charming rooms are available for booking, with the unmistakable names of "Mrs. Clay", "Mrs. Smith", "Sir Walter Elliot" and "Captain Wentworth".

Information on www.95sydneyplace.uk

• Situated six miles from Bath, in Norton St. Philip, **The George Inn** is one of the oldest inns still in operation in England. This is the place that Captain Wentworth, the Musgroves and Anne visited. Dating back to the Tudor era, the inn has thirteen rooms, a restaurant and a garden.

Information at butcombe.com/the-george-inn-somerset

Persuasion, BBC, 2007, 93 minutes

This TV film is the shortest of all the *Persuasion* adaptations. Like the previous one, it includes a passage from the deleted chapter.

Directed by: Adrian Shergold

Script: Simon Burke

Cast: Sally Hawkins (Anne Elliot), Rupert Penry-Jones (Frederick Wentworth), Anthony Head (Sir Walter Elliot), Amanda Hale (Mary Musgrove), Jennifer Higham (Louisa Musgrove), Alice Krige (Lady Russell), Tobias Menzies (Mr. Elliot).

Anecdotes:

♦ Playing a secondary role in this adaptation, Nicholas Farell (Mr. Musgrove) plays the hero Edmund Bertram in *Mansfield Park* (1983).

♦ Tobias Menzies, who portrays Mr. Elliot met Sally Hawkins, the heroine, at the Royal Academy of Dramatic Art (RADA) in London London, where they became friends. He is best known for his role as Black Jack Randall in the hit series *Outlander*.

♦ The dark green jacket worn by Sally Hawkins in the final scene of the film is the same as that worn by Amanda Root (*Persuasion*, 1995) in a scene shot on a street in Bath.

Shooting locations:

♦ **Sheldon Manor**, about eighteen miles from Bath in Chippenham, was the location for the Musgrove family's **Uppercross Hall**. Built in the 17th century, it is still inhabited, and only the park is open to the public. Funnily enough, this mansion hosted the team from the 1995 adaptation when it was used for Uppercross Hall.

♦ Anne's bedroom at Uppercross Cottage and the meal scene at the Lyme Regis Inn were shot in the same location. **Manor House** in Great Chalfield is a 15th century house, restored in the 20th century. The manor house and park are open from April to September, from Tuesday to Thursday and on Sundays. Information at nationaltrust.org.uk/visit/wiltshire/great-chalfield-manor-and-garden

Manor House

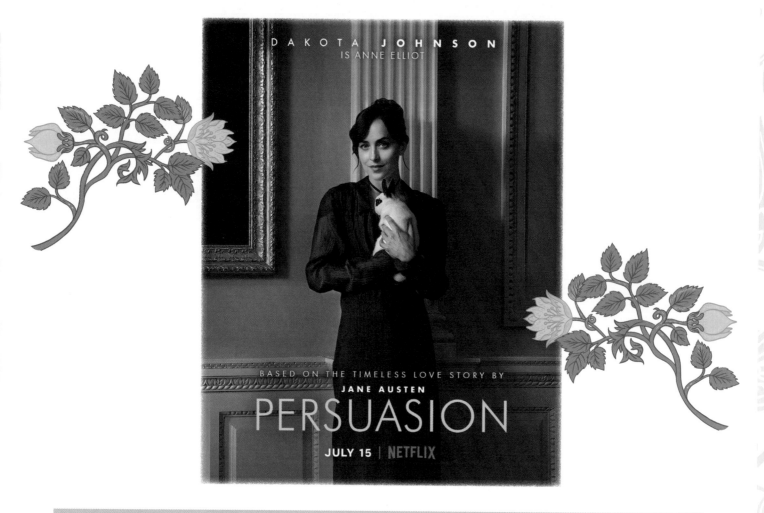

Persuasion, Netflix, 2022, 108 minutes

This latest adaptation is more modern. The photography is more colourful and attractive.

Directed by: Carrie Cracknell

Script: Ron Bass, Alice Victoria Winslow

Cast: Dakota Johnson (Anne Elliot), Cosmo Jarvis (Frederick Wentworth), Richard E. Grant (Sir Walter Elliot), Mia McKenna-Bruce (Mary Musgrove), Nia Towle (Louisa Musgrove), Nikki Amuya-Bird (Lady Russell), Henry Golding (Mr. Elliot).

Anecdotes:

♦ The Primark clothing chain in Bath Street took a step back in time during filming. Just a stone's throw from the Roman Baths, some of the store's windows were transformed for the Bath shoot. Accessories, fabrics and ribbons replaced crop-tops, skirts and trousers. To mark the occasion, the store-front was transformed and given the name "Madam Lefroy".

♦ Anne Elliot's white rabbit does not exist in the novel. In fact, the only pet Jane Austen mentions in her novels is Lady Bertram's pug in *Mansfield Park*. The director included this animal to appeal to new generations.

Chenies Manor

Shooting locations:

- The **Assembly Rooms** in Bath were actually filmed in London, at **Osterley Park and House**. This original Tudor manor house was built in the 1570s and renovated in 1761. The park and the house are open to visitors: flats, servants' quarters and the long gallery, some forty metres long, are waiting to be discovered. The estate is complemented by a second-hand bookshop, shops and restaurants.
Information at
nationaltrust.org.uk/visit/london/osterley-park-and-house

- **Chenies Manor** in Rickmansworth is the setting for Charles and Mary Musgrove's **Uppercross Cottage**. Open Mondays and Tuesdays in summer, this manor house is famous for having welcomed Henry VIII and then his daughter, Queen Elizabeth I.
Information at cheniesmanorhouse.co.uk

LOOSE ADAPTATIONS

- In 1972, a Spanish mini-series was broadcast on television in black and white. It was loosely based on *Persuasion* and consisted of ten episodes.

- *Rational Creature* is a 2019 web series comprising eighteen episodes ranging in length from three to eleven minutes.

- *Modern Persuasion* is a loose, modern television adaptation, released in 2020.

Did you know?

Released in 2006, *The Lake House* found inspiration in *Persuasion*. The film starred Sandra Bullock and Keanu Reeves. After moving out, Kate leaves her new address in the letterbox for the next tenant, Alex, so that he can forward her mail. But the two protagonists do not share the same space-time. Alex lives in 2004 and Kate in 2006, and their only means of communication is through this letterbox. The references to *Persuasion* are subtle and no scenes are taken from the original novel. The analogy between the treatment of lost time and feelings forms the essence of the film.

WHEN *PERSUASION* INSPIRES CONTEMPORARY WRITERS

- *Captain Wentworth's Diary* by Amanda Grange. Not only does this diary reveal all the Captain's thoughts and feelings on his return to Kellynch, it also recounts his first meeting with Anne eight years earlier. (Robert Hale, 2007)

- *For Darkness Shows the Stars* by Diana Peterfreund. For fans of dystopian tales, this novel takes up the key elements of the original story and plunges readers into a unique world. Comprising several volumes, only the first is derived from *Persuasion*. (Balzer + Bray, 2012)

- *Persuading Austen* by Brigid Coady. This modern retelling features Annie Elliot and Austen Wentworth, transporting them to the 21st century and the world of cinema. (Harper Collins, 2017)

Did you know?

Helen Fielding, author of *Bridget Jones's Diary*, was not only inspired by *Pride and Prejudice* for her story. Several passages from *Persuasion* are introduced in the second volume of Bridget's adventures, *The Edge of Reason*, including some key scenes:

- The most similar scene takes place at a birthday party, when Bridget is attacked by two children. Mark Darcy saves her from the assault, as Captain Wentworth does for Anne, freeing her from one of his nephews at Uppercross Cottage.

- Louisa's fall onto the Cobb is replaced by a scene when Bridget's sworn enemy, Rebecca, sprains her ankle diving into the water.

- Finally, Wentworth's poignant letter is replaced by a small note from Mark Darcy, on which a poem is written.

These references, which aren't all that numerous in the end, pop up in the course of a few pages like amusing passing nods. At least one positive argument in favour of the films based on Helen Fielding's books? Colin Firth plays the role of Mark Darcy every time!

Log book

Lyme Regis

Most of Jane Austen's characters live in imaginary places invented and created by the author. In *Persuasion*, while Kellynch and Uppercross are fictional towns, the novel's main scenes take place in the famous spa town of Bath and the cosy little seaside resort of Lyme Regis.

Beautifully dubbed "the pearl of Dorset", Lyme Regis welcomed the Musgrove family and Anne Elliot, who travelled there in the company of Captain Wentworth, who instigated the visit, to visit friends staying in the town.

"THE PEARL OF DORSET"

Lyme Regis is a charming little seaside town with a population of around five thousand. It lies in the south-west of England, in Dorset, around a sixty miles south of Bath. Once renowned as a trading port, particularly for wine and wool, it later became a meeting place for high society, seeking the benefits of the sea and the entertainment organised by the town.

Among the earliest records of Lyme Regis, one of the most notable concerns the construction of a jetty between the 13th and 14th centuries. First made of wood, then stone, it is nicknamed "the Cobb". Providing essential protection for the town and port for the developing trade, it allowed boats to moor without fear. Gradually, however, the ships became larger and the port could no longer accommodate them. The city was changing course and modernising.

In the 18th century, high society loved spa towns, and Lyme Regis understood this. From then on, the seaside resort invested in the construction of new homes and shops, expanded its activities and, little by little, welcomed a new class of visitor. Like Bath, holidaymakers come here to relax and enjoy the health benefits of the water. As well as bathing in the open sea, from 1806 onwards, three spas were built to offer more privacy to more affluent customers. The oldest and most spacious of these venues consisted of a room used for public events, and three or four separate areas in the basement where seawater was pumped in. Today, none of these facilities are still in operation. One is now a theatre, while another has been converted into holiday accommodation.

The Cobb

The Granny's Teeth

A stay in this seaside resort was also an opportunity to meet some great people. Built around 1775, the Assembly Rooms, although not quite the same size, were just as majestic as those in Bath. Balls and card games were organised there. The Cobb, meanwhile, was becoming a legendary place for strolling and socialising. In *Persuasion*, the climax of the tale occurs on this pier. As this has changed over the years, it is not known exactly where the steps from the top of which Louisa fell are located. However, the place that most closely resembles it today, linking the upper and lower parts of the Cobb, is known as "Granny's Teeth". These "Granny's Teeth" are genuinely dangerous. Be particularly vigilant because, depending on the weather, even a walk along the pier can be dangerous.

Today, Lyme Regis is a little paradise on Earth. From the Cobb, the view of Charmouth and the cliffs of the Golden Cap is breathtaking. The charm of the town centre with its colourful houses, the beach and the warm welcome of the residents make it the perfect location for a memorable holiday. Unfortunately, the town still suffers from erosion and landslides. Numerous preservation plans have been undertaken and are still under way. The Church Cliff promenade is a new seawall built in 2015, providing easy access to the "fossil beach". As its name suggests, this beach is a place where numerous fossils have been found, some of them millions of years old, first discovered by Mary Anning, a famous palaeontologist and native of Lyme Regis. Since 2001, the Dorset and East Devon coastline, known as the Jurassic Coast, of which Lyme Regis is a part, has been a UNESCO World Heritage Site.

JANE AUSTEN AND LYME REGIS

In a letter to her sister in January 1801, when the Austen family were on the point of moving to Bath, Jane Austen raved about the "prospect of spending future summers by the sea".[93] Breathing in the sea air and walking on the beach were activities that made the novelist happy.

According to her correspondence, Jane Austen visited Lyme Regis on at least two occasions. Her first visit took place in November 1803. She recalled a fire that occurred while she was staying there. Research has established that a major fire broke out on 5 November 1803, destroying many homes in its path. Apart from this mention, there is no additional information about this trip.

Her second encounter with the seaside resort took place around September 1804. In the company of her parents, as well as Cassandra, Henry and Eliza, she went on holiday to the south coast. They stopped at Lyme Regis and, although there is no evidence to support this, may have rented Pyne House at 10 Broad Street. Above the door, a plaque now proudly states that "This is the most likely lodging of Jane Austen, whose visits to Lyme in 1803 and 1804 gave birth to her novel *Persuasion*". Today, this house is privately owned.

The Austen family enjoyed the coast and the surrounding area. On a trip to the surrounding countryside, Cassandra drew a picture of her sister seen from behind. This information was gathered from a letter from Anna Lefroy, Jane Austen's niece, to James Edward Austen-Leigh. Some time after their arrival, Henry, Eliza and Cassandra set off again for Weymouth, leaving Jane Austen and her parents to enjoy the pleasures and distractions of the town for a few more weeks. All three would then have moved on, but no location is given.

Only one letter has survived from this period, addressed to Cassandra. On 14 September 1804, Jane Austen told her about her daily life and activities: walks, sea bathing and socialising. She recounted going to a ball at the Assembly Rooms and remarking that it "was pleasant, but not full for Thursday".[94] At the ball, she said that she had no partner for the first two dances, but that she was invited for the next two by a Mr. Crawford. Sadly, nothing remains of the building as a violent storm destroyed the Assembly Rooms in 1928. Today, the site is a car park. The novelist also talked about meeting the parents of Miss Armstrong, a woman with whom she became friends. Together, they strolled along the Cobb, chatting and enjoying the mild late-season weather. We also learn that Jane Austen regularly used bathing machines. "The bathing was so delightful this morning and […] I stayed in rather too long, as since the middle of the day I have felt unreasonably tired".[95] She added that she would be more careful next time. Information about this holiday ends with this letter. We don't know how long she stayed there or when she left. This pretty seaside resort undoubtedly made a big impression on her. Through her words in *Persuasion*, the novelist conveys the happiness felt at Lyme Regis.

---

93 *Jane Austen's Letters*, Deirdre le Faye, *op. cit.*
94 *Ibid.*
95 *Ibid.*

Bathing machines: the latest craze

You dream of diving into the sea, but unfortunately you're an 18th century woman and it's not the done thing! Well, this elegant bathing machine is made for you!

Even if you were wearing a "swimming costume" —a long dress made of cotton, flannel or wool— it was inconceivable for a woman to go to the beach and slip into the water in front of the gentlemen. Probably developed in the 1750s in Margate, Kent, these bathing machines were created to allow women to bathe and protect themselves from prying eyes. These were small wheeled vehicles made of wood and canvas, with a door at the front and rear, and often a window and canvas awning.

The process was simple. You entered the machine in your street clothes, changed inside, and horses would pull the carriage through the water. The bather could then exit through the other door, going down the small steps. If she couldn't swim, a rope was tied around her waist. To get the full experience, people could be literally pushed out of the machine or submerged under water by their attendant - an experience that could be quite traumatic. Men also used these machine for privacy, notably King George III, who is said to have started the trend around 1789.

Diving into the sea was not simply for pleasure. Doctors prescribed and encouraged their patients to bathe for health reasons. Water was said to be beneficial in particular for skin problems and stomach upsets. Bathing was also highly recommended for people who studied too much. Constantly being cooped up in a room, with no fresh air and no physical activity... This was the proposed remedy! Swimming usually took place in the morning, and lasted between fifteen minutes and an hour. According to the doctor treating Eliza de Feuillide, Jane Austen's cousin, it was even advisable to go there out of season, when the water was very cold. Invigorating, yes, but dangerous all the same.

Apart from that, when the town's establishments were full, bathing machines were an alternative for men who had nowhere to stay. Basic, but effective!

At the beginning of Queen Victoria's reign, a law was promulgated. It was now forbidden for men and women to

bathe less than twenty metres apart. In 1901, the year of the sovereign's death, the law was repealed. Shortly afterwards, bathing machines lost their usefulness and disappeared from use. Queen Victoria's still exists. First converted into a chicken coop before being restored, it is now on display at Osborne Beach, the royal family's residence on the Isle of Wight.

A TRIBUTE

♦ A bust of Jane Austen was erected in 1975 in Jane Austen's Garden[96] to mark the bicentenary of her birth. The opening was hosted by Hugh Smiley, then President of the Jane Austen Society. To round off the event, a short play based on the novelist's visit to Lyme Regis was staged. In 2006, the garden was redeveloped and the bust was removed. Unfortunately, it has not been found since. Was it lost or stolen? A mystery. This charming square is nevertheless ideal for relaxing, admiring the view out to sea and reading a few pages of *Persuasion*.

♦ The town's museum has a "literary room" devoted to the writers who stayed at Lyme Regis, including Jane Austen. Some objects that once belonged to the Austen family have been bequeathed to the museum by Diana Shervington, a descendant of Edward Knight, the novelist's brother. Diana inherited these objects and donated them to the museum so that as many people as possible could benefit from them. On display are board games, gloves, a pair of Cassandra's glasses and a cockade that probably belonged to Jane Austen. Diana Shervington organised small events, talking about her ancestor to the delight of visitors, until her death in 2018 at the venerable age of ninety-nine.

♦ On the long avenue by the sea, Marine Parade, two small houses with pretty pink façades bear the names of captains Harville and Benwick. These were built after 1830 and therefore have no connection with the characters in *Persuasion*. This is simply a tribute to the novelist.

♦ In the summer, Fred Humphrey, a member of the research team at Lyme Regis Museum, organises guided tours in the footsteps of Jane Austen.

LITERARY ANECDOTES

♦ Henry Fielding (1707-1754), author of *The History of Tom Jones, the Foundling*, to which Jane Austen refers in one of her letters, visited Lyme Regis for a short time. In 1725, the writer fell madly in love with a beautiful young girl, Sarah, and wanted to run away with her. But her uncle wanted to marry her off to his son, John Tucker. Strongly rebuffed, Henry Fielding left the city the very next day, publicly depositing the following note: "This is to give notice to the World that Andrew Tucker and his Son John Tucker are Clowns, and Cowards. Witness my hand Henry Feilding".[97]

♦ Alfred, Lord Tennyson (1809-1892), the famous poet laureate of the Victorian era, was a great admirer of Jane Austen's novels. Freshly arrived at Lyme Regis, he came to visit friends. As soon as his suitcases were deposited, he couldn't help exclaiming: "Show me the steps from which Louisa Musgrove fell!".[98]

---

[96] In 1902, Constance and Ellen G. Hill published *Jane Austen: Her Homes and Her Friends*. The guidebook stated that the house, which had previously stood on this site, had been the one rented by Jane Austen and her parents in 1804. However, it was established years later that the dwelling had only been built after 1817.

[97] Note exhibited at the Lyme Regis Museum. The author later changed the spelling of his surname.

[98] *Alfred Lord Tennyson: A Memoir by his Son*, Hallam Tennyson, MacMillan & co. 1905.

Practical information

TRANSPORT

The easiest way to reach Lyme Regis is by car. However, it's also possible to travel there by train and then by bus. The town has no rail links, and the nearest station is Axminster. From there, buses run every hour and the journey takes around thirty minutes. If you choose this option, pay close attention to the timetables.

Information on lymeregistowncouncil.gov.uk/travel

ACCOMMODATION

Why not stay at The Royal Lion Hotel, just opposite the house that Henry, Eliza, Cassandra, Jane Austen and their parents probably rented?
Information on royallionhotel.com

There are plenty of small hotels and rooms to rent in the town, so you're sure accommodation to suit you.

EATING OUT

Would you like some tea? Experience Jane's Café, which, according to the geographical description in the novel, is the home of the Harville family, Bay Cottage. You can also grab a bite to eat and relax on the beach or at Jane Austen's Garden, just a few steps away.

The unfinished novels

Jane Austen gave six novels to literary history.
But that didn't mean that other stories, characters and places
didn't exist in her imagination. Thanks to the meticulousness
of her family who, after her death, ensured that every
last one of her writings was cherished, the manuscripts
of two unfinished novels have been preserved.
Although these fragments are not very well developed,
they nevertheless give us a glimpse of her stunning talent.

The Watsons

The Watsons, the first of Jane Austen's two unfinished novels, leaves no one indifferent. Emma Watson, like Elizabeth Bennet, is frank and spontaneous, while Lord Osborne is as proud and cold as Mr. Darcy. Robert Watson and his wife have an air of déjà vu about them, echoing *Sense and Sensibility's* John and Fanny Dashwood.

Did the novelist draw inspiration from this tale for her subsequent stories? A bit of *Mansfield Park* here, a bit of *Persuasion* there. How can you resist the *Watsons* and not imagine the sequel Jane Austen might have written?

Incipit 1871

The first winter assembly in the Town of D., in Surrey, was to be held on Tuesday 13 October, and it was generally expected to be a very good one; a long list of Country Families was confidently run over as sure of attending, and sanguine hopes were entertained that the Osbornes themselves would be there.[1]

WHAT'S IT ABOUT?

Raised from an early age in luxury by a wealthy aunt, Emma Watson is then sent home to her family of modest means in Stanton. Her aunt's new husband is leaving England to go back to Ireland, and he doesn't want to bother with a young girl. She now has to learn to live with strangers, who are her three sisters and her sick father.

As soon as she arrives, Emma is invited to a ball attended by the whole neighbourhood. An injustice she witnesses prompts her to ask a young boy to dance with her, even though she doesn't know him. This is noticed by everyone, and she finds that a simple gesture such as this will turn her life upside down.

---

[1] *The Watsons – A Fragment by Jane Austen & Concluded by L. Oulton.* Hutchinson & Co, London 1923.

Character Gallery
THE LADIES

EMMA WATSON: **a nineteen-year-old young woman, the youngest of the family.**
Emma has brown eyes and a dark, yet radiant complexion. She is of medium height and a little chubby. With her friendly face and sweet smile, Emma is described as a pretty girl. She is a well-educated young woman with a kind and caring nature. Honest and impulsive, she does not seek to please the person she is talking to when the situation exasperates her.

ELIZABETH WATSON: **twenty-eight years old, Emma's sister.**
At a critical age, Elizabeth is still not married. When she was younger, she fell in love with a certain Mr. Purvis, but his sister Penelope kept him out of her way. Elizabeth hopes to find a husband so that she can leave home and to longer be a burden to her father. According to her, Mr. Purvis will always be close to her heart, but she never stops talking about Mr. Musgrave. She talks a lot and seems to exaggerate a little, but she is kind to Emma, whom she welcomes with affection. Physically, they have some features in common.

MARGARET WATSON: **Emma's sister.**
This young woman has fair skin, a slim figure and is not ugly. In social situations, she is pleasant and gentle. But as soon as a situation doesn't suit her or doesn't interest her, she becomes grumpy and unsociable.

PENELOPE WATSON: **Emma's sister.**
According to Elizabeth, Penelope has no qualms about turning things to her advantage. This makes it difficult to trust her. She has her sights set on marrying Dr. Harding, a wealthy old man.

JANE WATSON: **Emma's sister-in-law.**
Jane has an ordinary physique, a pretentious air and affected manners. With an income of £6,000, Jane is proud of her high position in life and attaches great importance to etiquette. She is married to Robert, the elder brother of the Watson family. Together they have a daughter, Augusta.

LADY OSBORNE: **a widow, aged fifty.**
Despite her "age", Lady Osborne is a beautiful woman who commands respect. She has two children, a daughter (Miss Osborne) and a son who inherited his father's title, Lord Osborne. When they do the honour of going to a ball, they always arrive late and leave early.

MRS. BLAKE: **a widow, aged thirty-five or thirty-six.**
Small in stature, Mrs. Blake looks pleasant and gentle. She is the sister of Mr. Howard and lives with him, his daughter and his three sons.

MARY EDWARDS: **a young woman aged twenty-two.**
An only child, she has a modest spirit and no lack of discernment. Mary seems to have her heart set on a certain gentleman who is not to her parents' liking.

MRS. EDWARDS: **Mary's mother.**
A friend of the Watson family, Mrs. Edwards is polite and reserved, but a little stilted. She takes great pleasure in accompanying the Watson girls in society on the arm of her husband. Although they often argue, decorum soon calls them to order.

Character Gallery
THE GENTLEMEN

TOM MUSGRAVE: **a charming young man.**
Handsome and distinguished, Tom loves to please and woo young women, all of whom fall under his spell, except Emma. He is financially independent and enjoys all that life has to offer. Playful and reckless, Tom is also impertinent and full of himself.

LORD OSBORNE: **Tom Musgrave's friend.**
Lord Osborne's good looks do not go unnoticed. He's not lacking in common sense, but he's cold and clumsy. He doesn't like the company of women, nor does he take pleasure in dancing. At the ball, he only observes. He is soon attracted to Emma, who shows no interest in him.

MR. HOWARD: **a young clergyman, just over thirty.**
Previously Lord Osborne's tutor, he becomes a clergyman in the parish in the same village as the Osborne estate. He takes his role very seriously and gives a wonderful sermon. Mr. Howard, always appears cheerful, and is a pleasure to behold.

ROBERT WATSON: **the elder brother of the Watson children.**
Robert has a kindly manner, but is tactless when he sees his sister Emma again. A solicitor by profession, he talks a lot about business and money and seems indifferent to his surroundings. He is married to Jane, his employer's daughter.

SAMUEL WATSON: **Emma's brother.**
Samuel is a surgeon. We learn from his appearance that he bears little resemblance to Emma. He has grey eyes, a long face and a big mouth. He is very attracted to Miss Edwards.

MR. EDWARDS: **Mary's father.**
Open and courteous, much more so than his wife, he loves to gossip. Close to the Watsons, he looks after the girls if they need escorting, particularly at balls.

The Watsons
IN A NUTSHELL

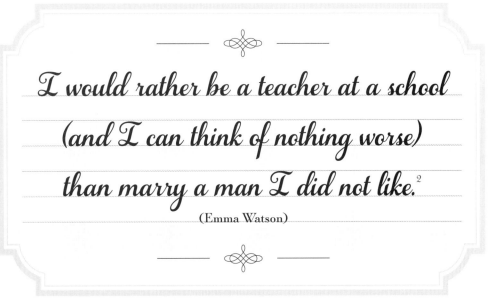

I would rather be a teacher at a school (and I can think of nothing worse) than marry a man I did not like.[2]

(Emma Watson)

---

[2] *The Watsons*, Jane Austen, Penguin Classics, 1975. *op. cit.*

A BRIEF HISTORY

Jane Austen had been living in Bath for several years when, in 1804, at the age of twenty-eight, she began writing a new novel. She only wrote seventeen thousand five hundred words. The story of *The Watsons* came to an abrupt end in 1805. The novelist never finished it. No explanation has been given as to why she took this decision. A few hypotheses have been offered. Of these, the two most likely are bereavements. On 17 December 1804, the day after her birthday, Jane Austen learned of the sudden death of her close friend Madam Lefroy. She had died the day before in an accident with a horse. A few weeks later, on 21 January 1805, Reverend Austen, her father, died suddenly.

Cassandra, the novelist's sister, writes about the destiny Jane Austen imagined for Emma Watson and the other characters: "Mr. Watson was soon to die; and Emma to become dependent for a home on her narrow-minded sister-in-law and brother. She was to decline an offer of marriage from Lord Osborne, and much of the interest of the tale was to arise from Lady Osborne's love for Mr. Howard, and his counter affection for Emma, whom he was finally to marry".[3]

Did the sad events that took place during the writing of *The Watsons* prevent Jane Austen from finishing the story? Did she think it wasn't worth it? In any case, the novel was shelved and did not see the light of day again until Cassandra bequeathed it to her niece Caroline, the daughter of her elder brother James Austen.

The Watsons was first published in 1871 in the second edition of *A Memoir of Jane Austen*, by James Edward Austen-Leigh, the novelist's nephew. He chose the title himself and also added the deleted chapter from *Persuasion*.

Did you know?

In 1818, the youngest Austen's brother, Francis, and his first wife, Mary Gibson, had a daughter, Catherine Anne. At the age of twenty-four, she married John Hubback, a lawyer. Unfortunately, he died a few years later, leaving his wife and children penniless. Catherine Anne had no choice but to return to her parents. In 1850, with the hope of earning some income, she had the idea of rewriting *The Watsons*. According to Anna Lefroy, Jane Austen's niece, she copied the story she had overheard at family gatherings and used it without permission. The book was published under the title *The Younger Sister*. However, this was not a sequel. It takes the original story and transposes it into the Victorian era. Catherine Anne dedicated it to her aunt, declaring that although she did not know her, she greatly admired her.

Available on gutenberg.org

Caroline's nephew, William Austen-Leigh, inherited the manuscript and offered the first six pages at a charity auction in aid of the Red Cross in 1915. The Morgan Library in New York acquired them in 1925. The other section, previously held on deposit at the British Library, belonged to William Austen-Leigh's nephew and nieces. It was then sold at auction on several occasions. It is now part of Oxford University's Bodleian Library collection.

Jane Austen's fine handwriting left little room for corrections. She crossed out certain words or passages, but for bigger revisions, she used a separate piece of paper that she pinned to the precise spot where she wanted to make the change.

More information at treasures.bodleian.ox.ac.uk/treasures/the-watsons

---

[3] *Jane Austen, a Family Record*, Deirdre Le Faye, Cambridge University Press, 2004

THE BIG PICTURE

Carriages

In *The Watsons*, there's a lot about vehicles and carriages, which are an indicator of wealth. A carriage was expensive and maintaining horses was a luxury that not everyone could afford. Here are a few examples of the transport that was available in Jane Austen's time.

Curricles were the most common two-wheeled vehicles. They were easy to get around in and perfect for short trips. They were lightweight and had two seats: one for the driver and one for the passenger. A gig was pulled by a horse. A curricle was faster with two horses.

The phaeton was a light, four-wheeled, open-topped vehicle with a retractable hood, pulled by one or two horses. It had two seats.

Engraving showing a curricle

Chaise-and-four

Meals

Nowadays, we have breakfast between 7am and 8am, lunch between 12pm and 1pm, perhaps a snack around 4pm (not just for children) and dinner around 7pm. In Jane Austen's time, meal times varied according to social class. Those at the bottom of the ladder who worked ate earlier.

Breakfast was served between 9am and 10.30am. It was not unusual to go for a walk or deal with correspondence before the first meal of the day. Breakfast might have included tea, coffee, hot chocolate, bread and butter. Some families also ate savoury foods such as cold pork and eggs.

The barouche also had four wheels and a hood, but could accommodate up to four people facing each other with a coachman at the front.

Berlin carriages and **chaise-and-four** were the ideal vehicles for long journeys. They were covered and enclosed with windows. Mounted on four wheels, they could accommodate three or four people. The driver sat on a seat outside.

For those who didn't have the means, public transport existed, such as **mail coaches** that carried the mail and four or five passengers. **Stagecoaches** were only used for passengers, but some crews crammed people in to make the journey more profitable, which made it longer and less comfortable.

Lunch was more of a snack, and the time it was eaten depended on when you chose to eat dinner. Lunch was a simple, informal meal, with no need to set the table. You might eat sandwiches, soup, cold meats, fruit and cakes.

Dinner was usually served around 5pm, but the upper classes ate between 6pm and 8pm. In *The Watsons*, Tom Musgrave decides that he will have his dinner at 8pm, which he considers to be more "fashionable". The Watson family, on the other hand, eat early, from 3.30pm. In 1798, Jane Austen wrote to her sister Cassandra, who was visiting her brother Edward in Godmersham: "We dine now at half after Three, & have done dinner I suppose before you begin. We drink tea at half after six. I am afraid you will despise us."[4]

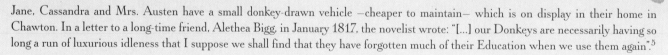

Did you know?

Jane, Cassandra and Mrs. Austen have a small donkey-drawn vehicle —cheaper to maintain— which is on display in their home in Chawton. In a letter to a long-time friend, Alethea Bigg, in January 1817, the novelist wrote: "[...] our Donkeys are necessarily having so long a run of luxurious idleness that I suppose we shall find that they have forgotten much of their Education when we use them again".[5]

---

[4] *Jane Austen's Letters*, Deirdre Le Faye, Oxford University Press, 2011.
[5] *Ibid.*

The dishes served comprised local produce, game, poultry and fish. Pies, soup, beef puddings, etc. were all prepared. The unusual part was that there was no "starter, main course, dessert", everything was served at the same time and everyone choose what they wanted to eat. For dessert, there were cakes, biscuits, fruit, apple pie, jelly...

As the drinking water could be harmful, tea or coffee were preferred as the water was boiled. To avoid risk, alcohol was common: wine, liqueur, rum, beer... These drinks were not just for men: women drank them too in reasonable quantities. The day after a ball, Jane Austen confided to her sister that she had certainly had too much wine the night before. In another letter, she remarked: "By the bye, as I must leave off being young, I find many douceurs in being a sort of chaperon, for I am put on the sofa near the fire and can drink as much wine as I like".[6]

A SEQUEL TO *THE WATSONS*?

♦ In 2018, a play was produced by English playwright Laura Wade. When the actors reached the last pages written by Jane Austen, another actor came on stage to ask them how the story should continue. The play was such a success that it was staged again in 2019 and 2020. However, the last tour had to be cancelled due to the Covid-19 pandemic. The play is available as a script on online purchasing platforms.

♦ John Coates (*The Watsons*, 1958) and Joan Aiken (*Emma Watson*, 1996), for example, both tried their hand at finishing the story.

---

[6] *Jane Austen's Letters*, Deirdre Le Faye, *op cit*

Sanditon

What do people say about hypochondriacs? That they are concerning? Annoying? Under Jane Austen's pen, they're funny! As well as caricaturing these figures, she also shows the repercussions of property speculation in *Sanditon*. Her last story is the most intriguing, yet it was unfinished and the one we know nothing about, except that it would undoubtedly have been another masterpiece of irony and criticism of the evils of society.

Incipit 1925

A gentleman and a lady travelling from Tunbridge towards that part of the Sussex coast which lies between Hastings and Eastbourne, being induced by business to quit the high road and attempt a very rough lane...[7]

WHAT'S IT ABOUT?

One fine day in July, the Heywoods' routine is disrupted when a horse-drawn carriage crashes on the lane beside their estate. Inside is a couple of travellers, the Parkers. Unfortunately, they are unable to return home as the husband has sprained his ankle. He and his wife are forced to spend two weeks in the home of their rescuers.

As they set off for Sanditon, the new seaside resort co-founded by Mr. Parker and Lady Denham, they are keen to take one of the Heywood girls to enjoy the sea air and fine sand. Charlotte, the lucky one chosen, is delighted. It's a chance for her to see the countryside and discover the glorious Sanditon, about which Mr. Parker insists that "nature chose it".[8]

---

[7] *Jane Austen's Sanditon – A Fragment of a Novel.* Oxford, 1925.
[8] *Ibid.*

It's also an opportunity for Charlotte to meet new people and be introduced to a variety of different characters: Lord Denham, his sister Esther and Clara Brereton, all waiting to inherit a fortune from their relative, Lady Denham; as well as Mr. Parker, an entrepreneur, and his siblings, including Diana, Susan and Arthur, the latter three with health concerns. What are we to make of these characters and their future, lost forever in Jane Austen's death?

Character Gallery
THE LADIES

CHARLOTTE HEYWOOD: **a young woman of twenty-two, the eldest of the Heywood daughters.**
Despite being the heroine, Charlotte is not developed much in these first pages. All we know about her looks is that she's pretty. Her nature is simple, gentle and sensible. Although not as romantic as some young women, Charlotte reads a lot of novels. She is observant and can easily guess what is behind the personalities of those around her. Sometimes mocking, Charlotte is nonetheless polite and respectful.

LADY DENHAM: **an elderly woman of seventy in very good health.**
Co-founder of Sanditon, Lady Denham, née Brereton, is very wealthy. After burying her first husband, Mr. Hollis and acquiring his fortune, she lives comfortably. Her second marriage, to the late Sir Denham, gave her the title of "Lady". She is of medium height, stout and upright. She is cordial and polite, but has no education or culture. Despite her income of £30,000, Lady Denham is nevertheless careful with every penny. She has no direct descendants and potential heirs are jostling for position. However, she is mean-spirited, and nobody knows quite what to expect from her.

CLARA BRERETON: **a relative of Lady Denham.**
This young woman is tall and elegant. Her delicate complexion and blue eyes give her unrivalled beauty. Graceful and modest, Clara is a pleasant companion for Lady Denham, with whom she has been staying with for over six months.

ESTHER DENHAM: **Lady Denham's niece.**
Reserved and lacking warmth, Esther is a young woman who lives with her brother. She is proud of her position, but her meagre dowry does not allow her to maintain an appropriate lifestyle. She hopes to win Lady Denham's favour and is all smiles when she was in her presence.

DIANA PARKER: **thirty-four years old, sister of Tom Parker.**
Medium-sized and slim, Diana is a woman with a pleasant face and bright eyes. She suffers from a thousand and one ailments, including biliary colic, but is nevertheless very active. Diana is charitable, does favours for her brother and tells her acquaintances about Sanditon. She's determined to do everything on her own and to dictate what her older sister and younger brother, Arthur, do.

SUSAN PARKER: **Diana Parker's elder sister.**
Poor Susan has three teeth pulled, hoping to cure her migraines. She looks a lot like Diana, but is thinner and more weary. Her treatment with six leeches a day for ten days is certainly due to her condition. The two sisters know how to make themselves useful, but hypochondria is their favourite occupation.

MRS. MARY PARKER: **wife of Tom Parker.**
Mary's character is not very well developed, but she is described as a kind and likeable woman. She is not very thoughtful and lacks self-control. Happily married for seven years, Mrs. Parker follows her beloved husband around and allows herself to be led without objection. They leave the family home to live in Trafalgar House, a newly-built house in Sanditon. They have four children.

MRS. GRIFFITHS: chaperone to Miss Lambe and the Beaufort sisters.
The distinguished Mrs. Griffiths has a perfect education and uses it to earn a living. She takes in young girls to teach them good manners.

MISS LAMBE: a seventeen-year-old girl.
Living under the supervision of Mrs. Griffiths, Miss Lambe, a young woman of mixed race, is extremely wealthy and seems to have a weak constitution.

Character Gallery
THE GENTLEMEN

TOM PARKER: almost thirty-five years old, devoted to Sanditon.
Mr. Parker is open, enthusiastic, friendly, generous, eloquent, passionate and, above all, an eternal optimist. When he travels to Willingden, he hopes to recruit a doctor for his beloved Sanditon. He talks incessantly about his new seaside resort, which he co-founded with Mrs. Denham. Although she is determined not to need one, he feels that a doctor would be a great asset. Tom insists that sea air and swimming are indispensable to every human being, even those with a good constitution, and that it is imperative to spend six weeks a year in a seaside town.

SYDNEY PARKER: twenty-seven or twenty-eight years old, the youngest of the Parkers.
This very handsome young man is a pleasant person to talk to. Always dressed in the latest fashion and with good manners, he knows how to charm. Sydney is cheerful and supportive of his brother, but that's not his priority. He's unpredictable and never stands still.

ARTHUR PARKER: about twenty years old, youngest of the Parkers.
The youngest member of the family lives with his two sisters. They fear for his liver and fragile nerves. He also suffers from rheumatism and excessive sweating. For these reasons, he avoids all physical effort. Arthur has a strong

MISS BEAUFORT AND LETITIA BEAUFORT: Mrs. Griffiths' lodgers.
The two sisters, not very pretty but very pretentious, attach a great deal of importance to their finery and anything that might attract them attention. The eldest acquires a harp and the youngest, drawing paper, to show off their "talents" when the opportunity arises.

build, he's tall and very greedy. As soon as his sisters turn their backs, he rushes off to butter his toast more than he should. He is entirely mothered by his sisters, who leave him little freedom to act and think for himself.

SIR EDWARD DENHAM: Lady Denham's nephew.
After the death of his uncle, Edward inherited the title of baronet. But the rest of the estate still belongs to his aunt. He has no money, but his beautiful smile and his good manners commend him. Edward is charming and softly-spoken, but too romantic. When he's deep in conversation and inspired by his reading, it's impossible to stop his ramblings. He seeks to seduce his audience at all costs, in particular Clara Brereton, Lady Denham's heir apparent.

MR. HEYWOOD: fifty-seven years old, father of the Heywood family.
A handsome, courteous man who is always in a good mood, Mr. Heywood lives in Willingden with his wife and their fourteen children. Simple and very kind, the family warmly welcomes Tom and Mary Parker. Mr. Heywood makes fun of Sanditon and all the new seaside towns, and deplores the rising cost of living there.

> *It should seem that they must either be very busy for the Good of others or else extremely ill themselves.*[9]

Sanditon IN A NUTSHELL

A BRIEF HISTORY

About six months after completing *Persuasion*, on 27 January 1817, Jane Austen began working on a new story. This text, which later became *Sanditon*, took the form of three notebooks. Almost all of the text is written in her confident, neat handwriting, although a few lines in pencil reveal a more fragile state. The novelist was ill. After twenty-four thousand words over twelve chapters, she suffered an attack of fever that forced her to shelve the manuscript. She died almost four months later.

When Cassandra Austen, the novelist's sister, died in 1845, she bequeathed this final manuscript, along with the deleted chapters of *Persuasion*, to her niece Anna Lefroy. According to a descendant of Francis Austen, the last son of the Austen siblings, the original title chosen by Jane Austen was *The Brothers*. Perhaps her intention had been to concentrate on the Parker brothers. In any case, the text was renamed *Sanditon*, probably by Anna.

She and her half-brother James Edward Austen-Leigh decided to include a summary and a few quotations from the story in the republication of their aunt's biography in 1871, under the title *The Last Work*. It was not until 1925 that the complete manuscript was published by Robert Chapman, this time entitled *Fragment of a Novel*. The current name of *Sanditon* did not appear until 1954, published by Oxford University Press. A facsimile can be consulted online, produced by King's College Cambridge in 1975.

---

[9] *Sanditon*, Jane Austen, Penguin Classics, 1975. *op. cit.*

ANNA LEFROY AND HER VAIN ATTEMPT TO CONTINUE HER AUNT'S WORK

In 1862, Anna Lefroy, Jane Austen's favourite niece, mentioned the possible publication of *Sanditon* in a letter to James Edward Austen-Leigh. She also recounted that one of their cousins, Catherine Anne Austen, the daughter of Francis the novelist's younger brother, was present when Cassandra read aloud the stories by her sister. According to Anna, Catherine Anne, who had become a novelist under the name of Mrs. Hubback, after her marriage, appropriated *The Watsons* manuscript without authorisation. In 1850, she published *The Younger Sister*, in which she took the beginning of this novel and invented a continuation of her own. Anna Lefroy feared that Catherine Anne Hubback would do the same with the *Sanditon* manuscript.

In the end, it was Anna who tried to invent a future for the *Sanditon* characters, writing the continuation. She applied her aunt's style and irony, but wasn't able to match her talent. In the first section, she added a number of characters and foresaw a relationship between Clara and Edward, as well as between Charlotte and Sydney. This part concluded with the appearance, at a party, of a certain Mr. Woodcock, owner of the Sanditon Hotel. He and Sydney hurriedly leave the reception. The second section is devoted to Clara Brereton. After about twenty thousand words, Jane Austen's niece put the manuscript down and never returned to it.

This writing was discovered at a Sotheby's auction in 1977. In 1983, *Sanditon: A Continuation* was transcribed and published in a limited edition of five hundred copies, but no further printings were made. For a subscription fee, it is available online at **scribd.com**.

THE BIG PICTURE

Medicine and health

In Jane Austen's time, anaesthesia and antibiotics did not exist. Treatments were being designed to relieve pain and cure diseases, but medical advancement was slow. The list below is not exhaustive and a number of medications were used for different health problems.

Many remedies are still used today, with only the ingredients sometimes differing. To relieve coughs, people drank herbal teas made from leaves, flowers, bark or roots, to which salts or animal substances were sometimes added. You could also swallow potions made from infusions or distilled water, which may contain syrups or salts. These potions were used to treat digestive disorders, fever, convulsions and even hysteria. For the skin, ointments or poultices made from flour mixed with water, milk, oils or fats were applied.

It was necessary, as pointed out by Mr. Parker in *Sanditon*, to enjoy the benefits of the sea air and take a dip in the sea. They were recommended for all types of ailments. Many holidaymakers visited seaside resorts or spas for gout treatment. This disease, which causes inflammation of the joints, could also be treated with an alcoholic solution made from onion juice and vinegar. It was then heated and applied to the painful areas. Vinegar —sometimes combined with flavourings such as cinnamon or rosemary— was also a miracle solution for women prone to fainting. A sponge was soaked in it and then encased in an accessory called a "vinaigrette". This accessory, usually made of silver, was then placed under the nose of the unfortunate woman. Salts also worked wonders if you felt unwell.

Photograph of a vinaigrette, Birmingham, circa
1824-1825.

Some practices were more dangerous and harmful. Fumigation with sulphur, mercury or alcohol was a treatment given to those suffering from skin problems or venereal diseases. Arsenic was also commonly used to combat syphilis, arthritis and diabetes. Finally, laudanum, an alcoholic tincture of opium, could be used to relieve pain and was recommended for patients suffering from nervous breakdowns. Unfortunately, addiction to this drug caused a great deal of devastation.

Apart from the wealthy who could call on the services of a doctor, the most disadvantaged had no option but to resort to their own remedies or, if they could afford it, to the medicines of an apothecary. This professional could only provide advice. Their income came from the sale of various treatments. As a result, they belonged to the lower social classes.

However, being a surgeon did not automatically command respect. Working with their hands, they were not considered gentlemen. They worked on external injuries, applying bandages for example, or operating on patients to treat various illnesses. The only decent profession was that of doctor, because it was an intellectual profession, not a manual one. Their job was to examine the patient, but without any physical contact.

BLOODLETTING AND LEECHES

Bloodletting had been a common medical practice for many centuries. Several techniques were used, depending on the patient's symptoms. Leeches were the preferred remedy for skin inflammation or fever. The skin was rubbed with sugar water or milk to encourage the leech to cling to it. The creature would fall off when it was gorged with blood.

For rheumatism or problems with the internal organs, a suction cup was used. After cutting into the skin, this dome-shaped glass cup was heated and then placed on the cut to create a vacuum. Another procedure, to treat headaches, involved tying the patient's arm to enlarge the veins. The doctor then made an incision to allow the blood to drain away.

DENTISTRY OR THE ART OF PULLING TEETH

The French were among the first in Europe to be concerned about their teeth. In 1728, the French physician Pierre Fauchard published *Le Chirurgien Dentiste, ou Traité des Dents* (The Dental Surgeon, or Treatise on Teeth), considered to be the first work to bring together knowledge of the dental system, treatments and intervention techniques. In 1791, the Frenchman Nicolas Dubois de Chémant obtained the first patent for porcelain teeth. In England, the first modern toothbrush was invented by a certain William Addis in 1780.

But the practice of dental care was atrocious, particularly for people who couldn't afford the services of a dentist. When a tooth hurt, you went to the village blacksmith who would extract it, sometimes at risk of breaking your jaw. In *Sanditon*, Diana Parker suffers from migraines, and the extraction of three teeth seems to be a possible remedy, probably unsuccessful.

The wealthiest consulted those trained as dentists. They obtained children's teeth for a few shillings to use as replacement teeth. A common alternative was to use "Waterloo teeth", the teeth of brave soldiers who died on the battlefield.

Did you know?

THE ORIGIN OF VACCINATIONS

Smallpox was an epidemic virus which was fatal in around 30% of cases. At the end of the 18th century, Edward Jenner, an English country doctor, observed that people who contracted the virus known as vaccinia were subsequently immune to smallpox. The etymology of vaccinia comes from the Latin *vacca*: cow, whose udders were infected.

To confirm his theory, in 1797 Edward Jenner inoculated a child with a drop of vaccinia pus. A few weeks later, he injected him with smallpox. The young boy did not develop any symptoms. The doctor published the results of his *variola vaccine*. This is how the term "vaccination" came about. The first official vaccine was thus introduced.

ADAPTATIONS

Although the novel was never completed, it has been adapted into a play, a web series and a TV series.

Sanditon, ITV, 2019-2022

The series is divided into three seasons, the first of which comprises eight episodes and the next two, six episodes of one hour each. Several directors and scriptwriters were involved in the project, but only those who worked on the three seasons are mentioned here.

Although *Sanditon* is a short manuscript, Jane Austen had time to establish the main characters and create the expository scenes. Only half of the first episode of the series was based on these few pages. The rest was created from scratch. The film team researched the Regency period extensively and drew inspiration from the novelist's other works. Andrew Davies wanted to create a Jane Austen story, but in a modern way.

Directed by: Charles Sturridge

Script: Andrew Davies, Justin Young, Andrea Gibb

Casting: Rose Williams (Charlotte Heywood), Kris Marshall (Mr. Parker), Kate Ashfield (Mrs. Parker), Turlough Convery (Arthur Parker), Theo James (Sydney Parker), Anne Reid (Lady Denham), Jack Fox (Sir Edward Denham), Charlotte Spencer (Esther Denham), Lily Sacofsky (Clara Brereton), Crystal Clarke (Miss Lambe).

To celebrate the launch of our new drama, Sanditon, artist David Downes brings the fictional seaside town to life by painting a bespoke artwork inspired by the series.

New main characters: Leo Suter (James Stringer), Mark Stanley (Lord Babington), Ruth Kearney (Eliza Campion), Sophie Winkleman (Lady Susan), Tom Weston-Jones (Colonel Francis Lennox), Frank Blake (Captain Declan Fraser), Ben Lloyd-Hughes (Alexander Colbourne), Eloise Webb (Augusta Markham), Cai Brigden (Ralph Starling), Edward Davis (Lord Harry Montrose), James Ball (Rowleigh Pryce).

Anecdotes:

• In Diana Parker's house is a real first edition of *Pride and Prejudice*.

• The second and third seasons almost never saw the light of day. In 2019, after the first season was broadcast, ITV announced that the series would not be recommissioned. The audience was disappointed. However, a year and a half later, thanks to an online campaign to "save *Sanditon*", the adaptation returned for two more seasons.

• Most of the scenes were shot in the Bristol studio: Trafalgar House, Denham Place and the Assembly Rooms.

• Production Designer Grant Montgomery was also involved in the 2013 mini-series *Pemberley (Death comes to Pemberley)*.

• There are many nods to Jane Austen throughout the series, not least in the names of the characters. In Tom Parker's office, you can see a map of the resort as it will look when completed. All the streets, such as Darcy Place, refer to Jane Austen's novels. The shop signs also allude to this.

Shooting locations:

• Some of the beach and cliff scenes were shot at **Brean Beach, Sand Point** and **Weston-Super-Mare's Marine Lake**, all in Somerset.

• On the **Bowood** estate in Calne, Wiltshire, you'll find a fairytale shell grotto, a waterfall and a lake. This was used for the **regatta** in the first season. The estate also includes a house, a hotel and a golf course. Bowood House and its gardens are open to visitors from April to the end of October. There are plenty of activities on offer for children.

Information on bowood.org

Bowood Estate

Iford Manor

• **Iford Manor,** near Bradford-on-Avon in Wiltshire, is the setting for the Heywood family's home. In the 15th century, the building was a woollen mill that made the fortune of the Horton family. It was the subsequent owners who modified and fitted out the current residence. Its gardens are exceptional and open from April to September. You can stay at Rowler Cottage, which is on the estate, or simply enjoy the restaurant and café.

Information on ifordmanor.co.uk

• One of the ball scenes in season two was filmed at **Leigh Court** in Bristol. This estate has a fascinating history. The original building was constructed in the 11th century. It became a retirement home for monks. In 1651, the new owner George Norton unknowingly took in Charles II, who was fleeing to France. By 1812, the building had fallen into disrepair and the new owner, Philip John Miles, decided to demolish it and build the current house in the Palladian style. Around 1917, the Miles family left the premises, which were then transformed into a hospital for mentally disabled patients. Since 2000, the house has been used for private events, conferences and weddings.

Information on leighcourt.co.uk

Dyrham Park

♦ **Dyrham Park**, at Chippenham in Gloucestershire, is an exceptional site. The current Baroque residence was built in 1691 for William Blathwayt, secretary to King William III. The architect of the east façade is none other than William Talman, known for his plans for the famous Chatsworth House. Dyrham Park, with its fine art collection and beautiful gardens, has been open to visitors since 1961. The house offers a wealth of experiences, with objects to touch and feel and the pleasure of listening to music in the great hall. There is a second-hand bookshop in the basement. The exterior of the estate is used for **Sanditon House**.

For more information, visit nationaltrust.org.uk/visit/bath-bristol/dyrham-park

♦ The interior of **Sanditon House** was shot at **Badminton House** in Gloucestershire, which was also the setting for *Bridgerton*. The manor house, mostly in the Palladian style, has belonged to the Dukes of Beaufort since the 17th century. Between 1939 and 1945, while war was raging in Europe, the wife of King George V, Queen Consort Mary de Teck, was invited by her niece to stay at the house. Another queen, Elizabeth II, regularly visited Badminton House for the annual horse show. The origins of the sport of badminton date back to ancient civilisations, but tradition has it that the name comes from this house after army officers played a derivative of the game. The site is not open to the public, but can be booked for private events.

Information on badmintonestate.com

Other adaptations:

- ◆ Chris Brindle is the great-great-great-grandson of the artist R. H. C. Ubsdell, who painted the miniature of Anna Lefroy in 1845. In 2014, Chris Brindle wrote a play using both Jane Austen's and Anna Lefroy's text, as well as his own content. In 2019, he turned it into a musical: *Jane Austen & Anna Lefroy's Sanditon 200 Years Later*.[10]

- ◆ *Welcome to Sanditon*,[11] made in 2013, is a sequel to the web series *The Lizzie Bennet Diaries*. Charlotte Heywood is ousted in favour of Gigi Darcy, who is holidaying in Sanditon. It consists of twenty-seven episodes of less than five minutes.

When *Sanditon* inspires contemporary writers

Several sequels have been written, here are two of the best:

- ◆ In 1975, Houghton Miffin published *Sanditon*, completed by "Another Lady". This book was also published with the "other lady" instead credited as Marie Dobbs and Anne Telscombe.

- ◆ In 2004, Virtualbookworm.com Publishing released *A Completion of Sanditon, Jane Austen's Unfinished Novel*. This continuation was completed by respected author and Austen expert Juliette Shapiro.

---

[10] *Sanditon by Jane Austen and Anna Lefroy 200 Years Later*. Both shows are available on YouTube.
[11] Available on YouTube.

Early works and other writings

Jane Austen's early writings are a real manifesto
of her first steps as a novelist.

In these texts, which are akin to exercises in style, she takes
side roads, allows herself to imitate, reproduces mechanisms,
puts her talent to the test and pushes back the boundaries.
In this way, she laid the foundations for her future work.

Lady Susan

This work of around a hundred pages is usually described as a novella. Because of its epistolary style and brevity, it cannot be ranked among Jane Austen's six great completed novels. In his notes for the Pléiade edition, French translator Pierre Goubert describes it as a "moral tale".

Incipit 1925

My dear brother,

I can no longer refuse myself the pleasure of profiting by your kind invitation, when we last parted, of spending some weeks with you at Churchill... [12].

WHAT'S IT ABOUT?

Lady Susan Vernon reconnects with her in-laws when her husband dies after a long illness. The couple only had one daughter, Frederica. Desperate for money, the young widow has to find a way to maintain her lifestyle. She thinks she has found it in Sir Martin, a rich but foolish young man who wants to marry Frederica. Can an alliance be forced where there is no love? After spending the first few months of her widowhood with friends, Lady Susan invites herself to Churchill to stay with her in-laws just before Christmas. As she flits from intrigue to intrigue, she forgets that it's easy to get burned.

[12] *Lady Susan*, Jane Austen, James Edward Austen-Leigh, 1871.

CHRISTMAS IN THE REGENCY

In *Lady Susan*, Christmas is described as a happy time when the Vernon and De Courcy families are all to meet at Parklands, the De Courcy castle.

In 1644, Oliver Cromwell banned Christmas. Parties, meetings and singing were prohibited and deemed to be against the law. The restoration of King Charles II in 1660 re-established this great family tradition. In Georgian times, it was once again an extremely popular festival.

Christmas lasted a whole month in England: from St Nicholas' Day on 6 December to 6 January, when the Epiphany is celebrated. However, the festivities intensified during the so-called *twelve days of Christmas*,[13] which gave rise to a famous song [14] of the same name.

This time of reunion and celebration began on Christmas Eve and ended on Three Kings' Day. It was a time for family, meals, sharing gifts and even dances. Houses were decorated, but there were no Christmas trees and cards were not exchanged. These traditions originated in Germany and were first imported by King George III's wife, Charlotte, but only within the Royal Family. Then, thanks to Prince Albert, they were popularised throughout the country during the Victorian period.

[13] The twelve days of Christmas.
[14] The oldest version dates back to 1780, but it was popularised in 1909 by a certain Frederic Austin.

Character Gallery
THE LADIES

LADY SUSAN VERNON: **not an unhappy widow.**
Considered extremely attractive for her thirty-five years, with her perfect complexion and grey eyes topped by black eyebrows, she charms everyone who meets her. A fine strategist, she has an art of leading her little world by the scruff of the neck. Spoilt as a child, married too young to a man she didn't love, her upbringing left something to be desired. Her financial status changed when her husband died, leaving her destitute. She has only one desire: to climb the social ladder. To achieve this, she is prepared to do anything. Perfidious, calculating and persuasive, she never loses her cool or her sense of repartee, not even when she's caught lying.

FREDERICA VERNON: **a shy teenager.**
Sixteen years old, she is considered very pretty, although not at all like her mother, Lady Susan. Her face is oval and her eyes are dark and soft. She takes refuge in reading, one of the few activities not forbidden to her by some stern maternal commandment. Often left alone or at boarding school, she becomes withdrawn. She is much loved by her father's family, especially her little cousins. If her own mother is to be believed, she has none of the talents that make a beautiful woman: grace and manners.

CATHERINE VERNON: **Lady Susan's sister-in-law.**
Six years earlier, when Catherine was engaged to Charles Vernon, Lady Susan did everything she could to prevent the union. This low blow has left its mark, and the young woman avoids her sister-in-law like the plague. She's one of the few women who won't allow herself to be manipulated, and can see through intentions and duplicity. On the other hand, she is very fond of her niece Frederica, whom she hopes to marry off to her younger brother Reginald. Catherine had several children with her husband, including a little Frederic, named after Lady Susan's husband.

MRS. ALICIA JOHNSON: **Lady Susan's best friend and confidante.**
As devious as her friend, Alicia delights in her adventures, sometimes advises her and constantly flatters her. Alicia's husband forbids her to associate with Lady Susan, threatening to send her back to the countryside. He is old and ill, suffering regular attacks of gout, which force him to take cures in Bath. Lady Susan is already looking forward to the day when another attack will be fatal.

MRS. DE COURCY: **mother of Catherine Vernon and Reginald De Courcy.**
This lady lives peacefully in the countryside, enjoying being a grandmother, and living close enough to her daughter for frequent visits. A loving mother, she is constantly worried about her children.

Character Gallery
THE GENTLEMEN

REGINALD DE COURCY: **a handsome and proud young man.**
A wealthy bachelor aged twenty-three, he lives with his parents, not far from his sister, Catherine Vernon. Lively, intelligent and a little impertinent, he burns with curiosity to meet the most accomplished coquette in England, Lady Susan, whose reputation precedes his own. He swears he won't let himself get caught in her net.

SIR JAMES MARTIN: **a naive country gentleman.**
A relatively well-to-do landowner, Sir James is invited, along with Lady Susan and her daughter, to the home of mutual friends. It is already understood that he will marry one of the ladies of the household. But he cannot resist Lady Susan's charm for long, and she convinces him that he is infatuated with Frederica.

MR. DE COURCY: **father of Catherine Vernon and Reginald De Courcy.**
As the patriarch of a close-knit family, his only concern is to do good for those around him. He owns a beautiful estate, Parklands, and a comfortable fortune. Although he is rather old, he is in excellent physical condition, which is a source of regret to Lady Susan, who wants Reginald to inherit as soon as possible.

CHARLES VERNON: **Lady Susan's brother-in-law.**
A wealthy banker, he has his own estate as well as Churchill Manor. He has a very good heart and wants to help his sister-in-law. He has no grievance against her, even though she tried to prevent his marriage to Catherine. Happily married and a fulfilled father, he is conciliatory and affectionate with his family.

MR. MANWARING: **an attractive married man.**
This gentleman is in Lady Susan's group of friends. She stayed with him for a few months at the beginning of her widowhood, as a friend of his wife, Mrs. Manwaring, and her sister. But no one is fooled that he is not her lover.

Lady Susan IN A NUTSHELL

There is exquisite pleasure in subduing an insolent spirit, in making a person pre-determined to dislike, acknowledge one's superiority.[15]

(Lady Susan)

---

[15] *Lady Susan*, Jane Austen, James Edward Austen-Leigh, 1871.

A BRIEF HISTORY

This short text consists of forty-one letters exchanged between seven characters. We don't know exactly whether it was intended to exist in this form, or even whether it was actually completed. There is a conclusion, but it seems a little rushed. This may not be the ending that was initially planned. In any case, it is in keeping with the series of writings that Jane Austen produced throughout her teenage years.

Lady Susan stands out for its epistolary style, the originality of its subject, its unusual anti-heroine and its relative brevity. One of the hypotheses put forward to explain the origin of this text is that Jane Austen was trying her hand at a writing exercise, challenging herself and, above all, giving free rein to her imagination, nourished by her many and varied readings.

The inspirational presence in Jane Austen's life of her cousin Eliza de Feuillide (later Eliza Austen), who lived for a time in France, cannot be underestimated. It is not impossible that it was Eliza who introduced her to the sulphurous epistolary novel *Les Liaisons Dangereuses* by Choderlos de Laclos (1779), which the future novelist could read in French, as she had a relatively good command of it. *Lady Susan* shares some traits with the famous Marquise de Merteuil.

The first version of *Lady Susan* was most probably written around 1794, when Jane Austen was only nineteen. Although the 1794 folios have now completely disappeared, the novelist took care to copy them again in 1805, in a new copy of one hundred and fifty-eight perfectly clean pages,

almost without erasures or corrections. But at that point, the text still had no title and did not seem destined for publication. However, the high quality of the paper used suggests that this was a gift for someone close to her. *Lady Susan* is the only complete hand-written work by Jane Austen that has survived.

Cassandra Austen left the manuscript to her favourite niece, Fanny Knight, now Lady Knatchbull. It was James Edward Austen-Leigh who decided to include it in the second printing of his biography of his aunt, *A Memoir of Jane Austen*.[16] He also chose the title *Lady Susan*. He wrote to his cousin Fanny to ask her permission. But all she found was a slightly different copy, not in Jane Austen's hand. Fanny wasn't in the best of health, she didn't have the strength to look for the original. It was only after her death in 1882, when her son Edward Knatchbull-Hugessen, the first Baron of Brabourne, inherited the estate, that it was found again, in his mother's papers.

The original was immediately loaned to Oxford University Press for printing. This was the definitive version and would be used for all subsequent editions and translations. After Lord Brabourne's death, part of his estate went to auction, including the famous manuscript, which was sold for £22.10.[17] In 1900, it was found again in a new sale, where it was went for 90 pounds.[18] In 1933, it was sold at Sotheby's. A Chicago bookseller bought it for £2,100.[19] In 1947, he sold it for 6,750 dollars[20] to the director of the Morgan Library in New York, librarian Bella da Costa Greene. It is still there, preciously preserved.

---

[16] James Edward Austen-Leigh also includes fragments of *The Watsons* and *Sanditon*.
[17] Approximately £3,175 today.
[18] Around £13,150 today.
[19] Around £187,600 today.
[20] Around £266,000 today.

EXCHANGES OF LETTERS BETWEEN THE CHARACTERS

Lady Susan is renowned for her eloquence, which she masters both orally and in writing. Throughout the text, she is the most prolific, writing a total of sixteen letters to three different recipients. Twelve of her letters are addressed to Mrs. Alicia Johnson, who replies five times. She also exchanges three letters with Reginald De Courcy, who only writes to her twice. She also writes a note to her brother-in-law, Charles Vernon, to warn him of her imminent arrival. For each of the letters sent by Lady Susan, we have a mirror image of the opinion of Catherine Vernon, her sister-in-law. In eleven letters to her mother, she recounts the same events from a different point of view, revealing the heroine's hypocrisy.

Lady Susan likes to be elegant, and part of that means using French words, which are supposed to add a touch of refinement. In letter XXXIII, addressed to her dear confidante Alicia, she uses the words "éclaircissement" (clarification) and "Adeiu", an alteration of the French "adieu". It's not the first time we've come across typos in Jane Austen's work, such as in the little text *Love and Freindship*, which she wrote at the age of fifteen.[21] Alicia Johnson, no doubt in an attempt to imitate her friend, makes the same spelling mistake. We remember that Lady Susan, despite her good manners, did not have the best of upbringings. This is Jane Austen's way of tactfully poking fun at her character, right down to the smallest details.

Letter from Lady Susan

Lady Susan to Mrs. Johnson
Upper Seymour St

This éclaircissement is rather provoking. How unlucky that you should have been from home! I thought myself sure of you at seven. I am undismayed however. Do not torment yourself with fears on my account. Depend upon it, I can make my own story good with Reginald. Manwaring is just gone; he brought me the news of his wife's arrival. Silly woman! what does she except by such manœuvres? Yet, I wish she had stayed quietly at Langford. Reginald will be a little enraged at first, but by tomorrow's dinner, everything will be well again.
Adeiu.
S. V.[22]

---

[21] The typo is Jane Austen's, and is regularly used in English-language editions.
[22] *Lady Susan*, Jane Austen, *op. cit.*

Did you know?

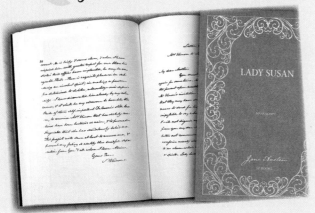

THERE IS A FRENCH FACSIMILE EDITION OF *LADY SUSAN*

In 2020, the Morgan Library in New York allowed Les Editions des Saints Pères to make a copy of the original manuscript. This French publisher is unique in that it only publishes texts in facsimile, in prestige boxes and in limited editions. It will cost you 180 euros to buy this book, and you'll get an impression of what it's like to leaf through the original.[23]

THE BIG PICTURE

Correspondence plays a key role in all Jane Austen's novels. Need we remind you that, at the time, this was the main way of getting news? People wrote letters mostly in the morning, before breakfast, which was served at ten o'clock. Writing and receiving letters was part of the daily routine. It was an activity that required time, effort, patience and concentration. It's what Jane Austen called "the true art of letter-writing".[24]

The postal service was invented towards the end of the 17th century, with horse-drawn carriages transporting mail from town to town. You could send or receive between four and eight letters a day, and it was usually a young boy who collected and delivered the mail —the post boy. The price varied depending on the weight of the letter and the distance to be covered. For an ordinary single-sheet letter

[23] www.lessaintsperes.fr
[24] *Jane Austen's Letters*, Deirdre Le Faye, Oxford edition, 2011.

WRITING A LETTER TO LADY SUSAN AND JANE AUSTEN

Once the letter had been properly folded and sealed, if it was destined for London or a major city, the person's name and address were written first.

> Lady Susan Vernon
> Upper Seymour Street
> Westminster, London

If the mail was going to the countryside, the destination would be written first, then the name of the recipient, then the name of the village and finally the county.

> Chawton Cottage
> Miss Jane Austen
> Chawton, Hampshire

Every gentry household had the necessary items for correspondence. The equipment included a sharp quill pen, with a small knife to sharpen it, a container for the ink, and sometimes a box that served as a writing surface. The nib had to be trimmed enough to hold the perfect amount of ink, but not so much that it ran everywhere, and this operation had to be repeated as often as necessary. The steel point was not mass-produced until after 1830. Writing required a certain amount of dexterity, because quill pens were very flexible. A nib generally lasted a week.

travelling a few thousand miles, it cost almost 17 pence.[25] Postage was usually paid by the recipient.[26] Envelopes were not used, in order to keep the price down. Both sides of the paper were written on, to use every centimetre. The letter was folded into a rectangle and then sealed with wax.

In the Regency period, it was not uncommon to practise the art of the "home-made". Martha Lloyd, a family friend and later sister-in-law, lived in Chawton with Mrs. Austen and her daughters. She took care of many domestic tasks, including making ink. It was easy and inexpensive to make, and could even be transported in powder form. Martha had her own recipe, which she kept in a precious notebook, now part of the Jane Austen Museum collection.

Ingredients for homemade ink, according to Martha Lloyd

❀ Walnuts

❀ Iron sulphate

❀ Gum arabic

❀ Sugar

❀ Water

❀ Fourteen-day-old chimney ash

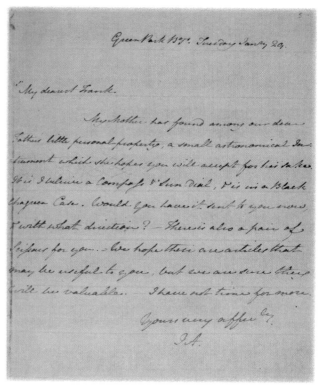

Letter from Jane Austen to her brother Francis 'Frank' Austen, 29 January 1805, after the death of their father.

Jane Austen used this ink, called iron gall, for her correspondence. It was made from the tannin of crushed oak gall nuts (gallic acid), iron sulphate (also known as vitriol), crushed gum arabic and water. We don't know exactly what Martha's little additions of sugar and ash were for (she particularly insists that the ash should be at least two weeks old). This ink then turned brown. Most of Jane Austen's letters that have stood the test of time were written with Martha's mixture.

---

[25] About £3.50 today.
[26] Peers of the Kingdom were exempt and did not pay their postage, like Lord Bertram in *Mansfield Park* for example.

Flirting and courtship during the Regency era

Lady Susan was considered "the most accomplished coquette in England."[27] Having been widowed three months at the start of the story, she wastes no time in getting back in the marriage market and securing her financial situation. She flits between Reginald De Courcy (her sister-in-law's brother), Lord Manwaring (her lover) and Lord James Martin (her daughter's suitor). Who will have the grace to receive her favours?

A young lady was considered to have faded by the end of her twenties. However, Lady Susan is proud of her youthful beauty, despite her age of thirty-five. She is free to remarry. But she needs a wealthy man, preferably the first born of a lineage, because he normally has an estate. During the Regency, marriage offered wives considerable freedom and independence, but only under certain conditions. Let's not forget that a wife remained the property of her husband and had to obey him. Alicia, Lady Susan's friend, was forced by her husband to give up her friendship with her. However, in the right circumstances, a woman could be financially independent thanks to her husband's money.

So how does one make clear one's desire? Lord Martin does not hesitate to pursue Frederica Vernon to the home of her aunt and uncle. For her part, she seems to find Reginald De Courcy to her liking. Although reserved, she dares to talk to him and give him a few pointed glances. If a gentleman had been properly introduced to a young woman, there was no reason why she would not be able to make conversation with him, or even go for a walk with him, or dance at a ball, under the watchful eye of a chaperone. Officially, there was no flirting, and the rules for encounters between men and women were codified. Unofficially, it was a different story, as *Lady Susan* implies.

---

[27] Jane Austen, *op. cit.*

CHATSWORTH, THE LOCATION OF A FAMOUS MÉNAGE À TROIS

At the beginning of *Lady Susan*, Jane Austen leaves no doubt that her heroine is living under the same roof as her lover, with his wife. Rumours are rife, but the coquette doesn't care, as her talent for repartee always saves her from all sorts of ambiguous situations.

One of the most famous threesomes in English history dates back to Jane Austen's time, and caused a huge scandal at the time. But, as happens in the very high aristocracy, the various protagonists retained their status and privileges. In 1774, William, the fifth Duke of Devonshire, the most eligible bachelor of his time, married the beautiful Georgiana Spencer. They had four children, including a son, the future sixth Duke.

A colourful character, the Duchess of Devonshire anonymously published three novels, wrote verse and, above all, took an interest in science. She had a small laboratory built where she gave free rein to her passion for the natural sciences, in particular mineralogy and geology. Lady Georgiana Spencer of Devonshire is also known to be the fourth-degree ancestor of Lady Diana Spencer, the mother of the current Prince of Wales, William.

In 1782, the Duchess met Lady Elizabeth Foster in Bath. She had been in a difficult situation since separating from her husband. She had also been deprived of seeing her sons. The two women would become inseparable. So much so that when Elizabeth was invited for a long stay at Chatsworth, she ended up sharing the Duke's bed. They had two illegitimate children together. Georgiana also had a daughter out of wedlock with her lover, Charles Grey. Elizabeth Foster eventually married the Duke of Devonshire on Georgiana's death in 1806.

This story inspired Saul Dibb to make a film in 2008, *The Duchess*, starring Keira Knightley, Ralph Fiennes and Hayley Atwell.

ADAPTATIONS

Lady Susan: Masterpiece by Jane Austen, 2013, 18 minutes

In 2013, documentary filmmaker Michelle Lambeau directed this docu-drama, which looks back at the genesis of the text, with the opinions of academics, specialists and Jane Austen fans. Professional actors portray *Lady Susan*'s characters in sketches.

Directed by: Michelle Lambeau

Script: Michelle Lambeau

Anecdotes:

♦ Originally from Arizona, the director is also a member of the Jane Austen Society of North America. She provides the voice-over for the film, in the role of Jane Austen.

♦ You can watch the documentary on YouTube.

♦ It was produced in part thanks to funds raised on a crowdfunding platform.

Love & Friendship, Westerly film, 2016, 90 minutes

This is the only screen adaptation of *Lady Susan*.

Directed by: Whit Stillman   **Script:** Whit Stillman

Casting: Kate Beckinsale (Lady Susan Vernon), Morfydd Clark (Frederica Vernon), Tom Bennet (Sir James Martin), Jenn Murray (Lady Manwaring), Lochlann O'Mearáin (Lord Manwaring), Chloë Sevigny (Alicia Johnson), Stephen Fry (Mr. Johnson), Xavier Samuel (Reginald De Courcy), Emma Greenwell (Catherine Vernon), Justin Edwards (Charles Vernon), Jemma Redgrave (Lady De Courcy), James Fleet (Lord De Courcy), Kelly Campbell (Mrs. Cross).

Anecdotes:

♦ Whit Stillman is a great admirer of Jane Austen. When he was very young, he read *Northanger Abbey*, but he admits that he didn't understand much of it. The second novel he discovered was *Mansfield Park*, which inspired his directorial debut, *Metropolitan*, in 1990.

♦ The director lives in Paris. He had the idea of adapting *Lady Susan* when he saw the book in the window of an English bookshop on rue de Rivoli in Paris. The story does not say whether it was at Smith&Son [28] or Galignani. [29]

♦ Kate Beckinsale and Chloë Sevigny previously starred in Whit Stillman's 1998 film *The Last Days of Disco*.

♦ The character of Alicia Johnston has American nationality in the film, specifically to match Chloë Sevigny's accent.

♦ Morfydd Clark (Frederica Vernon) and Emma Greenwell (Catherine Vernon) starred in *Pride and Prejudice and Zombies* in the same year, as Georgiana Darcy and Caroline Bingley respectively.

♦ Unlike most Austen adaptations, new female costumes were created especially for the film, under the direction of Eimer Ni Mhaoldomhnaigh, who also worked on Julian Jarrold's biopic *Jane* (2007).

♦ James Fleet played the role of John Dashwood in *Sense and Sensibility* (1995), and of Mr. Bennet in *Death Comes to Pemberley* (2013).

Did you know?

WHY ISN'T THE TITLE OF THE FILM THE SAME AS THAT OF THE BOOK?

Whit Stillman justifies the change of title by the fact that it was not Jane Austen herself who decided to call her text *Lady Susan*, but her nephew James Edward. He also points out that *Elinor and Marianne* became *Sense and Sensibility*. Jane Austen likes to link two concepts in her titles, like *Pride and Prejudice*, for example. So the natural choice was another title in the same genre: *Love and Friendship*, [30] two themes which, according to the director, are precisely the subject of his film, and are more in keeping with "the spirit of Jane Austen".

---

[28] Located at 248, rue de Rivoli in Paris, this bookshop has been in business since 1870.
[29] Galignani is the oldest English-language bookshop in the French capital, opening in 1801 at 224, rue de Rivoli.
[30] This is the title of the book he wrote before making his film.

Howth Castle

Shooting locations:

✦ **Howth Castle**, in Fingal, Ireland, became the Vernon's **Churchill** manor house. Eight hundred years old, this property originally belonged to a Norman count, Almeric, who arrived in Ireland with John de Courcy, the famous knight who also came from Normandy after the conquest of England. The location was particularly well chosen, reminiscent of Jane Austen's De Courcy, who was no doubt inspired by the name of this old French family. The furniture dates from the 18th century and is representative of Irish craftsmanship. Visits are by online reservation only.

Information on howthcastle.ie

✦ **Russborough House**, in Blessington, near Dublin, was also used to represent **Churchill**. The property is located in the heart of West Wicklow, south of Kildare. Built in the mid-18th century for the first Earl of Milltown, its Palladian style has earned it the reputation of being the finest Georgian house in Ireland. The site is open every day, as are the café, gardens and labyrinth.

Information on russborough.ie

✦ **The Royal Hospital Kilmainham** has existed since 1680 and was inspired by the Hôtel des Invalides in Paris. Thirty years ago, it became the Museum of Modern Irish art. It is surrounded by a sumptuous garden. In the film, it is used as a backdrop for the outdoor scenes when Lady Susan and her friend Alicia Johnson are in **London**.

Information on rhk.ie

Russborough House

Kilmainham Royal Hospital

WHEN *LADY SUSAN* INSPIRES CONTEMPORARY WRITERS

- Californian Phyllis Ann Karr, author of numerous *fantasy* novels, was the first to try her hand, in the Regency Romance style, at rewriting *Lady Susan*, which she described as "an unfinished novel" by Jane Austen (Everest House, 1980).

- Janet Todd is an academic who has published widely on Jane Austen, including an illustrated scrapbook, *Jane Austen, Her Life, Her Times, Her Novels* (Andre Deutsch, 2013). She picks up where *Lady Susan* left off in *Lady Susan Plays the Game* (Bloomsbury Reader, 2013), where she turns the wily widow into a card-playing enthusiast at her peril.

- A Harvard graduate, Whit Stillman is also a writer. In *Love & Friendship*: In Which Jane Austen's Lady Susan Vernon is Entirely Vindicated a book he wrote before making the film *Love & Friendship*, he imagines a nephew by marriage to Lady Susan who is overwhelmed with admiration for her, so much so that he reinvents the whole story from an entirely subjective and inevitably comic perspective (Hodder & Stoughton, 2016).

Did you know?

THERE ARE ALSO SOME FRENCH ADAPTATIONS.

There are many adaptations of *Lady Susan* as plays in the English-speaking world. Its epistolary nature lends itself particularly well to dialogue. In 2003, the French company Petits Bâtons, founded by Hélène van der Stichele, staged a French adaptation in the department of Isère.

Actress and playwright Chloé Lambert played Lady Susan in an audio adaptation in 2011, based on the text translated by Pierre Goubert for La Pléiade. Former Comédie-Française member Georgia Scalliet played the role of Alicia Johnson, along with five other actors —the exact number of characters exchanging letters.

Juvenilia

Juvenilia are writings from childhood, adolescence and young adulthood that Jane Austen probably began around the age of eleven or twelve. Inspired by her reading, they are essentially short parodies of varying length, sometimes just a few pages, sometimes just a few paragraphs. This seems to be a learning phase in which she allows herself a thousand and one fantasies. The earliest date from 1786 or 1787, shortly after the Austen girls went to school in Reading. They are not drafts, which proves Jane Austen's desire to keep them.

As an adult, she took the time to copy them down and put them together in three notebooks. It is also conceivable that, at this point, she may have been sorting through and eliminating some of the productions she didn't want to keep. On the front cover of each notebook, she writes: *Volume the First, Volume the Second* and *Volume the Third*. The first is now in the Bodleian Library, Oxford. The second and third are held at the British Library in London.

These three volumes contain a variety of short texts of varying lengths, genres and themes: short stories, sketches, poems, pastiches, etc. They are mostly amusing imitations or parodies of popular novels. For Jane Austen, it was as much about practising her writing skills as entertaining her friends and family with these writings, which were often read aloud to everyone, sometimes in theatrical form, like little shows. The young girl was constantly encouraged and supported by those close to her in her ambition to become a novelist. In these early writings, we can already see the seeds of the qualities of her great novels to come.

After Jane Austen's death and later, after that of her sister Cassandra, the nephews and nieces who inherited *Juvenilia* did not want these writings published. They considered them to be essays or fantasies, not writings intended for distribution outside the close-knit family circle. It was finally the academic Robert William Chapman, with the invaluable help of his wife Katherine, a long-time Janeite, who had the complete early works published by Clarendon Press in Oxford in 1933, along with part of the correspondence. Ten years earlier, he was behind the first university edition of Jane Austen's novels, published by the same firm.

It was Jane Austen who decided on the organisation of her early writings
The titles appear in an order of her own choosing.
The first volume consists of very concise novels, both humorous and satirical,
as well as short sketches and fragments of texts, some of them unfinished.

VOLUME THE FIRST

FREDERIC AND ELFRIDA

◆

JACK AND ALICE

◆

EDGAR AND EMMA

◆

HENRY AND ELIZA

◆

THE ADVENTURES OF MR. HARLEY

◆

SIR WILLIAM MOUNTAGUE

◆

MEMOIRS OF MR CLIFFORD

◆

THE BEAUTIFUL CASSANDRA

◆

AMELIA WEBSTER

◆

THE VISIT

◆

THE MYSTERY

◆

THE THREE SISTERS

◆

*FRAGMENTS: TO MISS JANE ANNA ELIZABETH AUSTEN
/A BEAUTIFUL DESCRIPTION OF THE DIFFERENT EFFECTS
OF SENSIBILITY ON DIFFERENT MINDS.*

◆

THE GENEROUS CURATE

◆

ODE TO PITY

The second, less varied volume contains more elaborate texts,
which today's publishers sometimes choose to publish separately.

VOLUME THE SECOND

LOVE AND FRIENDSHIP

This is a short novel that parodies the sentimental style, in epistolary form. Dated 13 June 1790, it
is lovingly dedicated by the author, then aged fourteen and a half, to her beloved cousin, the Countess
Eliza de Feuillide.

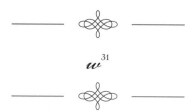

w [31]

In the English version, it stands out thanks to a small typo on the word 'friendship', *Love and Freindship*,
which is maintained in England from edition to edition. It's entirely plausible that this typo was deliberate,
given the quirky, parodic tone of this little text. However, some critics report that the young Jane Austen
sometimes reversed the order of the letters "i" and "e" when they followed each other in a word.[32] In this
writing, we also find the small alteration on the French word "adieu", as in *Lady Susan, adeiu*.

LESLEY CASTLE

◆

THE HISTORY OF ENGLAND

In this parody of a history textbook, *The History of England from the Reign of Henry IV to Charles I. By a
Partial, Prejudiced, and Ignorant Historian*,[33] Jane Austen amuses herself by recounting the biographies of
a number of historical figures who have left their mark on her country's history, with a great deal of humour
and a clear sense of subjectivity.

The work her pastiche was based on is probably Oliver Goldsmith's *History of England* (1764), available to
her in the library at Steventon Rectory. This copy was found in the family archives and is annotated in Jane
Austen's hand, with indignant little remarks when she disagrees with the eminent historian. There is a deep
aversion to Queen Elizabeth I, and a desire to rehabilitate the memory of Mary Stuart.

This book was also a collaboration between sisters. A dedicated watercolourist, Cassandra took regular classes.
She contributed thirteen colour illustrations in small medallions depicting the kings and queens of England.

---

[31] *Love and Freindship and Other Youthful Writings*, Jane Austen, Penguin Books, 2014. *op. cit.*
[32] *Jane Austen, op. cit.* 2014, information reported by Christine Alexander in her notes.
[33] *The History of England from the reign of Henry IV to Charles I. By a Partial, Prejudiced, and Ignorant Historian*, Jane Austen, 1791.

The parody is dated 26 November 1791. Jane Austen was not quite sixteen.

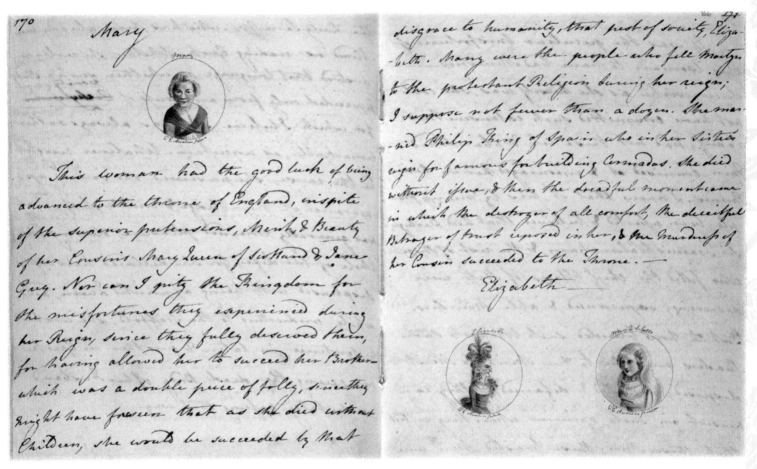

"The Reign of Queen Mary", *History of England [Volume The Second]*, with medallion portraits of Queen Mary, Queen Elizabeth and Mary, Queen of Scots, by Cassandra Austen.

An English edition includes text and colour drawings (Renard Press, 2022).

A COLLECTION OF LETTERS

◆

SCRAPS OF PAPER: *THE FEMALE PHILOSOPHER / THE FIRST ACT OF A COMEDY / A LETTER FROM A YOUNG LADY / A TOUR THROUGH WALES / A TALE*

The last volume contains two parodies of sentimental novels.

VOLUME THE THIRD

Evelyn
◆

This 'little' novel is a gift for Martha Lloyd, Jane Austen's dear friend. In a small fictional village in Sussex, everyone is far too nice. This is the beginning of a humorous story.

Catharine, or the Bower
◆

This last text is dedicated to Cassandra, Jane's beloved sister. Dated August 1792 (when Jane Austen was almost seventeen), it remained unfinished. We can recognise a few similarities with what would later become *Northanger Abbey*.

There are also a few poems, as well as a parodic letter, attributed to Jane Austen, dated 28 March 1789, signed under the pseudonym Sophia Sentiment, to the *Loiterer*, the satirical journal published by Henry and James Austen in Oxford. An amusing reading of the letter by Emma Corrin (who plays Lady Diana in the Netflix series *The Crown*) is available on the *Letters Festival* YouTube channel.[34]

Did you know?

THE FRENCH EDITIONS OF *JUVENILIA* ARE NOT QUITE THE SAME AS THE ENGLISH EDITIONS.

The publication of *Juvenilia* was a late arrival in France. It was the publisher Christian Bourgois who first had the works translated into French by Josette Salesse-Lavergne, in 1984. This is the translation still used today in all French editions. This edition is unusual in that it includes texts that are not in the British edition of *Juvenilia*. In a third part entitled *Miscellaneous Works*, the publisher added *Plan of a Novel According to Hints from Various Quarters*, which Jane Austen devised after 1816, following her correspondence with the Prince Regent's librarian, James Stanier Clarke. There are also some late poems, *Opinions of Emma* and *Opinions of Mansfield Park*,[35] which are not early works, since they were published after the publication of these two novels.[36] The British editions scrupulously respect the three-volume division created by Jane Austen herself.

These texts were passed down through several generations of the Austen family. As a result, they were ignored by readers and critics for many years. One of the novelist's nephews, James Edward Austen-Leigh, was the first to offer a few extracts, in 1871, in the second edition of his aunt's biography, *A Memoir of Jane Austen*. The remainder of these texts were published between 1922 and 1951, made public either by a rightful owner or by auction.

---

[34] *The Crown's* Emma Corrin reads a 13-year-old Jane Austen's letter
[35] As well as two fragments, one entitled *Poems* and the other *Prayers*.
[36] Published in English in *The Cambridge Edition of the Works of Jane Austen. Later Manuscripts*, Janet Todd and Linda Bree (eds), Cambridge, 2008.

Letters

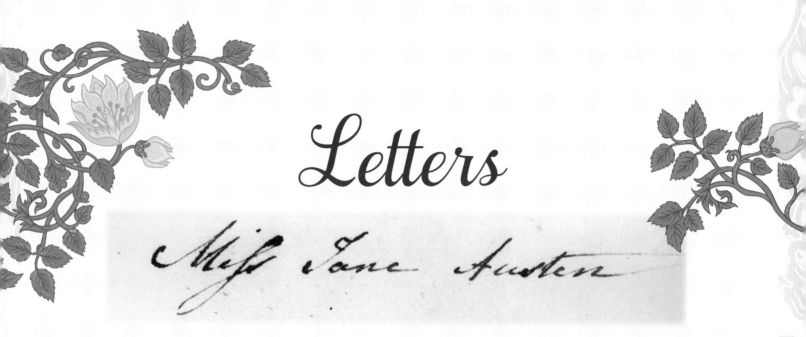

Jane Austen wrote some three thousand letters over the course of her life. Approximately[37] one hundred and sixty have been preserved, ninety-five of which are addressed to her sister. Deirdre Le Faye, a specialist in the subject, has studied this precious correspondence at length. She observed that the two sisters systematically wrote to each other when they were separated. A letter would arrive and a reply would then immediately be prepared. If Jane Austen was travelling, she immediately wrote to Cassandra, giving news of the family or relatives visited, and telling her some details about the trip. When Cassandra left, the novelist anticipated her sister's arrival, writing a missive in advance, that would sometimes await her when she arrived. She told her all that had happened since she left. So Jane Austen was almost always at the origin of their exchanges.

Why are there so few letters left out of these three thousand? In those days, it was not uncommon to throw your letters into the fireplace after reading them —it was a common practice. Cassandra also took her role as guardian of her sister's memory seriously. She knew that some letters contained information or comments about people close to her. These letters were personal, memories she didn't necessarily want to share. This was part of Cassandra's intimacy that she wanted to preserve, like the secrets the two sisters whispered to each other in the quiet of their bedroom at night. Caroline Austen, her niece, the daughter of James and Mary Lloyd, recounts that Cassandra told her that she had burnt some letters and crossed out others, after careful and thorough examination. These events took place two or three years before her death, in 1845.

The first very incomplete edition of Jane Austen's letters was published in 1884 thanks to Fanny Knight's son, Edward Knatchbull-Hugessen, the first Baron of Brabourne. This version is dedicated to Queen Victoria. This echoes Jane's dedication of *Emma* to the Prince Regent almost seventy years earlier. In 1946, one of Lord Brabourne's great-grandsons married one of Queen Victoria's great-great-granddaughters.

Other letters were subsequently discovered and added as editions were made, first in 1932 by Dr R.W. Chapman. A second edition was published in 1952 under his direction, with five additional letters. The first edition, edited and annotated by Deirdre Le Faye, dates from 1995, the second and most recent from 2011. She was working on a new version just before her death in 2020.

---

[37] Deirdre Le Faye explains in her 1995 edition of *Jane Austen's Letters* that there are still a handful of letters held by private individuals who do not wish to share them.

Letter from Jane Austen to her sister Cassandra, 30 November 1800

DEDICATION TO QUEEN VICTORIA

To The Queen's most excellent Majesty
Madam,

It was the knowledge that your Majesty so highly appreciated the works of Jane Austen which emboldened me to ask permission to dedicate to your Majesty these volumes, containing as they do numerous letters of that authoress, of which, as her grand-nephew, I have recently become possessed. These letters are printed, with the exception of a very few omissions which appeared obviously desirable, just as they were written, and if there should be found in them, or in the chapters which accompany them, anything which may interest or amuse your Majesty, I shall esteem myself doubly fortunate in having been the means of bringing them under your Majesty's notice.

I am, Madam,
Your Majesty's very humble 		*and obedient subject, Brabourne.*

DEIRDRE LE FAYE, THE JANE AUSTEN EXPERT.

Deirdre Le Faye's interest in Jane Austen began when she discovered documents relating to Jane Austen's paternal aunt, Philadelphia Hancock. She went to look for her grave, where her daughter Eliza de Feuillide and her grandson are also buried (see pages 26 and 27). So began her immense research work. While working full time at the British Library as an administrator in the Department of Medieval and Later Antiquities, she devoted her spare time to leafing through the family archives of the Austen descendants who gave her free access. Using the information she gathered, she set about completing the biography of William and Richard Austen-Leigh, adding to it everything she had been able to collect. She then took R.W. Chapman's letters, reorganised them chronologically, annotated them and added several indexes: biographical, topographical and by theme, such as clothing, religion and outdoor activities. These two works are benchmarks in the Austenian world.

She later became a patron of the library at Chawton House, the home of Jane Austen's brother Edward Knight, and bequeathed all her records to the descendants. Deirdre Le Faye devoted most of her life to studying the Austen family. Her meticulous and methodical work has been recognised by leading universities, which have given her the opportunity to publish books that are well documented and factual, full of small details and anecdotes. In addition to seventy articles, Deirdre Le Faye is also the author of several books devoted to the novelist.

Jane Austen did not enjoy any real success during her lifetime. The infatuation with her came after her death, and was literally exponential. Today, there are countless festivals, events, conferences and gatherings of Janeites all over the world. Jane Austen is an integral part of our everyday lives.

PART III

Jane Austen's legacy

Festivals

Festivals devoted to Jane Austen take place mainly
in the English-speaking world, with highlights
in the UK twice a year.
Janeites from all over the world gather here to celebrate
the memory of their favourite novelist and immerse
themselves in the Regency era for a few timeless days.

Log book
Bath Festival

Bath's Jane Austen Festival is a must for EVERY Janeite! It's just like going back in time to the Regency era. The whole city is euphoric, colourful and lively... It's both a trip back in time and an original cultural experience if you make the most of the occasion!

In 1894, George Saintsbury, professor of rhetoric and specialist in English literature at Edinburgh University, coined the English adjective Janeite in his introduction to a reprint of Pride and Prejudice. *In 1926, the famous British writer Rudyard Kipling took up this theme and entitled a short story* The Janeites. *The term was popularised in 1940 when Dorothy Darnell founded the Jane Austen Society in Chawton.*

A small group of us attended the Jane Austen Festival in Bath in 2022. Here's a step-by-step account of our preparations, with additional information and photos on our Instagram page ⓘ **jane_austen_france**.

It's best to draw up a fairly detailed plan well in advance, so as not to waste time on site. In a nutshell, it's all about organisation!

You might think it would be complicated to get to the Jane Austen Festival from outside the UK, but it's not.

General information

- The Jane Austen Festival takes place in Bath, Somerset.

- It was created in 2001 under the aegis of the Jane Austen Centre.

- It generally starts in the second week of September.

- It lasts ten days.

- It offers lectures, plays, meetings, a parade and a ball.

- It's a chance for Jane Austen fans from all over the world to meet up, in costume or not!

STEP 1: FOR MORE INFORMATION

→ First of all, and this is information to be taken seriously, the English are generally very polite and helpful. That's exactly what we love about them! If you have any questions before you leave, don't hesitate to contact the festival team at **contactus@janeausten.co.uk**.

→ Online, you'll find all the details (dates, programmes and all kinds of information) on the official website, in the *festival* section. The website reminds us that 2025 will mark the 250th anniversary of Jane Austen's birth. Don't miss the festival that year!

→ Taking part in this event requires a certain budget. In addition to travel and accommodation, you should expect to pay £20 for entry to the parade and £80 for the ball. However, many activities, such as lectures, are free of charge. Further information is also available on the **visitbath.co.uk** tourism website.

STEP 2: BOOK

The earlier you book, the cheaper it is, and this applies to both transport and accommodation.

→ By train on the Eurostar

If you are coming from continental Europe, you can buy tickets a year and a half in advance on the **eurostar.com** website or directly at the Gare du Nord in Paris. They can be exchanged, subject to price adjustments. Top tip: Subscribe to the Eurostar website newsletter to take advantage of special offers. Reduced-price tickets are sometimes available for as little as €39 (£33).

→ By plane

The nearest airport to Bath is Bristol. A shuttle bus can take you directly from the airport to Bath city centre. More information is available on the **airdecker.com** website, and return tickets cost £22.

→ By car on the Shuttle

Visit **eurotunnel.com** to book your journey from Coquelles (Pas-de-Calais) to Folkestone (Kent). The crossing takes thirty-five minutes, and everything is clearly explained —just follow the arrows. Travel time from Folkestone to Bath is around three and a half hours, via the M25 and M4 motorways. And don't forget, in England, we drive on the left!

→ By ferry

From Calais, visit **directferries.fr**; from Normandy or Brittany, visit **brittany-ferries.fr**.

STEP 3: TRAVEL

Travelling in England is not difficult, on the contrary, the rail and road networks are dense and the towns well connected:

→ For train travel in England, visit **national.co.uk**.

Once you're in London, you can get to Bath from Paddington station. If you arrive in London via St Pancras station, to reach Paddington, allow fifteen minutes on the Circle or Hammersmith & City lines, thirty minutes on the 205 bus, or between fifteen and thirty minutes by taxi, depending on traffic.

At Paddington station, take the opportunity to take a photo with the statue of the bear of the same name, on the left-hand side of the station near the toilets, under the big clock. It takes around two hours to get to Bath.

The National Express bus from Victoria station takes between three and four hours to Bath. The site is available at **nationalexpress.com/en**.

If you hire a car, it's best to collect it from the airport, so as to avoid central London, where traffic can be heavy at certain times of the day.

STEP 4: ACCOMMODATION

Rentals are literally packed during the festival. Fortunately, there is no shortage of specialist websites.

The affordable YMCA in Bath, which is fairly central and not far from the station, is a good option; information is available on the website at **ymcabath.org.uk**.

To join the parade at Sydney Gardens in the north of the city, it's best to stay in the city centre, especially if you're in costume. It's more practical and comfortable. Imagine, to add insult to injury, that you've forgotten your reticule, your fan, your parasol or your pommel cane —it'll be easier to go back and get them (I've been there!).

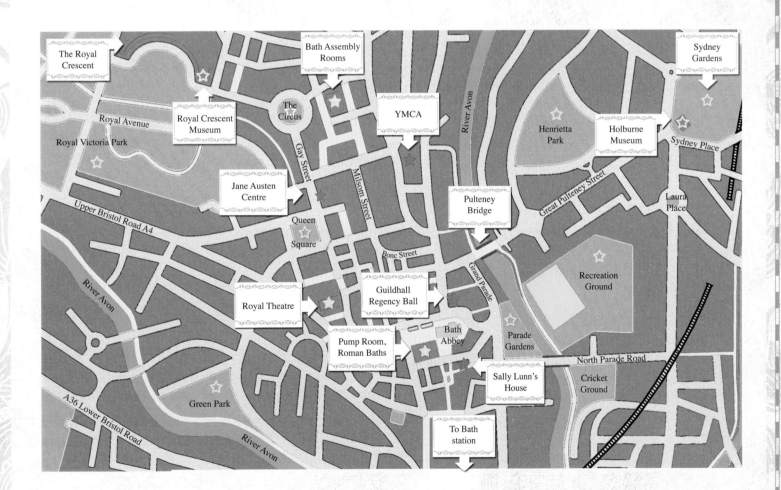

STEP 5: DRESSING UP

A lady's evening attire consists of:

a tiara and jewels

a dress with puffed sleeves

a belt

a fan

long gloves

a reticule

an embroidered shawl

A lady's evening undergarments consists of:

a long shirt

a bra worn over the shirt

a petticoat

white silk stockings

shoes laced with ribbons

➤ For a lady's outfit, you can always find a long, high-waisted dress with puffed sleeves, add a short blazer, a wide belt, a customised hat (flowers, feathers, ribbons —let your creativity run wild), a few accessories (jewellery, parasol, fan, gloves— fingerless are better for using your phone), a pair of simple ballet flats or ankle boots, and you're all set.

➤ If you want to take things to the next level, you can always hire a costume, or buy one from specialist websites.

➤ For examples of beautiful made-to-measure outfits, check out the website of Maureen Vinot, a Breton dressmaker and fan of Jane Austen and English culture, **boutiquemaureen.com**.

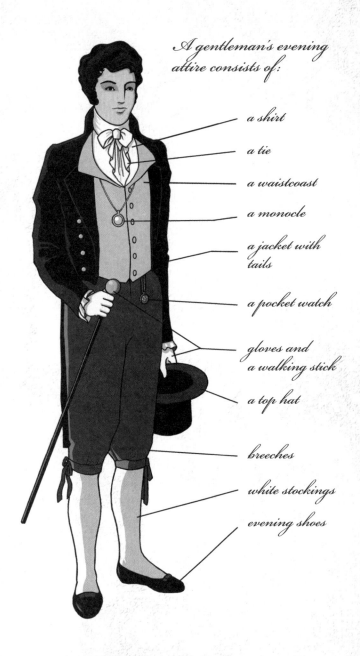

A gentleman's evening
attire consists of:

a shirt

a tie

a waistcoast

a monocle

a jacket with
tails

a pocket watch

gloves and
a walking stick

a top hat

breeches

white stockings

evening shoes

➤ For your hairstyle: a bun or hat? Bath can be windy —it's not that far from the coast— and you'll need your hands to take lots of photos and hold your reticule. Unless you're wearing a hat that sits well on your head, opt for a pretty hairstyle, preferably accessorised (ribbons, tiaras or feathers work very well).

➤ Finding a gentleman's outfit can be more complicated. Unless you're good at needlework, you'll need to use the rental sites. You'll need boots, a top hat, even a frock coat.

➤ You can also choose a themed costume, such as that of a military man or a clergyman (Mr. Collins, you've been found out).

On the **visit.somerset.co.uk** website, you'll find a link to a specialist site, Farthingale, which works directly with the Jane Austen Festival in Bath. A safe bet!

STEP 6: DO NOT FORGET

Here's our festival checklist with extra tips for international visitors:

❊ **Passport** (compulsory to enter the UK since 2021).

❊ **Bank card/Sterling** (top tip: choose a free card with no exchange fees).

❊ **Train or electronic tickets** (top tip: download the apps for your journey, Eurostar, Eurotunnel, etc., so that when there are delays, you will be informed in real time).

❊ **Hotel reservations or AirBnB.**

❊ **Programme and tickets for the festival.**

❊ **British plug adapters.**

❊ **Small sewing kit** (thread, needle, safety pins —these can save a whole outfit!)

❊ **Accessories,** these are important, especially if your outfit is modest. Don't skimp on tiaras, jewellery, ribbons, stoles, gloves, mittens, feathers, parasols, fans, reticules, etc.

❊ **Comfortable shoes** for the parade, because you walk as much as you stand, and that's for several hours.

❊ **Reading for the journey?** Why not dive back into *Persuasion* or *Northanger Abbey* which are partly set in Bath?

STEP 7: HAVE FUN

➤ Throughout the festival, the city of Bath is abuzz with activity. The atmosphere is extremely festive, joyful and good-natured. The crowds, the enthusiasm and, above all, the ingenuity of the British and foreign participants are impressive when it comes to celebrating Jane Austen and the Regency period. Costumes rival each other for elegance, colour and originality, but above all for historical accuracy. But nothing is imposed, there is no stress, everyone participates as they want.

➤ There is a charge for most of the festival's activities. The official website gives details of bookings and prices, and the full programme is online ahead of the event. There will be strolling plays, lectures, book signings and themed tours, as well as an authentic fair as in Jane Austen's time, where you'll find everything you need in muslins, ribbons and fans.

➤ The festival's main event is undoubtedly the parade, which invariably takes place on the first Saturday of the festival, when the costumed crowds gather to parade through the town in a movie-star atmosphere. Locals and tourists alike line the streets to capture the moment all the way to Queen Square, near the Jane Austen Centre at 40 Gay Street. Jane Austen and her family lived for a time at number 25. It now houses a dental practice!

➤ A little later, on Saturday evening, fans of period activities can meet up at the prestigious Regency Ball. You can attend to dance or just to watch. Express training courses and rehearsals are organised the afternoon before the ball, after the parade. So don't panic if you haven't yet mastered the steps of the quadrille or the boulangere! And don't forget to take a more refined outfit especially for the ball.

STEP 8: EXPLORING BATH

➤ There's plenty to do in Bath, which is a charming town. The historic city centre isn't very big, but it has everything, from supermarkets to bookshops. We can't recommend enough that you discover the joys of shopping in the many charity shops dotted around the city. They are full of little treasures at very affordable prices.

➤ The Theatre Royal offers a varied programme all year round, see **theatreroyal.org.uk**.

➤ An ancient Roman city, Bath boasts Roman baths dating back to the 1st century CE. It's best to plan ahead and book your ticket online at **romanbaths.co.uk**.

➤ In the same vein, you can also stop off at The Pump Room restaurant, just across the road (to sample the local water, known for its therapeutic properties but not really tasty on the palate), or simply to enjoy a good cup of tea.

➤ Sally Lunn's, **sallylunns.co.uk**, is also a must for tea time. Legend has it that in 1680, Solange Luyon, a Huguenot woman, fled persecution in France. She found work in the bakery that would later become Sally Lunn's. She also lived there and sold her bread rolls in the square next to the cathedral. The recipe was inspired by the French brioche. It was an immediate success. Solange Luyon became Sally Lunn, because the English couldn't pronounce her name, and her 'petits pains' became buns. The bakery changed its name several times over the years, until it became the tea room we know today. During renovation work carried out in 1937, the secret recipe for the buns was found in a cupboard hidden in the walls. In one of her letters, Jane Austen refers to a bunn (sic), tasted in Bath, certainly a Sally Lunn bun! In fact, in the tearoom, the upstairs room is called the Jane Austen room. It is also the oldest house in Bath, built in 1483.

IT'S TEA TIME?

You might think that in Jane Austen's day, people enjoyed the famous five o'clock tea. This is not the case.

Although tea has been a British favourite since the 18th century, the tea time *tradition is not Georgian, but Victorian, from 1840 onwards. Jane Austen never experienced this habit, which has become part of everyday life. The Duchess of Bedford, Queen Victoria's lady-in-waiting, was responsible for this invention. Towards the end of the afternoon, her Grace felt hungry. So a few sweet and savoury treats were prepared for her to be enjoyed with her tea. This pleased her enormously. The Duchess invited friends, who took up the concept themselves. The tradition had begun!*

Scones

INGREDIENTS
1 cup single cream
1 cup lemonade
3 cups self-raising flour
1 pinch of salt
A little extra flour
Egg yolk or butter (for glazing)
Jam, marmalade and clotted cream to serve.

Would you like a good scone recipe for your tea? We know one that's easy to make, with a secret: lemonade!

If you don't have clotted cream (a typically British speciality), Isigny cream, which is very rich in fat, will do the trick. Salted or unsalted butter (preferably spreadable), also works very well. And don't forget to serve it all with a nice cup of tea, just the right amount, in your finest china!

➤ Preheat the oven to 220°C (conventional oven) or 200°C (fan oven).

➤ Sift the flour three times into a large bowl. This step must not be neglected, otherwise the recipe will go wrong.

➤ Mix the lemonade, cream and salt with the flour in the bowl to make a soft, sticky dough.

➤ Roll out the pastry on a generously floured surface.

➤ Knead the dough very lightly until it is smooth.

➤ Shape it into a large square, about 3 cm thick.

➤ Then cut it into regular-sized squares.

➤ Place the squares on a baking tray lined with floured baking paper, leaving a little space between them.

➤ Brush lightly with a little butter or egg yolk.

➤ Place in the oven for ten to fifteen minutes, until the scones are golden brown.

Did you know?

So, cream on top or underneath the jam? There are two schools of thought on this thorny issue. In true Devon fashion, the cream goes first. Following Cornish tradition, it's the jam first. In fact, it comes down to logic. If the scone is warm, it's best to put the cream on top of the jam. If the scone is cold, put the cream first! And does the milk go in the cup before or after the tea? If the porcelain is fine, the tea comes first. If the cup is of lesser quality, the milk —cold— is poured in first to prevent the china from cracking.

STEP 9: EXPLORING FURTHER AFIELD

If you're feeling adventurous and the English countryside inspires you, don't hesitate, because the region is very lush and green.

➤ Just near the station is a little corner of paradise, Prior Park (entrance fee: £8). The Bath City 2 bus journey takes ten minutes. You can buy your £2 bus ticket on the bus with a bank card. This authentic 18th century English garden offers spectacular views over the city of Bath. Here you can admire one of the last four Palladian bridges.

➤ The second place to visit around Bath is Claverton Manor. It is a beautiful mansion that once belonged to a lawyer in the 19th century, in the heart of a huge park, which today houses the American Museum (bus U1 or U2, then fifteen minutes' walk). It offers a fine panorama of art and folklore from across the Atlantic (entrance fee: £13). A change of scenery is guaranteed!

Prior Park and its Palladian bridge

FOLLOWING IN THE FOOTSTEPS OF JANE AUSTEN:

◆ A two-and-a-half-hour guided tour is available from Friday to Sunday. This is a private tour for up to six people. Book on: **strictlyjaneausten.com**

◆ There is a free audio format for a visit of about an hour and a half with a pdf guide to download: **visitbath.co.uk/blog/read/2019/11/in-the-footsteps-of-jane-austen-a-free-audio-walking-tour-b124**

Even more festivals

JANE AUSTEN REGENCY WEEK

Every year at the end of June, the county of Hampshire organises this major Jane Austen event. The festival has grown in importance over the years. As is often the case, it all started modestly. In 2005, the Phoenix Theatre Company offered a performance of *Persuasion*. The success was encouraging. The following year, the event was a Regency-style dinner. In 2007, the phenomenon was extended over a weekend, with another themed dinner and a craft market. Each time, it was a great success. More volunteers and partners joined, including the town of Alton, Jane Austen's House Museum and Chawton House Library. As at the Jane Austen Festival in Bath, period costume is recommended to get the most out of the experience.

The programme is rich and varied and is spread across a number of venues between Alton and Chawton. On the first day, festival-goers gather in Alton town centre's High Street in the morning for a free costume walk —only carriage rides attract a fee. The Regency atmosphere can then be enjoyed, with re-enactments by locals, as well as the craft market. Dance workshops are also available on registration, in preparation for the ball at Alton's Assembly Rooms. Other walks, one of which is a highlight, aim to raise awareness of literacy. Lunches, cultural visits, readings, lectures, picnics, afternoon teas and workshops (would you like to learn how to make your own bonnet or reticule?) are also among the activities on offer.

Information, schedule and prices at janeaustenregencyweek.co.uk

The festival is working in conjunction with the Jane Austen Literacy Foundation, set up by Caroline Knight (the novelist's fifth great-niece) to promote literacy among the world's most vulnerable populations.

Information on janeaustenlf.org

Oakley Hall

JANE AUSTEN SOCIETIES

The North American Jane Austen Societies, commonly known as Jasna, are extremely popular and active. The first American society dates back to 1979. Spurred on by Canadian novelist Joan Austen-Leigh,[1] Jane Austen's great-great-great-niece, the first Jasna group was formed one evening in October at a gala dinner at the Gramercy Park Hotel in Manhattan. Around one hundred guests attended the event. The other two co-founders, lawyer Henry Gershon Burke and school headmaster Jack David Grey, were also present. Each of them had an encyclopedic knowledge of Jane Austen's work and life.

But the idea was born much earlier. The first Jane Austen Society was founded in 1940 by Dorothy Darnell in Chawton. Jack David Grey and Joan Austen-Leigh met in Hampshire in 1975, at a ball held on the estate of Oakley Hall to celebrate the bicentenary of Jane Austen's birth. They danced together and realised their shared love for the novelist. Joan Austen-Leigh was the owner of her ancestor's small portable writing desk, which she later donated to the British Library. She also lent it to the Morgan Library in New York for a bicentenary exhibition. It was there that they met the third co-founding member, Henry Gershon Burke, who, with his familiarity with the legal world, helped give the society a legal framework.

---

[1] Also known by her married name of Joan Mason-Hurley.

Jack David Grey became the first Chair, with Henry Gershon Burke and Joan Austen-Leigh as Vice-Chairs. Joan Austen-Leigh also founded the magazine *Persuasions*,[2] which she edited, enriching the first issues with personal family archives. As a novelist, her own literary output was substantial: around thirty plays, including one devoted to her illustrious relative, *Our Own Particular Jane* (1975), two very popular novels, and rewrites of *Emma*, *Letters of Highbury: Mrs. Goddard, Mistress of a School* (1993), *A Visit to Highbury* (1995), and *Last Days at Highbury* (1996). Fun fact: a keen sailor, she named her boat *Elizabeth Bennet* and her dinghy *Mr. Darcy*.[3] A literary prize, the Joan Austen-Leigh Award, was created in her memory and is presented at each General Meeting, following a Young Writers workshop.

The society is divided into eighty-one local groups in the United States and Canada, and has a European branch in Stuttgart, Germany. Anyone can become a member. If you live in North America, you will also be invited to events organised near you. Joining such a large community gives you a feeling of belonging to a secret society, yet one that is very open to the world and the future. The local groups are very active and regularly organise costume parties, lectures, tea parties, balls and, above all, trips to Jane Austen country. In her essay on the Jane Austen fandom, Deborah Yaffe simply explains the phenomenon by saying that "Perhaps because Jane Austen is one of the most accessible of great writers— easy to read, easy to love".[4]

Each year, Jasna invites all its members to join them in different cities in the United States and Canada for three days of meetings and conferences, each with a different theme, such as "*Pride and Prejudice*, a rocky romance" or "The literary, political and cultural origins of Jane Austen". Jane Austen's work seems inexhaustible. Jane Austen societies are also active in Argentina, Australia, Brazil, Italy, Japan, the Netherlands, New Zealand, Pakistan and the United Arab Emirates.

Information on jasna.org

Did you know?

THE JANE AUSTEN FESTIVAL IN FRANCE

In March 2009, actress, author and director Céline Devalan organised a *Jane Austen Festival* in Senlis. For one week, this small town in the Oise region was on British time. Festival-goers could enjoy a literary café, an exhibition on Jane Austen, and a showing of Julian Jarrold's film *Jane*, followed by a debate with Professor Alain Jumeau from the Sorbonne. Finally, these few timeless days came to an end with the revival of the play *Les Trois Vies de Jane Austen* and a concert of Celtic music.

---

[2] Many articles are available online: **jasna.org/publications-2/persuasions-online**
[3] Joan Austen-Leigh died in 2001. She was descended from the Austen branch through James Austen, the novelist's elder brother.
[4] *Among The Janeites*, Deborah Yaffe, HarperCollins, 2013.

Famous museums and collections

Jane Austen's legacy extends beyond her meticulously written stories. Many people have worked to preserve her original manuscripts and objects that once belonged to her. Her most fervent admirers have done everything in their power to perpetuate her memory and make the ground she walked on a place that is still rich in emotion and history. Thanks to museums, libraries and a handful of seasoned fans, Jane Austen's daily life and work are now available to all, reinforcing the admiration she has earned for over two hundred years.

The museums

Hampshire is the corner of England where Jane Austen's imprint is most evident. The presence of two museums, one of which was her home, as well as the proximity of her birthplace and Winchester Cathedral, where she is buried, make the county a must for Janeites from all over the world.

JANE AUSTEN'S HOUSE

Jane Austen's house, museum in Chawton

Ideally situated at the entrance to the market town of Chawton, this cottage was the last official residence of Jane Austen, her sister Cassandra and their mother. In 1808, Edward Knight, the brother adopted by wealthy cousins, made this comfortable house available to them. It was a time for her to rest, revise the novels already started and create new ones.

The site itself is very old, built on a former 16th century farm that was extended over the years. The farm then became a pub, The New Inn, where a terrible incident occurred in the form of two bloody murders. It was a very noisy area, and a well-known crossroads. The roads of London and Kent converged here.

Edward Knight bought the premises and had them refurbished, with new windows and a beautiful tapestry. Jane Austen only lived there for eight years, but Cassandra lived there for thirty-seven. After her death in 1845, the cottage reverted to the Knight family, who had no further use for it. The premises were emptied and it was used as housing for farm workers for a century. For a time, there was a gentlemen's club here.

It took the passion of one woman, Dorothy Darnell, who founded the first Jane Austen Society, to come up with the idea of restoring the cottage as a writer's house. But it was 1940, and the war put a temporary halt to the project. The premises are still owned by the Knight family, who continue to rent them out. The descendant at the time, Commander Edward Knight, had no objection to selling, but the price of £3,000[5] was too high for the fledgling society.

---

[5] Around £210,000 today.

Fortunately it, the village library, which occupied one of the spaces on the ground floor of the cottage, vacated it, providing Dorothy Darnell with a temporary office. The case aroused the interest of two Jane Austen specialists, Elizabeth Jenkins and R. W. Chapman. Thanks to them, in 1946 *The Times* launched an appeal for donations, which raised almost half the purchase price. Finally, in 1947, a London lawyer, Thomas Edward Carpenter, took it upon himself to buy the cottage for the society, with the intention of dedicating it to the memory of his son, who had been killed in action in 1944. This explains the plaque in tribute to Lieutenant Philip John Carpenter on the façade.

The tenants gradually vacated the premises, and the Jane Austen Society took over the entire site after carrying out a few repairs. Dorothy Darnell effectively supervised the work with her sister Beatrice, so that on 23 July 1949, the official inauguration took place under the patronage of the Duke of Wellington. Objects and furniture that once belonged to the Austen family were donated by descendants or gradually recovered at auction. It was an immediate success and the cottage quickly became a place of pilgrimage.

---

[6] Lizzy is the nickname of the heroine of *Pride and Prejudice*, Elizabeth Bennet.

PORTRAIT OF LIZZIE DUNFORD, DIRECTOR OF JANE AUSTEN'S HOUSE IN CHAWTON

Since 14 April 2020, Lizzie Dunford (what a perfect name![7]) has been doing her dream job. She is the director of Jane Austen's House, dedicated entirely to the English novelist. When asked to summarise her daily tasks, she invariably replies: collecting donations, carrying out research, preparing exhibitions, welcoming tourists and prestigious visitors, such as Queen Camilla, the wife of King Charles III, in 2022.

But her main role is to keep this house alive, to make it known and to accompany it along the way, so that it continues to spread the influence of Jane Austen's work. Lizzie Dunford sees herself as a kind of ambassador for the museum. In 2020, during the Covid-19 pandemic, she realised the need to broaden the horizons of the house, and introduced virtual tours and online events that were followed around the world. Around fifteen people work alongside her, half of them being volunteers.

What she particularly likes about Jane Austen's novels is that they are written from an exclusively female point of view, a rarity in the literature of the period. For her, Jane Austen succeeded in giving women a voice. What's more, although the heroes are not perfect, this makes them all the more endearing. Although for Lizzie Dunford *Pride and Prejudice* is in a class of its own, her favourite novel is *Mansfield Park*. She considers it to be very daring, as it can be read on various levels.

Jane Austen Memorial House Museum, Chawton, Hampshire, United Kingdom.

Today, the museum is continuing its preservation work, in particular by maintaining and renovating the various rooms in the cottage. One team, for example, recreated an entire wall tapestry from a period fragment. A private, independent museum, Jane Austen's House depends entirely on ticket sales and donations. In 2021, an online fundraising campaign to save the roof of the cottage raised over £67,000.

The museum offers the unique experience of being transported back in time, of walking in Jane Austen's footsteps, of getting up close to how she spent her daily life for eight years. On display are a number of objects that once belonged to her, including sixteen of her letters, and her fine gold ring topped with a turquoise stone. This delicate piece of jewellery has remained in the Austen family for a long time, handed down from generation to generation. It nevertheless ended up at Sotheby's in 2012, where it was bought by an American artist.[7] But the British government objected to the sale, declaring the jewel a "national treasure". Donations from all over the world enabled the museum to buy it back in 2013.

You can buy a copy at janeausten.co.uk

At the end of the tour, a quick trip to the shop is a must. The museum is not open every day; the calendar can be consulted online at **janeaustens.house**. Just opposite, don't miss the delicious tearoom: **cassandrascup.co.uk**.

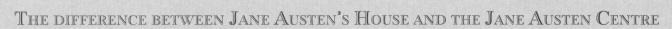

Did you know?

THE DIFFERENCE BETWEEN JANE AUSTEN'S HOUSE AND THE JANE AUSTEN CENTRE

Located in Bath, Somerset, and created in May 1999, the Jane Austen Centre is not strictly speaking an historic Austen site, although, the family did live in the same street, Gay Street. The centre offers a shop, a tea room, a short film telling Jane Austen's story, an collection explaining the Regency period and the novels, and a collection of objects and costumes related to the adaptations.

---

[7] Singer Kelly Clarkson.

CHAWTON HOUSE, THE KNIGHT MANOR

Chawton House, owned by Jane Austen's brother, Edward Knight, Chawton, Hampshire, southern England, United Kingdom.

This Elizabethan manor house is four hundred metres from Jane Austen's House. An important Austen family location, it was inherited by Edward Austen from his adoptive parents, Thomas and Catherine Knight. Edward had to change his surname when Catherine Knight died in 1812. This was the condition for inheriting the entire estate. Jane Austen was known to come here almost every day when her brother and his family were in the area.

Built for an ancestor, John Knight, the manor house dates back to 1580. It has been modified and extended several times over the centuries. The house was passed down from generation to generation, until Thomas Brodnax, who changed his name to Knight. It was his son Thomas Brodnax II, second cousin by marriage to Mr. Austen, who adopted Edward Austen. The house remained in the same family until 1992, when it was bought by a foundation.

The library has an impressive collection of almost nine thousand period books and works in partnership with the University of Southampton. In 2015, the manor house became a museum. Here you can see objects belonging to the Austen Knight family, as well as one of the novelist's favourite places: an armchair conveniently located near a window where she enjoyed reading every time she visited.

The manor house is also home to the study centre for English women's writing from 1600 to 1830, which organises regular exhibitions. The garden can be visited independently. A small tea room in the old kitchens serves delicious meals. When visiting Chawton House, volunteers are happy to explain the history of the site to tourists. If they are lucky, they may be welcomed by Jeremy Knight, a living descendant of this branch of the family.

Events calendar on chawtonhouse.org

Log book
Chawton

Chawton is situated in Hampshire, some eighty kilometres south of London, and is easily accessible from either Alton or Winchester.

STEP 1: TRAVEL

➤ **By train in England**, from London, to get to Alton or Winchester, the towns closest to Chawton which are served by train, visit the **nationalrail.co.uk** website.

➤ **The 64 bus** runs several times a day between Alton and Winchester via Chawton. The timetable can be consulted at **stagecoachbus.com**. Chawton can be reached in an hour from Winchester, or in around 15 minutes from Alton. Don't forget to press the Stop button to request the Chawton, Chawton Roundabout stop, otherwise the bus will continue on its way. The cost of the journey in either direction is £2.

➤ **Taxis to Chawton** from Alton station are very quick, taking around ten minutes and costing around £7.

➤ **By car**, it takes an hour and twenty minutes from London on the A31.

STEP 2: ACCOMMODATION

➤ **If you want to stay as close to Chawton as possible**, Alton is the place to be. Winchester is a little further afield, but this may allow you to include a visit to its cathedral, where Jane Austen is buried.

➤ **The Swan pub and hotel in Alton** offers a typically cosy British setting: **greenekinginns.co.uk/hotels/swan-hotel-alton/**

➤ **The Westgate pub and hotel in Winchester** has the advantage of being located in the city centre, five minutes' walk from the station, and the rooms, on the upper floors, are quiet: **westgatewinchester.com**

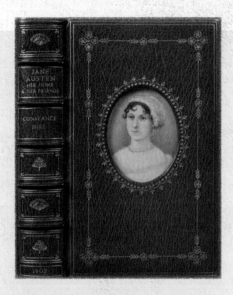

THE HILL SISTERS, THE FIRST TRAVELLING JANEITES

In 1901, the Hill sisters published what might be considered the first Austen travel guide, *Jane Austen, Her Home and Her Friends* (Dover Publications, 2018). Long before Shannon Hale and her *Austenland* (Charleston, 2013), they proposed the idea of an immersion in Austenland —they literally invented the word, since it is the title of the first chapter of their guide: *An Arrival in Austenland*. This travelogue, which follows in the footsteps of the novelist throughout the UK, was created by both sisters. Constance wrote the text and Ellen drew the illustrations.

Their testimony is all the more precious today because it tells of a bygone era, when these places were not tourist attractions and, above all, were much closer in time to Jane Austen's own life. The two young women talked to people connected to the family, gathered anecdotes and accessed unpublished documents and locations. They first went to Steventon, where Jane Austen spent a happy childhood. They then travelled to Bath, Lyme, Southampton, Chawton and Winchester. They visited all the places that were important to the author, and told the story of her life with emotion.

On the centenary of the novelist's death, 18 July 1917, the Hill sisters were invited to Chawton. They presented the house museum with a plaque, in solid oak and bronze, designed by Ellen and paid for by Janeite supporters from England and America. Several descendants of the Knight and Austen families were present. After the purchase of the plaque, there was enough money left over to fund a library in Jane Austen's name in the village of Steventon.

Constance and Ellen G. Hill also wrote books on women writers such as Fanny Burney, Maria Edgeworth and Mary Russell Mitford.

JANE AUSTEN

Lived here from 1809 to 1817, and hence all her works were sent into the world.

Her admirers in this country and in America have united to erect this tablet.

Such art as hers can never grow old.

FF THE BEATEN TRACK

Steventon, Jane Austen's birthplace

In 1808, the Austens chose Hampshire as their refuge, returning to the neighbourhood of Steventon, the parish where James Austen, who had succeeded his father, officiated. Walking through the Hampshire countryside, you really get the feeling that you're meeting a more intimate, secretive Jane Austen. Steventon is not a tourist destination, simply because there is nothing to see here other than the little 11th century church of St Nicholas.[8] At least, that's the impression you might get. In fact, we are literally following in the footsteps of a young Jane Austen, whose daily life is partly summed up in this isolated countryside.

On the way up to the church, you pass the site of the former vicarage, once home to the Reverend James Austen and his family. Demolished in 1823, it was replaced by a larger property. We can imagine the young woman walking the same route, from the rectory to the church, in the fields, at the risk of dirtying her dress, like Elizabeth Bennet, "six inches deep in mud".[9]

At the entrance to the church, a sign with a silhouette of the novelist at her desk pays tribute to her status as a literary woman. Presented in 1936 by her great-grandniece Emma Austen-Leigh, a plaque on an inside wall of the church reminds us that she was born in the village in 1775. Her brother James lies in the adjacent cemetery, his wife Mary beside him. We remember with emotion how she cared for Jane Austen with sisterly devotion in her final days.

Visit the village website for more information:
steventonvillage.co.uk

To get there, take the 76 bus from Basingstoke bus station, then walk for about twenty minutes. From Chawton, the journey takes around 30 minutes by car.

---

[8] Not to be confused with St Nicholas Church in Chawton House.
[9] *Pride and Prejudice*, Jane Austen, *op. cit.*

The *famous collections*

The English novelist left only six novels, which makes a simple text written in her own hand belonging to her family, or even the smallest fragment that mentions her from near or far, all the more precious. Thus, her work also finds its way into the collections of enthusiasts and universities, ready to do anything to acquire their own "little bit of ivory".[10]

ALBERTA H. BURKE AND HENRY G. BURKE COLLECTION

The American Alberta Hirschheimer Burke was probably the biggest collector ever of Jane Austen's work. Alberta was the wealthy heiress of a family that made its fortune in the agricultural machinery trade. In 1928, she was a student at Goucher University in Baltimore, Maryland. A year later, she was just beginning to take an interest in Jane Austen when she came across a bibliography, the first descriptive list of historical editions of her novels, by Geoffrey Keynes,[11] a British army doctor and author.

In 1930, she married the lawyer Henry Gershon Burke, the brother of one of her classmates. It was with him that she really began her collection, which in a way became her life's work: collecting everything she could find on the English novelist, her "Austen archives", as she called them.

---

[10] *Jane Austen's letters*, Deirdre Le Faye, Oxford, 2011.
[11] *Jane Austen, A Bibliography*, The Nonesuch Press, 1929.

In 1935, the couple travelled to England. No sooner had they arrived at Waterloo station than they came face to face with a W. H. Smith newsagent. On one of the shelves was Lord Cecil David's biography of *Jane Austen*,[12] just published by Cambridge University Press. This passion would never leave them. The couple made a habit of rereading Jane Austen's six novels aloud every year.

Alberta Burke bought the vast majority of her most precious pieces when the market was not yet too developed, during the 1930s and 1940s. To these treasures, she added anything she deemed worthy of interest. She listed all the newspaper and magazine articles relating to Jane Austen, grouping them together in ten albums; not a single scribble escaped her notice. Her collection also included drawings, posters, film stills and radio scripts. She also patiently compiled a catalogue of different editions from around the world, which she gathered on her travels.

But that's not all. When Alberta Burke was consider buying a piece, whether it was from another enthusiast, a bookseller or an academic, she carefully kept all her correspondence, including a copy of her own letters. These letters are packed with a thousand and one details, providing even more information about the origin and context of each book or object. The highlight of her collection is undoubtedly a copy of the first American edition of *Emma*, published in Philadelphia in 1816, which she found at an auction in 1945. She bought it from a British buyer, which led her to say that it would cross the Atlantic again.

In a letter to Eleanor Falley, the librarian at Goucher University, Alberta Burke wrote: "I am always enchanted by any little scrap of knowledge which has anything to do with Jane Austen".[13] She described herself as a passionate Janeite. She also owned a lock of the novelist's hair, bought at Sotheby's in 1948, which she later donated to Jane Austen's House Museum in Chawton. The anecdote about this is delightful. It took place during a meeting of the Jane Austen Society, at which the members expressed regret that an "American" had acquired this relic, without knowing that the buyer was actually in the room with them. After a while, Alberta Burke introduced herself as this "American", in front of the astonished audience, and offered this souvenir, which she had intended to donate to the museum anyway.

Her collection comprises more than a thousand items, including first editions of all of Jane Austen's novels, in several copies, as well as British books and periodicals from the Regency period, on subjects as varied as architecture, gardening and fashion. For nearly five decades, Alberta Burke patiently collected everything she deemed worthy of preservation. On her death in 1975, she bequeathed part of her precious collection to the Morgan Library in New York and the other part, known as the Jane Austen Collection, to Goucher University. Her husband, Henry Burke, was one of the founders of the Jane Austen Society of North America (Jasna) in 1979.

When he died in 1989, Goucher University inherited over a thousand of his books, all his wife's correspondence and the archives of the Jane Austen Society. In 1998, Jasna member Barbara Winn Adams added a further two hundred and seventy-five books to this already impressive collection. All these archives are now accessible to students and researchers.

Information on janeausten.goucher.edu

---

[12] Lord David Cecil published another biography forty-three years later, in 1978: *A Portrait of Jane Austen* (Hill and Wang, 1978).
[13] *Everybody's Jane: Austen in the Popular Imagination*, by Juliette Wells, Continuum Books, 2011.

THE RANSOM COLLECTION

The Harry Ransom Center is a library and archival preservation facility located at the University of Austin in Texas. Founded in 1957 by a former university president, Harry Huntt Ransom, this gigantic database holds some thirty-six million manuscripts, one million old and rare books, including a copy of the Gutenberg Bible, a collection of around five million photographs from all eras, and over one hundred thousand works of art. In particular, the centre holds the complete archives of several great writers, including John Steinbeck, T. H. Lawrence and Evelyn Waugh, including his own copy of the famous Peacock edition of *Pride and Prejudice* illustrated by Hugh Thomson.

Academic Janine Barchas[14] is one of the leading figures in this institution. A Jane Austen specialist, she organised an exhibition entitled *Austen in Austin* in 2019. The following year, she made a surprising discovery in the university archives: a script for a radio play of *Pride and Prejudice*, written by the famous playwright Arthur Miller,[15] based on Helen Jerome's play, the one used in the adaptation of the Robert Z. Leonard film in 1940, starring Laurence Olivier as Mr. Darcy. At the time, Arthur Miller's work was his bread and butter, but with hindsight it represents an unusual encounter between two very different literary geniuses. This sixty-minute piece was broadcast on 18 November 1945, on the occasion of Thanksgiving. Actress Joan Fontaine[16] is the voice of Elizabeth Bennet. This script forms part of the Arthur Miller archive, which was bequeathed to the Harry Ransom Centre on his death in 2005.

The Harry Ransom Center holds letters from James Edward Austen-Leigh, the novelist's nephew, a first edition of *Pride and Prejudice*, annotated in Cassandra Austen's hand, and various editions of Jane Austen's novels from all periods.

Information on the utexas.edu website

Did you know?

PRINCETON, THE OTHER AMERICAN UNIVERSITY COLLECTION

Princeton University in New Jersey has a copy of each of the first editions of Jane Austen's novels in its rare books section. In 1971, the bibliophile and philanthropist Robert H. Taylor bequeathed his collection of seven thousand books, manuscripts and drawings of English and American literature. Among these treasures are letters exchanged between Jane Austen's sister, Cassandra Austen, and her niece, Anna Austen Lefroy, known as Mrs. B. Lefroy, and two letters from Jane Austen to Cassandra.

Information on princeton.edu

---

[14] She and her students also launched the **whatjanesaw.org** website in 2013. See Part I, *Jane Austen in London*.
[15] A Pulitzer Prize-winning and prolific playwright, he was married to actress Marilyn Monroe.
[16] Five years earlier, she was Laurence Olivier's partner in Alfred Hitchcock's *Rebecca*, based on Daphne du Maurier.

MORGAN LIBRARY COLLECTION

The Morgan Library is a museum and library located at 225 Madison Avenue in New York. It is well known to Janeites as the only place with a complete manuscript in Jane Austen's handwriting, *Lady Susan*, as well as the eight sheets she wrote following her correspondence with James Stanier Clarke, *Plans of a Novel*, and a fragment of the *Watsons*. The museum's archives also hold fifty-one letters by the novelist, making it the largest collection of Jane Austen's letters in the world. This treasure trove is carefully preserved out of sight, and brought out for temporary exhibitions.

The history of the museum is also interesting. Banker John Pierpont Morgan bought the premises in 1880. He was a passionate collector. He created a library of rare and beautiful works, including a Gutenberg Bible, which he supplemented with prints, drawings and various objets d'art. In accordance with his father's wishes, J. P. Morgan Jr. transformed it into an institution that was open to the public in 1924. The museum also holds the original manuscript of *The Little Prince* by Antoine de Saint-Exupéry. A glass building, designed by architects Renzo Piano and Beyer Blinder Belle, completed the museum's structure in 2006. The interior decoration is grand, with rare floor-to-ceiling artwork and, in some rooms, creaking floors. It's a haven of peace in the heart of the hustle and bustle of the city.

Information on themorgan.org

Jane Austen's little portable desk (British Library)

BRITISH LIBRARY COLLECTION

London's British Library is a veritable institution. With nearly fourteen million books, it is one of the largest libraries in the world, alongside the Library of Congress in Washington. Originally a department of the British Museum, it became independent after 1973, but only moved to its current premises near St Pancras station in 1998. It also has an annexe in Yorkshire. The library systematically receives a copy of everything published in the UK, known as legal deposit.

The library's archives house a number of important items relating to Jane Austen: *The History of England* that she wrote as a teenager, with illustrations by her sister Cassandra, chapters X and XI of *Persuasion*, letters, as well as the notes that the novelist collected and which are 'opinions' on her novels and two volumes of Juvenilia. But the most precious object is undoubtedly the small portable desk that Reverend Austen gave his daughter for her nineteenth birthday. It was donated to the British Museum by a Canadian descendant, the novelist and playwright Joan Austen-Leigh. This object is usually on display in the museum's permanent collection, but may be moved when it is being maintained or on special loan.

Information on bl.uk

THE BODLEIAN COLLECTION

The oldest part of Oxford University is eight centuries old, and the university has a network of twenty-six libraries, bringing the total number of references to over thirteen million. Jane Austen's family has always had important connections with Oxford University, from Mrs. Austen's uncle, Principal of Balliol College, to Mr. Austen and two of the novelist's brothers who graduated there. We also remember Jane Austen and her sister Cassandra attended Mrs. Cawley's classes in Oxford.

The collection of Jane Austen's work includes Fanny Burney's copy of *Camilla* (1796) with an inscription in Cassandra Austen's hand,[17] a volume of Juvenilia, a large part of the unfinished *Watson* novel, the other being held by the Morgan Library in New York, as well as first editions of her novels. The *Sanditon* manuscript is in the possession of King's College Cambridge. A major retrospective of these collections took place in 2017.

Information at visit.bodleian.ox.ac.uk

Did you know?

One of the largest collections of Austen archives belongs to the British Royal Family, much of which is held at Windsor Castle. It is a dizzying array of ninety-four references, including first editions, such as that of *Emma* presented to the Prince Regent and specially dedicated to him.

Information on rct.uk

In addition to various English-language editions of novels and essays, the Bibliothèque Nationale de France in Paris has French-language copies of every one of Jane Austen's novels, from the first printing in 1815 to the most recent publications available.

Information on bnf.fr

AN INCREDIBLE COLLECTION OF AUSTEN FAMILY PHOTOS ON EBAY

In 2019, an American collector, Karen Levers, made an incredible discovery on the eBay website. She thought she was acquiring a series of photographs of 19th century Irish strangers. She had just begun researching her husband's Irish origins.

She didn't know it at the time, but for $1,000 she was getting to see faces of people who knew Jane Austen. Jane died around ten years before the invention of photography. Names and faces with familiar features emerged from this album: Edward Knight, Charles Knight, Fanny the much-loved niece, who looks like an old lady. So many years had passed since Jane Austen's death, and yet she seemed more alive than ever.

Karen Levers shared her discovery with researcher Sophia Hill from the University of Belfast. They discovered that this album existed thanks to a certain Lord George Augusta Hill, an Irishman who married two of Jane Austen's nieces successively, Cassandra Jane Knight and Louisa Knight, daughters of Edward Austen Knight and Elizabeth Bridges. One of the novelist's brothers, Charles Austen, also married two sisters in his time, Frances and Harriet Palmer.

---

[17] A copy given by Lady Austen (also known as Martha Lloyd before her marriage).

Influence

The inspiration that Jane Austen has generated around
the world is astonishing. Her six novels are still among
the best-selling, and the film and television adaptations
of them are a huge success.
But her impact is also measured by the devotion of her fans
and the enthusiasm of her admirers, who reappropriate
her stories and characters in every possible way: prequels,
sequels, modern rewrites, but also goodies and other fantasies.
Jane Austen's world seems to be limitless.

Welcome to Austenland [21]

Jane Austen has a place in today's world. For some contemporary writers, the novelist has even been reincarnated as a literary heroine, like Elizabeth Bennet. In an unusual twist, her fans —the Janeites— have also become fictional characters. You can even find traces of the author in everyday objects. The Austenian influence has spread like wildfire across the globe over the last two centuries. Jane Austen reinvents herself, again and again, and there are literally no limits to this.

WHEN JANE AUSTEN BECOMES A CHARACTER IN A NOVEL

❋ American Stephanie Barron (aka Francine Mathews) is the author of the *Jane Austen Mysteries*: fourteen volumes in which Jane Austen leads a case.

❋ The popularity of Jane Austen in France has seen many contemporary authors insert the writer into new tales. A great example of this is the series A League of Extraordinary Women Writers, with the volume *Jane Austen contre le Loup-garou (Jane Austen against the Werewolf)* (Moltinus, 2020). Marianne Ciaudo describes Jane Austen as a hunter of supernatural creatures, while still living in Steventon, her small country village. In the same vein and in the same collection, she also appears in the tome *Ann Radcliffe, Jane Austen and Mary Shelley versus Carmilla* by Élisabeth Ebory.

---

[18] Term borrowed from Constance and Ellen Hill and their guide *Jane Austen: Her Home and her Friends* (1902).

✤ In *Le Musée Imaginaire de Jane Austen* (The Imaginary Museum of Jane Austen, Albin Michel, 2017), Fabrice Colin takes us back to the English author's personal museum, with pastel and poetic illustrations by Nathalie Novi.

✤ In *I Was Jane Austen's Best Friend*, Cora Harrison recounts the adventures of Jenny Cooper, who receives the help of her 15 year-old cousin Jane Austen to conquer the heart of a Captain (Macmillan, 2010).

✤ Julia Golding, a former diplomat, is the author of several sagas. Her series *Jane Austen Investigates* (Lion Fiction, 2021) imagines the novelist as a teenager embroiled in various mysteries. Her logical mind, keen sense of observation and insatiable curiosity come in handy in many a sticky situation.

✤ Lucy Worsley depicts, in *The Austen Girls*, a mature and weathly Jane Austen who plays the detective to help her nieces Fanny and Anna in her adventures (Bloomsbury Children's Books, 2020).

Did you know?

First times

Do you know what the first thesis written on Jane Austen was? It was by an American from Boston, William Henry George Pellew, a student at Harvard. In 1883, he wrote a thesis entitled *Jane Austen's Novels*. The rest of his life was both sad and funny. Throughout his life, he was interested in the paranormal. Sadly, he died young, aged thirty-three. Just before, he made it known that, if at all possible, he would come back to haunt his friends. Several eyewitness accounts have corroborated the facts: George Pellew has returned from beyond the grave to give them signs. This story does not reveal whether he met Jane Austen in the other world.

The first thesis in French was written by Léonie Villard in 1915 and was entitled *Jane Austen, sa Vie, son Oeuvre* (Jane Austen: her life, her work). It is now held in the archives of the University of Lyon. Léonie Villard was also the first woman to become a professor of literature at a French university. In 1917, her thesis was awarded the Rose-Mary Crawshay Prize[19] by the British Academy. Claire Tomalin, one of Jane Austen's biographers, also received the award in 2003 for her work on Samuel Pepys.

The first Jane Austen fan fiction, published in 1913, was written by Sybil Grace Brinton. Entitled *Old Friends and New Fancies*. In this story, all the characters from Jane Austen's novels know each other and meet. The book received an appreciative review from Virginia Woolf in a literary supplement to the *Times*. We know almost nothing about Sybil Grace Brinton. She married George Percival Preen, a wool mill manager, in 1908 at the age of thirty-four. In frail health, she died twenty years later, without having had any descendants or published another novel.

---

[19] Born Rose Mary Yeates (1828-1907), this British philanthropist and suffragette fought all her life for the right to education for all women.

WHEN JANEITES BECOME CHARACTERS IN A NOVEL

※ *The Jane Austen Book Club* by Karen Joy Fowler (Penguin, 2005) tells the story of a group of Californian women who are Jane Austen fans. They end up welcoming a young man into their midst because they're short of a partner. Jocelyn, Bernadette, Sylvia, Prudie, Allegra and Grigg form an unusual group: the Jane Austen Book Club. These avid readers have half a year to read (or reread) all six of the British author's novels.

Each participant must defend their favourite novel. Grigg, a newcomer to the Austen scene, takes *Northanger Abbey*, which the others do not particularly like. Jocelyn, who likes to meddle in other people's lives, chooses *Emma*. Sylvia and Allegra, mother and daughter, share *Persuasion* and *Sense and Sensibility*. Prudie, a melancholy French teacher, takes *Mansfield Park*.[20] As for Bernadette, the eldest and, in a way, the leader of the group, she takes *Pride and Prejudice* for herself. As the pages turn, Jane Austen's words resonate in their personal lives and influence every decision they make.

※ In *The Missing Manuscript of Jane Austen* (Penguin, 2012), American Syrie James fulfils the ultimate fantasy of every Jane Austenite: to find an unpublished manuscript! This is what happens to her heroine Samantha on a trip to Oxford. Syrie James explores the Austen world in two other novels, *The Lost Memoirs of Jane Austen* (William Morrow Paperbacks, 2007) and *Jane Austen's First Love* (Berkley, 2014). She is currently adapting another of her stories into a screenplay, *The Secret Diaries of Charlotte Brontë* (William Morrow, 2009).

Emily Blunt and Marc Blucas as Prudie and Dean Drummond.

THE JANE AUSTEN BOOK CLUB

In 2007, director Robin Swicord turned this novel into a delightful feature film, *The Jane Austen Book Club* starring Hugh Dancy, Maria Bello, Amy Brenneman, Maggie Grace, Emily Blunt and Kathy Baker. Before filming, each cast member was invited to read the book assigned to their on-screen character. The large volume used by Hugh Dancy in the film is in fact the complete works of Shakespeare, the cover of which has been changed by the prop master. The reason given for using this book is that the reduced budget did not allow the purchase of the real Jane Austen anthology. The film asks the question *What would Jane do?* The result is an anthological scene, showing just how easily Jane Austen can break into the everyday lives of those who are passionate about her.

The director, who is also the scriptwriter, deliberately made the characters younger than in the book. For each, she used an Austen model to refine their character. Bernadette, for example, was inspired by Mrs. Gardiner in *Pride and Prejudice*, as Elizabeth Bennet's wise aunt. Jocelyn, the leading lady, is of course Emma Woodhouse. Sylvia compares herself to Fanny Price in *Mansfield Park*, while her daughter Allegra's enthusiasm is reminiscent of Marianne Dashwood in *Sense and Sensibility*. Prudie is going through a turbulent period in her relationship, which echoes Anne Elliot in *Persuasion*. Finally, Grigg brings out the best in every male Austen character.

---

[20] The breakdown of the novels is slightly different in the film.

※ In *Austenland: A Novel* (Bloomsbury, 2007), Shannon Hale invented a new concept. You can go on holiday in a world that mimics that of the Regency (albeit with modern facilities), in the aptly named Austenland Park. This is the experience of its heroine Jane Hayes, who travels from her small New York flat to the plush English countryside to satisfy her obsession with Mr. Darcy. A film was released in 2013, directed by Jerusha Hess and starring Keri Russell and J. J. Feild as a couple reminiscent of Elizabeth Bennet and Mr. Darcy. Shannon Hale also wrote a sequel, *Midnight in Austenland* (Bloomsbury, 2012).

※ In *The Jane Austen Society* (St Martin's Press, 2020), Natalie Jenner recounts how Jane Austen enthusiasts met and set up the first Jane Austen Society in Chawton in 1940.

※ Polly Shulman and *Enthusiasm* (Putnam, 2006) invite us to follow the adventures of two teenage girls who live their daily lives through the prism of Jane Austen, and above all who are in search of a Mr. Bingley and a Mr. Darcy 2.0.

※ In *Confessions of a Jane Austen Addict* (Dutton, 2007) and *Rude Awakenings of a Jane Austen Addict* by Laurie Viera Rigler (Dutton, 2009), two young women swap places, one from the Regency era, the other from the 21st century. In 2010, these two novels were adapted into a series of three- or four-minute episodes under the title *Sex and the Austen Girl*.

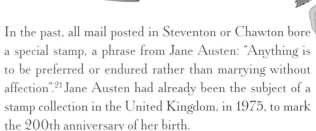

GOODIES AND OTHER ODDITIES

❋ Jane Austen is the only novelist to be recreated as a Funko Pop figurine. In her hand, she holds her greatest literary success, *Pride and Prejudice*. This brand of small figurines was created in 1998 in Washington State, USA. Around ten centimetres high, with a head disproportionately larger than its body, it is nonetheless very popular. The Jane Austen figurine was released in March 2021. It was an immediate success.

❋ To celebrate the two hundredth anniversary of *Pride and Prejudice* in 2013, the British Post Office released a series of collector's stamps depicting all six of Jane Austen's novels. The drawings were by Angela Barrett.

In the past, all mail posted in Steventon or Chawton bore a special stamp, a phrase from Jane Austen: "Anything is to be preferred or endured rather than marrying without affection".[21] Jane Austen had already been the subject of a stamp collection in the United Kingdom, in 1975, to mark the 200th anniversary of her birth.

❋ Jane Austen can be found in an infinite variety of forms: there are ephemeral tattoos in her likeness, plasters, candles, flower pots, hair clips, socks, telephone cases, cookie cutters, Christmas decorations, tea towels, tea tins, teapots, wallets, notebooks, pens, puzzles, card games, fortune telling sets, cookery books, and even books in which you are the hero, and more.

❋ The tote bag is undoubtedly the most popular item, especially the one that proclaims love for Mr. Darcy. Most of the official goodies can be found on the Bath Jane Austen Centre website **janeausten.co.uk**.

Did you know?

THERE ARE DIFFERENT PLACES IN THE WORLD NAMED AFTER JANE AUSTEN

There is a Jane Austen Street in Emfuleni, South Africa. In the United States, there is another Jane Austen Street in Houston and a Jane Austen Trail in Pflugerville, both in Texas. There is also a Jane Austen Course in Johnston, Iowa, and a Jane Austen Trail in Waldorf, Maryland. In England, a college in Norwich is named after Jane Austen. In France, there is an Allée Jane Austen in Strasbourg.

---

[21] Quote from *Pride and Prejudice*, Jane Austen, Egerton, 1813.

Jane Austen around the world

Jane Austen is now a real star, and not just among Janeites.
In the UK in 2003, *Pride and Prejudice* was voted Britain's favourite book, second only to
J. R. R. Tolkien's *Lord of the Rings*. In France, this same novel came nineteenth out of a list of
one hundred in the programme *Le Livre Favori des Français*, broadcast on France Télévisions in
December 2022. Finally, in 2023, there were no fewer than 683 million views of the hashtag
#janeausten on TikTok.

Jane Austen has inspired generations of fans. There have been countless rewritings, creations and even inspired vocations. An example was Georgette Heyer, who gave pride of place to the Regency era starting from her first novel. *The Black Moth* in 1921. Jane Austen's legacy can also be seen in the pool of romance specialists such as Mary Balogh, Loretta Chase, Lisa Kleypas and Julia Quinn. The modern British novel also owes a great deal to her, with the emergence of original writers such as

Elizabeth Jane Howard, Martin Amis, Jeffrey Eugenides and Tracy Chevalier.

We asked three questions to a number of Janeites from across the world to find out their 'first impressions' of the English novelist, the influence she has on their daily lives, and how they think Jane Austen would have reacted to the success she enjoys today.

FIRST QUESTION
What was the first Jane Austen novel you ever read?

SECOND QUESTION
What influence does Jane Austen have on your everyday life?

THIRD QUESTION
What do you think Jane Austen would say if she saw all the success and hype around her writing these days?

FRANCE

Céline Devalan

Author, actress and director

She wrote *Les Trois Vies de Jane Austen (The Three Lives of Jane Austen)*, performed Jane Austen on stage, and organised a Jane Austen festival in France.

1 I read *Emma* when I was fourteen and fell in love with the independence of this young woman, then at eighteen I read *Pride and Prejudice*, which I have ever since had to hand...

2 Jane Austen has considerably influenced, if not conditioned, my life as an artist and my personal life choices: to assert myself as a woman director and to be completely independent in my choice of artistic projects, to consider my shows as my children (as she spoke of her books when they were printed: "my own darling child"), giving up a life as a mother and a family in favour of creation (the difference Virginia Woolf emphasised between creation and procreation). And there's also a strong parallel between her relationship with her sister Cassandra and mine with my own sister, their unfailing support in our choices as artists.

3 I think she'd be flattered, but still humble, and above all, she'd discreetly laugh at those who think she's a "romantic" author in the "mawkish" sense of the term, ironically saying that they'd be better off rereading her books! I especially wonder how she would have reacted to seeing Darcy emerge from the water in the BBC series.

Lhattie Haniel

Novelist

She has written a fictionalised biography of Jane Austen, *Le Mystérieux Secret de Jane Austen (The Mysterious Secret of Jane Austen)*, and quotes the English novelist in each of her novels.

1 My first Jane Austen was *Pride and Prejudice*, but at the same time I also discovered *Sense and Sensibility* and her collection of essays *Juvenilia*.

2 Jane Austen has had, and continues to have, a certain influence on my life. Although my first admiration was for her writing, I have to admit that over time I began to appreciate the novelist for more than just this. She's part of my social life as a novelist, but she's also part of my day-to-day life: whenever I write or create something, I always wonder what she would think of it. She is a strong presence in my everyday life.

3 I think she would be humble enough not to express her joy, but deep down she would be happy and proud of the legacy she has left us and the passion that many people have for her, wether it is her writing or everything that revolves around her name. But I'm sure she'd have an ironic remark to say about it, and she'd even find the importance we attach to her world ridiculous, since she loved to laugh at everything.

Nathalie Novi

✿ Illustrator

✿ *A poet of images, with the novelist Fabrice Colin she created Le Musée Imaginaire de Jane Austen, un album empli de rêves et d'aquarelles (an album full of dreams and watercolours).*

1. My very first Jane Austen novel was of course *Pride and Prejudice*, as I think is the case for many. As the second youngest of a trio of tenderly humorous sisters, I took to this Bennet family straight away! I felt close to the reserved Jane, I admired Lizzie's tenacity and I fell in love with Mr. Darcy, whose uprightness I loved. I still love them in the same way, infinitely.

2. Jane Austen is my best friend, like a fifth sister in whom I might confide, and who, in return, might tell me all sorts of wonderful stories that I would enjoy painting, always (which is basically what I do!). She makes me laugh a lot, comforts me often, knows how to find the right words to convey a feeling, an emotion, shows me the way when I suddenly hesitate. I love walking alongside her, following her thoughts. I can read her novels again and again and never tire of them. I know every one of her characters. They could even cross paths in my life. Lizzie would then be friends with Anne Elliot, Captain Wentworth would enjoy Col. Brandon's company, Mr. Darcy would welcome them happily to Pemberley... Mrs. Bennet and Mrs. Jennings would be wallpapering, devouring little canapés and gossiping constantly. And I would be part of their circle, a happy spectator and official literary painter of their lives. In my daily life, I dance one step and then a counter step, to be as close as possible to her, who loved balls so much. And then I named my beige cat "Mr. Bingley", which allows me to refer to him familiarly as "my little Bibi"! I'm not sure whether Jane Bennet *herself* would have allowed it...

3. I think she would smile, if not laugh. Perhaps she wouldn't care most of the time and would probably laugh at herself. But I imagine her quietly pursuing her life as a writer in her cottage in Chawton, almost indifferent to the world, yet delighted to know that a woman can pass on such a wonderful legacy to her family. What a revenge on the inheritance system! She would probably be amused by self-important people who take the liberty of talking about her novels that they have never read, spraying them with rose and violet water for free. She would have the same caustic, tender gaze as the one she gives Mr. Collins for those who think they only know her from films, TV series and other fantasies, completely missing out on her wonderful writing and unfailing humour. I imagine that she would also feel some tenderness towards the (sometimes slightly ridiculous) Janeites. Perhaps they would have made great characters in a future novel? She would look kindly on all those directors and authors who, with beautiful Regency costumes and ultra-English landscapes, often simplify her work, reducing her novels to stories that always end in marriage, regularly forgetting her wit, her sharp, prickly, literary pen. But I think she'd be particularly fond of Ang Lee and Joe Wright, who have paid her a wonderful tribute in their film adaptation. The unconditional love for her by great artists like Virginia Woolf would probably have moved her, touched her heart. On the other hand, I'm not sure she would have liked to find out that some of her correspondence with her sister Cassandra had been published. What would she think of all the biographies and tributes devoted to her? I think she'd turn red. No doubt she would be surprised to know that her novels have been translated into so many languages. No doubt she would be amazed to find herself adored in countries so far from her native England, where she lived and set all her novels. And despite all the admirers who make her their own so easily, I sincerely hope that she would have agreed to be my best friend.

ABROAD

Syrie James

※ Writer

USA

※ Author of *The Lost Memoirs of Jane Austen*, *The Missing Manuscript of Jane Austen*, *Jane Austen's First Love* and the play, *Jane Austen in 48 minutes*.

1 In a college literature class, we read Pride and *Prejudice and Emma*. I knew at once they were special.

2 My life has been forever changed by Jane Austen. After reading her books, I fell in love with the 1995 BBC *Pride and Prejudice* and the film *Sense and Sensibility*. As a life member of JASNA I am thrilled to be immersed in Austen's world constantly, surrounded by like-minded people who have become forever friends. Although I follow Jane Austen's advice and rely on my own inner guide for most things, whenever I'm uncertain about something I ask myself, "What would Jane do?"

3 I think Jane Austen would be completely astonished, humbled, and amused by her popularity. She might say, "Who could have imagined that I would one day adorn the ten-pound note? My only regret is that the vast piles of pewter which have accumulated cannot revert to me posthumously."

Sonia Alain

※ Novelist

◖ Canada

※ She has been writing ever since she "fell in love" with the novels of Jane Austen and with *Angélique, the Marquise of the Angels* by Anne Golon.

1 *Pride and Prejudice* is a real favourite of mine.

2 I consider Jane Austen to be one of the first great female writers. I think her characters are magnificent and so well defined. That's how Jane Austen influences me when I create my own characters in my books. The realism of her stories is also a great template.

3 I think she would be happy about it, or at least feel some gratification. However, I also think that she would remain modest in the face of this success.

Amanda Grange

※ Novelist

🇬🇧 United Kingdom

※ She is the author of the famous *Diaries* of the Various Austen gentlemen.

1 My first Jane Austen novel was *Pride and Prejudice*. I found myself drawn in from page to page. It's the humour and the brilliant character portraits that I love most about this book.

2 Jane Austen teaches me not to take myself too seriously, and to see the bright side of life. I often find myself quoting her because she always has a *bon mot*[22] for every occasion.

3 Given her fabulous sense of humour, I'm sure she would laugh at this fame and popularity. At the same time, I think she would be quietly proud of the way she inspires generations of writers —and would still laugh at her own pride!

---

[22] A clever remark.

Abigail Reynolds

❧ Novelist

🇺🇸 United States

❧ She was a doctor before she started writing fan fiction in the 2000s. All her rewrites focus on *Pride and Prejudice*, especially the character of Mr. Darcy.

1 My first Jane Austen novel was *Pride and Prejudice*, when I was eleven.

2 Jane Austen has always been my favourite novelist, and I re-read her books every year. Her voice echoes in my head, and I often think about what she says about everything and anything. Writing about her characters has been a constant joy. I love researching her era and her books. In the process, I made some wonderful friends in the Janeite community.

3 After a phase of great astonishment, I think she would be very amused by this situation, and, given her sharp sense of humour wouldn't hold back with her family in making a few well-crafted remarks about attaching so much importance to books published so long ago. I think she'd be happy about it, but she'd also find a way of teasing us about it.

Mari Carmen Romero

❧ Essayist

🔵 Spain

❧ She is the author of an essay on the influence of the Janeite community in the Hispanic world, Historia de los Austenitas: *Una Cronica de Jane Austen en castellano y sus fans hispanohablantes*. She is also the founder of the Spanish Jane Austen Society **janeausten.org.es,** which is more than twenty years old.

1 In 1998, thanks to cable TV and the advice of my sister Almudena, I discovered the *Pride and Prejudice* series and immediately bought the book.

2 Jane Austen has had a huge influence on my life, not least through the **janeausten.org.es** website, which I set up with my sister. It has allowed me to meet a real community of people and friends, who may have different tastes or points of view, but Jane Austen unites us all.

3 I think she'd be happy to see her success, and that people like her books. At the same time, she'd be amazed, especially at all the people who take their inspiration from her. She would probably laugh at them a little.

Adriana Sales

❧ University Professor

🔵 Brazil

❧ She is the translator of *Emma* into Brazilian Portuguese and President of Jasbra (Jane Austen Society of Brazil).

1 In the early 1990s, I took an English literature course at university. The teacher presented a biography and books, with a focus on *Emma*. When I finished my degree, I read Jane Austen books for relaxation. From that day on, I fell in love with Jane Austen.

2 Jane Austen is an integral part of my life! I read or talk about her every day. As President of the Jane Austen Society in Brazil, I'm also in charge of our social media accounts, so I have to publish content every day.

3 I think she would have liked to see how her writings have influenced people around the world. I also think she was a rather reserved person, so interacting with people behind a keyboard would have suited her perfectly! A clever girl!

Prima Santika

⁂ Novelist

◗ Indonesia

⁂ *He is the author of a modern retelling of Sense and Sensibility in modern-day Indonesia, Three Weddings and Jane Austen.*

1 *Emma*, with Gwyneth Paltrow, for the films, and *Persuasion* for the books. I'm more of a film buff than an avid reader, which is why I know Jane Austen primarily through the films. I love romantic comedies from the 1990s and 2000s. After *Emma*, I watched *Sense and Sensibility*, and then *Pride and Prejudice*. After seeing *Sense and Sensibility*, I realised that I loved Jane Austen, so I bought all her novels. I ended up reading them just as I started writing mine. I couldn't rely on adaptations, so I had to read the books! At the time, I chose *Persuasion* because it was more contemplative and also shorter than the others. After that, I continued with *Pride and Prejudice, Emma, Sense and Sensibility, Mansfield Park* and finally *Northanger Abbey*.

2 Firstly, I'm a man, so I don't have a direct connection with Jane Austen from a personal experience. Secondly, I only know her books, I know nothing about her private life. I suppose she can't be reduced to two adaptations, like *Jane* or *Jane's Choice*. These are good films in my opinion, but certainly not enough to capture all the complexity of the real Jane Austen. That said, Jane Austen has had a huge influence on me. The adaptations of her novels and the various rewrites have helped me to understand women. I tried to imitate her writing style, I don't hesitate to express myself freely in long sentences. And I have so much sympathy for the characters that are mothers. Jane Austen's novels deal with being single and its problems, and writing a novel about women in Jane Austen's style gives me a broader perspective on the maternal point of view. The main character of my novel is a mother whose three daughters are single and looking for a loving marriage. Mothers play a crucial role in the education of girls, preparing

them for the realities of this world, and (in the case of my book) acting as matchmakers, because time is running out, whether they like it or not. I live in Indonesia, in the Javanese culture, where tradition plays an important role, particularly in marriage. Are we modern? We're modern! And we're feminists, for gender equality in both education and the workplace. As for marriage, we're pretty traditional, and in that I recognise the same values as in Jane Austen's time, when it was up to the man to make the first move. In my novel, this is one of the plot devices. Jane Austen has that spark, that quick wit, that intelligent point of view, in just a few words. She helps me understand what it's like to be a woman, a mother, a feminist in today's world.

3 I don't know Jane Austen's biography well enough to imagine what she would say, but in the films I've seen, there's a feminist aspect, independent, in control of her feelings and manners. She remained single, yet in each of her six novels, her heroines marry. They're all intelligent, educated, they know what they want, and that's a loving husband. So, in the end, I think Jane Austen might say to women, "Girls, do we always have to wait for men to make the first move?" But on the other hand, she could equally say "I knew the world wasn't going to change that much. All right, women have made progress, and that's good, very good! But still, what could be more beautiful than a loving marriage that lasts forever?".

Laaleen Sukhera

◈ Novelist

◗ Pakistan and the ◖ United Arab Emirates

◈ She is the founder of the Jane Austen Society of Pakistan and Emirates, and the author of a collection of short stories, *Austenistan*.

1 I was in England with my family one summer. At some point, I went to buy books with my Aunt Helen, who is English. For my twelfth birthday, she gave me a box set containing *Pride and Prejudice*, *Mansfield Park* and *Persuasion*, with magnificent illustrations by Hugh Thomson. So my very first novel was *Pride and Prejudice*, which I read straight away and then went on to read all the others. The mischievous repartee between Lizzie Bennet and Caroline Bingley caught my attention straight away and I sympathised with Kitty Bennet's excitement. To be honest, I didn't fall in love with Darcy until I saw Colin Firth play him. And when I read *Northanger Abbey*, I found I had a lot in common with Catherine Morland, in the sense that I had developed a real obsession with Agatha Christie at the time.

2 Everything that reminds me of Jane Austen and the Regency period fascinates me in everyday life. There's a part of me that constantly wants to escape into my own world, despite all the modern conveniences, in a *Lost in Austen* kind of way.

But I can also draw parallels with my own life and observations, in a postmodern way. For the first part of my life, I voraciously devoured the novels of Georgette Heyer, and all the Prinny biographies[23] that passed through my hands, coming to my university library from the United States. I still devour all the historical novels I can find. My favourite part of the day is tea time, if possible in an elegant setting with beautiful crockery. I'm hoping to organise a ball with waltzes this year. I love playing the matchmaker like Emma Woodhouse, and bringing people together. Some of them are now in a relationship! Oh, and I also prefer men in suits and dinner jackets.

3 Jane Austen would certainly have been highly amused and both shocked and flattered. Two hundred years on, she would see how many people from all over the world have come from so far away, and how many admirers continue to pay tribute to her in so many ways, in so many languages and in so many forms. But above all, she would have given us a witty take on the whole thing, while finding a way to invent memes of her own.

Teri Wilson

◈ Novelist

◗ United States

◈ She is a prolific writer of romance novels, including one based on the characters of Elizabeth Bennet and Mr. Darcy in contemporary America.

1 My very first Jane Austen novel was *Pride and Prejudice*, and it's still my favourite.

2 Jane Austen obviously has an impact on my everyday life. In truth, I owe her a great deal, not least because my most successful book, *Unleashing Mr. Darcy* is a retelling of *Pride and Prejudice* set in the world of dog shows. The book was adapted by Hallmark and made into two TV films. This book and these adaptations have literally changed my life and my career.

3 Sometimes I do wonder what Jane Austen would have thought if she knew she was so famous. I have a feeling that she would have some strong opinions about the treatment of women writers in her time.

---

[23] Prinny was the nickname given to the Prince-Regent during the Georgian period.

How well do you know
Jane Austen?

One hundred questions to test
your knowledge of the English novelist:
all the answers are in the book!

BIOGRAPHICAL QUESTIONS ABOUT JANE AUSTEN

1. Where was Jane Austen born?

2. What was Jane Austen's sister's first name?

3. How many brothers did Jane Austen have?

4. What was Jane Austen's star sign?

5. What was Jane Austen's mother's first name?

6. Who was the Duchess in Jane Austen's family tree?

7. Where did Jane Austen's paternal family come from?

8. What colour was Jane Austen's mother's wedding dress?

9. Which of Jane Austen's brothers were in love with their cousin, the beautiful Eliza?

10. What name did Edward Austen take when he inherited from his wealthy cousins?

11. Who was Jane Austen's favourite brother?

12. Where is Charles Austen, the youngest brother, buried?

13. What was the name of Cassandra Austen's fiancé?

14. Where was the beautiful cousin Eliza, Countess De Feuillide, born?

15. Where did Thomas Lefroy, Jane Austen's first crush, come from?

16. Jane Austen was briefly engaged, but for how long?

17. Who was Mrs. La Tournelle?

18. What happened at Enham House in 1792?

19. Who took over from Mr. Austen in Steventon in 1800?

20. What was the name of the master of ceremonies at the Assembly rooms in Jane Austen's time?

21. Who gave Chawton Cottage to Jane Austen, her sister and their mother?

22. How did Jane Austen start her day?

23. What was Jane Austen's favourite way of relaxing?

24. To which saint is Jane Austen's last book dedicated?

25. Where is Jane Austen buried?

26. What was the name of the shop where Jane Austen bought her tea in London, still in existence today?

27. Which book did Jane Austen buy from Hatchards?

28. Which famous playwright did Jane Austen read?

29. How old was Jane Austen when her first novel was published?

30. Who is behind the pseudonym Sophia Sentiment?

31. How many letters did Jane Austen write in her lifetime?

32. What was the name of Jane Austen's niece, Fanny Knight, after her marriage?

33. What is the name of the little church in Steventon where Jane Austen was baptised?

⋙ NOVELS AND ADAPTATIONS ⋙

34. In which novel(s) does Jane Austen evoke the city of Bath?

35. Which two novels did Jane Austen write reviews of in a notebook?

36. Which book did the translator, Isabelle de Montolieu, change the ending of?

37. What are the first names of the Dashwood sisters in *Sense and Sensibility*?

38. In *Sense and Sensibility*, what is the surname of Mrs. Dashwood's cousin?

39. What is the first name of Lucy Steele's sister?

40. Where does Ang Lee, the director of *Sense and Sensibility* (1995) come from?

41. What is the name of the most famous edition of *Pride and Prejudice*, published in 1894?

42. What instruments does Georgiana Darcy play?

43. What is the first name of the handsome Mr. Wickham?

44. What was the original title of *Pride and Prejudice*?

45. Who was the first actress to play Elizabeth Bennet?

46. What great name in British literature was involved in the screenplay for the film adaptation of *Pride and Prejudice* in 1940?

47. How old is Fanny Price when she arrives at Mansfield Park?

48. Who is the richest Austen gentleman?

49. Which actor plays Tom Bertram in the 2007 version of *Mansfield Park*?

50. What is Mr. Knightley's first name?

51. Who is *Emma* dedicated to?

52. What award did Rachel Portman win for the film *Emma* in 1997?

53. Who was the first on-screen Emma?

54. Where was Jonny Flynn, Mr. Knightley 2020, born?

55. In *Northanger Abbey*, how many children make up the Morland siblings?

56. Which famous mystery writer wrote a modern version of *Northanger Abbey*?

57. In *Persuasion*, how long are Anne Elliot and Captain Wentworth apart?

58. What is Sir Walter Elliot's title in *Persuasion*?

59. Which actor plays Captain Wentworth in the 1995 version of *Persuasion*?

60. A famous English actress is named after an Austen character. Which one?

61. What is the first name of the heroine of *Sanditon*?

62. What was the original title chosen by Jane Austen for *Sanditon*?

63. In which year was *Lady Susan* first published?

64. Which British actor, who is also a writer, plays the role of Mr. Johnson in *Love and Friendship* by Whit Stillman, in 2016?

65. Who illustrated Jane Austen's parodic work, *The History of England*?

66. Which famous American playwright wrote a radio version of *Pride and Prejudice*?

67. What is the name of the character played by J. J. Feild in *Austenland*?

⤜ AUSTEN CULTURE ⤛

68. Which actresses were the first to play Jane and Cassandra Austen in the theatre?

69. What was the title of the magazine founded and written by James and Henry Austen?

70. Who was the author of *Selected Fables*, a French grammar book given to Jane Austen by her cousin Eliza?

71. How many books did George Austen have in his library?

72. Which of Frances Burney's novels did Jane Austen help to publish by subscription?

73. Which of Jane Austen's contemporaries admired her most?

74. Who was the most famous poet of Jane Austen's time?

75. What kind of novels is Ann Radcliffe known for, which Jane Austen used as inspiration for *Northanger Abbey*?

76. What literary technique did Jane Austen use throughout her work?

77. Which famous Regency princess saw herself in Marianne Dashwood?

78. In which town did André Gide buy his copy of *Pride and Prejudice*?

79. Which Russian writer gave a course on Jane Austen at Cornell University in 1948?

80. Which author was Jane Austen's most fervent critic?

81. What was the name of John Murray's quarterly literary magazine in which an article was published about *Emma*?

82. In which famous castle is the Double Cube room, where (among other films) *Sense and Sensibility* (1995), *Pride and Prejudice* (2005) and *Emma* (2020) were filmed?

83. Who was the first theatre personality to stage a play based on a work by Jane Austen?

84. What is a *syllabub*?

85. What is a boulangere?

86. Which famous library houses the original manuscript of *Lady Susan*?

87. In which city is the biggest annual Jane Austen festival held?

88. What specialities can you try at Sally Lunn?

89. In which year were the Jasna (Jane Austen Societies of North America) founded?

90. Who is the current director of Jane Austen's House Museum in Chawton?

91. Which sisters wrote the first travel guide to Jane Austen, in 1901?

92. Who is Austin's most famous collector?

93. Where is the largest collection of letters written by Jane Austen held?

94. Which library has the original unfinished manuscript of *Sanditon*?

95. Which country produced the first illustrated edition of a Jane Austen novel in 1821?

96. Which American author turned Jane Austen into an amateur detective in a series of fourteen books?

97. Who are the authors of *Le Musée Imaginaire de Jane Austen*?

98. In what year was the first fan fiction adapted from the works of Jane Austen published?

99. Who wrote the short story *The Janeites*?

100. In which French town is there a street named after the novelist, "Allée Jane Austen"?

Answers

BIOGRAPHICAL QUESTIONS ABOUT JANE AUSTEN

1. In Steventon, Hampshire.

2. Jane Austen's sister was called Cassandra.

3. Jane Austen had five older brothers and one younger brother.

4. Jane Austen was born on 16 December 1775, making her a Capricorn.

5. Jane Austen's mother was also called Cassandra, and it was customary at the time to give the eldest daughter her mother's name.

6. The Duchess in Jane Austen's family tree is Cassandra Willoughby, the surname of the *bad boy* in *Sense and Sensibility*.

7. Jane Austen's paternal family came from Kent.

8. Jane Austen's mother's wedding dress was red, and it probably her most beautiful garment at the time.

9. It was Jane Austen's brothers James and Henry who were in love with their cousin, the beautiful Eliza.

10. Edward Austen became Edward Knight.

11. Jane Austen's favourite brother was Henry.

12. Charles Austen is buried in Burma, the site of his last Royal Navy mission.

13. Cassandra Austen's fiancé was Tom Fowle.

14. The beautiful cousin Eliza, Countess De Feuillide, was born in India.

15. Thomas Lefroy was Irish.

16. Jane Austen was engaged for one night.

17. Mrs. La Tournelle was the headmistress of the Abbey School in Reading, where Jane Austen and her sister studied.

18. In Enham House in 1792, Jane Austen made her debut in society.

19. Mr. Austen passed the parish of Steventon to his eldest son James in 1800.

20. The master of ceremonies of the *Assembly Rooms* in Jane Austen's time was called Mr. King.

21. It was Edward Knight who gave Chawton Cottage to Jane Austen, her sister and their mother.

22. Jane Austen began her day playing the piano.

23. Jane Austen's favourite way to relax was to play bilboquet.

24. Jane Austen's last book is dedicated to Saint Swithin.

25. Jane Austen is buried in Winchester, in the north wing of the cathedral.

26. Jane Austen's favourite tea shop was Twinings on the Strand.

27. Jane Austen bought *The Mysteries of Udolpho* (1794) by Ann Radcliffe from Hatchards Bookshop.

28. Jane Austen often read Shakespeare.

29. Jane Austen was thirty-six when her first novel was published.

30. It seems to have been Jane Austen who hid behind the pseudonym Sophia Sentiment in a letter to *The Loiterer*, the magazine run by her brothers James and Henry. She was thirteen at the time.

31. Over the course of her life, Jane Austen wrote some three thousand letters.

32. Jane Austen's niece, Fanny Knight, married Lord Knatchbull.

33. The little church in Steventon where Jane Austen was baptised is called St Nicholas.

NOVELS AND ADAPTATIONS

34. Jane Austen evokes the city of Bath in *Emma* (it's the place where Mr. Elton meets his wife), *Northanger Abbey* and *Persuasion*.

35. Jane Austen wrote down the opinions of her readers on *Emma* and *Mansfield Park* in a notebook.

36. Translator Isabelle de Montolieu changed the ending of *Sense and Sensibility*.

37. The Dashwood sisters in *Sense and Sensibility* are Elior, Marianne and Margaret.

38. In *Sense and Sensibility*, Mrs. Dashwood's cousin's surname is Middleton.

39. Lucy Steele's sister is called Anne.

40. Ang Lee, the director of *Sense and Sensibility* (1995), was originally from Taiwan.

41. The most famous edition of *Pride and Prejudice*, published in 1894, is known as the Peacock edition.

42. Georgiana Darcy plays the harp and the piano.

43. The handsome Mr. Wickham's first name is George.

44. *Pride and Prejudice*'s original title was *First Impressions*.

45. The first actress to play Elizabeth Bennet was Curigwen Lewis in 1938.

46. Aldous Huxley wrote the screenplay for the film adaptation of *Pride and Prejudice* in 1940. He is the author of the famous dystopian work *Brave New World*.

47. Fanny Price was nine years old when she arrived at Mansfield Park.

48. The richest Austen gentleman is Mr. Rushworth, Maria's suitor in *Mansfield Park*, who owns £12,000 in annuities.

49. James D'Arcy plays Tom Bertram in the 2007 version of *Mansfield Park* .

50. Mr. Knightley is called George, as is Mr. Austen.

51. *Emma* is dedicated to the Prince-Regent.

52. Rachel Portman won the Oscar for Best Musical Score for the film *Emma* in 1997.

53. The first on-screen Emma was Judy Campbell, mother of actress and singer Jane Birkin.

54. Johnny Flynn was originally from South Africa.

55. In *Northanger Abbey*, there are ten children in the Morland family.

56. Val McDermid wrote a modern version of *Northanger Abbey* (2014).

57. In *Persuasion*, Anne Elliot and Captain Wentworth are separated for eight years.

58. Sir Walter Elliot, in *Persuasion*, is a baronet.

59. Ciarán Hinds plays Captain Wentworth in the 1995 version of *Persuasion* .

60. Emma Watson is a character in the unfinished novel *The Watsons*.

61. The heroine of *Sanditon* is Charlotte Heywood.

62. The original title chosen by Jane Austen for *Sanditon* was *The Brothers*.

63. *Lady Susan* was published in 1871.

64. It was the great British actor Stephen Fry who played Mr. Johnson in *Love and Friendship*.

65. Cassandra Austen illustrated Jane Austen's parodic *The History of England*.

66. Arthur Miller wrote a radio version of *Pride and Prejudice*.

67. The character played by J. J. Feild in *Austenland* is Henry Nobley.

AUSTEN CULTURE

68. Josephine Hutchinson and Eva Le Gallienne were the first to play Jane and Cassandra Austen in the theatre.

69. The title of the magazine written and founded by James and Henry was *The Loiterer*.

70. *The Fables chosen* were those of La Fontaine.

71. George Austen had a library of five hundred books.

72. The novel by Frances Burney for which Jane Austen took part in the publication by subscription was *Camilla*.

73. Walter Scott admired Jane Austen's work and made this known.

74. The most famous poet of Jane Austen's time was Lord Byron.

75. Ann Radcliffe wrote Gothic novels.

76. Jane Austen uses free indirect discourse.

77. King George III's granddaughter, Princess Charlotte, recognised herself in Marianne Dashwood.

78. André Gide bought his copy of *Pride and Prejudice* in Algiers.

79. The author of *Lolita*, Vladimir Nabokov, gave a course on Jane Austen at Cornell University in 1948.

80. Jane Austen's most fervent critic was Mark Twain, the author of *The Adventures of Tom Sawyer*.

81. John Murray's quarterly literary journal was *The Quarterly Review*.

82. Wilton House is home to the famous Double Cube room.

83. Rosina Filippi wrote the first play about Jane Austen, in 1895.

84. A *syllabub* was a popular dessert at picnics.

85. A boulangere is a dance.

86. The original manuscript of *Lady Susan* is in the Morgan Library in New York.

87. The biggest festival devoted to Jane Austen takes place in Bath every year at the beginning of September.

88. You can eat *buns* there.

89. The Jasna (Jane Austen Societies of North America) were created in 1979.

90. The current Director of Jane Austen's House Museum in Chawton is Lizzie Dunford.

91. The Hill sisters wrote the first Jane Austen travel guide.

92. The most famous Austen collector was Alberta Burke.

93. The largest collection of letters written by Jane Austen is in New York.

94. The original of the unfinished *Sanditon* manuscript is in the possession of King's College Cambridge.

95. France produced the first illustrated edition of a Jane Austen novel.

96. Stephanie Barron turns Jane Austen into an amateur detective in her *Jane Austen Mysteries*.

97. The authors of *Le Musée Imaginaire de Jane Austen* are Fabrice Colin (text) and Nathalie Novi (drawings).

98. The first fan fiction adapted from the works of Jane Austen was published in 1913.

99. The short story *The Janeites* was written by Rudyard Kipling.

100. There is an Allée Jane Austen in Strasbourg.

Conclusion

The portrait of Jane Austen that emerges, as we see her today, is that of an extremely intelligent person, a woman of strong convictions, a literary woman who made no compromise to achieve her dream. She is a role model, an inspiration and an icon. So it was no coincidence that in 1908, suffragettes from the Women Writers' Suffrage League embroidered her name alongside those of Fanny Burney, Maria Edgeworth and Mary Wollstonecraft on their banners[1] during the first battles for women's suffrage in the United Kingdom.

Surprisingly, however, one of the Austen family's descendants was vehemently opposed to women's suffrage, the granddaughter of Anna Lefroy, one of Jane and Cassandra Austen's beloved nieces. Her name was Florence Emma Austen-Leigh and she married one of her cousins, Augustus Austen-Leigh.[2] However, as president of the Cambridge Women's Opposition to Women's Suffrage, Florence Austen-Leigh never mentioned her illustrious ancestor's name. Would Jane have vindicated her for this? We'll never know. However, Jane Austen inevitably became a feminist icon,[3] without having been a feminist herself. Yet, the themes she constantly developed in her novels subtly denounced the lack of consideration given to the women of her time.

Jane Austen has not always been as famous as she is today. When we think of her now, we think of a whole world, an idea of British refinement, a bucolic England, the elegance of a cashmere shawl as much as a warm scone on a delicate Wedgwood plate. Could little Jane, daughter of the Reverend George Austen and Cassandra née Leigh, ever have imagined what the mere mention of her name would imply? Her name surpasses her, even precedes her. You don't need to have read her work to know it. For a novelist who died more than two centuries ago, her ever-increasing popularity has certainly not ceased to surprise us.

---

[1] These banners are now kept at the Women Library London School of Economics.
[2] The son of James Edward Austen-Leigh, her husband was Provost of King's College Cambridge from 1889 to 1905.
[3] The term did not appear until 1872, with Alexandre Dumas *fils*. It is however the first feminist activist Hubertine Auclert who popularised it in 1882.

Bibliography

WORKS BY JANE AUSTEN

- *Emma*, John Murray, 1815.
- *Juvenilia*, translation by Josette Salesse-Lavergne, 10-18, 1999.
- *Lady Susan*, Penguin Classics, 2016.
- *Love and Freindship and Other Youthful Writings*, Penguin Books, 2014.
- *Mansfield Park*, Thomas Egerton, 1814.
- *Northanger Abbey*, John Murray, 1818.
- *Œuvres romanesques complètes I*, edited by Pierre Goubert with the collaboration of Pierre Arnaud and Jean-Paul Pichardie, Gallimard, 2000, (Bibliothèque de la Pléiade).
- *Œuvres romanesques complètes II*, edited by Pierre Goubert with the collaboration of Guy Laprevotte and Jean-Paul Pichardie, Gallimard, 2013, (Bibliothèque de la Pléiade).
- *Persuasion*, John Murray, 1817.
- *Pride and Prejudice*, Cambridge University Press, 2006.
- *Pride and Prejudice*, Thomas Egerton, 1813.
- *Sanditon*, Penguin Classics, 1975.
- *Sense and Sensibility*, Thomas Egerton, 1811.
- *The Cambridge Edition of the Works of Jane Austen. Later Manuscripts*, edited by Janet Todd and Linda Bree, Cambridge, 2008.
- *The Watson*, James Edward Austen-Leigh, 1871.

EXCLUSIVE COLLECTIONS OF LETTERS FROM JANE AUSTEN

- *Du Fond de mon Cœur: Lettres à ses Nièces*, Deirdre Le Faye, Finitude, 2015 (From the bottom of my heart: Letters to her Nieces).
- *Les sautes d'humour de Jane Austen*, Payot et Rivages, 2014 (The Wicked wit of Jane Austen, compiled by Dominique Enright, Michael O'Mara Books limited, 2002).
- *Pas de femmes parfaites, s'il vous plaît*, translated by Delphine Ménage, Éditions L'Orma, 2020 (No perfect women, please).
- *Jane Austen's Letters*, edited by Deirdre Le Faye, Oxford Editions, 2011.

BOOKS ON JANE AUSTEN, HER WORKS AND HER TIMES

- Austen Caroline, *My Aunt Jane Austen, A Memoir,* 1867.
- Austen-Leigh James Edward, *A Memoir of Jane Austen*, Richard Bentley & Son, 1869.
- Birtwistle Sue and Susie Conklin, *The Making of Pride and Prejudice*, Penguin Books BBC Books, 1995.
- Bradbrook Frank W., *Jane Austen and her Predecessors*, Cambridge University Press, 1966.
- Byrne Paula, *The Real Jane Austen,* Harper Perennial, 2014.
- Cecil David, *A Portrait of Jane Austen*, Will and Wang, 1978.
- Cecil David, *Jane Austen's 'Sir Charles Grandison,'* Oxford University Press, 1981.
- Clery E.J., *Jane Austen: The Banker's Sister*, Biteback Publishing, 2017.
- Fullerton Susannah, *Happy Ever After, Celebrating Jane Austen's Pride and Prejudice*, Frances Lincoln Limited, 2013.
- Greeves Lydia, *Houses of the National Trust*, National Trust, 2013.
- Greany Michael, *An A-Z of Jane Austen,* Bloomsbury, 2023.
- Halperin John, *Jane Austen*, Plon, 1992.
- Halsey Katie, *Jane Austen and her Readers*, 2012.
- Harman Claire, *Jane's Fame*, Canongate, 2009.
- Heald Henrietta, *Amazing and Extraordinary Facts, Jane Austen*, Rydon Publishing, 2016.
- Hill Constance and Ellen G., *Jane Austen, Her Home and Her Friends*, Dover Publications, 2018.
- Ivins Holly, *The Jane Austen Pocket Bible*, Pocket Bibles, 2011.
- Jenkins Elizabeth, *Jane Austen*, Victor Gollancz, 1949.
- Jennings Charles, *Jane Austen, The Life and Times of the World's Favourite Author*, Hachette, 2012.
- Johnson Claudia L., *Jane Austen's Cults and Cultures*, 2012.
- Kennedy Margaret, *Jane Austen*, Arthur Barker, 1950.
- Kloester Jennifer, *Georgette Heyer's Regency World*, Arrow Books, 2008.

- Lane Maggie, *Jane Austen and Lyme Regis*, The Jane Austen Society, 2003.
- Le Faye Deirdre, *Jane Austen, a Family Record*, Cambridge University Press, 2004.
- Le Faye Deirdre, *A Chronology of Jane Austen and her Family*, Cambridge University Press, 2013.
- Looser Devoney, *The Making of Jane Austen*, John Hopkins University Press, 2017.
- Lynch Deidre, *Janeites: Austen's Disciples and Devotees*, Princeton University Press, 2000.
- Martin Lydia, *Jane Austen's Novels on Screen: Aesthetics and Ideology*, L'Harmattan, 2007.
- Mullan John, *What Matters in Jane Austen?*, Bloomsbury, 2014.
- Quint Karin, *Jane Austen's England: A Travel Guide*, ACC Art Books, 2019.
- Reynolds Sophie, *Jane Austen's House, Souvenir Guidebook*, Jane Austen's House, 2022.
- Ross Josephine, *Jane Austen and her World,* National Portrait Gallery, 2017.
- Tomalin Claire, *Jane Austen, A Life*, Viking, 1997.
- Sheridan Sara, *The World of Sanditon*, Trapeze, 2019.
- Shields Carol, *Jane Austen*, Viking, 2002.
- Stafford, Fiona, *Jane Austen, A Brief Life*, Yale University Press, 2017.
- Sutherland Kathryn (ed.), *Jane Austen Writer in the World*, Bodleian Library, 2017.
- Thompson Emma, *Sense and Sensibility. The Screenplay and Diaries*, Bloomsbury, 1995.
- Todd Janet, *Jane Austen, her Time, her Life, her Novels*, Andre Deutsch, 2013.
- Watkins Susan, *Jane Austen in Style*, Thames and Hudson, 1990.
- Wells Juliette, *Everybody's Jane: Austen in the Popular Imagination*, Continuum Books, 2011.
- Worsley Lucy, *Jane Austen at Home*, Hodder & Stoughton, 2017.
- Yaffe Deborah, *Among The Janeites*, HarperCollins, 2013.

OTHER

- *Alfred Lord Tennyson: A memoir by his son,* Hallam Tennyson, MacMillan & co, 1905.
- *André Gide, Journal,* 1889-1939, Gallimard, 1939.
- *Austen, Dickens, Flaubert, Stevenson,* Vladimir Nabokov, Stock, 1999, translation by Hélène Pasquier.
- *Brummell ou le prince des dandys,* Jacques de Langlade, Presses de la Renaissance, 1985.
- *Henry Crabb Robinson on Books and their Writers,* London Dent, 1938.
- *Georgette Heyer's Regency World, Jennifer Kloester,* Arrow Books, 2008.
- *Maria Edgeworth: Letters from England 1813-1844,* Oxford, Clarendon Press, 1971.
- *The Brontës: A life in Letters,* edited by Juliet Baker, The Overlook Press, 1997.
- *The Complete Letters of Mark Twain,* Echo Library, 2007.
- *The Journal of Sir Walter Scott,* Oxford Clarendon Press, 1972.
- *The Letters of Princess Charlotte 1811-1817,* London: Home and Van Thal, 1949.
- *The Life and Letters of Maria Edgeworth,* London Arnold, 1894.
- *A Room of One's Own.* Virginia Woolf, 1929. London: Hogarth Press.

ONLINE RESOURCES

- *Jane Austen and her world,* **janeausten.fr.** **janeaustenandherworld.wordpress.com**.
- *Jane Austen Society of North America,* **jasna.org**.
- *Jane Austen's house,* **janeaustens.house**.
- *Jane Austen's world,* **janeaustensworld.com**.
- *Lise Antunes Simoes,* **liseantunessimoes.com**.
- *Onirik,* **onirik.net**.
- *Regency World,* **janeaustenmagazine.co.uk**.
- *The British Library,* **bl.uk**.
- *The Jane Austen centre,* **janeausten.co.uk/en**.
- *The Morgan Library,* **themorgan.org**.
- *The Republic of Pemberley,* **pemberley.com**.
- *The Inn at Lambton,* **https://the-inn-at-lambton.1fr1.net/**
- *Whoopsy Daisy,* **https://whoopsy-daisy.forumactif.org/**

Acknowledgements

We would like to express our gratitude to Lizzie Dunford and Jeremy Knight for welcoming us so warmly to Chawton, and for taking the time to answer our (many!) questions. Our thanks also to Graham Davies, director of the research team at the Lyme Regis Museum, for his invaluable help and patience.

Many thanks also to Christine Hobson and Audrina Canaux for their expertise and support, and to Joyce Hobson and Bob, our wanderings deep in the Hampshire countryside will remain unforgettable.

Lucie, thank you for believing in us and giving us the opportunity to take part in this project, we'll always be grateful to you. Sophie, your illustrations make this encyclopaedia the most beautiful that has ever existed.

We'd also like to thank the people around us, our loyal network of Janeites (who know who they are), our families and Lana Del Rey.

Our passionate collaboration, made up of intense exchanges both day and night, our constant encouragement and our unshakeable trust in each other, made writing this book an extraordinary adventure. It would never have existed without you, without me, without us.

To the memory of Deirdre Le Faye for her colossal work, her unfailing devotion and all those years spent dissecting the slightest piece of information, the slightest clue about Jane Austen, with the aim of sharing it with as many people as possible.

And finally, to Jane Austen, for her immense talent and the indelible mark she has left on us and on the whole world.

Gwen and Claire

MANAGER: Catherine Saunier-Talec
PROJECT MANAGER: Timothée Le Mière
ARTISTIC DIRECTOR: Mélissande Mestas
PROJECT MANAGER: Lucie Levron
ILLUSTRATIONS: Sophie Koechlin
COVER AND PAGE DESIGN AND LAYOUT: Studio POLI&CO
PROOF-READING: Anne-Sophie Guénégès
PRODUCTION: Anne-Laure Soyez
TRANSLATION: Helen Moss for ABAQUE GROUP

Printed in China
Published by Titan Books, London, in 2024.

TITAN
BOOKS

A division of Titan Publishing Group Ltd
144 Southwark Street
London SE1 0UP
www.titanbooks.com
Find us on Facebook: www.facebook.com/titanbooks
Follow us on X: @TitanBooks
Published by arrangement with Hachette Heroes:
www.hachetteheroes.com
A CIP catalogue record for this title is available from the British Library.
ISBN: 9781835410639

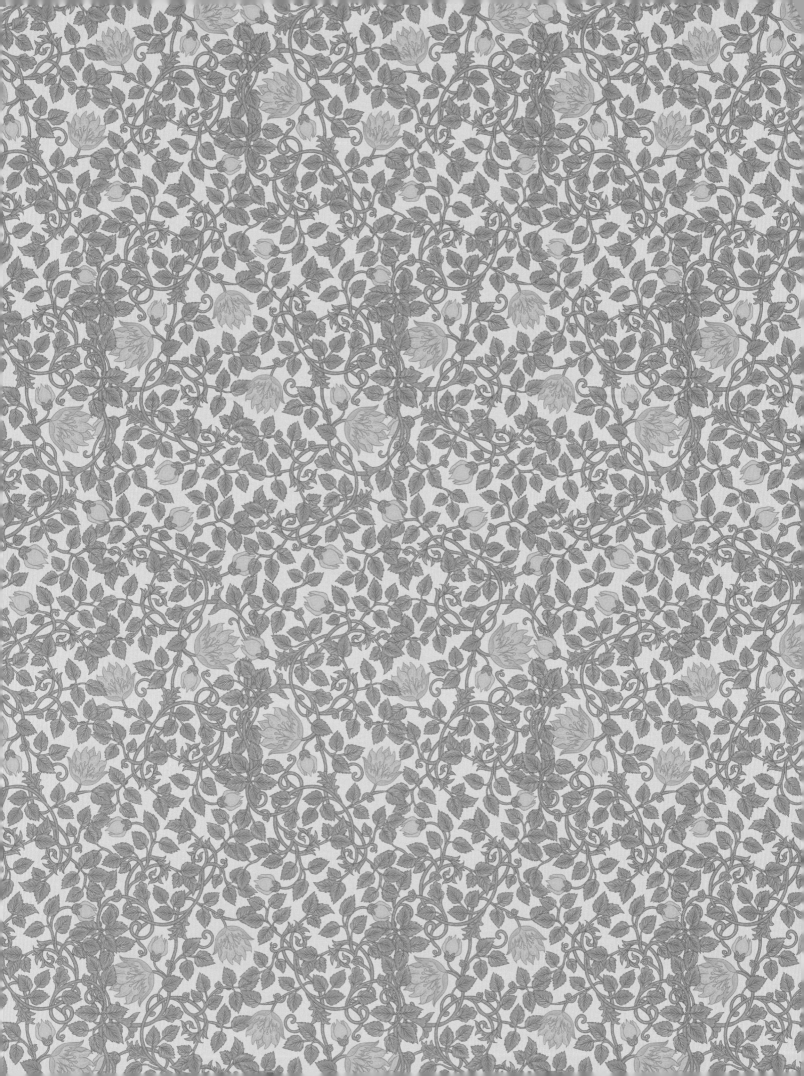

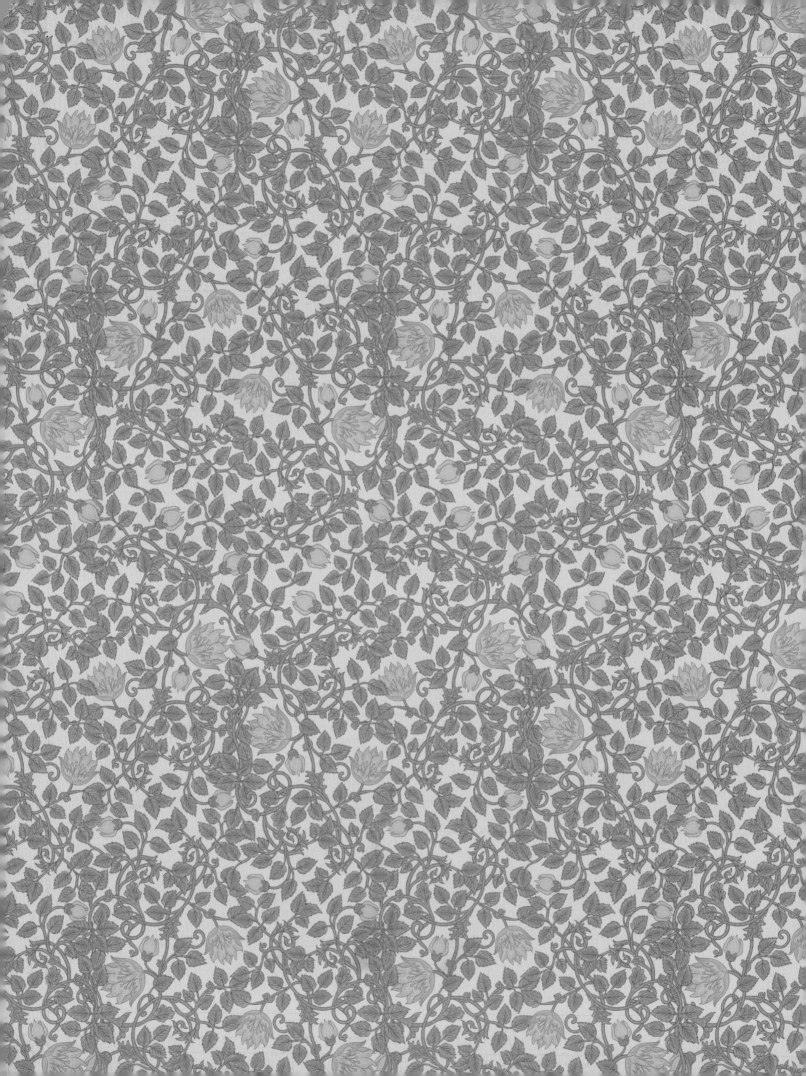